W9-AIA-522

The Literary Book of Economics

The Literary Book of Economics

Including Readings from Literature and Drama on Economic Concepts, Issues, and Themes

Edited, with commentary, by Michael Watts

ISI Books

2003

Cataloging-in-Publication Data

The literary book of economics: including readings from literature and drama on economic concepts, issues, and themes / edited by Michael Watts —1st ed. —Wilmington, DE : ISI Books, 2003.

p. ; cm.

ISBN 1-932236-02-3

1. Economics in literature. 2. Economics—Literary collections.

I. Watts, Michael.

PN51 .L58 2003 2003102918

808.80355—dc21 CIP

Interior design by: Kara Beer

Published by: ISI Books
Intercollegiate Studies Institute
3901 Centerville Road
Wilmington, Delaware 19807
www.isibooks.org

Printed in the United States of America

For Deirdre Watts, who reads more than I do,
and has especially supported this particular project.

Malthus is the right organ of English proprietors. But we shall never understand political economy until we get Beranger or Burns or some poet to teach it in songs; and they won't teach Malthuism.

And there is no subject that does not belong to the Poet; manufacturers and stock brokerage, as much as sunsets and souls; only the things placed in their true order are poetry; but displaced, or put in kitchen-order, they are unpoetic.

Ralph Waldo Emerson

Contents

I. Public Goods, Externalities, and the Coase Theorem

J. Government Regulation and the Legal and Social Framework for Markets

K. Principal-Agent Problems

L. Government Failure and the Economics of Public Choice

M. Labor Markets, Unions, and Human Capital

N. Discrimination

O. Immigration

P. Income Inequality, Poverty, and Income Redistribution Policies

Q. Barter, Money, and Inflation

R. Real versus Nominal Values

S. Unemployment and Fiscal Policy

T. Free Trade versus Protectionism

U. Cost-Benefit Analysis

Epilogue

Appendices

Acknowledgments

What a long, strange road led to this book, which was always the book I most wanted to do. For a long time it was the book I thought I would try to put together and get published just before I retired, because in some sense literature and drama has always been a hobby and pleasure for me, not work. This volume did take about twenty-five years, but as I still hope to have another decade or more before I retire, it is coming out a little early. The clear reason is because since conceiving it I have received special encouragement for this project from family members, friends, teachers, and colleagues. Then two or three years ago—out of the blue and beyond any reasonable expectations—a publisher sought me out about the project, provided generous support to make the publication possible, and put me in the hands of an unfailingly patient and supportive editorial and marketing staff. None of this is the usual academic or publishing experience, which makes me that much more grateful for it.

I cannot begin to name, or even remember, all of those who have suggested literary passages dealing with economics to me, some of which have been included here and others of which could have been but were not. I sincerely thank everyone who made recommendations to me, as well as those who will, I am sure, recommend passages to me in the future. It seems to be deeply ingrained in people who like to read literature and drama *and* economics to share their own favorite passages.

There are many people I must thank by name, however, starting with some of my favorite professors at Louisiana State University: Robert F. Smith and William F. Campbell in economics; and Don D. Moore, James Gilbert, and Lawrence A. Sasek in English. Then there are some of my favorite colleagues, including Gerald Lynch at Purdue University, John Siegfried at Vanderbilt University, William Becker at Indiana University, William Walstad at the University of Nebraska, John McMillan at Stanford University, Don Leet at California State University at Fresno, Vann Seawell at Indiana University–Purdue University at Indianapolis, and Robert Duvall at the National Council for Economic Education (a former English professor). The faculty at Robert Morris University invited me to present this material to over one hundred economists at their annual conference on teaching in 2002, and presentations on the material included here were also invited at meetings of the American Economic Association, the Midwest Economics Association, the National Association of Teachers of English, and the National Council on Economic Education. Every time I thought about putting these materials aside until retirement, or letting them slide further down in my stack of things to do, one of these people or organizations would come along to ask me to give a talk, write a paper, or teach a graduate or undergraduate economics or English class (or both). As a result, the manuscript never quite got put in the bottom drawer. Instead it got larger, and there were always some people saying "this is interesting," or that it was "fun" or "important" and asking, "What new passages have you found?" and, "When are you going to bring this out so that more people can use it?" Looking back, all of that was very important in keeping the work alive and on this schedule, and I deeply appreciate it.

At ISI, Jeff Nelson, Jeremy Beer, Anne Krulikowski, Doug Schneider, and for all I know others whose names I have never heard have been an incredibly generous and supportive group to work with. To put it bluntly they have always been at least as committed to the project as I am, and I confess there were times when I thought they were even more committed. More importantly, though, they always seemed to have exactly the same vision for the book that I did, in signing, editing, and promoting it. That's a rare thing, which I have only encountered with one other publisher and a handful of editors. What a pleasure it is to say and mean this.

And this. I have been blessed with three great secretaries in my twenty-two years at Purdue. Two of them, Julie Huffer and April Fidler, spent countless hours preparing excerpts and checking dozens of references for this volume, not to mention dealing with the unwieldy set of papers and transparencies I use in presentations on this material.

Finally, or first, are the family members. My mother taught me to read, and to like reading. She says my first favorite book was Frieda Friedman's *Bobbie Had a Nickel,* which starts (as I have been able to recite as long as I can remember): "Bobbie had a nickel/All his very own – / Should he buy some candy/ Or an ice cream cone?" The language certainly isn't Robert Frost's in "The Road Not Taken," which appears later in this work, but the ideas of choice and opportunity cost are exactly the same.

My wife has earned the dedication to this volume in more ways than I can say. I could have written this kind of dedication to her in other volumes, too; but I saved it for this book because of the large and special places in my heart that I hold for it and for her. It also helped that in marrying me she brought along her father, Robert Berner, who retired not so long ago as a professor of English at the University of Wisconsin–Oshkosh. He graciously endured (and improved) the appendices, and had numerous long discussions on the other materials with me. I look forward to presenting him with his "free" copy of the published book, and to thanking him and Connie, once again, for Deirdre.

Introduction
The Inevitable but Uneasy Relationship between Economics and Literature and Drama

Why Economics Appears in Literature and Drama

The central part of Alfred Marshall's famous definition of economics is "the study of mankind in the ordinary business of life."[1] While some literature and drama deals with extraordinary people in extraordinary situations, ordinary people engaged in the ordinary business of life—including the rest of Marshall's definition, "the attainment and . . . use of the material requisites of well-being"—make up a large part of what literary writers and critics often refer to as the human condition.

Like economists, literary writers—including novelists, dramatists, poets, and literary critics—often write about such topics as work, income, consumption, production, markets, trading, poverty, unemployment, money, prices, inflation, businesspeople, profits, and government programs and policies that make an economic system better or worse, or would make it better or worse if they were implemented. On rare occasions some literary authors and critics even write about economists and economics, and some economists occasionally return the favor. From both sides, however, these references are frequently less than complimentary.

Although such antipathy is in some cases related to individual personalities or particular historic events, more often it stems from factors deeply rooted in the different professions themselves. For one thing, while the subject matter of these seemingly disparate disciplines often overlaps, there are clearly major differences in the methodology of their analysis, presentation, and discussion.[2] And occasionally—but not always, as I will argue—the friction between economists and literary writers is based in the discrepancy between their fundamental attitudes about, or knowledge of, economics and economic issues, and in particular the role of markets and government.

The appendices to this volume briefly review the relatively small (in volume) but nevertheless broad (in scope) range of work by economists, literary historians, and literary critics in which these scholars consider each other's work. But the real reason for this book is the large selection of primary works from literature and drama it presents. These selections will, I hope, serve as a pleasurable and instructive way for many students, teachers, and other interested readers to enhance their knowledge of key economic concepts, and will also add to their appreciation for the many ways economic ideas affect daily life for individuals, businesses, and policymakers. For economists, who already are thoroughly familiar with the economic ideas illustrated here, I hope these readings will not only be a pleasant consumable, but will also be of use in their own teaching and writing.

The brief introductions to sections and individual readings that I have provided usually suggest in non-technical language a few key points about mainstream economists' views on the topics and issues described in the excerpts. Economists may therefore want to skip these introductions and let the passages speak for themselves, with no external "framing" or pre-suggestion, and then perhaps compare their interpretations of the passages with mine.[3]

But as I say, my primary motivation in compiling this anthology has been to demonstrate just how often literature and drama deal with economic concepts and issues, and frequently (but not always) deal with them very well. I hope that readings such as these will become more widely used by economists as they teach their courses, as well as by English and other humanities teachers who would like to build more economics into their courses in order to show students that literature and drama, no less than economics, speaks to the ordinary business of life.

To the surprise of some of my economist and English-professor friends, colleagues, and acquaintances, it was not especially difficult to find literary passages dealing with economic themes, simply because economics is such a basic part of life that literary authors have to, and often want to, deal with it. Indeed, there are many other passages I could have used but did not (occasionally because of steep copyright fees or outright prohibitions against reprints), and I am sure there are far more passages of which I am simply not aware. Few months pass when I do not discover at least one more text that could have been included, regardless of whether I am reading contemporary authors or those long deceased. And whenever I have presented this material to meetings of either economists or literature professors, it is typical for at least one new (to me) example to be suggested by someone in the group. All of which leads me to a confession and warning: the selections presented here are mainly a reflection of my own choices and tastes in literature or, in some cases, my own long-past academic coursework.[4]

As is obvious from the list of readings, my interests lean mainly to writers from the United States and the United Kingdom. I am keenly aware that there are few writers represented here, even in translation, who do not write in English. Some have suggested that women authors and critics are also underrepresented. If that is true, *mea culpa*. I also decided not to include passages from science fiction and fantasy literature, although I have found some suitable passages in those works, despite the fact that I did not begin to read in those genres until the relatively old age of about 25. I am certain that suitable passages could be found among all of these groups of authors, too, but my publisher has already been very generous in spending money for reprint permissions. Perhaps, in the not-too-distant future, a thicker, subsequent edition of this work will appear that addresses some of these concerns, featuring additional selections suggested by readers of this edition.

Differences and Similarities in Economics, Literature, and Drama— in Ends As Well As Means

Another necessary warning is that, despite the frequent similarities in the topics they consider, the important differences between economics and literature and drama should not be minimized. Nothing in this volume is meant to suggest that we should rely on literary authors to do what economists do, or vice versa. Through long years of training and practice, but probably also because of different inclinations and talents, the methods and skills the disciplines employ have become so unlike that it can be difficult for these specialists to understand each other, even when they do write about the same thing. As Adam Smith pointed out in 1776, and Alexander Pope several decades earlier, there are important and substantial costs as well as benefits associated with specialization and the division of labor.

Beyond the obviously far greater use of mathematics and statistics in economics, there are methodological differences related to the *ends* of the disciplines, not just to the tools they use. Most modern economics analysis is intentionally designed to be limited to positive (what is), rather than normative (what ought to be), analysis and discussion. For example, economists assume that individual consumers maximize utility; but exactly what goes into the consumer's utility functions—in other words, what things will make consumers happy—and how it gets there is rarely studied, and even more rarely questioned.[5]

That is not as limiting as it may sound to people hearing it for the first time. For example, if some goods or activities are judged to be illicit and declared illegal by political authorities, economists can show how that judgment will affect prices and the production and consumption of these goods and services. Conceivably some economists might even conclude, as some have with respect to Prohibition during the 1920s or perhaps with heroin today, that the costs of making a product illegal outweigh the pragmatic and financially measurable benefits of such a policy. Or they might show how economic interests lead to coalitions with the power to ban or legalize certain products.

Sometimes economists accept without questioning the appropriateness of a political authority's determination about the legality of certain goods and services. For example, markets in slaves are banned because that violates our notion of basic human rights. And markets for directly buying and selling votes on election days are prohibited because that violates democratic ideals—despite the fact that most third-year undergraduate economics majors can explain how such markets would make individual buyers and sellers better off, at least in their own judgments.[6]

In all such cases, however, no amount of training as a professional economist could confer any special expertise allowing an economist to say definitively that a good or service should be prohibited or legalized. Nor, to consider the mundane kind of choices that are quite possibly more important in the ordinary business of life, can an economist make a professional judgment that consumers are wrong to spend fifteen dollars for a pink flamingo to put in their front yard rather than a paperback copy of the latest novel to win the Pulitzer Prize. If the price of the plastic bird and the book are the same, the question comes down to which product the consumer—not the economist or any other kind of expert—believes will provide more satisfaction.

Generally, literary authors neither seek nor accept such restrictions. Their canvas is the entire range of human experience: normative and positive, material and spiritual, utilitarian and aesthetic. Once a subject has been chosen, literary authors present material from the standpoint of "human interest," developing characters and plots to present studies of people, themes, and institutions, rather than collecting and then analyzing quantitative data. It might surprise literary authors to learn that in this they are working much like economic theorists, though unlike empirical economists and other social scientists. The typical practice of the economic theorist is also to begin with the individual (buyer, seller, worker, voter, firm, or representative of whatever group is being studied), to try to understand what motivates that individual "unit of analysis," and then to determine how that decision-making unit would respond to different opportunities and constraints. Both the literary author and the economic theorist must try to strip away thousands of the insignificant details that crowd into our daily lives and focus on the key causes and effects of what people do.

Unlike economic theorists, however, literary authors write poetry, dialogue, or rich and emotionally evocative prose. The theorists use mathematics to formalize their models of human behavior and rigorously establish consistent behaviors and equilibrium outcomes, subject to such constraints as limited incomes and the costs of purchasing or producing different products. Then, to communicate clearly and convincingly with other economists, theoretical and empirical economists write articles for academic journals, or sometimes books, featuring formulas, graphs, tables of data and statistics, and simple declarative sentences. There is a premium on the efficient and economical use of language in these articles.[7] Still, economists like good stories and examples, too, and frequently tell them in establishing the motivation for the topics of their articles and books, or in explaining the intuition behind their methods of analysis or results. Academic economists especially like to tell stories in the classes they teach, partly because those who aren't good storytellers and opt instead to use exclusively math and graphs usually get poor teaching evaluations from students, at least at the undergraduate level.[8]

One final similarity helps to explain some of the ways and reasons economists have occasionally used literature and drama in their own professional writings, and qualifies the assertion that literary authors are not bound by some of the disciplinary restrictions economists have adopted. The similarity is simply that once a literary author has established a character or situation, in order to make characters, situations, and dialogue believable the author is inexorably bound by many of the same restrictions that confront economists: Do characters understand the incentives and trade-offs they face? Is their behavior understandable (or in other words, is it rational)? Can it be explained by what has been said or shown in the rest of the work, or by what readers can be assumed to know from their own experience? Are the situations and actions depicted consistent with what people do, or at least with what they believe happens, "in the real word"? Are the situations and the overall work interesting and important?

All of these questions are asked by both literary authors and economists. And the more successful a literary author who chooses to write about an economic concept, issue, or theme is in answering these questions, the easier it is for an economist to recognize and use that author's work to illustrate or even analyze economic behavior—albeit often recast in specialized terms that the literary author would either not know or not use in the same way. Literary authors have the further advantage of being able to show why characters develop the beliefs and preferences that motivate them, and how and why those values and tastes change as a character ages and grows. In this sense, the literary author gets to create and "mine" his or her own data. And readers evaluate literary works based in part on whether that is done well or poorly, which in turn affects authors' reputations and their popularity in the marketplace.

Of course, some literary authors and critics are not particularly successful or perhaps even interested in recognizing economic incentives, or the way in which competitive markets work to channel self-interest into socially useful outcomes and to automatically and impersonally establish a new equilibrium when something changes in the economy. Some literary authors accept (or at least some of the characters in some of their writings accept, which is an important distinction to make) ideas that a majority of the public and political leaders may also espouse, but a majority of economists do not—for example, restrictions on international trade in the belief that such policies will increase employment, production, and standards of living for everyone in the economy, not just for workers and firms in the sectors protected from foreign competition.[9] Finally, like economists, some literary writers and critics are political liberals, while others are political conservatives. Not surprisingly, conservative economists are more likely to criticize liberal literary authors, and vice versa.

All of these factors have played a part in establishing the long-standing distrust between economists and literary authors and critics, a distrust that occasionally breaks out into open hostility. It was, after all, Carlyle, Ruskin, and Dickens who were most responsible for hanging the "dismal science" tag on economics, although not for the reasons most people now believe.[10] Partly because of that, and because of literary depictions casting business and economic activities in a negative light, economists, historians, and other social scientists have not infrequently claimed that literary authors are either ignorant of, or biased against, business, economics, and markets.

If such a pervasive bias really does exist—not just in writings by a few writers and not only in literary works narrowly defined, but also in movies, television programs, magazines, and other media outlets—that is a very serious matter for economists, for there is some evidence that these cultural sources are more influential in shaping public opinion about economic issues than are economists.[11] Frankly, given the discrepancy between the sales figures for leading works of fiction and periodicals and the best-selling works of economists, that difference in influence is not especially surprising. And to the extent that the reading public—that is, the more articulate and influential citizenry—is strongly influenced by what literary and journalistic writers and teachers say about economics, there is even more reason for economists to learn what literary authors and those who study, interpret, and teach literary works are saying about economic ideas.

These questions about the relationship between literary authors and economists are considered in the epilogue. For now, enough has been said to suggest why the relationship between economics and literature and drama is both inevitable and uneasy, as it has been since the time economics began to emerge as an autonomous academic discipline.[12]

I want to conclude this introduction on a more optimistic note, however, and in doing so set the stage for the excerpts that follow. Because taken as a group, I believe the readings from literature and drama in this section help to establish that there is no single or uniform literary point of view on economics issues, concepts, and themes. Instead, one finds basically the same range of opinions among these authors that one finds among economists.

One could, if one were so inclined, read a steady diet of works casting economic ideas and market activity in a harsh, sinister, or paranoid light. One could also, without too much trouble, read only authors sympathetic to markets and economics. But most writers are, I find, somewhere in the middle, using characters, situations, and dialogue more with an eye to what makes a particular story work than with an eye toward promoting this or that economic idea. Especially in longer literary works, or across several works, authors are likely to present a more balanced mix of characters and situations. Interestingly, as critics have pointed out (see Appendix B) concerning the few authors who set out to strongly support markets (such as Rand) or to condemn them (such as Brecht), the more strident the defense or attack, the less successful a particular work or author often becomes, considered on purely literary grounds.

Who Benefits by Using Literature and Drama with Economics?

There are two major ways economists can use literature and drama. First, for a literary work to endure it must tell a memorable story or paint a memorable image or picture. In large part, as Samuel Johnson once said, an author does that by making things that are new seem familiar and things that are familiar seem new. Few people write well enough to do that in any field, but in a technical field like economics, where data, issues, and even institutions change so rapidly, writing and saying things that are memorable is a tall order indeed. Literary works often describe human behavior and motivations more eloquently, powerfully, or humorously than economists typically do, even when dealing with economic subjects.

Literature is therefore a rich resource to economists as writers and researchers. As discussed in Appendix A, economists have used literary passages as evidence of how individuals act in response to particular economic conditions and institutions in a particular place and time; they have evaluated whether literary authors have described characters and behaviors that are in line with economists' predictions and understandings of rational action; and they have attempted to determine whether there is, as some economists and economic historians have claimed, a pervasive anti-economics, anti-market, or at least anti-business orientation throughout literature.

The second way economists can use passages from literature and drama is to help teach economics more effectively at the secondary and college level. Most of my earlier writings on this subject have focused on this application, but I am by no means the first economist to use literature and drama to do this. In fact, when I took my first university course in economics in 1968 I used an early edition of Paul Samuelson's textbook—a path breaking book in many ways—and there as a preface to one chapter was the passage from W. S. Gilbert's (of Gilbert and Sullivan fame) "Up Goes the Price of Shoddy," which is reprinted here in the passage from *Songs of a Savoyard*. Other principles textbooks or ancillaries have reprinted passages from Kurt Vonnegut's "Harrison Bergeron," which is also included here, and excerpts from some works that are not here, such as Thomas Wolfe's *From Death To Morning* (on the men of Catawba's debate over the market, legal, and fair price of a mule).

When George Stigler became coeditor of the *Journal of Political Economy* in 1973, that prestigious journal began to run short excerpts from different books and articles on its back cover, including the passage from Rabelais' *Gargantua and Pantagruel* that is reprinted in this volume.

These literary passages are wonderfully effective teaching tools both because they are well written and memorable and because they introduce variety in the economics classroom, compared to the typical steady diet of textbook prose, graphs, tables of numbers, and math. Perhaps even more important in considering students' general education, they help make the point that the ability to explain economic concepts verbally as well as graphically and mathematically is important, useful, and sometimes pleasing in and of itself.

Some of the passages—especially scenes from plays and many poems—lend themselves to "active learning" methods of instruction, such as skits or role-playing, and small group discussions. Other passages deal with introductory material that, in my opinion, gets too little time and space in most textbooks and economics classes; when I want to do more on the idea of opportunity cost or property rights, I turn to the two famous poems by Robert Frost that are reprinted here.

Despite these advantages, there isn't time in most standard economics courses to use more than a handful of these readings, and I must admit they might lose some of their effectiveness if an entire economics course were taught via literature. As the Table of Contents should make clear, however, it really *would* be possible to teach such a course. In fact, I once taught a one-credit course on economics in literature and drama for secondary economics and English teachers in Indianapolis. They loved the material and enjoyed being brought together to work on a common set of material as allies, for once—not something that happens often for economics and English teachers at any level.

That brings me to the last question I want to consider in this introduction: What do English and other language teachers and professors have to gain from a study of economic concepts, issues, and themes in literature and drama? Several things, I believe. First, the secondary English teachers in my Indianapolis course appreciated the chance to use readings that their students would find more relevant to their own lives and worlds than they would many of the readings in literature textbooks, especially those dealing with such topics as romantic love, the duties of kings and queens, etc. That is not meant to imply that I, or any of these teachers, advocate a wholesale change in the content of existing literature classes—just a bit more breadth and variety, in exactly the same way these passages can be used to add variety to typical economics courses.

As I show in Appendix B, it also turns out that in recent decades many literary critics have once again taken up the study of economic issues and themes in literature and drama, just as Ruskin, Carlyle, Shaw, and other influential critics did a century or more ago. The simple reason for that, I believe, is because economic concepts, issues, and themes inevitably find their way into primary literary sources, which means literary critics have to deal with such material. It is worth noting here, however, that literary critics often have different backgrounds, write for different audiences, and therefore face different incentives than the authors of poems, novels, and plays. That turns out to be important in considering whether there is a literary bias against markets, economics, or business.

While I have always found the issue of such bias to be an interesting question, as a matter of perspective it has always seemed to me to be at most only an occasionally important side issue. For most people who like to read literature and drama—which includes a very large number of economists—the real pleasure is in seeing how people who write so well use language to talk about the same ideas and issues that economists discuss all the time.

Literary passages on economic topics are not, however, a substitute for either formal economic theory or empirical analysis. They cannot prove what economic theorists prove nor quantify what empirical economists quantify, and in doing that work economists make a substantial and often unique contribution to understanding what consumers, workers, firms, and policymakers do well—and sometimes not so well. At best, literary passages like those included here complement economic analysis, and today they are clearly weaker complements than material from such fields as statistics and mathematics.

But in teaching economics, and more broadly, in the attempt to develop an articulate citizenry,[13] literature may well be indispensable. In fact, in their efforts to influence public opinion and explain to noneconomists why what they do is important, economists may need literature and drama more than literature and drama need economists.[14] Literary treatments (including "good stories" told by economists) are often more convincing to noneconomists than are mathematical models and statistical evidence. The surprising thing is that economists have failed for so long to recognize that, or at least to try to use it to their advantage.

Notes

1. *Principles of Economics,* 8th ed. (London: Macmillan, 1920). Although other definitions are more widely used today, Marshall's is still popular more than a century after it was first published, and regularly appears in textbooks for students taking their first course in economics.

2. As D. McCloskey and others have argued for the past two decades, there is perhaps also more similarity in the methods of proof and argument in the subjects than most economists would like to admit. See *The Rhetoric of Economics* (Madison, Wis.: University of Wisconsin Press, 1985).

3. To proceed in this fashion is a common practice in reading literature and drama, but not in economics, where the standard practice (with good reason) is to provide readers with an overview of what you will say, then say it, and then summarize the key points of what you have said. By contrast, perhaps one of the most fascinating things about literature and drama is that readers and critics often notice or discover diverse themes, images, or allusions. There is a story about the noted author and critic Robert Penn Warren, who supposedly asked another author whether he had intentionally meant to suggest a theme that Warren had just identified in one of this writer's works. When the writer said no, Warren asked "But it is there, isn't it?" The author agreed. This anecdote is not meant to support the claim—often expressed by struggling students in their first university survey courses on literature and drama—that a poem or novel means one thing to one reader, something else to other readers, and one person's interpretation is as good as anyone else's. In the twentieth century Warren was, in fact, perhaps the most influential early proponent of close textual readings to determine exactly what was said in a literary work and how that meaning was developed. It is also true, however, that literary works reflect historical influences and ideas on the one hand, while on the other hand current events can make us appreciate something in Shakespeare or other classic authors in a new light. For similar reasons, an economist reading literary passages dealing with economic topics or issues may well find more interest and importance in some words, motivations, or outcomes than do most other readers.

4. Mainly as an English minor throughout graduate school, by special dispensation of the economics department at Louisiana State University. That dispensation would probably not have been granted at most economics Ph.D. programs in the 1970s, and certainly would not be granted by most Ph.D. programs today, quite possibly even at LSU.

5. A classic article on this method, co-authored by two Nobel laureates, has an equally classic title: "De Gustibus Non Est Disputandum," by George Stigler and Gary Becker (*American Economic Review* 67 [September 1977]: 76–90). But some prominent economists have pushed the boundaries of these limiting assumptions, for example James Dusenberry's work on how an individual's consumption and saving is affected by comparisons to his or her friends and colleagues (*Income, Saving and the Theory of Consumer Behavior* [Cambridge, Mass.: Harvard University Press, 1952]), and Robert Frank's works on such topics as *Choosing the Right Pond: Human Behavior and the Quest for Status* (New York: Oxford University Press, 1985) and *Passions Within Reason: The Strategic Role of the Emotions* (New York: W. W. Norton, 1988).

6. These examples are taken from Arthur Okun, *Equality and Efficiency: The Big Tradeoff* (Washington, D.C.: Brookings, 1975).

7. See D. McCloskey, "Economical Writing," *Economic Inquiry* 23 (April 1985): 187–222.

8. Again, this is one of the main themes in McCloskey's *Rhetoric of Economics.* And as William Becker and I have shown in several studies, virtually no other college and university professors are as fond of teaching using only—or almost only—"chalk and talk" as are academic economists. "Chalk and Talk: A National Survey on Teaching Undergraduate Economics,"

American Economic Review 86 (May 1996): 448–53; "Teaching Economics: What Was, Is, and Could Be," in *Teaching Economics to Undergraduates: Alternatives to Chalk and Talk,* W. E. Becker and M. Watts, eds. (Cheltenham, U.K. and Northampton, Mass.: Edward Elgar, 1998), 1–10; "Teaching Economics at the Start of the 21st Century: Still Chalk and Talk," *American Economic Review* 91 (May 2001): 446–51.

9. For a non-technical summary of the economic analysis of this issue, and other issues such as environmental regulations and policies to deal with unemployment and inflation, as well as a discussion of how the consensus view of economists on many of these issues differs from public and political opinion, see Alan Blinder, *Hard Heads, Soft Hearts: Tough-Minded Economics for a Just Society* (Reading, Mass.: Addison-Wesley Publishing, 1987).

10. On this topic, see D. Levy, *How the Dismal Science Got Its Name: Classical Economics and the Ur-text of Racial Politics* (Ann Arbor, Mich.: University of Michigan Press, 2001).

11. W. E. Becker, W. B. Walstad, and M. Watts. "A Comparison of the Views of Economists, Economic Educators, Teachers, and Journalists on Economic Issues." In *An International Perspective on Economic Education,* W. Walstad, ed. (Boston: Kluwer Academic Publishers, 1994), 65–87.

12. For example, see Jonathan Swift's "A Modest Proposal," reprinted here, which predates Adam Smith's *Wealth of Nations* but satirizes the inappropriate use of financial measures of costs and benefits.

13. For example, see A. B. Ferguson, *The Articulate Citizen in the English Renaissance* (Durham, N.C.: Duke University Press, 1965).

14. This is a paraphrase of the quotation by noted economist Philip Wicksteed that appears at the end of the epilogue. In the same book (*The Common Sense of Political Economy* [London: Macmillan, 1910]), Wicksteed makes it clear that he also values economics as much as anyone: "I have maintained from first to last that the laws of Economics are the laws of life." (vol. 2, bk. 2, ch. 1, 404).

Literary Passages on Economic Concepts, Issues, and Themes

A. Scarcity, Wants, and Resources

The fundamental economic problem is scarcity. By that statement economists mean that human wants that can be satisfied with material goods and services are unlimited, at least compared to the finite level of resources available to produce those goods and services. Because of scarcity, every parent has to teach his or her children that they can't have everything they want; but for that matter no nation has ever been able to provide its citizens with all the goods and services they want, either.

The basic premise of scarcity might well be enough to make people view economics as a "dismal science," one always telling people and nations something they don't want to hear. But scarcity is only the starting point of economics, not the end. The real rationale for the study of economics is that just because you can't have everything you want doesn't mean you can't have some of the things you want, and over time have more of those things. The key is to make good choices, and the key to good economic choices is a careful consideration of how to use resources in ways that will provide the greatest satisfaction, not only today but also in the future.

Economists classify productive resources into three or four different groups. The first group consists of natural resources or "gifts of nature," such as land, mineral deposits, virgin forests, wildlife, and scenic views of mountains, deserts, oceans, and rivers. Some economists discuss two types of human resources, labor and entrepreneurship, while others just consider both kinds of activity under the heading of human resources. Either way, a key distinction is made between routine types of labor (both manual and intellectual) and entrepreneurship. Entrepreneurs are those who make the risk-taking decisions involved in the production of goods and services, earning profits if they are successful and incurring losses if they are not. The income payments received for routine types of labor are wages and salaries. The final type of productive resource is capital. Capital goods are intermediate goods—things made to produce other goods and services, rather than for direct consumption. Factories and machinery are the most common type of physical capital. Human capital refers to the quality of labor and activities that improve it, such as education, training, and healthcare. All of these activities can increase workers' future productivity but, like physical capital, entail costs or investments to acquire—and carry the risk that the investment may turn out to be unprofitable.

While economists usually accept wants as something determined by individual consumers, or in the case of goods and services provided by the government, by voters and political leaders, literary authors are far more willing to explore normative issues related to how wants are developed and which desires are more deserving and important than others. In the excerpt below from John Milton's masque, Comus, *we see a discussion of how different kinds of resources can be used to satisfy human wants, and encounter the claim that not to satisfy those wants would be unnatural and ungrateful. That theme may surprise those who remember Milton as a Puritan who himself chose to wear simple clothing rather than to indulge in vain displays of style and fashion, like the courtiers and Charles I. But in fact there is no contradiction between these lines from the masque and Milton's personal beliefs, because they are spoken by the title character, Comus, who is the god of the underworld. This disreputable character is making this argument for a most unseemly purpose—he is attempting to seduce a virgin. In this particular passage, therefore, it seems that Milton might not have approved of the basic premise and goal of economics, to satisfy more wants despite the fundamental problem of scarcity. But on the other hand, Max Weber and other economic historians and sociologists later identified the Puritan ethic as a key factor in the development of capitalism and market societies, because that ethic also stressed the value of work, saving, and investment.*

Comus
(1634)
John Milton

Resources are available to satisfy many, but not all, human wants. Choosing which wants to satisfy and which to forgo is a question that all individuals and societies must answer, in the recognition that choices made today not only affect the economic situation they will face in the future, but also their characters and the character of their society.

Comus. O foolishness of men! that lend their ears
To those budge doctors of the Stoic fur,
And fetch their precepts from the Cynic tub,
Praising the lean and sallow Abstinence!
Wherefore did Nature pour her bounties forth
With such a full and unwithdrawing hand,
Covering the earth with odours, fruits, and flocks,
Thronging the seas with spawn innumerable,
But all to please and sate the curious taste?
And set to work millions of spinning worms,
That in their green shops weave the smooth-haired silk,
To deck her sons; and, that no corner might
Be vacant of her plenty, in her own loins

She hutched the all-worshipped ore and precious gems,
To store her children with. If all the world
Should, in a pet of temperance, feed on pulse,
Drink the clear stream, and nothing wear but frieze,
The All-giver would be unthanked, would be unpraised,
Not half his riches known, and yet despised;
And we should serve him as a grudging master,
As a penurious niggard of his wealth,
And live like Nature's bastards, not her sons,
Who would be quite surcharged with her own weight,
And strangled with her waste fertility:
The earth cumbered, and the winged air darked with
plumes,
The herds would over-multitude their lords;
The sea o'erfraught would swell, and the unsought
diamonds
Would so emblaze the forehead of the deep,
And so bestud with stars, that they below
Would grow inured to light, and come at last
To gaze upon the sun with shameless brows.

B.
Choice and Opportunity Cost

Inevitably, using scarce resources to produce or consume a particular good or service means that those resources cannot be used to produce anything else or to satisfy other consumer wants. The opportunity cost of using a resource is the next most valuable thing the resource could have been used to produce or do, because that is what has been given up.

Every economic choice entails an opportunity cost, whether it is something as simple as deciding whether to buy a hamburger or a hot dog, or something as important as choosing a career or a spouse. Robert Frost's famous poem, "The Road Not Taken," is a perfectly clear description of a choice involving an opportunity cost. Most people remember that in this poem the speaker takes the road "less traveled by," which makes "all the difference." Few remember an earlier line, which states that the roads were worn "about the same." That line suggests another basic idea in economics—an automatic process of equalizing differences among returns (after adjusting for risks) that occurs among workers with similar qualifications or investors with similar amounts of funds to invest. Whenever the overall returns become higher down one path than another, more people will start to choose that path until the roads are, in fact, worn about equally. Even then, of course, because of individual differences in skills, interests, and the willingness to accept risks, people must try to choose the road that suits them best. So perhaps Frost implies here that because of these subjective factors the choices people make are more a matter of personal perception than of how much different "roads" are actually traveled and worn. In any case, each person who comes to a crossroad must make a choice for it is impossible to travel down two roads at the same time, and the road that is chosen today often leads a person to different roads and choices tomorrow.

The Road Not Taken
(1916)
Robert Frost

Every choice has a cost because choosing to do one thing entails giving up the opportunity to do something else. Faced with the same option, different people often make different choices because they place different values on each alternative's cost and expected outcome.

Two roads diverged in a yellow wood,
And sorry I could not travel both
And be one traveler, long I stood
And looked down one as far as I could
To where it bent in the undergrowth;

Then took the other, as just as fair,
And having perhaps the better claim,
Because it was grassy and wanted wear;
Though as for that the passing there
Had worn them really about the same,

And both that morning equally lay
In leaves no step had trodden black.
Oh, I kept the first for another day!
Yet knowing how way leads on to way,
I doubted if I should ever come back.

I shall be telling this with a sigh
Somewhere ages and ages hence:
Two roads diverged in a wood, and I—
I took the one less traveled by,
And that has made all the difference.

Self-Interest and Economic Systems

A derogatory synonym for self-interest is greed. Stated more positively, self-interest encourages people to work hard and watch their pennies, and rewards them for doing it. Economists and literary authors have written about self interest in both harsh and gentle terms, discovering a social "silver lining" to many kinds of self-interested behavior and a dark side to the many activities undertaken by people who claim to be acting out of altruistic motives, but in fact are not.

Adam Smith became known as the father of economics due in large part to his emphasis on the role of competitive markets in channeling self-interested behavior into socially desirable and useful forms of behavior. In one famous example, Smith noted that we depend on a butcher to be pleasant to customers and provide a good product at a reasonable price not because of any innate goodwill the butcher has toward the rest of humanity, but rather because it is in the butcher's self-interest to be pleasant and sell good products at reasonable prices; otherwise, he would lose business to other butchers. More than seventy years before Smith published his Wealth of Nations *(1776), Bernard Mandeville expressed some of the same general ideas, somewhat more harshly, in a variety of literary formats eventually published as two volumes titled* The Fable of the Bees: Or, Public Vices, Public Benefits. *Mandeville's poem from this work, "The Grumbling Hive: Or, Knaves turn'd Honest," is reprinted below. Similar statements on self-interest appear in many surprising places in literature and drama, such as the passage from Emily Brontë's* Wuthering Heights.

Explicit and more formal discussions of different types of economic systems are somewhat rarer in literature and drama, but are represented here in excerpts from Ayn Rand's Atlas Shrugged *and T. H. White's* The Book of Merlyn. *The twentieth century may well be viewed by future historians as the greatest period of struggle between market systems based on individual rights and self-interest and command economies based on central planning and Karl Marx's famous dictum, "From each according to his abilities, to each according to his needs." But the struggle between these systems goes back almost as far as recorded history, at least to the time of ancient Sparta—which had a command economy endorsed by Plato—and Athens, the home of a market economy and the birthplace of democracy.*

Edward Bellamy's most famous work, Looking Backward, *is a modern example of a utopian novel depicting a society in which the fundamental economic problem of scarcity has been solved by reforming society, and perhaps even human nature.* Looking Backward *was extremely influential when it was first published, and led to the formation of Bellamy Societies in many communities in Europe and in the United States. Bellamy's "Parable of the Water Tank," reprinted here, is a shorter—and considerably funnier—satire of market systems, capitalists, and economists.*

Thomas Mann's Doctor Faustus *is a historical and cultural investigation of how Germany fell under Nazi control after World War I. Mann notes the presence of inflation that John Maynard Keynes, writing in 1919, had predicted would precipitate World War II. But Mann points to many other contributing factors, including the central problem that during this period of extreme isolation and dislocation in Germany the ideas of individualism and freedom were no longer seen as providing viable foundations for economic and social order. Instead, those who stayed in Germany felt that they faced a Hobson's choice (in Mann's view) between socialism and nationalism.*

The Grumbling Hive: Or, Knaves turn'd Honest: (1705)

Bernard Mandeville

Mandeville's claim that private vices result in public benefits—seen as somewhat scandalous in his day—has long been recognized as an important precursor to Adam Smith's more staid claim that competitive market systems channel self-interest into behaviors promoting general economic welfare, even when that outcome is no part of the self-interested person's original intention. Smith also shared Mandeville's skeptical view of those who claim to "trade for the publick good," concluding that he had "never known much good" to be done by them.

A Spacious Hive well stockt with Bees,
That liv'd in Luxury and Ease;
And yet as fam'd for Laws and Arms,
As yielding large and early Swarms;
Was counted the great Nursery
Of Sciences and Industry.
No Bees had better Government,
More Fickleness, or less Content:
They were not Slaves to Tyranny,
Nor rul'd by wild *Democracy*;
But Kings, that could not wrong, because
Their Power was circumscrib'd by Laws.

These Insects liv'd like Men, and all
Our Actions they perform'd in small:
They did whatever's done in Town,
And what belongs to Sword or Gown:
Tho' th' Artful Works, by nimble Slight
Of minute Limbs, 'scap'd Human Sight;
Yet we've no Engines, Labourers,
Ships, Castles, Arms, Artificers,
Craft, Science, Shop, or Instrument,
But they had an Equivalent:
Which, since their Language is unknown,
Must be call'd, as we do our own.
As grant, that among other Things,
They wanted Dice, yet they had Kings;
And those had Guards; from whence we may
Justly conclude, they had some Play;
Unless a Regiment be shewn
Of Soldiers, that make use of none.

Vast Numbers throng'd the fruitful Hive;
Yet those vast Numbers made 'em thrive;
Millions endeavouring to supply
Each other's Lust and Vanity;
While other Millions were employ'd,
To see their Handy-works destroy'd;
They furnish'd half the Universe;
Yet had more Work than Labourers.
Some with vast Stocks, and little Pains,
Jump'd into Business of great Gains;
And some were damn'd to Sythes and Spades,
And all those hard laborious Trades;
Where willing Wretches daily sweat,
And wear out Strength and Limbs to eat:
While others follow'd Mysteries,
To which few Folks bind 'Prentices;
That want no Stock, but that of Brass,
And may set up without a Cross;
As Sharpers, Parasites, Pimps, Players,
Pick-pockets, Coiners, Quacks, South-sayers,
And all those, that in Enmity,
With downright Working, cunningly

Convert to their own Use the Labour
Of their good-natur'd heedless Neighbour.
These were call'd Knaves, but bar the Name,
The grave Industrious were the same:
All Trades and Places knew some Cheat,
No Calling was without Deceit.

The Lawyers, of whose Art the Basis
Was raising Feuds and splitting Cases,
Oppos'd all Registers, that Cheats
Might make more Work with dipt Estates;
As wer't unlawful, that one's own,
Without a Law-Suit, should be known.
They kept off Hearings wilfully,
To finger the refreshing Fee;
And to defend a wicked Cause,
Examin'd and survey'd the Laws,
As Burglars Shops and Houses do,
To find out where they'd best break through.

Physicians valu'd Fame and Wealth
Above the drooping Patient's Health,
Or their own Skill: The greatest Part
Study'd, instead of Rules of Art,
Grave pensive Looks and dull Behaviour,
To gain th' Apothecary's Favour;
The Praise of Midwives, Priests, and all
That serv'd at Birth or Funeral.
To bear with th' ever-talking Tribe,
And hear my Lady's Aunt prescribe;
With formal Smile, and kind How d'ye,
To fawn on all the Family;
And, which of all the greatest Curse is,
T' endure th' Impertinence of Nurses.

Among the many Priests of *Jove*,
Hir'd to draw Blessings from Above,
Some few were Learn'd and Eloquent,
But thousands Hot and Ignorant:
Yet all pass'd Muster that could hide
Their Sloth, Lust, Avarice and Pride;

For which they were fam'd as Tailors
For Cabbage, or for Brandy Sailors:
Some, meagre-look'd, and meanly clad,
Would mystically pray for Bread,
Meaning by that an ample Store,
Yet lit'rally received no more;
And, while these holy Drudges starv'd,
The lazy Ones, for which they serv'd,
Indulg'd their Ease, with all the Graces
Of Health and Plenty in their Faces.

THE SOLDIERS, that were forc'd to fight,
If they surviv'd, got Honour by't;
Tho' some, that shunn'd the bloody Fray,
Had Limbs shot off, that ran away:
Some valiant Gen'rals fought the Foe;
Others took Bribes to let them go:
Some ventur'd always where 'twas warm,
Lost now a Leg, and then an Arm;
Till quite disabled, and put by,
They liv'd on half their Salary;
While others never came in Play,
And staid at Home for double Pay.

THEIR KINGS were serv'd, but Knavishly,
Cheated by their own Ministry;
Many, that for their Welfare slaved,
Robbing the very Crown they saved:
Pensions were small, and they liv'd high,
Yet boasted of their Honesty.
Calling, whene'er they strain'd their Right,
The slipp'ry Trick a Perquisite;
And when Folks understood their Cant,
They chang'd that for Emolument;
Unwilling to be short or plain,
In any thing concerning Gain;
For there was not a Bee but would
Get more, I won't say, than he should;
But than he dar'd to let them know,
That pay'd for't; as your Gamesters do,

That, tho' at fair Play, ne'er will own
Before the Losers what they've won.

BUT WHO can all their Frauds repeat?
The very Stuff, which in the Street
They sold for Dirt t'enrich the Ground,
Was often by the Buyers found
Sophisticated with a quarter
Of good-for-nothing Stones and Mortar;
Tho' *Flail* had little Cause to mutter,
Who sold the other Salt for Butter.

JUSTICE HER self, fam'd for fair Dealing,
By Blindness had not lost her Feeling;
Her Left Hand, which the Scales should hold,
Had often dropt 'em, brib'd with Gold;
And, tho' she seem'd Impartial,
Where Punishment was corporal,
Pretended to a reg'lar Course,
In Murther, and all Crimes of Force;
Tho' some, first pillory'd for Cheating,
Were hang'd in Hemp of their own beating;
Yet, it was thought, the Sword she bore
Check'd but the Desp'rate and the Poor;
That, urg'd by meer Necessity,
Were ty'd up to the wretched Tree
For Crimes, which not deserv'd that Fate,
But to secure the Rich and Great.

THUS EVERY Part was full of Vice,
Yet the whole Mass a Paradise;
Flatter'd in Peace, and fear'd in Wars,
They were th' Esteem of Foreigners,
And lavish of their Wealth and Lives,
The Balance of all other Hives.
Such were the Blessings of that State;
Their Crimes conspir'd to make them Great;
And Virtue, who from Politicks
Had learn'd a Thousand Cunning Tricks,
Was, by their happy Influence,

Made Friends with Vice: And ever since,
The worst of all the Multitude
Did something for the Common Good.

THIS WAS the State's Craft, that maintain'd
The Whole of which each Part complain'd:
This, as in Musick Harmony,
Made Jarrings in the main agree;
Parties directly opposite,
Assist each other, as 'twere for Spight;
And Temp'rance with Sobriety,
Serve Drunkenness and Gluttony.

THE ROOT of Evil, Avarice,
That damn'd ill natur'd baneful Vice,
Was Slave to Prodigality,
That noble Sin; whilst Luxury
Employ'd a Million of the Poor,
And odious Pride a Million more:
Envy it self, and Vanity,
Were Ministers of Industry;
Their darling Folly, Fickleness,
In Diet, Furniture and Dress,
That strange ridic'lous Vice was made
The very Wheel that turn'd the Trade.
Their Laws and Clothes were equally
Objects of Mutability;
For, what was well done for a time,
In half a Year became a Crime;
Yet while they alter'd thus their Laws,
Still finding and correcting Flaws,
They mended by Inconstancy
Faults, which no Prudence could foresee.

THUS VICE nurs'd Ingenuity,
Which join'd with Time and Industry,
Had carry'd Life's Conveniencies,
It's real Pleasures, Comforts, Ease,
To such a Height, the very Poor
Liv'd better than the Rich before,
And nothing could be added more.

HOW VAIN is Mortal Happiness!
Had they but known the Bounds of Bliss;
And that Perfection here below
Is more than Gods can well bestow;
The Grumbling Brutes had been content
With Ministers and Government.
But they, at every ill Success,
Like Creatures lost without Redress,
Curs'd Politicians, Armies, Fleets;
While every one cry'd, *Damn the Cheats,*
And would, tho' conscious of his own,
In others barb'rously bear none.

ONE, THAT had got a Princely Store,
By cheating Master, King and Poor,
Dar'd cry aloud, *The Land must sink*
For all its Fraud; And whom d'ye think
The Sermonizing Rascal chid?
A Glover that sold Lamb for Kid.

THE LEAST thing was not done amiss,
Or cross'd the Publick Business;
But all the Rogues cry'd brazenly,
Good Gods, Had we but Honesty!
Merc'ry smil'd at th' Impudence,
And others call'd it want of Sense,
Always to rail at what they lov'd:
But Jove with Indignation mov'd,
At last in Anger swore, *He'd rid*
The bawling Hive of Fraud; and did.
The very Moment it departs,
And Honesty fills all their Hearts;
There shews 'em, like th' Instructive Tree,
Those Crimes which they're asham'd to see;
Which now in Silence they confess,
By blushing at their Ugliness:
Like Children, that would hide their Faults,
And by their Colour own their Thoughts:
Imag'ning, when they're looked upon,
That others see what they have done.

But, Oh ye Gods! What Consternation,
How vast and sudden was th' Alteration!
In half an Hour, the Nation round,
Meat fell a Peny in the Pound.
The Mask Hypocrisy's flung down,
From the great Statesman to the Clown:
And some in borrow'd Looks well known,
Appear'd like Strangers in their own.
The Bar was silent from that Day;
For now the willing Debtors pay,
Ev'n what's by Creditors forgot;
Who quitted them that had it not.
Those, that were in the Wrong, stood mute,
And dropt the patch'd vexatious Suit:
On which since nothing less can thrive,
Than Lawyers in an honest Hive,
All, except those that got enough,
With Inkhorns by their sides troop'd off.

Justice hang'd some, set others free;
And after Goal delivery,
Her Presence being no more requir'd,
With all her Train and Pomp retir'd,
First march'd some Smiths with Locks and Grates,
Fetters, and Doors with Iron Plates:
Next Goalers, Turnkeys and Assistants:
Before the Goddess, at some distance,
Her chief and faithful Minister,
'Squire Catch, the Law's great Finisher,
Bore not th' imaginary Sword,
But his own Tools, an Ax and Cord:
Then on a Cloud the Hood-wink'd Fair,
Justice her self was push'd by Air:
About her Chariot, and behind,
Were Serjeants, Bums of every kind,
Tip-staffs, and all those Officers,
That squeeze a Living our of Tears.

Tho' Physick liv'd, while Folks were ill,
None would prescribe, but Bees of skill,
Which through the Hive dispers'd so wide,

That none of them had need to ride;
Wav'd vain Disputes, and strove to free
The Patients of their Misery;
Left Drugs in cheating Countries grown,
And us'd the Product of their own;
Knowing the Gods sent no Disease
To Nations without Remedies.

THEIR CLERGY rous'd from Laziness,
Laid not their Charge on Journey-Bees;
But serv'd themselves, exempt from Vice,
The Gods with Pray'r and Sacrifice;
All those, that were unfit, or knew
Their Service might be spar'd withdrew:
Nor was there Business for so many,
(If th' Honest stand in need of any,)
Few only with the High-Priest staid,
To whom the rest Obedience paid:
Himself employ'd in Holy Cares,
Resign'd to others State-Affairs.
He chas'd no Starv'ling from his Door,
Nor pinch'd the Wages of the Poor;
But at his House the Hungry's fed,
The Hireling finds unmeasur'd Bread,
The needy Trav'ler Board and Bed.

AMONG THE King's great Ministers,
And all th' inferior Officers
The Change was great; for frugally
They now liv'd on their Salary:
That a poor Bee should ten times come
To ask his Due, a trifling Sum,
And by some well-hir'd Clerk be made
To give a Crown, or ne'er be paid,
Would now be call'd a downright Cheat,
Tho' formerly a Perquisite.
All Places manag'd first by Three,
Who watch'd each other's Knavery,
And often for a Fellow-feeling,
Promoted one another's stealing,
Are happily supply'd by One,
By which some thousands more are gone.

No Honour now could be content,
To live and owe for what was spent;
Liv'ries in Brokers Shops are hung,
They part with Coaches for a Song;
Sell stately Horse by whole Sets;
And Country-Houses, to pay Debts.

Vain Cost is shunn'd as much as Fraud;
They have no Forces kept Abroad;
Laugh at th' Esteem of Foreigners,
And empty Glory got by Wars;
They fight, but for their Country's sake,
When Right or Liberty's at Stake.

Now mind the glorious Hive, and see
How Honesty and Trade agree.
The Shew is gone, it thins apace;
And looks with quite another Face.
For 'twas not only that They went,
By whom vast Sums were Yearly spent;
But Multitudes that liv'd on them,
Were daily forc'd to do the same.
In vain to others Trades they'd fly;
All were o'er-stocked accordingly.

The Price of Land and Houses falls;
Mirac'lous Palaces, whose Walls,
Like those of Thebes, were rais'd by Play,
Are to be let; while the once gay,
Well-seated Houshold Gods would be
More pleas'd to expire in Flames, than see
The mean Inscription on the Door
Smile at the lofty ones they bore.
The building Trade is quite destroy'd,
Artificers are not emply'd;
No Limner for his Art is fam'd,
Stone-cutters, Carvers are not nam'd.

Those, that remain'd, grown temp'rate, strive,
Not how to spend, but how to live,
And, when they paid their Tavern Score,

Resolv'd to enter it no more:
No Vintner's Jilt in all the Hive
Could wear now Cloth of Gold, and thrive;
Nor *Torcol* such vast Sums advance,
For *Burgundy and Ortelans*;
The Courtier's gone, that with his Miss
Supp'd at his House on *Christmas* Peas;
Spending as much in two Hours stay,
As keeps a Troop of Horse a Day.

The haughty *Chloe*, to live Great,
Had made her Husband rob the State:
But now she sells her Furniture,
Which th' Indies had been ransack'd for;
Contracts th' expensive Bill of Fare,
And wears her strong Suit a whole Year:
The slight and fickle Age is past;
And Clothes, as well as Fashions, last.
Weavers, that join'd rich Silk with Plate,
And all the Trades subordinate,
Are gone. Still Peace and Plenty reign,
And every Thing is cheap, tho' plain:
Kind Nature, free from Gard'ners Force,
Allows all Fruits in her own Course;
But Rarities cannot be had,
Where Pains to get them are not paid.

As Pride and Luxury decrease,
So by degrees they leave the Seas.
Not Merchants now, but Companies
Remove whole Manufactories.
All Arts and Crafts neglected lie;
Content, the Bane of Industry,
Makes 'em admire their homely Store,
And neither seek nor covet more.

So few in the vast Hive remain,
The hundredth Part they can't maintain
Against th' Insults of numerous Foes;
Whom yet they valiantly oppose:
'Till some well-fenc'd Retreat is found,

And here they die or stand their Ground.
Nor Hireling in their Army's known;
But bravely fighting for their own,
Their Courage and Integrity
At last were crown'd with Victory

THEY TRIUMPH'D not without their Cost,
For many Thousand Bees were lost.
Hard'ned with Toils and Exercise,
They counted Ease it self a Vice;
Which so improv'd their Temperance;
That, to avoid Extravagance,
They flew into a hollow Tree,
Blest with Content and Honesty.

THE MORAL

THEN LEAVE Complaints: Fools only strive
To make a Great an Honest Hive
T'enjoy the World's Conveniences,
Be fam'd in War, yet live in Ease,
Without great Vices, is a vain
EUTOPIA seated in the Brain,
Fraud, Luxury and Pride must live,
While we the Benefits receive:
Hunger's a dreadful Plague, no doubt,
Yet who digests or thrives without?
Do we not owe the Growth of Wine
To the dry shabby crooked Vine?
Which, while its Shoots neglected stood,
Chok'd other Plants, and ran to Wood;
But blest us with its noble Fruit,
As soon as it was ty'd and cut:
So Vice is beneficial found,
When it's by Justice lopt and bound;
Nay, where the People would be great,
As necessary to the State,
As Hunger is to make 'em eat.
Bare Virtue can't make Nations live

In Splendor; they, that would revive
A Golden Age, must be as free,
For Acorns, as for Honesty

FINIS

Wuthering Heights (1847)

Emily Brontë

Love stories are not the most likely source in literature for passages on economic ideas but even that sometimes happens, frequently built around the kinds of themes included in this brief passage. Without a foundation of shared and compatible interests—regardless of whether those interests are mild and generous or domineering—marriages based only on love prove to be no more enduring or happy than those based on mutual interests but without love.

Catherine had seasons of gloom and silence, now and then; they were respected with sympathizing silence by her husband, who ascribed them to an alteration in her constitution, produced by her perilous illness, as she was never subject to depression of spirits before. The return of sunshine was welcomed by answering sunshine from him. I believe I may assert that they were really in possession of deep and growing happiness.

It ended. Well, we *must* be for ourselves in the long run; the mild and generous are only more justly selfish than the domineering; and it ended when circumstances caused each to feel that the one's interest was not the chief consideration in the other's thoughts.

Atlas Shrugged
(1957)
Ayn Rand

Rand's writings defend individualism on philosophical, ethical, and economic grounds and, as in the passage below, attack the idea of organizing society and business on any other basis, including the notion that we ought to try to provide for other people's needs.

"Well, there was something that happened at that plant where I worked for twenty years. It was when the old man died and his heirs took over. There were three of them, two sons and a daughter, and they brought a new plan to run the factory. They let us vote on it, too, and everybody—almost everybody—voted for it. We didn't know. We thought it was good. No, that's not true, either. We thought that we were supposed to think it was good. The plan was that everybody in the factory would work according to his ability, but would be paid according to his need. We—what's the matter, ma'am? Why do you look like that?"

"What was the name of the factory?" she asked, her voice barely audible.

"The Twentieth Century Motor Company, ma'am, of Starnesville, Wisconsin."

"Go on."

"We voted for that that plan at a big meeting, with all of us present, six thousand of us, everybody that worked in the factory. The Starnes heirs made long speeches about it, and it wasn't too clear, but nobody asked any questions. None of us knew just how the plan would work, but every one of us thought that the next fellow knew it. And if anybody had doubts, he felt guilty and kept his mouth shut—because they made it sound like anyone who'd oppose the plan was a childkiller at heart and less than a human being. They told us that this plan would achieve a noble ideal. Well, how were we to know otherwise? Hadn't we heard it all our lives—from our parents and our schoolteachers and our ministers, and in every newspaper we ever read and every movie and every public speech? Hadn't we always been told that this was righteous and just? Well, maybe there's some excuse for what we did at that meeting. Still, we voted for the plan—and what we got, we had it coming to us. You know, ma'am, we are marked men, in a way, those of us who lived through the four years of that plan in the Twentieth Century factory. What is it that hell is supposed to be? Evil—plain, naked, smirking evil, isn't it? Well, that's what we saw and helped to make—and I think we're damned, every one of us, and maybe we'll never be forgiven. . . .

"Do you know how it worked, that plan, and what it did to people? Try pouring water into a tank where there's a pipe at the bottom draining it out faster than you pour it, and each bucket you bring breaks that pipe an inch wider, and the harder you work the more is demanded of you, and you stand slinging buckets forty hours a week, then forty-eight, then fifty-six—for your neighbor's supper—for his wife's operation—for his child's measles—for his mother's wheel chair—for his uncle's shirt—for his nephew's schooling—for the baby next door—for the baby to be born—for anyone anywhere around you—it's theirs to receive, from diapers to dentures—and yours to work, from sunup to sundown, month after month, year after year, with nothing to show for it but your sweat, with nothing in sight for you but their pleasure, for the whole of your life, without rest, without hope, without end .... From each according to his ability, to each according to his need....

"We're all one big family, they told us, we're all in this together. But you don't all stand working an acetylene torch ten hours a day—together, and you don't all get a bellyache—together. What's whose ability and which of whose needs comes first? When it's all one pot, you can't let any man decide what his own needs are, can you? If you did, he might claim that he needs a yacht—and if his feelings is all you have to go by, he might prove it, too. Why not? If it's not right for me to own a car until I've worked myself into a hospital ward, earning a car for every loafer and every naked savage on earth—why can't he demand a yacht from me, too, if I still have the ability not to have collapsed? No? He can't? Then why can he demand that I go without cream for my coffee until he's replastered his living room? . . . Oh well. . . . Well, anyway, it was decided that nobody had the right to judge his own need or ability. We *voted* on it. Yes, ma'am, we voted on it in a public meeting twice a year. How else could it be done? Do you care to think what would happen at such a meeting? It took us just one meeting to discover that we had become beggars—rotten, whining, sniveling beggars, all of us, because no man could claim his pay as his rightful earning, he had no rights and no earnings, his work didn't belong to him, it belonged to 'the family,' and they owed him nothing in return, and the only claim he had on them was his 'need'—so he had to beg in public for relief from his needs, like any lousy moocher, listing all his troubles and miseries, down to his patched drawers and his wife's head colds, hoping that 'the family' would throw him the alms. He had to claim miseries, because it's miseries, not work, that had become the coin of the realm—so it turned into a contest among six thousand panhandlers, each claiming that *his* need was worse than his brother's. How else could it be done? Do you care to guess what happened, what sort of men kept quiet, feeling shame, and what sort got away with the jackpot?

"But that wasn't all. There was something else that we discovered at the same meeting. The factory's production had fallen by forty per cent, in that first half-year, so it was decided that somebody hadn't delivered 'according to his ability.' Who? How would you tell it? 'The family' voted on that, too. They voted which men were the best, and these men were sentenced to work overtime each night for the next six months. Overtime without pay—because you weren't paid by time and you weren't paid by work, only by need.

"Do I have to tell you what happened after that—and into what sort of creatures we all started turning, we who had once been human? We began to hide whatever ability we had, to slow down and watch like hawks that we never worked any faster or better than the next fellow. What else could we do, when we knew that if we did our best for 'the family,' it's not thanks or rewards that we'd get, but punishment? We knew that for every stinker who'd ruin a batch of motors and cost the company money—either through his sloppiness, because he didn't have to care, or through plain incompetence—it's we who'd have to pay with our nights and our Sundays. So we did our best to be no good.

"There was one young boy who started out, full of fire for the noble ideal, a bright kid without any schooling, but with a wonderful head on his shoulders. The first year, he figured out a work process that saved us thousands of man-hours. He gave it to 'the family,' didn't ask anything for it, either, couldn't ask, but that was all right with him. It was for the ideal, he said. But when he found himself voted as one of our ablest and sentenced to night work, because we hadn't gotten enough from him, he shut his mouth and his brain. You can bet he didn't come up with any ideas, the second year."

The Book of Merlyn (1941)*

T. H. White

White's literary device of having Merlyn train King Arthur by turning him into animals, made famous in the animated Disney movie, The Sword in the Stone, *was used to raise a basic economic and political question: Is private property truly a natural right for human beings, if not for all species? That in turn leads to key questions about free trade and nationalism. In White's work, the following discussion takes place when Arthur is very old, after he has lost his kingdom.*

"Do we find, as badger's famous communists would postulate, that it is the species which owns individual property that fights? On the contrary, we find that the warfaring animals are the very ones which tend to limit or to banish individual possessions. It is the ants and bees, with their *communal* stomachs and territories, and the men, with

---

* In 1941, White submitted the complete manuscript of this work as the fifth volume of *The Once and Future King*, which was not published until 1958. That printing still did not include *The Book of Merlyn*, which was first published in 1977.

their *national* property, who slit each other's throats; while it is the birds, with their private wives, nests and hunting grounds, the rabbits with their own burrows and stomachs, the minnows with their individual homesteads, and the lyre-birds with their personal treasure houses and ornamental pleasure-grounds, who remain at peace. You must not despise mere nests and hunting grounds as forms of property: they are as much a form of property to the animals as a home and business is to man. And the important thing is that they are private property. The owners of private property in nature are pacific, while those who have invented public property go to war. This, you will observe, is exactly the opposite of the totalist doctrine.

"Of course the owners of private property in nature are sometimes forced to defend their holdings against piracy by other individuals. This rarely results in bloodshed, and men themselves need not fear it, because our king has already persuaded them to adopt the principal of a police force.

"But you want to object that perhaps the link which binds the warfaring animals together is not the link of nationalism: perhaps they go to war for other reasons—because they are all manufacturers, or all owners of domestic animals, or all agriculturalists like some of the ants, or because they all have stores of food. I need not trouble you with a discussion of possibilities, for you must examine them for yourself. Spiders are the greatest of manufacturers, yet do no battle: bees have no domestic animals or agriculture, yet go to war: many ants who are belligerent have no stores of food. By some such mental process as this, as in finding out the Highest Common Factor in mathematics, you will end with the explanation which I have offered: an explanation which is, indeed, self-evident when you come to look at it. War is due to communal property, the very thing which is advocated by nearly all the demagogues who peddle what they call the New Order.

"I have out-run my examples. We must return to the concrete instances, to examine the case. Let us look at rookery.

"Here is a gregarious animal like the ant, which lives together with its comrades in airy communities. The rookery is conscious of its nationalism to the extent that it will molest other rooks, from distant congeries, if they attempt to build in its own trees. The rook is not only gregarious but also faintly nationalistic. But the important thing is that it does not make any claim to *national property* in its feeding grounds. Any adjacent field that is rich in seed or worms will be frequented not only by the rooks of this community but also by those of all nearby communities, and, indeed, by the jackdaws and pigeons of the neighbourhood, without the outbreak of hostilities. The rooks, in fact, do not claim national property except to the minor extent of their nesting site, and the result is that they are free from the scourge of war. They agree to the obvious natural truth, that access to raw materials must be free to private enterprise.

"Then turn to the geese: one of the oldest races, one of the most cultured, one of the best supplied with language. Admirable musicians and poets, masters of the air for millions of years without ever having dropped a bomb, monogamous, disciplined, intelligent, gregarious, moral, responsible, we find them adamant in their belief that the natural resources of the world cannot be claimed by any particular sect or family of their tribe. If there is a good bed of *Zostera marina* or a good field of stubble, there may be two hundred geese on it today, ten thousand tomorrow. In one skein of geese which is moving from feeding ground to resting place, we may find white-fronts mingled with pink-feet or grey-lags or even with the bernicles. The world is free to all. Yet do not suppose that they are communists. Each individual goose is prepared to assault his neighbour for the possession of a rotten potato, while their wives and nests are strictly private. They have no communal home or stomach, like the ants. And these beautiful creatures who migrate freely over the whole surface of the globe without making a claim to any part of it, have never fought a war.

"It is nationalism, the claims of small communities to parts of the indifferent earth as communal property, which is the curse of man. The petty and driveling advocates of Irish or Polish nationalism: these are the enemies of man. Yes, and the English, who will fight a major war ostensibly for 'the rights of small nations,' while erecting a monument to a woman who was martyred for the remark that patriotism was not good enough, these people can only be regarded as a collection of benevolent imbeciles conducted by bemused crooks. Nor is it fair to pick on the English or the Irish or the Poles. All of us are in it. It is the general idiocy of *Homo impoliticus*. Aye, and when I speak rudely of the English in this particular, I would like to add at once that I have lived among them during several centuries. Even if they are a collection of imbecile crooks, they are at least bemused and benevolent about it, which I cannot help thinking is preferable to the tyrannous and cynical stupidity of the Huns who fight against them. Make no mistake about that."

"And what," asked the badger politely, "is the practical solution?"

"The simplest and easiest in the world. You must abolish such things as tariff barriers, passports and immigration laws, converting mankind into a federation of individuals. In fact, you must abolish nations, and not only nations but states also; indeed, you must tolerate no unit larger than the family. Perhaps it will be necessary to limit private incomes on a generous scale, for fear that the very rich people might become a kind of nation themselves. That the individuals should be turned into communists or anything less is quite unnecessary, however, and it is against the laws of nature. In the course of a thousand years we should hope to have a common language if we were lucky, but the main thing is that we must make it possible for a man living at Stonehenge to pack up his traps overnight and to seek his fortune without hindrance in Timbuktu. . . .

"Man might become migratory," he added as an afterthought, with some surprise.

"But this would spell disaster!" exclaimed the badger. "Japanese labour . . . Trade would be undercut!"

"Fiddlesticks. All men have the same physical structure and need of nourishment. If a coolie can ruin you by living on a bowl of rice in Japan, you had better go to Japan and buy a bowl of rice. Then you can ruin the coolie, who will by then, I suppose, be sporting it in London in your Rolls-Royce."

"But it would be the deathblow of civilisation! It would lower the standard of living. . . ."

"Fudge. It would raise the coolie's standard of living. If he is as good a man as you are in open competition, or a better one, good luck to him. He is the man we want. As for civilisation, look at it."

"It would mean an economic revolution!"

"Would you rather have a series of Armageddons? Nothing of value was ever yet got in this world, my badger, without being paid for."

"Certainly," agreed the badger suddenly, "it seems the thing to do."

"So there you have it. Leave man to his petty tragedy, if he prefers to embrace it, and look about you at two hundred and fifty thousand other animals. They, at any rate, with a few trifling exceptions, have political sense. It is a straight choice between the ant and the goose, and all our king will need to do, when he returns, will be to make their situation obvious."

The badger, who was a faithful opponent to all kinds of exaggeration, objected strongly.

"Surely," he said, "this is a piece of muddled thinking, to say that man may choose between ants and geese? In this first place man can be neither, and secondly, as we know, the ants are not unhappy as themselves."

Merlyn covered his argument at once.

"I should not have said so. It was a manner of speaking. Actually there are never more than two choices open to a species: either to evolve along its own lines of evolution, or else be liquidated. The ants had to choose between being ants or being extinct, and the geese had to choose between extinction and being geese. It is not that the ants are wrong while the geese are right. Antism is right for ants and goosyness is right for geese. In the same way, Man will have to choose between being liquidated and being manly. And a great part of being manly lies in the intelligent solution of these very problems of force, which we have been examining through the eyes of other creatures. That is what the king must try to make them see."

The Parable of the Water Tank

Edward Bellamy

(1897)

Bellamy's satire of capitalism and mainstream economists includes many key ideas put forward by Karl Marx, including the view that only labor creates wealth, profits represent a surplus value, markets produce or soon become monopolies, and the inherent cyclical instability and inevitable eventual downfall of industrialized market economies. Ironically, in many ways the collapse of the Soviet Union in the early 1990s fits the predictions of Bellamy (and Marx), far more than has the historical experience of market economies.

There was a certain very dry land, the people whereof were in sore need of water. And they did nothing but to seek after water from morning until night, and many perished because they could not find it.

Howbeit, there were certain men in that land who were more crafty and diligent than the rest, and these had gathered stores of water where others could find none, and the name of these men was called capitalists. And it came to pass that the people of the land came unto the capitalists and prayed them that they would give them of the water they had gathered that they might drink, for their need was sore. But the capitalists answered them and said:

"Go to, ye silly people! why should we give you of the water which we have gathered, for then we should become even as ye are, and perish with you? But behold what we will do unto you. Be ye our servants and ye shall have water."

And the people said, "Only give us to drink and we will be your servants, we and our children." And it was so.

Now, the capitalists were men of understanding, and wise in their generation. They ordered the people who were their servants in bands with captains and officers, and some they put at the springs to dip, and others did they make to carry the water, and others did they cause to seek for new springs. And all the water was brought together in one place, and there did the capitalists make a great tank for to hold it, and the tank was called the Market, for it was there that the people, even the servants of the capitalists, came to get water. And the capitalists said unto the people:

"For every bucket of water that ye bring to us, that we may pour it into the tank, which is the Market, behold! we will give you a penny, but for every bucket that we shall draw forth to give unto you that ye may drink of it, ye and your wives and your children, ye shall give to us two pennies, and the difference shall be our profit, seeing that if it were not for this profit we would not do this thing for you, but ye should all perish."

And it was good in the people's eyes, for they were dull of understanding, and they diligently brought water unto the tank for many days, and for every bucket which they did bring the capitalists gave them every man a penny; but for every bucket that the capitalists drew forth from the tank to give again unto the people, behold! the people rendered to the capitalists two pennies.

And after many days the water tank, which was the Market, overflowed at the top, seeing that for every bucket the people poured in they received only so much as would buy again half a bucket. And because of the excess that was left of every bucket, did the tank overflow, for the people were many, but the capitalists were few, and could drink no more than others. Therefore did the tank overflow.

And when the capitalists saw that the water overflowed, they said to the people:

"See ye not the tank, which is the Market, doth overflow? Sit ye down, therefore, and be patient, for ye shall bring us no more water till the tank be empty."

But when the people no more received the pennies of the capitalists for the water they brought, they could buy no more water from the capitalists, having naught wherewith to buy. And when the capitalists saw that they had no more profit because no man brought water of them, they were troubled. And they sent forth men in the highways, and byways, and the hedges, crying, "If any thirst let him come to the tank and buy water of us, for it doth overflow." For they said among themselves, "Behold, the times are dull; we must advertise."

But the people answered, saying: "How can we buy unless ye hire us, for how else shall we have wherewithal to buy? Hire ye us, therefore, as before, and we will gladly buy water, for we thirst, and ye will have no need to advertise." But the capitalists said to the people: "Shall we hire you to bring water when the tank, which is the Market, doth already overflow? Buy ye, therefore, first water, and when the tank is empty, through your buying, we will hire you again." And so it was because the capitalists hired them no more to bring water that the people could not buy the water they had brought already, and because the people could not buy the water they had brought already, the capitalists no more hired them to bring water. And the saying went abroad, "It is a crisis."

And the thirst of the people was great, for it was not now as it had been in the days of their fathers, when the land was open before them, for every one to seek water for himself, seeing that the capitalists had taken all the springs, and the wells, and the water wheels, and the vessels and the buckets, so that no man might come by water save from the tank, which was the Market. And the people murmured against the capitalists and said: "Behold, the tank runneth over, and we die of thirst. Give us, therefore, of the water, that we perish not."

But the capitalists answered: "Not so. The water is ours. Ye shall not drink thereof unless ye buy it of us with pennies." And they confirmed it with an oath, saying, after their manner, "Business is business."

But the capitalists were disquieted that the people bought no more water, whereby they had no more profits, and they spake one to another, saying: "It seemeth that our profits have stopped our profits, and by reason of the profits we have made, we can make no more profits. How is it that our profits are become unprofitable to us, and our gains do make us poor? Let us therefore send for the soothsayers, that they may interpret this thing unto us," and they sent for them.

Now, the soothsayers were men learned in dark sayings, who joined themselves to the capitalists by reason of the water of the capitalists, that they might have thereof and live, they and their children. And they spake for the capitalists unto the people, and did their embassies for them, seeing that the capitalists were not a folk quick of understanding neither ready of speech.

And the capitalists demanded of the soothsayers that they should interpret this thing unto them, wherefore it was that the people bought no more water of them, although the tank was full. And certain of the soothsayers answered and said, "It is by reason of overproduction," and some said, "It is a glut"; but the significance of the two words is the same. And others said, "Nay, but this thing is by reason of the spots on the sun." And yet others answered, saying, "It is neither by reason of glut, nor yet of spots on the sun that this evil hath come to pass, but because of lack of confidence."

And while the soothsayers contended among themselves, according to their manner, the men of profit did slumber and sleep, and when they awoke they said to the soothsayers: "It is enough. Ye have spoken comfortably unto us. Now go ye forth and speak comfortably likewise unto this people, so that they be at rest and leave us also in peace."

But the soothsayers, even the men of the dismal science—for so they were named of some—were loath to go forth to the people lest they should be stoned, for the people loved them not. And they said to the capitalists:

Masters, it is a mystery of our craft that if men be full and thirst not but be at rest, then shall they find comfort in our speech even as ye. Yet if they thirst and be empty, find they no comfort therein but rather mock us, for it seemeth that unless a man be full our wisdom appeareth unto him but emptiness." But the capitalists said: "Go ye forth. Are ye not our men to do our embassies?"

And the soothsayers went forth to the people and expounded to them the mystery of overproduction, and how it was that they must needs perish of thirst because there was overmuch water, and how there could not be enough because there was too much. And likewise spoke they unto the people concerning the sun spots, and also wherefore it was that these things had come upon them by reason of lack of confidence. And it was even as the soothsayers had said, for to the people their wisdom seemed emptiness. And the people reviled them, saying: "Go up, ye bald-heads! Will ye mock us? Doth plenty breed famine? Doth nothing come out of much?" And they took up stones to stone them.

And when the capitalists saw that the people still murmured and would not give ear to the soothsayers, and because also they feared lest they should come upon the tank and take of the water by force, they brought forth to them certain holy men (but they were false priests), who spake unto the people that they should be quiet and trouble not the capitalists because they thirsted. And these holy men, who were false priests, testified to the people that this affliction was sent to them of God for the healing of their souls, and if they should bear it in patience and lust not after the water, neither trouble the capitalists, it would come to pass that after they had given up the ghost they would come to a country where there should be no capitalists but an abundance of water. Howbeit, there were certain true prophets of God also, and these had compassion on the people and would not prophesy for the capitalists, but rather spake constantly against them.

Now, when the capitalists saw that the people still murmured and would not be still, neither for the words of the soothsayers nor of the false priests, they came forth themselves unto them and put the ends of their fingers in the water that overflowed in the tank and wet the tips thereof, and they scattered the drops from the tips of their fingers abroad upon the people who thronged the tank, and the name of the drops of water was charity, and they were exceedingly bitter.

And when the capitalists saw yet again that neither for the words of the soothsayers, nor of the holy men who were false priests, nor yet for the drops that were called charity, would the people be still, but raged the more, and crowded upon the tank as if they would take it by force, then took their counsel together and sent men privily forth among the people. And these men sought out the mightiest among the people and all who had skill in war, and took them apart and spake craftily with them, saying:

"Come, now, why cast ye not your lot in with the capitalists? If ye will be their men and serve them against the people, that they break not in upon the tank, then shall ye have abundance of water, that ye perish not, ye and your children."

And the mighty men and they who were skilled in war harkened unto this speech and suffered themselves to be persuaded, for their thirst constrained them, and they went within unto the capitalists and became their men, and staves and swords were put in their hands and they became a defense unto the capitalists and smote the people when they thronged upon the tank.

And after many days the water was low in the tank, for the capitalists did make fountains and fish ponds of the water thereof, and did bathe therein, they and their wives and their children, and did waste the water for their pleasure.

And when the capitalists saw that the tank was empty, they said, "The crisis is ended"; and they sent forth and hired the people that they should bring water to fill it again. And for the water that the people brought to the tank they received for every bucket a penny, but for the water which the capitalists drew forth from the tank to give again to the people they received two pennies, that they might have their profit. And after a time did the tank again overflow even as before.

And now, when many times the people had filled the tank until it overflowed and had thirsted till the water therein had been wasted by the capitalists, it came to pass that there arose in the land certain men who were called agitators, for that they did stir up the people. And they spake to the people, saying that they should associate, and then would have no need to be servants of the capitalists and should thirst no more for water. And in the eyes of the capitalists were the agitators pestilent fellows, and they would fain have crucified them, but durst not for fear of the people.

And the words of the agitators which they spake to the people were on this wise:

"Ye foolish people, how long will ye be deceived by a lie and believe to your hurt that which is not? for behold all these things that have been said unto you by the capitalists and by the soothsayers are cunningly devised fables. And likewise the holy men, who say that it is the will of God that ye should always be poor and miserable and athirst, behold! they do blaspheme God and are liars, whom he will bitterly judge though he forgive all others. How cometh it that ye may not come by the water in the tank? Is it not because ye have no money? And why have ye no money? Is it not because ye receive but one penny for every bucket that ye bring to the tank, which is the Market, but must render two pennies for every bucket ye take out, so that the capitalists may have their profit? See ye not how by this means the tank must overflow, being filled by that ye lack and made to abound out of your emptiness? See ye not also that the harder ye toil and the more diligently ye seek and bring the water, the worse and not the better it shall be for you by reason of the profit, and that forever?"

After this manner spake the agitators for many days unto the people, and none heeded them, but it was so that after a time the people hearkened. And they answered and said unto the agitators:

"Ye say truth. It is because of the capitalists and of their profits that we want, seeing that by reason of them and their profits we may by no means come by the fruit of our labor, so that our labor is in vain, and the more we toil to fill the tank the sooner doth it overflow, and we may receive nothing because there is too much, according to the words of the soothsayers. But behold, the capitalists are hard men and their tender mercies are cruel. Tell us if ye know any way whereby we may deliver ourselves out of our bondage unto them. But if ye know of no certain way of deliverance we beseech you to hold your peace and let us alone, that we may forget our misery."

And the agitators answered and said, "We know a way."

And the people said: "Deceive us not, for this thing hath been from the beginning, and none hath found a way of deliverance until now, though many have sought it carefully with tears. But if ye know a way, speak unto us quickly."

Then the agitators spake unto the people of the way. And they said:

"Behold, what need have ye at all of these capitalists, that ye should yield them profits upon your labor? What great thing do they wherefore ye render them this tribute? Lo! it is only because they do order you in bands and lead you out and in and set your tasks and afterward give you a little of the water yourselves have brought and not they. Now, behold the way out of this bondage! Do ye for yourselves that which is done by the capitalists—namely, the ordering of your labor, and the marshaling of your bands, and the dividing of your tasks. So shall ye have no need at all of the capitalists and no more yield to them any profit, but all the fruit of your labor shall ye share as brethren, every one having the same; and so shall the tank never overflow until every man is full, and would not wag the tongue for more, and afterward shall ye with the overflow make pleasant fountains and fish ponds to delight yourselves withal even as did the capitalists; but these shall be for the delight of all."

And the people answered, "How shall we go about to do this thing, for it seemeth good to us?"

And the agitators answered: "Choose ye discreet men to go in and out before you and to marshal your bands and order your labor, and these men shall be as the capitalists were, but, behold, they shall not be your masters as the capitalists are, but your brethren and officers who do your will, and they shall not take any profits, but every man his share like the others, that there may be no more masters and servants among you, but brethren only. And from time to time, as ye see fit, ye shall choose other discreet men in place of the first to order the labor."

And the people hearkened, and the thing was very good to them. Likewise seemed it not a hard thing. And with one voice they cried out, "So let it be as ye have said, for we will do it!"

And the capitalists heard the noise of the shouting and what the people said, and the soothsayers heard it also, and likewise the false priests and the mighty men of war, who were a defense unto the capitalists; and when they heard they trembled exceedingly, so that their knees smote together, and they said one to another, "It is the end of us!"

Howbeit, there were certain true priests of the living God who would not prophesy for the capitalists, but had compassion on the people; and when they heard the shouting of the people and what they said, they rejoiced with exceeding great joy, and gave thanks to God because of the deliverance.

And the people went and did all the things that were told them of the agitators to do. And it came to pass as the agitators had said, even according to all their words. And there was no more any thirst in that land, neither any that was ahungered, nor naked, nor cold, nor in any manner of want; and every man said unto his fellow, "My brother," and every woman said unto her companion, "My sister," for so were they with one another as brethren and sisters which do dwell together in unity. And the blessing of God rested upon that land forever.

Doctor Faustus
(1947)
Thomas Mann

How could a political party like the Nazis come to power in a nation with the level of cultural and economic development enjoyed by Germany in the 1920s? Mann notes the hyperinflation and other economic dislocations related to the reparations imposed on the country after World War I. But he explores even more deeply the breakdown of traditional cultural norms and ideas, set against the popular appeal and political pressure from socialist ideas and political parties on the one hand, and nationalist ideas and political parties on the other.

"He's right!" declared Matthäus Arzt candidly, whom the others called "social *Arzt,*" the "social doctor," because social concerns were his passion; he was a Christian Socialist, and often quoted Goethe's statement that Christianity had been a political revolution that, having failed, became a moral one. And, as he said now, it had to become political again, that is socialist—that was the true and sole means for disciplining the religious impulse, whose possible dangerous degenerations Leverkühn had not done a bad job of describing. Religious socialism, religiosity committed to social concerns, that was the thing, for it all depended on finding the right commitment, and the theonomous bond had to be joined to the social bond, to the task God had imposed on us to perfect society. "Believe me," he said, "everything depends on the development of a responsible industrial population, of an international industrial nation that can someday create a genuine and just European economic society. In it will be found the impulses—indeed their seeds are already found—for shaping not just the technical realization of a new economic organization, not just for a thoroughgoing cleansing of the natural interrelations of life, but also for the founding of new political orders."

I am reproducing the speeches of these young men just as they were given, along with the terms that were part of a learned jargon whose bombast they were not in the least aware of; rather they used it quite naturally, with total satisfaction and ease, flinging stilted, pretentious phrases at one another with unpretentious virtuosity. "Natural interrelations of life" and "theonomous bond" were typical affectations; one could have put it more simply, but then it would not have been the language of their theological science. They loved to put the "existential question," spoke of "sacral space" or "political space" or "academic space," of "structural principle," of "didactic tension," of "ontological correspondences," and so forth. And so now, with hands clasped behind his head, Deutschlin put the existential question about the genetic origin of Arzt's economic society. It was really nothing other than common business sense, and nothing else could ever be represented in an economic society. "We must be clear on this point, Matthäus," he said, "that the social ideal of an economic social organization arises from the Enlightenment's autonomous mode of thought, in short, from rationalism, which still never has been grasped by the powerful forces beyond or beneath reason. You believe that out of mere human insight and reason, that by equating 'just' and 'socially useful,' you can build a just order from which, you think, will come new political forms. Economic space, however, is totally different from political, and there is no direct access from ideas of economic usefulness to a political consciousness related to history. I do not understand how you can fail to see that. Political order is related to the state, which is a given form of power and control that is not based in utility and in which quite different qualities are represented than those known to the agents of industrialists or to secretaries of labor unions—honor and dignity for example. For such qualities, my good man, people in the economic space do not bring with them the necessary ontological correspondences."

"Ah, Deutschlin, what are you talking about," Arzt said. "As modern sociologists we know quite well that the state is likewise determined by its useful functions. There is the administration of justice, there is the maintenance of security. And just in general, we really do live in an economic age; the economic is simply the historical character of our age, and honor and dignity won't help the state one whit if it does not know on its own how to recognize and guide economic relationships correctly."

Deutschlin admitted as much. But he denied that utilitarian functions were the essential basis of the state. The state's legitimacy lay in its sovereignty, its authority, which was therefore independent of the value judgments of the individual, since—in contradistinction to the humbug of the *contract social*—it preceded the individual. Connections above and beyond the individual had, in fact, as much existential primality as individuals, and an economist could therefore understand nothing about the state, since he understood nothing about its transcendent foundation.

To which Teutleben said, "I am certainly not without sympathy for the social-religious bond that Arzt advocates; it is better than none at all, and Matthäus is only too right when he says that everything depends on finding the right bond. But to be right, to be concurrently religious and political, it must come from the people, and what I now ask myself is, whether a new national character can arise out of an economic society. Look at the Rhur. There you have a reservoir of human beings but no new cells of national character. Take a train sometime from Leuna to Halle. You'll see workers sitting together who can speak quite well about the question of wages, but that they might have drawn any sort of national popular strength from their common activity—that is not evident in their conversations. In economics, more and more it is the nakedly finite that holds sway. . . ."

"But nationality is finite, as well," someone else recalled, either Hubmeyer or Schappeler, I cannot say for certain. "Nationality as eternal—we can't accept that as theologians. A capacity for enthusiasm is very good and the need for faith very natural for youth, but it is also a temptation, and one must take a very close look at the substance of these new bonds offered up on all sides nowadays as liberalism dies off—whether a bond is genuine as well and whether the object establishing such a commitment is something real or perhaps merely the product of, let us say, structural romanticism, which creates ideological objects by nominalistic, if not to say, fictional means. It is my opinion, or my fear, that the people as an idol and the state as a utopia are just such nominalistic bonds, and to profess faith in them—faith in Germany, shall we say—provides no real binding commitment because it has nothing whatever to do with personal substance and qualitative content. For *that* there is no demand whatever, and when someone says 'Germany!' and declares it to be a bond of commitment, he need not prove—and no one asks, not even he of himself—how much Germanness he actually realizes in the personal, that is, in the qualitative sense and to what extent he is capable of serving the affirmation of a German form of life in the world. That is what I call nominalism, or better, making a fetish of a name, and it is, in my opinion, ideological idolatry."

"Fine, Hubmeyer," Deutschlin said, "what you say is all quite correct, and in any case I will grant you that your critique has brought us closer to the problem. I disputed Matthäus Arzt because the ascendancy of the utilitarian principle in economic space is not to my liking; but I will agree with him totally that the theonomous bond *per se*, that is, religiosity in general, has something formalistic and insubstantive about it, that it needs down-to-earth, empirical repletion or application or verification, some act of obedience to God. And so Arzt has chosen socialism and Carl Teutleben nationalism. And those are the commitments between which we have to choose at present. I deny that we have a surplus of ideologies, now that the slogan of freedom no longer washes. There are, in fact, only these two possibilities of religious obedience and religious attainment: the socialist and the nationalist. As bad luck will have it, however, they both entail questions and dangers, and very serious ones. Hubmeyer spoke very cogently about a certain nominalistic hollowness and personal insubstantiality frequently found in professions of nationalistic faith, and one should add that as a general principle it means nothing to side with life-enhancing objectivism if that has no bearing on the shaping of one's personal life but is intended merely for solemn occasions, among which I would even include the frenzy of sacrificial death. Two constituent values and qualitative components are required for genuine sacrifice: the cause, and the object sacrificed. We know of cases, however, where the personal substance of, let us say, Germanness, was very great and quite spontaneously objectivized itself as sacrifice, yet where not only was there a total lack of a professed faith in the nationalist bond, but the sacrifice also took place under the most violent negation of it, so that the tragedy consisted precisely in the contradiction between one's being and one's professed faith. . . . But enough for this evening about the nationalist commitment. As for the socialist, the hitch there is that once everything is regulated as well as possible in economic space, the question of a meaningful fulfillment of existence and of a life worthily led will remain just as open as it is today. We shall one day have the universal economic administration of earth, the complete victory of collectivism—fine, and with it will vanish man's relative insecurity, which the capitalist system with its inherent social catastrophes lets stand. That means: The last memories of the perils of human life will have vanished and with them, the spiritual problem in general. One asks oneself, why go on living. . . ."

"What I'd like to know," von Teutleben remarked, "is whether the youth of other nations . . . torment themselves with problems and antinomies."

"Hardly," Deutschlin replied dismissively. "For them everything is intellectually much easier and cozier."

"One should make the exception," Arzt suggested, "of Russia's revolutionary youth. There you'll find, if I'm not mistaken, an untiring interest in discussion and one hell of a lot of dialectic tension."

"The Russians," Deutschlin said sententiously, "have depth, but no form. Those to our west have form, but no depth. Only we Germans have both together."

"Well, if that isn't a nationalist commitment!" Hubmeyer said with a laugh.

D.
Property Rights and Incentives

One of the most basic institutional foundations of market economies is private property. The right to buy and sell things in the market presumes, of course, that what you sell is yours to sell, and what you buy becomes yours to use or keep as long as you want to keep it. More specifically, when you buy something you typically acquire two rights. The first is the right to exclude other people from using the product—forever if you buy and eat a hamburger, or for some period of time if you are buying a time-share condo in a popular vacation and resort area. The second is the right to transfer the property to someone else if you choose to do so, such as your family, heirs, friends, or favorite charity.

One longstanding debate about property rights still arises on occasion to occupy the attention of economists, policymakers, and people at neighborhood bars. In more formal terms than these arguments are usually couched, the issue is whether property rights are a "natural right," as the English philosopher John Locke argued in his list of unalienable rights: life, liberty, and property. If property rights are not a part of some natural or divine order, then they are simply a socially established institution that can be legitimately modified for purely pragmatic purposes (such as the use of eminent domain laws to secure a right-of-way for a new road or public park). They may also be severely limited as part of more sweeping social reforms, such as was seen in ancient Sparta under Lycurgus, and in the twentieth century in the Soviet Union.

A second debate about property rights concerns the incentive effects of letting people own, buy, and sell property, or of taking away people's property, including the wages, salaries, or other income they receive from owning land, financial securities, or other kinds of assets. Most literary and *economic writers who have dealt with this topic have called for some type of government transfer programs to low-income families, although there are certainly disagreements about what kinds of programs, and what levels of transfers. These writers also generally expect the transfer programs to be financed by a system of taxes that is to some degree progressive (i.e., programs that take a larger percentage of income from high-income families than from low-income families).*

The problem, as experience has shown time and again, is that taxing people's income establishes a significant disincentive to work, save, and invest. Similarly, income transfers to people who aren't working reduce their financial incentives to work, especially when transfers are reduced on a dollar-for-dollar basis when recipients do begin to earn more income. (Amazingly, at least to economists, that's exactly the kind of transfer program that prevailed in the United States through much of the second half of the twentieth century, and in many other countries as well.) If these transfers are viewed as "entitlements"—a basic right owed to anyone who lives in the country—these disincentive effects may be even stronger.

While there is a fairly high degree of consensus among economists about the best ways to design income transfer programs to support low-income families, such programs are inherently costly and entail some disincentives to work. The question of how severe are the disincentives associated with varying levels of income transfers and tax rates on wages and other earnings is much more open to debate. Neither studies of the effects of such programs in the United States, nor studies that compare programs in different nations, have provided simple, clear answers.

The passages below touch on many of these issues. Robert Frost's poem, "Mending Wall," features mostly unspoken debate between the narrator and his neighbor. The narrator sees private property as something often not loved by nature or man. Well-defined and enforced property rights may be undeniably necessary in cases where what's on one side of the wall could do harm to what's on the other, but that's not the case with these two neighbors, who are making annual repairs to a wall between one neighbor's pine trees and the other's cherry trees. The narrator's neighbor is an old man who walks "in darkness" and "will not go beyond his father's saying," which is "good fences make good neighbors." In the neighbor's mind, well-defined and maintained property rights seem to be part of the natural order. The narrator questions this, but he admits that he questions in a sense of spring-induced "mischief," and we learn that he does, in fact, repair the wall with his neighbor year after year. In fact, it is he who takes the initiative to schedule the day for repairing the wall. One wonders whether he would continue to repair the wall with another neighbor. For despite what the narrator says to his neighbor in trying to make him think about what is being walled in and walled out, if we were to judge the narrator by his actions, it seems that he too believes "good fences make good neighbors."*

In Sebastian Junger's Perfect Storm *there is a contemporary example of what the biologist Garett Hardin labeled "the tragedy of the commons." Throughout history, first with the commons areas in medieval villages, and later with buffalo, whales, and, in Junger's example, swordfish, it has been seen that when resources are held in common, rather than as private property, they are systematically overused and sometimes completely depleted. The economic reason for that is simple—when everyone has as much claim to the resource as anyone else, the incentive each person faces is to use up as much of the resource as he or she can before someone else does. Exactly the same problem confronted a parent whose two children stuffed their faces with the sugar-coated cereal their mother brought home from the store each week—until the*

---

*This passage is quite similar to sections of a famous article on property rights and externalities by Nobel laureate Ronald Coase. One of Coase's examples involved a wheat farmer whose neighbor was a rancher, and how these two neighbors might deal with the problem of the cattle eating and damaging the wheat. One possible solution was to build a fence/wall, but Coase showed that there are other alternatives that will, in many cases, be less expensive.

mother decided to divide the cereal into two containers, giving one to each child. Once half the box of cereal was their private property, the children had the incentive (and security, with their parents' help in enforcing property rights) to make the cereal last the entire week.

Some broader environmental issues, however, must be addressed with government policies such as those Junger describes in The Perfect Storm; *it is simply too difficult to use only private property incentives to deal with roaming animals and "flowing" resources such as water and air. Nevertheless, Ducks Unlimited and similar organizations have used private and public contributions to buy and improve land to address some of these problems on an extensive scale. Similarly, in the passage from Ivan Doig's* Ride with Me, Mariah Montana, *a retiring rancher decides to transfer his land to the Nature Conservancy, with the stipulation that it be used to graze buffalo. The bequest motive in Erskine Caldwell's* God's Little Acre*—religious charity—is not so pure.*

The final passage in this section is a simple but powerful example of what literary authors and critics refer to as the "sense of place." In many important ways land and culture own and shape people, sometimes over generations or even centuries. Relocations and dislocations caused by economic and technological forces are serious and sometimes traumatic episodes in a person's or a family's life. This is powerfully shown in a section from an early chapter of John Steinbeck's Grapes of Wrath, *set during the worst period of economic dislocation of the past century, the Great Depression.*

Mending Wall
(1914)
Robert Frost

A wall is Frost's symbol for private property, which gives rise to many other questions: Is this particular wall necessary, or at least useful? Is any wall? What are the costs of keeping something in and something out, and of maintaining walls? Do "good fences make good neighbors?" Could that in fact be the only major benefit of this particular wall?

Something there is that doesn't love a wall,
That sends the frozen-ground-swell under it
And spills the upper boulders in the sun,
And makes gaps even two can pass abreast.
The work of hunters is another thing:
I have come after them and made repair
Where they have left not one stone on a stone,
But they would have the rabbit out of hiding,
To please the yelping dogs. The gaps I mean,
No one has seen them made or heard them made,

But at spring mending-time we find them there.
I let my neighbor know beyond the hill;
And on a day we meet to walk the line
And set the wall between us once again.
To keep the wall between us as we go.
To each the boulders that have fallen to each.
And some are loaves and some so nearly balls
We have to use a spell to make them balance:
"Stay where you are until our backs are turned!"
We wear our fingers rough with handling them.
Oh, just another kind of out-door game,
One on a side. It comes to little more:
There where it is we do not need the wall:
He is all pine and I am apple orchard.
My apple trees will never get across
And eat the cones under his pines. I tell him.
He only says, "Good fences make good neighbors."
Spring is the mischief in me, and I wonder
If I could put a notion in his head:
"*Why* do they make good neighbors? Isn't it
Where there are cows? But here there are no cows.
Before I built a wall I'd ask to know
What I was walling in or walling out,
And to whom I was like to give offense.
Something there is that doesn't love a wall,
That wants it down." I could say "Elves" to him,
But it's not elves exactly, and I'd rather
He said it for himself. I see him there
Bringing a stone grasped firmly by the top
In each hand, like an old-stone savage armed.
He moves in darkness as it seems to me,
Not of woods only and the shade of trees.
He will not go behind his father's saying,
And he likes having thought of it so well
He says again, "Good fences make good neighbors."

The Perfect Storm (1997)

Sebastian Junger

Like the commons that were once used by everyone in a village to graze their sheep, cows, and goats, resources owned in common—which is to say not really owned by any one person, company, or organization at all—will be systematically "overgrazed," perhaps to the point of extinction. Ocean fishing grounds offer a contemporary but classic example of this problem, as well as an extremely difficult legal context in which to find solutions, given the number of countries with fishing fleets that try to use these resources. Changes in health and environmental regulations and in the technology of ocean fishing have further complicated the problem.

Finally, in 1978, the U.S. government relaxed the standards for acceptable mercury contamination in fish, and the gold rush was on. In the interim fishing had changed, though; boats were using satellite navigation, electronic fish finders, temperature-depth gauges. Radar reflectors were used to track gear, and new monofilament made it possible to set thirty or forty miles of line at a time. By the mid-eighties, the U.S. swordfish fleet alone was up to 700 boats fishing around fifty million hooks a year. "The technological change appears to be bumping up against the limits of the resource," as one government study put it at the time.

Until then the fishery had been relatively unregulated, but a new drift-entanglement net in the early eighties finally got the wheels of bureaucracy turning. The nets were a mile long, ninety feet wide, and set out all night from the stern of a converted longliner. Although the large mesh permitted juveniles to escape, the National Marine Fisheries Service was still leery of its impact on the swordfish population. They published a management plan for the North Atlantic swordfish that suggested numerous regulatory changes, including limiting the use of drift nets, and invited responses from state and federal agencies, as well as individual fishermen. A series of public hearings were held up and down the East Coast throughout 1983 and 1984, and fishermen who couldn't attend—those who were fishing, in other words—sent in letters. One of the people who responded was Bob Brown, who explained in a barely legible scrawl that he'd made fifty-two sets that year and there seemed to be plenty of mature fish out there, they just stayed in colder water than people realized. Alex Bueno of the *Tiffany Vance* wrote a letter pointing out, among other things, that draggers weren't likely to switch over to drift nets because they cost too much, and that swordfish population estimates were inaccurate because they didn't take into account fish outside the two-hundred-mile limit. Sportsfishermen accused commercial fishermen of raping the oceans, commercial fishermen accused sportsfishermen of squandering a resource, and almost everyone accused the government of gross incompetence.

In the end, the Fishery Management Plan did not include a catch quota for Atlantic swordfish, but it required all sword boats to register with the National Marine Fisheries Service, a division of the Department of Commerce. Boat owners who had never swordfished in their lives scrambled for permits just to keep their options open, and the number of boats nearly doubled while, by all indications, the swordfish stock continued to decline. From 1987 to 1991, the total North Atlantic swordfish catch went from 45 million pounds to 33 million pounds, and their average size dropped from 165 pounds to 110. This was what resource management experts know as *tragedy of the commons,* a reference to overgrazing in eighteenth-century England. "In the case of common grazing areas," explained one fisheries-management pamphlet, "grass soon disappeared as citizens put more and more sheep on the land. There was little incentive to conserve or invest in the resource because others would then benefit without contributing."

That was happening throughout the fishing industry: haddock landings had plummeted to one-fiftieth of what they were in 1960, cod landings had dropped by a factor of four. The culprit—as it almost always has been in fishing—was a sudden change in technology. New quick-freeze techniques allowed boats to work halfway around the world and process their fish as they went, and this made the three-mile limit around most countries completely ineffectual. Enormous Russian factory ships put to sea for months at a time and scoured the bottom with nets that could take thirty tons of fish in a single haul. They fished practically within sight of the American coast, and within years the fish populations had been staggered by fifty-percent losses. Congress had to take action, and in 1976 they passed the Magnuson Fishery Conservation and Management Act, which extended our national sovereignty to two hundred miles offshore. Most other nations quickly followed suit.

Of course the underlying concern wasn't for fish populations, it was for the American fleet. Having chased out the competition, America set about constructing an industry that could scrape Georges Bank just as bare as any Russian factory ship. After the passage of the Magnuson Act, American fishermen could take out federally guaranteed loans and set themselves up for business in quarter-million-dollar steel boats. To make matters worse, the government established eight regional fishing councils that were exempt from conflict-of-interest laws. In theory, this should have put fisheries management in the hands of the people who fished. In reality, it showed the fox into the chicken coop.

Within three years of Magnuson, the New England fleet had doubled to 1,300 boats. Better equipment resulted in such huge takes that prices dropped and fishermen had to resort to more and more devastating methods just to keep up. Draggers raked the bottom so hard that they actually leveled outcrops and filled in valleys—

the very habitats where fish thrived. A couple of good years in the mid-eighties masked the overall decline, but the end was near, and many people knew it. The first time anyone—at least any fisherman—suggested a closure was in 1988, when a Chatham fisherman named Mark Simonitsch stood up to speak at a New England Fisheries Council meeting. Simonitsch had fished off Cape Cod his whole life; his brother, James, was a marine safety consultant who had worked for Bob Brown. Both men knew fishermen, knew fish, and knew where things were headed.

Simonitsch suggested that Georges Bank be closed to all fishing, indefinitely. He was shouted down, but it was the beginning of the end.

The swordfish population didn't crash as fast as some others, but it crashed all the same. By 1988, the combined North Atlantic fleet was fishing over one hundred million hooks a year, and catch logs were showing that the swordfish population was getting younger and younger. Finally, in 1990, the International Commission for the Conservation of Tunas suggested a fishing quota for the North Atlantic swordfish. The following year the National Marine Fishery Service implemented a quota of 6.9 million pounds of dressed swordfish for U.S.-licensed sword boats, roughly two-thirds of the previous year's catch. Every U.S.-licensed boat had to report their catch when they arrived back in port, and as soon as the overall quota was met, the entire fishery was shut down. In a good year the quota might be met in September; in bad years it might not be met at all. The result was that not only were fishing boats now racing the season, they were racing each other.

Ride with Me, Mariah Montana (1990)

Ivan Doig

Despite the inherent problems of preserving migratory birds and other animals that cannot, or at least historically have not, been considered private property, there are many ways for individuals, private organizations, and government to take actions that help guarantee their survival. For example, breeding and grazing grounds where hunting is entirely prohibited can be purchased and set aside from other uses, and regulations and licenses can be used to protect species from overhunting. The case of the buffalo is particularly interesting because it has now become possible to fence in the animals and raise them for display in private or public parks, or to sell them for food or other commercial uses. As Doig delights in pointing out, however, it is still more difficult, expensive, and dangerous to work with buffalo than with cattle.

The sentences surprised me with their readiness, as if I was being told word by word right then instead of all those decades ago when Toussaint was yet alive. As if the telling was not at my own instigation. "'When it came the season to hunt, I rode to the Sweetgrass Hills. From up there, the prairie looked burnt. Dark with buffalo, here, there, everywhere. It was the last time. Nobody knew so, but it was. The buffalo were so many, the tribes left each other alone. No fighting. Each stayed in place, around the buffalo. Gros Ventres and Assiniboines at the northeast. Piegans at the west. Crees at the north. Flatheads at the south. For seven days, there was hunting. The herd broke apart in the hunting. I rode west, home, with the Piegans. They drove buffalo over the cliffs, there at the Two Medicine River. That, now. That was something to see."

It was not seen again, by Toussaint's young eyes or any others. Killed for their hides or killed off by disease caught from cattle, the buffalo in their millions fell and fell as the cutting edges of the American frontier swathed westward into them. That last herd, in the last west called Montana, was followed by summers of scant and scattered buffalo, like crumbs after a banquet. Then came the Starvation Winter of 1883, hundreds of the Piegan Blackfeet dying of deprivation and smallpox in their creekside camps. A hunting society vanished there in the continent-wide shadow of a juggernaut society.

Say the slaughter of the buffalo, then, for what it was: they were land whales, and when they were gone our sea of life was less rich. The herds that took their place were manmade—ranch aggregates of cattle, sheep, horses—and to this day they do not fit the earth called Montana the way the buffalo did. In the words of the old man the color of leather:

"Those Indians, they said the buffalo best. They said, when the buffalo were all here the country looked like one robe."

Enumerating is one thing and making it all add up is a hell of another. Oh, I had tried. I'd even had the ranch put through a computer earlier this year. A Bozeman outfit in the land analysis business programmed it all for me and what printed out was that, no, the place couldn't be converted into a dude ranch because with the existing Choteau dudity colonies in one direction and Glacier National Park in the other, Noon Creek was not "destination-specific" enough to compete; that maybe a little money could be made by selling hay from the ranch's irrigated meadows, if the drought cycle continued and if I wanted to try to live on other people's misfortune; that, yes, when you came right down to it, this land and locale were best fitted to support Animal Units, economic lingo for cattle or the band of sheep I already had on the place (wherever the hell they were at the moment). In short, the wisdom of the microchips amounted to pretty much the local knowledge I already possessed. That to make a go of the ranch, you had to hard-learn its daily elements. Pace your body through one piece of work after another, paying heed always to the living components—the sheep, the grass, the hay—but the gravitational wear and tear on fences and sheds and roads and equipment also somehow attended to, so that you are able to reliably tell yourself at nightfall, that was as much of a day as I can do. Then get up and do it again 364 tomorrows in a row. Sitting there seeing the ranch in its every detail, knowing every ounce of work it required. Jesus but how I right then wished for fifteen years off my age. I'd have settled for five. Yet truth knows every way to nag. Even if I had seen that many fewer calendars, would it do any good in terms of the ranch ultimately? Maybe people from now on are going to exist on bean sprouts and wear polyester all over themselves, and lamb and wool belong behind glass in a museum. Maybe what I have known how to do in life, which is ranching, simply does not register any more.

I wasn't much more than in motion before a voice called out:

"Talk to you a minute can I, Jick?"

I was beginning to wonder: was there a procession all the way out into the street of people lined up to take aim on me?

This voice was that of Shaun Finletter from the Double W and so I at least knew what the sought minute of talk was going to be about. I turned around to Shaun's faceful of blondish fuzz—some of these beardgrowers were maybe going to need a deadline extension to Montana's *bi*centenntial—and responded as civilly as I could manage: "How's tricks?"

"Oh, not bad, Jick. Yourself?"

"Just trying to stay level."

Shaun then plunged right down to business, which was the way Finletters were.

"Jick, I been hearing from headquarters. They're still real interested in making you an offer on your place."

"Are they." I felt like adding, are you sure that was headquarters making itself heard instead of hindquarters? But Shaun was a neighbor, even if I did wish his bosses in big offices would take a long walk off a short balcony.

Shaun rattled it off to me. "It's nothing against you at all, Jick . . . just a matter of big-scale economics . . . better able to put maximum animal units on that land. . . ." The Double Dub had a great history of that, all right. Running more cattle than it had country for. The original Williamson, Warren, had practically invented overgrazing, and his son Wendell got in on buying up bankrupt smaller ranches during the Depression and *really* sandwiched cattle along Noon Creek from hell to breakfast, and now the corporation computers doubtless were unitizing cows and calves onto every last spear of grass.

Yet it was their business and none of my own, how the Williamsons or the corporaiders comported themselves on WW land they had title to. The patch of earth *I* held title to was the matter here, and Shaun now stated the dollars per acre, a damn impressive sum of them, that WW, Inc. would pay to take the ranch off my hands. "You know that's top dollar, the way things are, Jick."

Shaun was a nice enough human being. Someone who would look you square in the eye, as he was now while I scanned back at him and noticed he was growing beefier, a little more face, a bit more belly, than since I'd last seen him. Actually just a year or so older than Mariah, he and she had gone together a while in high school. My God, the way things click or don't. If that had worked out into marriage instead of her going on to photography and him to an ag econ degree at Bozeman, Shaun might well have been the answer to run my ranch; might have become the one to perpetually tell the Williamsons and WW, Inc. of the world to go to hell, instead of being their errand boy to me.

If I had pounds more of brains I might be smarter, too. I struggled to get myself back on the necessary train of thought. How to reply to the dollar sign. It wasn't as if I hadn't had practice closing one or both eyes to money. The first corporate guy, who'd acted as if he already owned my ranch and me as well, I'd told to stick his offer where the sun doesn't shine. All the others since, one or two every year, I'd just told nothing doing. But now here I was being perfectly polite with Shaun because even though he was the current factotum, I had known his family and him from when he was a waggy pup. Even I had to admit I seemed to be trending away from that original stick-it stance.

Click.

Shaun gave a little jump as if he'd been goosed. For once I didn't even mind that Mariah included me in her picture ambush. It was worth it to see the caught-while-sucking-eggs expression on Shaun.

"Don't let me interrupt Noon Creek man talk," Mariah put forth coolly with the camera still up to her eye. This was a different one than I'd yet seen her use tonight. Did she possibly have a calibre for every occasion?

"It'll keep," said Shaun, wincing at the next *click*. Maybe it had been purely coincidental but after splitting up with Mariah he all but instantly married Amber, who notably stayed home and raised kids. "Think the proposition over and let me know, Jick. Mariah, it's always an event to see you," and he headed rapidly off out of pointblank range.

"He always was about halfway to being a dork," Mariah mentioned as we watched Shaun retreat. "He even necked like he was doing math."

"Yeah, well, he's maybe getting better at his calculations," I let her know. "You sure you don't want a ranch?"

"You saw how far I've gotten from the place," Mariah answered after a moment. "On the way into town."

It took me a moment, too, to discard that incident at the Double W gate. "I guess when you get to my age you're a little touchy about skulls."

"Quit that," she directed quickly. "You're much too young to be as old as you are."

Didn't I wish. But I let that pass and instead took Mariah by the elbow and turned her around to the golder flood of flag cloth. "Something I need you to do." I indicated to the panel where I'd sewn Jericho Reef halfway to completion; the panel for the McCaskills to have their stitches ride the wind on. "Sit down there and immortalize yourself."

"You promise I won't get a reputation for domesticity?" she kidded, but I could see she was tickled pink to be included in the centennial stitchwork.

"Probably not much danger," I said, and we laughed together as we hadn't for a long time.

So Mariah sat and had at it, the needle disappearing and then tugging through another dark dash of the mountainline above the ranch earth where we were both born. "It's like putting ourselves on a quilt, isn't it," her similar thought came out quietly.

"Kind of, yeah." I stood and watched her neat intense work with the needle. "But the next hundred years don't look that simple."

She knew I meant the ranch and whether to sell now or stagger on. "How are you leaning?"

"Both directions. Any advice from somebody redheaded would be a whole lot welcome."

Mariah crinkled a little face and I thought she'd stuck herself. But it turned out to be the topic that was sharp.

"You know I couldn't wait to get off the place when I was growing up," she mused. "Away to college. Away to—where I've been. I got over that and before I knew it I was fond of the place again. The ranch meant, well, it meant you and Mother, in a way. As if it was part of you—some member of the family you and she made out of the land." Now Mariah addressed downward as if reasoning to the sliver of metal passing in and out of the cloth. "But it'll never be part of me in that same way. It hurts to say, but I'm just a visitor at the ranch any more. Lexa and I dealt ourselves out of it by going off to our own lives. That's what happens. You and Mother maybe didn't know you were raising an Alaskan and a Missoulian, but that's how we turned out, didn't we. So it has to be up to you what to do with the place, Dad. It's yours. Not ours in any way that we should have a say."

"You want me to walk over there and tell Shaun the Double Dub's got itself a deal, is that it?"

Mariah swallowed, but both the tug of her needle and the look she sent me stayed steady. "It's up to you," she stood by.

Maybe I would have made that journey across the room to Shaun, right then and there, if Mariah had not abruptly put down her needle in exchange for her camera, twirled a lens on, and aimed in sudden contemplation of something occurring behind me. In curiosity, not to mention self-defense, I shifted half-around to see.

•

The Nature Conservancy guy on the other end of the phone the night before had sounded simultaneously enthused and curious, as if he wished he could peer across the distance from Helena to Noon Creek and gauge me face to face.

"Naturally we're interested in a piece of country like yours, Mr. McCaskill. We try to keep real track of what's left of the original biology there along the Rocky Mountain Front, and those native grasses on the prairie part of your place qualify for the kind of preservation we want to do. We know how you've taken care of that land. What, ah, did you have in mind?"

When I told him for comparison what the Double Dub through Shaun was offering me, he responded: "We don't always have the dollars to pay market value like that, but there's a way of doing it called a bargain sale. What that is, the differential between the market value of a ranch such as yours and what the Conservancy can afford to pay qualifies as a charitable gift; it comes off your income tax load, you net out on it. Let me run some numbers by you, okay?"

After that trot across the calculator, I said to him:

"Good enough. The outfit is yours, if you can do a couple of other things for me."

"And those are?"

I laid it on him that Kenny and Darleen had to be kept for at least a year, given a chance to perform the upkeep or caretaking or whatever on the place. "They aren't either one exactly whiz kids, but they're hell for work." My figuring was that the two of them would be able to show their worth okay within a year, but also that it conceivably might take every minute of that span.

"We can stand them, it sounds like," the Conservancy director granted in a dry tone. "And the other thing?"

When I told him, his voice sat up straighter.

"Actually, we've been thinking about a preserve for those someplace on this side of the mountains, if we could manage to get enough land together out north from Pine Butte."

"It's got to be part of the deal," I made good and sure. "The name and everything."

Through the phone earpiece I could all but hear the land preservation honcho thinking *Holy smoke, we don't get many ranchers who are such a big buddy of*.... Then with determination he said: "We'll do it."

I took a pleasant moment to cast a gaze east from the ranch house, out across the moonlit hay meadows and grass country between there and my fenceline with the

Double W. If Pine Butte could be kept a fen, this ranch could be kept a ranch. After all, W W Inc. wanted to see maximum animal units on this piece of land, didn't it? It was about to have them. Buffalo. A whole neighboring ranchful. Right in here next to a corporate cow pasture would now be the Toussaint Rennie Memorial Bison range, original inhabitants of this prairie, nice big rambunctious butting ones. Let the sonofabitching Double W tend *its* fences against those, for a change.

The Nature Conservancy headman, trying to keep delight out of his tone, carefully checked to see that we were really concluded. "That's all the details of our transaction then, Mr. McCaskill? We sure appreciate your doing this."

"One more thing," I said into the phone. "Happy next hundred years."

God's Little Acre
(1933)
Erskine Caldwell

Charitable acts are good for the soul and make people feel better, which creates strong incentives for making donations. But for some people charity always begins at home, to the point that their motives become suspect and their actions humorous, if not hypocritical.

"I've always been a religious man, all my life I have. I've always done the best I could, no matter how much I was provoked, and I've tried to get my boys and girls to do the same. You see that piece of ground over yonder, Pluto? Well, that's God's little acre. I set aside an acre of my farm for God twenty-seven years ago, when I bought this place, and every year I give the church all that comes off that acre of ground. If it's cotton, I give the church all the money that cotton brings at market. The same with hogs, when I raised them, and about corn, too, when I plant it. That's God's little acre, Pluto. I'm proud to divide what little I have with God."

"What's growing on it this year?"

"Growing on it? Nothing, Pluto. Nothing but maybe beggar-lice and cockleburs now. I just couldn't find the time to plant cotton on it this year. Me and the boys . . . have been so busy with other things I just had to let God's little acre lie fallow for the time being."

Pluto sat up and looked across the field towards the pine woods. There were such great piles of excavated sand and clay heaped over the ground that it was difficult to see much further than a hundred yards without climbing a tree.

"Where'd you say that acre of land was, Ty Ty?"

"Over there near the woods. You won't be able to see much of it from here."

"Why did you put it 'way over there? Ain't that a sort of out-of-the-way place for it to be, Ty Ty?"

"Well, I'll tell you, Pluto. It ain't always been where it is now. I've been compelled to shift it around a heap during the past twenty-seven years. When the boys get to discussing where we'll start digging anew, it seems like it always falls on God's little acre. I don't know why that is, either. I'm set against digging on His ground, so I've been compelled to shift it around over the farm to keep from digging it up."

"You ain't scared of digging on it and striking a lode, are you, Ty Ty?"

"No, I wouldn't say that, but I'd hate to have to see the lode struck on God's little acre the first thing, and be compelled to turn it over to the church. That preacher's getting all he needs like it is. I'd hate something awful to have to give all the gold to him. I couldn't stand for that, Pluto."

❧

"That lode might be thirty feet in the ground, and at a place we haven't started digging into yet."

"It might be on God's little acre," Buck said. "What would you do about that? You wouldn't dig nuggets when they were all going to the preacher and the church, would you? I know I wouldn't. All the gold I get is going into my pockets, at least my share of it. I wouldn't be giving it to the preacher at the church."

"We ought to give up that piece of ground till we can dig on it and make sure," Shaw said. "God's not in need of it, and the first thing you know, we're going to strike a lode on it. I'll be dog-goned if I'm going to dig for nuggets and see that preacher get them. I'm in favor of shifting that piece of land till we can see what's in it."

"All right, boys," Ty Ty agreed, "I'll move it again, but I ain't aiming to do away with God's little acre altogether. It's His and I can't take it away from him after twenty-seven years. That wouldn't be right. But there ain't nothing wrong with shifting it a little, if need be. It would be a heathen shame to strike the lode on it, to be sure, the first thing, and I reckon I'd better shift it so we won't be bothered."

"Why don't you put it over here where the house and barn are, Pa?" Griselda suggested. "There's nothing under this house, and you can't be digging under it, anyway."

"I'd never thought of doing that, Griselda," Ty Ty said, "but it sure sounds fine to me. I reckon I'll shift it over here. Now, I'm pretty much glad to get that off my mind."

Pluto turned his head and looked at Ty Ty.

"You haven't shifted it already, have you, Ty Ty?" he asked.

"Shifted it already? Why, sure. This is God's little acre we're sitting on right now. I moved it from over yonder to right here."

"You're the quickest man of action I've ever heard about," Pluto said, shaking his head. "And that's a fact."

THE GRAPES OF WRATH
(1939)
John Steinbeck

Economists who study worker and family mobility have long recognized that there are few things more cumbersome and expensive to uproot and move than people, and especially large families. One reason for this is the attachment to a place—a house or town or piece of land, no matter how ugly and poor it may seem to others—that people often develop after living there for many years. In that sense land comes to own people as much or more than people own land, making the prospect of leaving a place a very difficult one to bear. Historically, however, Americans have been far more mobile than the citizens of other nations, even ones with market economies and similar levels of income and wealth.

At noon the tractor driver stopped sometimes near a tenant house and opened his lunch: sandwiches wrapped in waxed paper, white bread, pickle, cheese, Spam, a piece of pie branded like an engine part. He ate without relish. And tenants not yet moved away came out to see him, looked curiously while the goggles were taken off, and the rubber dust mask, leaving white circles around the eyes and a large white circle around nose and mouth. The exhaust of the tractor puttered on, for fuel is so cheap it is more efficient to leave the engine running than to heat the Diesel nose for a new start. Curious children crowded close, ragged children who ate their fried dough as they watched. They watched hungrily the unwrapping of the sandwiches, and their hunger-sharpened noses smelled the pickle, cheese, and Spam. They didn't speak to the driver. They watched his hand as it carried food to his mouth. They did not watch him chewing; their eyes followed the hand that held the sandwich. After a while the tenant who could not leave the place came out and squatted in the shade beside the tractor.

"Why, you're Joe Davis's boy!"

"Sure," the driver said.

"Well, what you doing this kind of work for—against your own people?"

"Three dollars a day. I got damn sick of creeping for my dinner—and not getting it. I got a wife and kids. We got to eat. Three dollars a day, and it comes every day."

"That's right," the tenant said. "But for your three dollars a day fifteen or twenty families can't eat at all. Nearly a hundred people have to go out and wander on the roads for your three dollars a day. Is that right?"

And the driver said, "Can't think of that. Got to think of my own kids. Three dollars a day, and it comes every day. Times are changing, mister, don't you know? Can't make a living on the land unless you've got two, five, ten thousand acres and a tractor. Crop land isn't for little guys like us any more. You don't kick up a howl because you can't make Fords, or because you're not the telephone company. Well, crops are like that now. Nothing to do about it. You try to get three dollars a day someplace. That's the only way."

The tenant pondered. "Funny thing how it is. If a man owns a little property, that property is him, it's part of him, and it's like him. If he owns property only so he can walk on it and handle it and be sad when it isn't doing well, and feel fine when the rain falls on it, that property is him, and some way he's bigger because he owns it. Even if he isn't successful he's big with his property. That is so."

And the tenant pondered more. "But let a man get property he doesn't see, or can't take time to get his fingers in, or can't be there to walk on it—why, then the property is the man. He can't do what he wants, he can't think what he wants. The property is the man, stronger than he is. And he is small, not big. Only his possessions are big—and he's the servant of his property. That is so, too."

The driver munched the branded pie and threw the crust away. "Times are changed, don't you know? Thinking about stuff like that don't feed the kids. Get your three dollars a day, feed your kids. You got no call to worry about anybody's kids but your own. You get a reputation for talking like that, and you'll never get three dollars a day. Big shots won't give you three dollars a day if you worry about anything but your three dollars a day."

"Nearly a hundred people on the road for your three dollars. Where will we go?"

"And that reminds me," the driver said, "you better get out soon. I'm going through the dooryard after dinner."

"You filled in the well this morning."

"I know. Had to keep the line straight. But I'm going through the dooryard after dinner. Got to keep the lines straight. And—well, you know Joe Davis, my old man, so I'll tell you this. I got orders wherever there's a family not moved out—if I have an accident—you know, get too close and cave the house in a little—well, I might get a couple of dollars. And my youngest kid never had no shoes yet."

"I built it with my hands. Straightened old nails to put the sheathing on. Rafters are wired to the stringers with baling wire. It's mine. I built it. You bump it down—I'll be in the window with a rifle. You even come too close and I'll pot you like a rabbit."

"It's not me. There's nothing I can do. I'll lose my job if I don't do it. And look—suppose you kill me? They'll just hang you, but long before you're hung there'll be another guy on the tractor, and he'll bump the house down. You're not killing the right guy."

"That's so," the tenant said. "Who gave you orders? I'll go after him. He's the one to kill."

"You're wrong. He got his orders from the bank. The bank told him, 'Clear those people out or it's your job.'"

"Well, there's a president of the bank. There's a board of directors. I'll fill up the magazine of the rifle and go into the bank."

The driver said, "Fellow was telling me the bank gets orders from the East. The orders were, 'Make the land show profit or we'll close you up.'"

"But where does it stop? Who can we shoot? I don't aim to starve to death before I kill the man that's starving me."

"I don't know. Maybe there's nobody to shoot. Maybe the thing isn't men at all. Maybe, like you said, the property's doing it. Anyway I told you my orders."

"I got to figure," the tenant said. "We all got to figure. There's some way to stop this. It's not like lightning or earthquakes. We've got a bad thing made by men, and by God that's something we can change." The tenant sat in his doorway, and the driver thundered his engine and started off, tracks falling and curving, harrows combing, and the phalli of the seeder slipping into the ground. Across the doorway the tractor cut, and the hard, foot-beaten ground was seeded field, and the tractor cut through again; the uncut space was ten feet wide. And back he came. The iron guard bit into the house-corner, crumbled the wall, and wrenched the little house from its foundation so that it fell sideways, crushed like a bug. And the driver was goggled and a rubber mask covered his nose and mouth. The tractor cut a straight line on, and the air and the ground vibrated with its thunder. The tenant man stared after it, his rifle in his hand. His wife was beside him, and the quiet children behind. And all of them stared after the tractor.

E. Specialization, the Division of Labor, and Economies and Diseconomies of Scale

Adam Smith, the founding father of economics as an autonomous academic discipline, viewed specialization and the division of labor as one of the most important sources of increased productivity, which translates into higher levels of national output (or in Smith's terms, the true "wealth of nations") and material standards of living. Specialization is simply the idea of people or nations producing a narrower range of goods and services than they consume. The division of labor refers to breaking down a production process into many small steps and performing those steps separately, with different workers doing different tasks, as on an assembly line.

With specialization and the division of labor, workers become more experienced and skilled at what they do. New tools and machinery are often developed to do these specialized jobs more efficiently, further increasing productivity and allowing more and more goods and services to be produced by fewer and fewer workers. In the short run, that can mean some workers are displaced from their current jobs by the introduction of new kinds of machinery and technology. As long as the fundamental economic problem of scarcity exists, however, workers who are displaced from one kind of labor can—perhaps with additional education and training—be moved to the production of other goods and services. In other words, despite centuries-old concerns about technological unemployment, the ability to produce more goods and services with less labor and other resources is clearly a blessing, not a curse. That has obviously been the experience of the United States and other industrialized nations since the industrial revolution, where full employment is still the norm after such revolutionary inventions as railroads, automobiles, airplanes, and computers. During that period, the world's leading economies moved from an employment base in which most workers and their families worked in agricultural occupations, first to economies where most jobs were in manufacturing, and finally in recent decades to economies dominated by the professional and service sectors.

Smith and other economists have always recognized that there is, however, a serious downside to specialization and the division of labor. Workers can become so specialized that it becomes difficult for them to communicate with workers in other occupations, and while many specialized jobs are both financially and intellectually rewarding, the jobs held by unskilled workers can be incredibly tedious and dull. Smith even said bluntly that specialization makes workers in some kinds of jobs as stupid as it is possible for human beings to be.

Specialization also leads to issues of size and standardization. Not always, but in some cases, the least expensive way to produce a good or service turns out to be in very high levels of volume, in order to take advantage of what economists call "economies of scale." In such cases it takes fewer producers to meet the demand for a product in a nation, and as a result small, independent producers come under increasing pressure from large national, or even international, concerns. There were hundreds of small automobile producers in the United States during the first quarter of the twentieth century, but their cost of producing cars was so high, compared to Henry Ford's assembly line production methods, that today there are only a few U.S. automobile companies, and fewer than twenty large producers of automobiles in the entire world. In other kinds of markets the advantages of large-scale production are important but not so pervasive—for example, there are nationwide chains of fast-food restaurants, but in most cities there are still independent restaurants and drive-ins selling similar kinds of food. In still other kinds of markets, such as medicine, law, and construction, national chains remain rare.

Many literary authors have recognized both the advantages and disadvantages of specialization, the division of labor, and economies and diseconomies of scale. In a passage from Winesburg, Ohio, Sherwin Anderson shows two characters with highly specialized skills and insights, George Willard and "Wing" Biddlebaum, trying to talk to each other. George is, in fact, one of the few people that Wing is able to talk to, and he warns George not to deny or waste his special gifts by trying to be like everyone else. In the passage from John Steinbeck's East of Eden, Steinbeck's characters describe both the importance of specialization, given the increasing difficulty of keeping up with information from many different fields, and the need to maintain broader understandings of how different topics and fields are related and how they affect people's lives and fundamental desires. Several of the poems from Edgar Lee Master's Spoon River Anthology deal with workers from different occupations whose outlooks have been shaped, at least in part, by their jobs. In Sister Carrie, Theodore Dreiser recognized, as did Adam Smith, that the degree of specialization is limited by the extent of the market. The larger the city, the more specialized the shops, restaurants, and other kinds of firms and jobs can be. And what has seemed large and impressive in a smaller city can be small and inadequate in a much larger market. The "Tin Lizzie" passage on Henry Ford, from John Dos Passos's U.S.A., is included in the next section on entrepreneurship and profits, but it also contains interesting material on specialization and assembly line production. In Travels with Charley, John Steinbeck considers another trade-off associated with specialization and economies of scale in operating many kinds of businesses as national franchises: the gains from providing a known, standardized product come with a corresponding diminution of local and regional diversity and sense of identity.

Winesburg, Ohio
(1919)
Sherwood Anderson

At social or professional events where people from different occupations and fields of specialization are brought together, typically the doctors will talk to other doctors, lawyers to other lawyers, economists to other economists, etc. It is often difficult to find common interests, experiences, or even a common vocabulary when approaching people from other walks of life, even when their education and income levels are similar to one's own. In Anderson's passage, the differences in specialization are even more extreme: Wing Biddlebaum is renowned for his physical skills, while George Willard is a gifted young journalist with special talents in communicating with others. Like Adam Smith's famous example of philosophers and street porters, these two characters, who seem to be such opposites, have a great deal in common; but they find that hard to recognize or admit.

In the presence of George Willard, Wing Biddlebaum, who for twenty years had been the town mystery, lost something of his timidity, and his shadowy personality, submerged in a sea of doubts, came forth to look at the world. With the young reporter at his side, he ventured in the light of day into Main Street or strode up and down on the rickety front porch of his own house, talking excitedly. The voice that had been low and trembling became shrill and loud. The bent figure straightened. With a kind of wriggle, like a fish returned to the brook by the fisherman, Biddlebaum the silent began to talk, striving to put into words the ideas that had been accumulated by his mind during long years of silence.

Wing Biddlebaum talked much with his hands. The slender expressive fingers, forever active, forever striving to conceal themselves in his pockets or behind his back, came forth and became the piston rods of his machinery of expression.

The story of Wing Biddlebaum is a story of hands. Their restless activity, like unto the beating of the wings of an imprisoned bird, had given him his name. Some obscure poet of the town had thought of it. The hands alarmed their owner. He wanted to keep them hidden away and looked with amazement at the quiet inexpressive hands of other men who worked beside him in the fields, or passed, driving sleepy teams on country roads.

When he talked to George Willard, Wing Biddlebaum closed his fists and beat them upon a table or on the walls of his house. The action made him more comfortable. If the desire to talk came to him when the two were walking in the fields, he sought out a stump or the top board of a fence and with his hands pounding busily talked with renewed ease.

The story of Wing Biddlebaum's hands is worth a book in itself. Sympathetically set forth it would tap many strange, beautiful qualities in obscure men. It is a job for a poet. In Winesburg the hands had attracted attention merely because of their activity. With them Wing Biddlebaum had picked as high as a hundred and forty quarts of strawberries in a day. They became his distinguishing feature, the source of his fame. Also they made more grotesque an already grotesque and elusive individuality. Winesburg was proud of the hands of Wing Biddlebaum in the same spirit in which it was proud of Banker White's new stone house and Wesley Moyer's bay stallion, Tony Tip, that had won the two-fifteen trot at the fall races in Cleveland.

As for George Willard, he had many times wanted to ask about the hands. At times an almost overwhelming curiosity had taken hold of him. He felt that there must be a reason for their strange activity and their inclination to keep hidden away and only a growing respect for Wing Biddlebaum kept him from blurting out the questions that were often in his mind.

Once he had been on the point of asking. The two were walking in the fields on a summer afternoon and had stopped to sit upon a grassy bank. All afternoon Wing Biddlebaum had talked as one inspired. By a fence he had stopped and beating like a giant woodpecker upon the top board had shouted at George Willard, condemning his tendency to be too much influenced by the people about him. "You are destroying yourself," he cried. "You have the inclination to be alone and to dream and you are afraid of dreams. You want to be like others in town here. You hear them talk and you try to imitate them."

On the grassy bank Wing Biddlebaum had tried again to drive his point home. His voice became soft and reminiscent, and with a sigh of contentment he launched into a long rambling talk, speaking as one lost in a dream.

Out of the dream Wing Biddlebaum made a picture for George Willard. In the picture men lived again in a kind of pastoral golden age. Across a green open country came clean-limbed young men, some afoot, some mounted upon horses. In crowds the young men came to gather about the feet of an old man who sat beneath a tree in a tiny garden and who talked to them.

Wing Biddlebaum became wholly inspired. For once he forgot the hands. Slowly they stole forth and lay upon George Willard's shoulders. Something new and bold came into the voice that talked. "You must try to forget all you have learned," said the old man. "You must begin to dream. From this time on you must shut your ears to the roaring of the voices."

Pausing in his speech, Wing Biddlebaum looked long and earnestly at George Willard. His eyes glowed. Again he raised the hands to caress the boy and then a look of horror swept over his face.

With a convulsive movement of his body, Wing Biddlebaum sprang to his feet and thrust his hands deep into his trousers pockets. Tears came to his eyes. "I must be getting along home. I can talk no more with you," he said nervously.

East of Eden
John Steinbeck
(1952)

Education can be aimed at developing narrow, specialized skills in a particular vocation, such as accounting or engineering, or it can stress general skills and outlooks, such as liberal arts and communications. The relative value of these approaches to education has been discussed for centuries by educators, philosophers, and, as here, by members of the same family.

To Cal the day was endless. He wanted to leave the house and couldn't. At eleven o'clock Adam went to the closed draft-board office to brood over the records of a new batch of boys coming up.

Aron seemed perfectly calm. He sat in the living room, looking at cartoons in old numbers of the *Review of Reviews*. From the kitchen the odor of the bursting juices of roasting turkey began to fill the house.

Cal went into his room and took out his present and laid it on his desk. He tried to write a card to put on it. "To my father from Caleb"—"To Adam Trask from Caleb Trask." He tore the cards in tiny pieces and flushed them down the toilet.

He thought, Why give it to him today? Maybe tomorrow I could go to him quietly and say, This is for you, and then walk away. That would be easier. "No," he said aloud. "I want the others to see." It had to be that way. But his lungs were compressed and the palms of his hands were wet with stage fright. And then he thought of the morning when his father got him out of jail. The warmth and closeness—they were the things to remember—and his father's trust. Why, he had even said it. "I trust you." He felt much better then.

At about three o'clock he heard Adam come in and there was the low sound of voices conversing in the living room. Cal joined his father and Aron.

Adam was saying. "The times are changed. A boy must be a specialist or he will get nowhere. I guess that's why I'm so glad you're going to college."

Aron said, "I've been thinking about that, and I wonder."

"Well, don't think any more. Your first choice is right. Look at me. I know a little about a great many things and not enough about any one of them to make a living in these times."

Cal sat down quietly. Adam did not notice him. His face was concentrated on his thought.

"It's natural for a man to want his son to succeed," Adam went on. "And maybe I can see better than you can."

Lee looked in. "The kitchen scales must be way off," he said. "The turkey's going to be done earlier than the chart says. I'll bet that bird doesn't weigh eighteen pounds."

Adam said, "Well, you can keep it warm" and he continued, "Old Sam Hamilton saw this coming. He said there couldn't be any more universal philosophers. The weight of knowledge is too great for one mind to absorb. He saw a time when one man would know only one little fragment, but he would know it well."

"Yes," Lee said from the doorway, "and he deplored it. He hated it."

"Did he now?" Adam asked.

Lee came into the room. He held the big basting spoon in his right hand, and he cupped his left under the bowl for fear it would drip on the carpet. He came into the room and forgot and waved his spoon and drops of turkey fat fell to the floor. "Now you question it, I don't know," he said. "I don't know whether he hated it or I hate it for him."

"Don't get so excited," said Adam. "Seems to me we can't discuss anything any more but you take it as a personal insult."

"Maybe the knowledge is too great and maybe men are growing too small," said Lee. "Maybe, kneeling down to atoms, they're becoming atom-sized in their souls. Maybe a specialist is only a coward, afraid to look out of his little cage. And think what any specialist misses—the whole world over his fence."

"We're only talking about making a living."

"A living—or money," Lee said excitedly. "Money's easy to make if it's money you want. But with a few exceptions people don't want money. They want luxury and they want love and they want admiration."

"All right. But do you have any objection to college? That's what we're talking about."

"I'm sorry," said Lee. "You're right, I do seem to get too excited. No, if college is where a man can go to find his relation to his whole world, I don't object. Is it that? Is it that, Aron?"

"I don't know," said Aron.

Spoon River Anthology
(1915)
Edgar Lee Masters

Many family names are based on the occupation of a distant ancestor, for example, a tailor, smith, baker, or fisher. To a large extent—some say far too large—even today a person becomes defined by what he does. But by the same token a person's interests, abilities, skills, and character also play a major role in determining what kind of occupation he will have.

Walter Simmons

My parents thought that I would be
As great as Edison or greater:
For as a boy I made balloons
And wondrous kites and toys with clocks
And little engines with tracks to run on
And telephones of cans and thread.
I played the cornet and painted pictures,
Modeled in clay and took the part
Of the villain in the "Octoroon."
But then at twenty-one I married
And had to live, and so, to live
I learned the trade of making watches
And kept the jewelry store on the square,
Thinking, thinking, thinking, thinking,—
Not of business, but of the engine
I studied the calculus to build.
And all Spoon River watched and waited
To see it work, but it never worked.
And a few kind souls believed my genius
Was somehow hampered by the store.
It wasn't true. The truth was this:
I didn't have the brains.

"Butch" Weldy

After I got religion and steadied down
They gave me a job in the canning works,
And every morning I had to fill
The tank in the yard with gasoline,

That fed the blow-fires in the sheds
To heat the soldering irons.
And I mounted a rickety ladder to do it,
Carrying buckets full of the stuff.
One morning, as I stood there pouring,
The air grew still and seemed to heave,
And I shot up as the tank exploded,
And down I came with both legs broken,
And my eyes burned crisp as a couple of eggs.
For someone left a blow-fire going,
And something sucked the flame in the tank.
The Circuit Judge said whoever did it
Was a fellow-servant of mine, and so
Old Rhodes' son didn't have to pay me.
And I sat on the witness stand as blind
As Jack the Fiddler, saying over and over,
"I didn't know him at all."

Schroeder the Fisherman

I sat on the bank above Bernadotte
And dropped crumbs in the water,
Just to see the minnows bump each other,
Until the strongest got the prize.
Or I went to my little pasture,
Where the peaceful swine were asleep in the wallow,
Or nosing each other lovingly,
And emptied a basket of yellow corn,
And watched them push and squeal and bite,
And trample each other to get the corn.
And I saw how Christian Dallman's farm,
Of more than three thousand acres,
Swallowed the patch of Felix Schmidt,
As a bass will swallow a minnow.
And I say if there's anything in man—
Spirit, or conscience, or breath of God
That makes him different from fishes or hogs,
I'd like to see it work!

Eugene Carma

Rhodes' slave! Selling shoes and gingham,
Flour and bacon, overalls, clothing, all day long
For fourteen hours a day the three hundred and thirteen days
For more than twenty years.
Saying "Yes'm" and "Yes, sir" and "Thank you"
A thousand times a day, and all for fifty dollars a month.
Living in this stinking room in the rattle-trap "Commercial."
And compelled to go to Sunday School, and to listen
To the Rev. Abner Peet one hundred and four times a year
For more than an hour at a time,
Because Thomas Rhodes ran the church
As well as the store and the bank.
So while I was tying my neck-tie that morning
I suddenly saw myself in the glass:
My hair all gray, my face like a sodden pie.
So I cursed and cursed: You damned old thing!
You cowardly dog! You rotten pauper!
You Rhodes' slave! Till Roger Baughman
Thought I was having a fight with some one,
And looked through the transom just in time
To see me fall on the floor in a heap
From a broken vein in my head.

☙

"Ace" Shaw

I never saw any difference
Between playing cards for money
And selling real estate,
Practicing law, banking, or anything else.
For everything is chance.
Nevertheless
Seest thou a man diligent in business?
He shall stand before Kings!

☙

Davis Matlock

Suppose it is nothing but the hive:
That there are drones and workers
And queens, and nothing but storing honey—
(Material things as well as culture and wisdom)—

For the next generation, this generation never living,
Except as it swarms in the sun-light of youth,
Strengthening its wings on what has been gathered,
And tasting, on the way to the hive
From the clover field, the delicate spoil.
Suppose all this, and suppose the truth:
That the nature of man is greater
Than nature's need in the hive;
And you must bear the burden of life,
As well as the urge from your spirit's excess—
Well, I say to live it out like a god
Sure of immortal life, though you are in doubt,
Is the way to live it.
If that doesn't make God proud of you
Then God is nothing but gravitation,
Or sleep is the golden goal.

Sister Carrie
(1900)
Theodore Dreiser

A very old but always popular theme in literature and popular music can be summarized in two short questions: Can the small-town boy or girl make it in the big city? Is it better to be a big fish in a small pond than a little (or even eaten) fish in a large pond? The larger the pond the more scope and scale there is for higher levels of specialization, but there is also more competition.

Whatever a man like Hurstwood could be in Chicago, it is very evident that he would be but an inconspicuous drop in an ocean like New York. In Chicago, whose population still ranged about 500,000, millionaires were not numerous. The rich had not become so conspicuously rich as to drown all moderate incomes in obscurity. The attention of the inhabitants was not so distracted by local celebrities in the dramatic, artistic, social, and religious fields as to shut the well-positioned man from view. In Chicago the two roads to distinction were politics and trade. In New York the roads were any one of a half-hundred, and each had been diligently pursued by hundreds, so that celebrities were numerous. The sea was already full of whales. A common fish must needs disappear wholly from view—remain unseen. In other words, Hurstwood was nothing.

There is a more subtle result of such a situation as this, which, though not always taken into account, produces the tragedies of the world. The great create an atmosphere which reacts badly upon the small. This atmosphere is easily and quickly felt. Walk among the magnificent residences, the splendid equipages, the gilded ships, restaurants, resorts of all kinds; scent the flowers, the silks, the wines; drink of the laughter springing from the soul of luxurious content, of the glances which gleam like light from defiant spears; feel the quality of the smiles which cut like glistening swords and of strides born of place, and you should know of what is the atmosphere of the high and mighty. Little use to argue that of such is not the kingdom of greatness, but so long as the world is attracted by this and the human heart views this as the one desirable realm which it must attain, so long, to that heart, will this remain the realm of greatness. So long, also, will the atmosphere of this realm work its desperate results in the soul of man. It is like a chemical reagent. One day of it, like one drop of the other, will so affect and discolour the views, the aims, the desire of the mind, that it will thereafter remain forever dyed. A day of it to the untried mind is like opium to the untried body. A craving is set up which, if gratified, shall eternally result in dreams and death. Aye! dreams unfulfilled—gnawing, luring, idle phantoms which beckon and lead, beckon and lead, until death and dissolution dissolve their power and restore us blind to nature's heart.

A man of Hurstwood's age and temperament is not subject to the illusions and burning desires of youth, but neither has he the strength of hope which gushes as a fountain in the heart of youth. Such an atmosphere could not incite in him the cravings of a boy of eighteen, but in so far as they were excited, the lack of hope made them proportionately bitter. He could not fail to notice the signs of affluence and luxury on every hand. He had been to New York before and knew the resources of its folly. In part it was an awesome place to him, for here gathered all that he most respected on this earth—wealth, place, and fame. The majority of the celebrities with whom he had tipped glasses in his day as manager hailed from this self-centered and populous spot. The most inviting stories of pleasure and luxury had been told of places and individuals here. He knew it to be true that unconsciously he was brushing elbows with fortune the livelong day; that a hundred or five hundred thousand gave no one the privilege of living more than comfortably in so wealthy a place. Fashion and pomp required more ample sums, so that the poor man was nowhere. All this he realised, now quite sharply, as he faced the city, cut off from his friends, despoiled of his modest fortune, and even his name, and forced to begin the battle for place and comfort all over again. He was not old, but he was not so dull but that he could feel he soon would be. Of a sudden, then, this show of fine clothes, place, and power took on peculiar significance. It was emphasized by contrast with his own distressing state.

And it was distressing. He soon found that freedom from fear of arrest was not the *sine qua non* of his existence. That danger dissolved, the next necessity became the grievous thing. The paltry sum of thirteen hundred and some odd dollars set against the need of rent, clothing, food, and pleasure for years to come was a spectacle little calculated to induce peace of mind in one who had been accustomed to spend five times that sum in the course of a year. He thought upon the subject rather actively the first few days he was in New York, and decided that he must act quickly. As a consequence, he consulted the business opportunities advertised in the morning papers and began investigations on his own account.

That was not before he had become settled, however. Carrie and he went looking for a flat, as arranged, and found one in Seventy-eighth Street near Amsterdam Avenue. It was a five-story building, and their flat was on the third floor. Owing to the fact that the street was not yet built up solidly, it was possible to see east to the green tops of the trees in Central Park and west to the broad waters of the Hudson, a glimpse of which was to be had out of the west windows. For the privilege of six rooms and a bath, running in a straight line, they were compelled to pay thirty-five dollars a month—an average, and yet exorbitant, rent for a home at the time. Carrie noticed the difference between the size of the rooms here and in Chicago and mentioned it.

"You'll not find anything better, dear," said Hurstwood, "unless you go into one of the old-fashioned houses, and then you won't have any of these conveniences."

Carrie picked out the new abode because of its newness and bright woodwork. It was one of the very new ones supplied with steam heat, which was a great advantage. The stationary range, hot and cold water, dumb-waiter, speaking tubes, and call-bell for the janitor pleased her very much. She had enough of the instincts of a housewife to take great satisfaction in these things.

Hurstwood made arrangements with one of the installment houses whereby they furnished the flat complete and accepted fifty dollars down and ten dollars a month. He then had a little plate, bearing the name of G.W. Wheeler, made, which he placed on his letter-box in the hall. It sounded exceedingly odd to Carrie to be called Mrs. Wheeler by the janitor, but in time she became used to it and looked upon the name as her own.

These house details settled, Hurstwood visited some of the advertised opportunities to purchase an interest in some flourishing down-town bar. After the palatial resort in Adams Street, he could not stomach the commonplace saloons which he found advertised. He lost a number of days looking up these and finding them disagreeable. He did, however, gain considerable knowledge by talking, for he discovered the influence of Tammany Hall and the value of standing in with the police. The most profitable and flourishing places he found to be those which conducted anything but a legitimate business, such as that controlled by Fitzgerald and Moy. Elegant back rooms and private drinking booths on the second floor were usually adjuncts of very profitable places. He saw by portly keepers, whose shirt fronts shown with large diamonds, and whose clothes were properly cut, that the liquor business here, as elsewhere, yielded the same golden profit.

At last he found an individual who had a resort in Warren Street, which seemed an excellent venture. It was fairly well-appearing and susceptible of improvement. The owner claimed the business to be excellent, and it certainly looked so.

"We deal with a very good class of people," he told Hurstwood. "Merchants, salesmen, and professionals. It's a well-dressed class. No bums. We don't allow 'em in this place."

Hurstwood listened to the cash-register ring, and watched the trade for a while.

"It's profitable enough for two, is it?" he asked.

"You can see for yourself if you're any judge of the liquor trade," said the owner. "This is only one of the two places I have. The other is down in Nassau Street. I can't tend to them both alone. If I had some one who knew the business thoroughly I wouldn't mind sharing with him in this one and letting him manage it."

"I've had experience enough," said Hurstwood blandly, but he felt a little diffident about referring to Fitzgerald and Moy.

"Well, you can suit yourself, Mr. Wheeler," said the proprietor.

He only offered a third interest in the stock, fixtures, and good-will, and this in return for a thousand dollars and managerial ability on the part of the one who should come in. There was no property involved, because the owner of the saloon merely rented from an estate.

The offer was genuine enough, but it was a question with Hurstwood whether a third interest in that locality could be made to yield one hundred and fifty dollars a month, which he figured he must have in order to meet the ordinary family expenses and be comfortable. It was not the time, however, after many failures to find what he wanted, to hesitate. It looked as though a third would pay a hundred a month now. By judicious management and improvement, it might be made to pay more. Accordingly he agreed to enter into partnership, and made over his thousand dollars, preparing to enter the next day.

His first inclination was to be elated, and he confided to Carrie that he thought he had made an excellent arrangement. Time, however, introduced food for reflection. He found his partner to be very disagreeable. Frequently he was the worse for liquor, which made him surly. This was the last thing which Hurstwood was used to in business. Besides, the business varied. It was nothing like the class of patronage which he had enjoyed in Chicago. He found that it would take a long time to make friends. These people hurried in and out without seeking the pleasures of friendship. It was no gathering or lounging place. Whole days and weeks passed without one such hearty greeting as he had been wont to enjoy every day in Chicago.

For another thing, Hurstwood missed the celebrities—those well-dressed, *elite* individuals who lend grace to the average bars and bring news from far-off and exclusive circles. He did not see one such in a month. Evenings, when still at his post, he would occasionally read in the evening papers incidents concerning celebrities whom he knew—whom he had drunk a glass with many a time. They would visit a bar like Fitzgerald and Moy's in Chicago, or the Hoffman House, uptown, but he knew that he would never see them down here.

Again, the business did not pay as well as he thought. It increased a little, but he found he would have to watch his house-hold expenses, which was humiliating.

In the very beginning it was a delight to go home late at night, as he did, and find Carrie. He managed to run up and take dinner with her between six and seven, and to remain home until nine o'clock in the morning, but the novelty of this waned after a time, and he began to feel the drag of his duties.

The first month was scarcely passed before Carrie said in a very natural way: "I think I'll go down this week and buy a dress."

"What kind?" said Hurstwood.

"Oh, something for street wear."

"All right," he answered, smiling, although he noted mentally that it would be more agreeable to his finances if she didn't. Nothing was said about it the next day, but the following morning he asked:

"Have you done anything about your dress?"

"Not yet," said Carrie.

He paused a few moments, as if in thought, and then said:

"Would you mind putting it off a few days?"

"No," replied Carrie, who did not catch the drift of his remarks. She had never thought of him in connection with money troubles before. "Why?"

"Well, I'll tell you," said Hurstwood. "This investment of mine is taking a lot of money just now. I expect to get it all back shortly, but just at present I am running close."

"Oh!" answered Carrie. "Why, certainly, dear. Why didn't you tell me before?"

"It wasn't necessary," said Hurstwood.

For all her acquiescence, there was something about the way Hurstwood spoke which reminded Carrie of Drouet and his little deal which he was always about to put through. It was only the thought of a second, but it was a beginning. It was something new in her thinking of Hurstwood.

Other things followed from time to time, little things of the same sort, which in their cumulative effect were eventually equal to a full revelation. Carrie was not dull by any means. Two persons cannot long dwell together without coming to an understanding of one another. The mental difficulties of an individual reveal themselves whether he voluntarily confesses them or not. Trouble gets in the air and contributes gloom, which speaks for itself. Hurstwood dressed as nicely as usual, but they were the same clothes he had in Canada. Carrie noticed that he did not install a large wardrobe, though his own was anything but large. She noticed, also, that he did not suggest many amusements, said nothing about the food, seemed concerned about his business. This was not the easy Hurstwood of Chicago—not the liberal, opulent Hurstwood she had known. The change was too obvious to escape detection.

Travels with Charley: In Search of America (1962)

John Steinbeck

When John Steinbeck and his dog Charley set out on their journey around the country, national (now international) fast food chains were revolutionizing restaurants and eating habits in the United States, especially for travelers. Reliable quality in food and restrooms, and knowing what would be on the menu no matter where you were, were important factors to many consumers. But in time many customers and writers began to lament the decline of independent drive-ins and restaurants run by local "characters," places that sometimes achieved the status of being local "institutions." Actually, many of these independent businesses still survive and receive loyal patronage from the same "locals" who go to the national chains whenever that is more convenient, especially when they are traveling.

From the beginning of my journey, I had avoided the great high-speed slashes of concrete and tar called "thruways," or "super-highways." Various states have different names for them, but I had dawdled in New England, the winter grew apace, and I had visions of being snowbound in North Dakota. I sought out U.S. 90, a wide gash of a super-highway, multiple-lane carrier of the nation's goods. Rocinante bucketed along. The minimum speed on this road was greater than any I had previously driven. I drove into a wind quartering in from my starboard bow and felt the buffeting, sometimes staggering blows of the gale I helped to make. I could hear the sough of it on the square surfaces of my camper top. Instructions screamed at me from the road once: "Do not stop! No stopping. Maintain speed." Trucks as long as freighters went roaring by, delivering a wind like the blow of a fist. These great roads are wonderful for moving goods but not for inspection of a countryside. You are bound to the wheel and your eyes to the car ahead and to the rear-view mirror for the car behind and the side mirror for the car or truck about to pass, and at the same time you must read all the signs for fear you may miss some instructions or orders. No roadside stands selling squash juice, no antique stores, no farm products or factory outlets. When we get these thruways across the whole country, as we will and must, it will be possible to drive from New York to California without seeing a single thing.

At intervals there are places of rest and recreation, food, fuel and oil, postcards, steam-table food, picnic tables, garbage cans all fresh and newly painted, rest rooms and lavatories so spotless, so incensed with deodorants and with detergents that it takes a time to get your sense of smell back. For deodorants are not quite correctly named; they substitute one smell for another, and the substitute must be much stronger and more penetrating than the odor it conquers. I had neglected my own country too long. Civilization had made great strides in my absence. I remember when a coin in a slot would get you a stick of gum or a candy bar, but in these dining palaces were vending machines where various coins could deliver handkerchiefs, comb-and-nail file sets, hair conditions and cosmetics, first-aid kits, minor drugs such as aspirin, mild physics, pills to keep you awake. I found myself entranced with these gadgets. Suppose you want a soft drink; you pick your kind—Sungrape or Cooly Cola—press a button, insert the coin, and stand back. A paper cup drops into place, the drink pours out and stops a quarter of an inch from the brim—a cold, refreshing drink guaranteed synthetic. Coffee is even more interesting, for when the hot black fluid has ceased, a squirt of milk comes down and an envelope of sugar drops beside the cup. But of all, the hot-soup machine is the triumph. Choose among ten—pea, chicken noodle, beef and veg., insert the coin. A rumbling hum comes from the giant and a sign lights up that reads "Heating." After a minute a red light flashes on and off until you open a little door and remove the paper cup of boiling-hot soup.

It is life at a peak of some kind of civilization. The restaurant accommodations, great scallops of counters with simulated leather stools, are as spotless as and not unlike the lavatories. Everything that can be captured and held down is sealed in clear plastic. The food is oven-fresh, spotless and tasteless; untouched by human hands. I remembered with an ache certain dishes in France and Italy touched by innumerable human hands.

These centers for rest, food, and replenishment are kept beautiful with lawns and flowers. At the front, nearest the highway, are parking places for passenger automobiles together with regiments of gasoline pumps. At the rear the trucks draw up, and there they have their services—the huge overland caravans. Being technically a truck, Rocinante took her place in the rear, and I soon made acquaintance with the truckers. They are a breed set apart from the life around them, the long-distance truckers. In some town or city somewhere their wives and children live while the husbands traverse the nation carrying every kind of food and product and machine. They are clannish and they stick together, speaking a specialized language. And although I was a small craft among monsters of transportation they were kind to me and helpful.

I learned that in the truck parks there are showers and soap and towels—that I could park and sleep the night if I wished. The men had little commerce with local people, but being avid radio listeners they could report news and politics from all parts of the nation. The food and fuel centers on the parkways or thruways are leased by the various states, but on other highways private enterprise had truckers' stations that offer discounts on fuel, beds, baths, and places to sit and shoot the breeze. But being a specialized group, leading special lives, associating only with their own kind, they would have made it possible for me to cross the country without talking to a local town-bound man. For the truckers cruise over the surface of the nation without being a part of it. Of course in the towns where their families live they have whatever roots are possible—clubs, dances, love affairs, and murders.

I liked the truckers very much, as I always like specialists. By listening to them talk I accumulated a vocabulary of the road, of tires and springs, of overweight. The truckers over long distances have stations along their routes where they know the service men and the waitresses behind the counters, and where occasionally they meet their opposite numbers in other trucks. The great get-together symbol is the cup of coffee. I found I often stopped for coffee, not because I wanted it but for a rest and a change from the unrolling highway. It takes strength and control and attention to drive a truck long distances, no matter how much the effort is made easier by air brakes and power-assisted steering. It would be interesting to know and easy to establish with modern testing methods how much energy in foot pounds is expended in driving a truck for six hours. Once Ed Ricketts and I, collecting marine animals, turning over rocks in an area, tried to estimate how much weight we lifted in an average collecting day. The stones we turned over were not large—weighing from three to fifty pounds. We estimated that on a rich day, when we had little sense of energy expended, each of us had lifted four to ten tons of rock. Consider then the small, unnoticed turning of the steering wheel, perhaps the exertion of only one pound for each motion, the varying pressure of foot on accelerator, not more than half a pound perhaps but an enormous total over a period of six hours. Then there are the muscles of shoulders and neck, constantly if unconsciously flexed for emergency, the eyes darting from road to rear-view mirror, the thousand decisions so deep that the conscious mind is not aware of them. The output of energy, nervous and muscular, is enormous. Thus the coffee break is a rest in many senses.

Quite often I sat with these men and listened to their talk and now and then asked questions. I soon learned not to expect knowledge of the country they passed through. Except for the truck stops, they had no contact with it. It was driven home to me how like sailors they were. I remember when I first went to sea being astonished that the men who sailed over the world and touched the ports to the strange and exotic had little contact with that world. Some of the truckers on long hauls traveled in pairs and took their turns. The one off duty slept or read paperbacks. But on the roads their interests were engines, and weather, and maintaining the speed that makes a predictable schedule possible. Some of them were on regular runs back and forth while others moved over single operations. It is a whole pattern of life, little known to the settled people along the routes of the great trucks. I learned only enough about these men to be sure I would like to know much more.

It is a rare house or building that is not rigged with spiky combers of air. Radio and television speech becomes standardized, perhaps better English than we have ever used. Just as our bread, mixed and baked, packaged and sold without benefit of accident or human frailty, is uniformly good and uniformly tasteless, so will our speech become one speech.

I who love words and the endless possibility of words am saddened by this inevitability. For with local accent will disappear local tempo. The idioms, the figures of speech that make language rich and full of the poetry of place and time must go. And in their place will be a national speech, wrapped and packaged, standard and tasteless. Localness is not gone but it is going. In the many years since I have listened to the land the change is very great. Traveling west along the northern routes I did not hear a truly local speech until I reached Montana. That is one of the reasons I fell in love again with Montana. The West Coast went back to packaged English. The Southwest kept a grasp but a slipping grasp on localness. Of course the deep south holds on by main strength to its regional expressions, just as it holds and treasures some other anachronisms, but no region can hold out for long against the highway, the high-tension line, and the national television. What I am mourning is perhaps not worth saving, but I regret its loss nevertheless.

Even while I protest the assembly-line production of our food, our songs, our language, and eventually our souls, I know that it was a rare home that baked good bread in the old days. Mother's cooking was with rare exceptions poor, that good unpasteurized milk touched only by flies and bits of manure crawled with bacteria, the healthy old-time life was riddled with aches, sudden death from unknown causes, and that sweet local speech I mourn was the child of illiteracy and ignorance. It is the nature of a man as he grows older, a small bridge in time, to protest against change, particularly change for the better. But it is true that we have exchanged corpulence for starvation, and either one will kill us. The lines of change are down. We, or at least I, can have no conception of human life and human thought in a hundred years or fifty years. Perhaps my greatest wisdom is knowledge that I do not know. The sad ones are those who waste their energy in trying to hold it back, for they can only feel bitterness in loss and no joy in gain.

"Just for ducks, let's try a little of what my boys would call this generality jazz. Under heads and subheads. Let's take food as we have found it. It is more than possible that in the cities we have passed through, traffic-harried, there are good and distinguished restaurants with menus of delight. But in the eating places along the roads the food has been clean, tasteless, colorless, and of a complete sameness. It is almost as though the customers had no interest in what they ate as long as it had no character to embarrass them. This is true of all but the breakfasts, which are uniformly wonderful if you stick to bacon and eggs and pan-fried potatoes. At the roadsides I never had a really good dinner or a really bad breakfast. The bacon or sausage was good and packaged at the factory, the eggs fresh or kept fresh by refrigeration, and refrigeration was universal." I might even say roadside America is the paradise of breakfast except for one thing. Now and then I would see a sign that said "home-made sausage" or "home-smoked bacons and hams" or "new-laid eggs" and I would stop and lay in supplies. Then, cooking my own breakfast and making my own coffee, I found that the difference was instantly apparent. A freshly laid egg does not taste remotely like the pale, battery-produced refrigerated egg. The sausage would be sweet and sharp and pungent with spices, and my coffee a wine-dark happiness. Can I then say that the America I saw has put cleanliness first, at the expense of taste? And—since all our perceptive nerve trunks including that of taste are not only perfectible but also capable of trauma—that the sense of taste tends to disappear and that strong, pungent, or exotic flavors arouse suspicion and dislike and so are eliminated?

"Let's go a little farther into our fields, Charley. Let's take the books, magazines, and papers we have seen displayed where we have stopped. The dominant publication has been the comic book. There have been local papers and I've bought and read them. There have been racks of paperbacks with some great and good titles but overwhelmingly outnumbered by the volumes of sex, sadism, and homicide. The big-city papers cast their shadows over large areas around them, the *New York Times* as far as the Great Lakes, the *Chicago Tribune* all the way here to North Dakota. Here, Charley, I give you a warning, should you be drawn to generalities. If this people has so atrophied its taste buds as to find tasteless food not only acceptable but desirable, what of the emotional life of the nation? Do they find their emotional fare so bland that it must be spiced with sex and sadism through the medium of the paperback? And if this is so, why are there no condiments save ketchup and mustard to enhance their foods?

"We've listened to local radio all across the country. And apart from a few reportings of football games, the mental fare has been as generalized, as packaged, and as undistinguished as the food." I stirred Charley with my foot to keep him awake.

Next day I walked in the old port of Seattle, where the fish and crabs and shrimps lay beautifully on white beds of shaved ice and where the washed and shining vegetables were arranged in pictures. I drank clam juice and ate the sharp crab cocktails at stands along the waterfront. It was not much changed—a little more run-down and dingy than it was twenty years ago. And here a generality concerning the growth of American cities, seemingly true of all of them I know. When a city begins to grow and spread outward, from the edges, the center which was once its glory is in a sense abandoned to time. Then the buildings grow dark and a kind of decay sets in; poorer people move in as the rents fall, and small fringe businesses take the place of once flowering establishments. The district is still too good to tear down and too outmoded to be desirable. Besides, all the energy has flowed out to the new developments, to the semi-rural supermarkets, the outdoor movies, new houses with wide lawns and stucco schools where children are confirmed in their illiteracy. The old port with narrow streets and cobbled surfaces, smoked-grimed, goes into a period of desolation inhabited at night by the vague ruins of men, the lotus eaters who struggle daily toward unconsciousness by way of raw alcohol. Nearly every city I know has such a dying mother of violence and despair where at night the brightness of the street lamps is sucked away and policemen walk in pairs. And then one day perhaps the city returns and rips out the sore and builds a monument to its past.

F. Entrepreneurship and Profits

"Captains of industry," "robber barons," eccentrics, social and psychological misfits, inventors, innovators, profiteers—entrepreneurs have been described in all of these ways. Successful entrepreneurs leave a trail of what the Austrian economist Joseph Schumpeter described as "creative destruction." Old products, old ways of doing business, and old jobs are often destroyed by entrepreneurs as they create new products, new jobs, and new ways of organizing businesses or even homes.

In the long run, entrepreneurial and technological innovations are a wellspring of economic growth and improved standards of living, and quite possibly the single most important source of that progress. In the short run, the most successful entrepreneurs sometimes build up business and financial empires, occasionally to the point of raising concerns about monopoly power in the economy's leading industries. A century ago that was the case in the petroleum, railroad, and banking industries. In later decades the automobile, radio, motion picture, television, fast food, beer, and soft drink industries carried the personal stamp of larger-than-life entrepreneurs. Today the computer and computer software industries offer similar examples. Many other industries have come under the influence of leaders who are not so well known among the general public, but who nevertheless attain legendary status among those who work in their particular fields. At the local level, many small businesses are developed by entrepreneurs who are content to operate as big fish in small ponds, or just as owners and operators of small "mom and pop" firms.

We know much more about the effects entrepreneurs have on markets and the overall economy than we do about how to create more entrepreneurs. It isn't at all clear, for example, that we can teach people how to be successful entrepreneurs. Business schools graduate thousands of new managers every year, but entrepreneurs are a different breed than managers, who by definition are content to work for a salary and bonuses. Financially, the reward that successful entrepreneurs earn is profits; and no less important to the working of the economy is the risk they bear of incurring losses if their innovations or business ventures prove unsuccessful.

To economists, profit is defined as a reward for accepting risks in combining factors of production to produce goods and services that customers may, or may not, buy. Profit that is higher than what can be earned in other markets with comparable risks attracts more resources—as long as legal or economic barriers to entry are not prohibitive. As more entrepre-

neurs and businesses start producing and trying to improve production of the more profitable goods and services, the increased competition and, in some cases, technological or organizational breakthroughs developed by entrepreneurs will eventually bring those profits back in line with earnings in other markets. Losses have the opposite but equally important effect of driving resources out of a market into greener pastures.

Literary authors have long recognized the important role of entrepreneurship in the economy, and have written about both real and fictional entrepreneurs. They often recognize the accomplishments of these figures, but also raise questions about the adverse effects of their success. In the passages below, Shakespeare's merchant of Venice is Antonio, not Shylock. Antonio is well aware of the risks of his business, and tries to spread his risks across several investments. He borrows as little as possible to meet his business and personal commitments, and more generally "holds the world but as the world." Balaam, the merchant in Alexander Pope's "Moral Essays," starts out well enough, but with unexpected success he falls victim to pride and ostentation, since Satan is "wiser now than of yore, and tempts by making rich, not making poor." In the epistle on the use of riches, Pope contrasts works done "for pride or show" with a wide range of useful and noble private and public projects, ranging from simple farming and forestry to national projects of building navies, harbors, temples, and roads. John Dos Passos describes the life, work, charities, and eccentricities of Andrew Carnegie ("Prince of Peace") and Henry Ford ("Tin Lizzie"). Joseph Heller's Milo Minderbinder cuts through the command economy of the U.S. military in World War II, and the traditional economies of Italian villages, like a hot knife through soft butter. He does this with other people's money and resources, repeatedly claiming that "everyone has a share." But it isn't clear that he practices what he preaches. In Banker, *Dick Francis succinctly explains the risks of and returns to successful investments in racing stallions. Arthur Miller's* All My Sons *explores the tragic consequences of a businessman's attempt to save his firm from bankruptcy by fraudulently reporting inspection results for aircraft parts during World War II. (A hilarious discussion of what level of profit is fair, not just legally but "mawrally," appears in Thomas Wolfe's* From Death to Morning. *Unfortunately, that passage was too long and expensive to reprint here.)*

THE MERCHANT OF VENICE (1598)*

William Shakespeare

The Renaissance was a period of economic expansion and exploration as much as cultural rebirth. Fortunes could be made with shiploads of merchandise from distant ports—and as easily lost when ships were sunk by storms or pirates. Joint stock companies were formed to spread the risks of some voyages, but financial markets and institutions were still in their infancy. Prudent merchants and ship owners, like Shakespeare's Anto-

nio, tried to diversify their risks; but they knew that they regularly risked losing everything they owned. Antonio discovers that acts of friendship and love also carry risks and rewards, which can be even harder to bear.

[I. I.] A quay in Venice

ANTONIO, SALERIO, *and* SOLANIO *approach, talking together*

ANTONIO: In sooth, I know not why I am so sad.
It wearies me, you say it wearies you;
But how I caught it, found it, or came by it,
What stuff 'tis made of, whereof it is born,
I am to learn:
And such a want-wit sadness makes of me,
That I have much ado to know myself.

SALERIO: Your mind is tossing on the ocean,
There, where your argosies with portly sail—
Like signiors and rich burghers on the flood,
Or, as it were, the pageants of the sea—
Do overpeer the petty traffickers,
That curtsy to them, do them reverence,
As they fly by them with their woven wings.

SOLANIO: Believe me, sir, had I such venture forth,
The better part of my affections would
Be with my hopes abroad. I should be still
Plucking the grass to know where sits the wind,
Peering in maps for ports and piers and roads:
And every object that might make me fear
Misfortune to my ventures, out of doubt,
Would make me sad.

SALERIO: My wind, cooling my broth,
Would blow me to an ague when I thought
What harm a wind too great might do at sea.
I should not see the sandy hour-glass run
But I should think of shallows and of flats,
And see my wealthy Andrew docked in sand,
Vailing her high-top lower than her ribs

---

* *The Merchant of Venice* was probably written around 1595 or 1596, but there is no definite evidence of date until it was entered in the Stationer's Register on July 22, 1598. The earliest recorded performance was in 1605. For more on the historical background of the play, see G. B. Harrison, ed., *Shakespeare: The Complete Works* (New York: Harcourt, Brace & World, 1968), 579–82.

To kiss her burial . . . Should I go to church
And see the holy edifice of stone,
And not bethink me straight of dangerous rocks,
Which touching but my gentle vessel's side
Would scatter all her spices on the stream,
Enrobe the roaring waters with my silks,
And, in a word, but even now worth this,
And now worth nothing? Shall I have the thought
To think on this, and shall I lack the thought
That such a thing bechanced would make me sad?
But tell not me—I know Antonio
Is sad to think upon his merchandise.

ANTONIO: Believe me, no—I thank my fortune for it—
My ventures are not in one bottom trusted,
Nor to one place, nor is my whole estate
Upon the fortune of this present year:
Therefore my merchandise makes me not sad.

SOLANIO: Why then you are in love.

ANTONIO: Fie, fie!

SOLANIO: Not in love neither? then let us say you are sad
Because you are not merry; and 'twere as easy
For you to laugh, and leap, and say you are merry,
Because you are not sad. Now, by two-headed Janus,
Nature hath framed strange fellows in her time:
Some that will evermore peep through their eyes,
And laugh like parrots at a bag-piper;
And other of such vinegar aspect,
That they'll not show their teeth in way of smile,
Though Nestor swear the jest be laughable. . . .

BASSANIO, LORENZO, *and* GRATIANO *are seen approaching*

Here comes Bassanio, your most noble kinsman,
Gratiano, and Lorenzo. . . . Fare ye well,
We leave you now with better company.

SALERIO: I would have stayed till I had made you merry,
If worthier friends had not prevented me.

ANTONIO: Your worth is very dear in my regard.
I take it your own business calls on you,
And you embrace th'occasion to depart.

SALERIO: Good morrow, my good lords.

BASSANIO: [*coming up*] Good signiors both, when shall we laugh? say, when?
You grow exceeding strange: must it be so?

SALERIO: We'll make our leisures to attend on yours.

SALERIO and SOLANIO bow and depart

LORENZO: My Lord Bassanio, since you have found Antonio,
We two will leave you, but at dinner-time
I pray you have in mind where we must meet.

BASSANIO: I will not fail you.

GRATIANO: You look not well, Signior Antonio,
You have too much respect upon the world:
They lose it that do buy it with much care,
Believe me you are marvelously changed.

ANTONIO: I hold the world but as the world, Gratiano—
A stage, where every man must play a part,
And mine a sad one.

MORAL ESSAYS (1733 & 1731)

Alexander Pope

Money isn't the root of all evil, but the love of money, or the even older sin of pride, may be. Economists are clearly more hesitant and restrained than are poets in identifying the immoral uses of material wealth, but most literary writers also recognize a wide range of wealth's appropriate uses, both for individuals and for public and charitable works.

EPISTLE III: OF THE USE OF RICHES (1733)

To Allen, Lord Bathurst

There dwelt a Citizen of sober fame,
A plain good man, and Balaam was his name.
Religious, punctual, frugal, and so forth,
His word would pass for more than he was worth;
One solid dish his week-day meal affords,
An added pudding solemnized the Lord's;
Constant at Church and 'Change; his gains were sure,

His givings rare, save farthings to the poor.
The Devil was piqued such saintship to behold,
And long'd to tempt him like good Job of old;
But Satan now is wiser than of yore,
And tempts by making rich, not making poor.
Rous'd by the Prince of Air, the whirl-winds sweep
The surge, and plunge his Father in the deep;
Then full against his Cornish lands they roar,
And two rich shipwrecks bless the lucky shore.
Sir Balaam now, he lives like other folks,
He takes his chirping pint, and cracks his jokes.
"Live like yourself," was soon my Lady's word;
And lo! two puddings smoked upon the board.
Asleep and naked as an Indian lay,
An honest factor stole a Gem away:
He pledg'd it to the knight; the knight had wit,
So kept the Diamond, and the rogue was bit.
Some scruple rose, but thus he eas'd his thought:
"I'll now give sixpence where I gave a groat;
Where once I went to church I'll now go twice—
And am so clear too of all other vice."
The Tempter saw his time; the work he plied;
Stocks and subscriptions pour on ev'ry side,
Till all the Demon makes his full descent
In one abundant shower of Cent. per Cent.,
Sinks deep within him, and possesses whole,
Then dubs Director, and secures his soul.
Behold Sir Balaam, now a man of Spirit,
Ascribes his gettings to his parts and merit;
What late he call'd a Blessing now was Wit,
And God's good Providence a lucky hit.
Things change their titles as our manners turn,
His counting-house employ'd the Sunday morn:
Seldom at church ('twas such a busy life),
But duly sent his family and wife.
There (so the Devil ordain'd) one Christmas-tide
My good old lady catch'd a cold and died.
A Nymph of Quality admires our Knight;
He marries, bows at Court, and grows polite;
Leaves the dull cits, and joins (to please the fair)
The well-bred cuckolds in St. James's air:

First for his Son a gay Commission buys,
Who drinks, whores, fights, and in a duel dies;
His daughter flaunts a viscount's tawdry wife;
She bears a Coronet and P—x for life.
In Britain's Senate he a seat obtains,
And one more Pensioner St. Stephen gains.
My Lady falls to play; so bad her chance,
He must repair it; takes a bribe from France;
The house impeach him; Coningsby harangues;
The Court forsake him, and Sir Balaam hangs.
Wife, son, and daughter, Satan, are thy own,
His wealth, yet dearer, forfeit to the Crown:
The Devil and the King divide the prize,
And sad Sir Balaam curses God and dies.

Epistle IV: Of the Use of Riches (1731)

To Richard Boyle, Earl of Burlington

'Tis Use alone that sanctifies Expense,
And Splendour borrows all her rays from Sense.
His Father's Acres who enjoys in peace,
Or makes his Neighbours glad, if he increase;
Whose cheerful Tenants bless their yearly toil,
Yet to their Lord owe more than to the soil;
Whose ample Lawns are not ashamed to feed
The milky heifer and deserving steed;
Whose rising Forests, not for pride or show,
But future Buildings, future Navies grow:
Let his plantations stretch from down to down,
First shade a Country, and then raise a Town,
You, too, proceed! make falling Arts your care;
Erect new wonders, and the old repair;
Jones and Palladio to themselves restore
And be whate'er Vitruvius was before:
Till kings call forth th' Ideas of your mind
(Proud to accomplish what such hands design'd),
Bid Harbours open, public Ways extend,
Bid Temples, worthier of the God, ascend,

Bid the broad arch the dangerous flood contain,
The Mole projected break the roaring Main,
Back to his bounds their subject Sea command,
And roll obedient Rivers thro' the land.
These Honours, Peace to happy Britain brings;
These are Imperial Works, and worthy Kings.

U.S.A.

John Dos Passos

In two brief sketches, Dos Passos vividly paints the sweeping impacts made by two early giants in the American steel and automotive industries, Andrew Carnegie and Henry Ford, on business, philanthropy, politics, and the national way of life.

"Prince of Peace" (1930)

Andrew Carnegie
was born in Dunfermline in Scotland,
came over to the States in an immigrant
ship worked as bobbinboy in a textile factory
fired boilers
clerked in a bobbin factory at $2.50 a week
ran round Philadelphia with telegrams as a Western Union messenger
learned the Morse code was telegraph operator on the Pennsy lines
was a military telegraph operator in the Civil War and

always saved his pay;
whenever he had a dollar he invested it.

Andrew Carnegie started out buying Adams Express and Pullman stock when they were in a slump;

he had confidence in railroads,
he had confidence in communications,
he had confidence in transportation,
he believed in iron.

Andrew Carnegie believed in iron, built bridges Bessemer plants blast furnaces rolling mills;

Andrew Carnegie believed in oil;
Andrew Carnegie believed in steel;
always saved his money
whenever he had a million dollars he invested it.
Andrew Carnegie became the richest man in the world
and died.

Bessemer Duquesne Rankin Pittsburgh Bethlehem Gary
Andrew Carnegie gave millions for peace
and libraries and scientific institutes and endowments and thrift
whenever he made a billion dollars he endowed an institution to promote universal peace
always
except in time of war.

"Tin Lizzie"
(1936)

"*Mr. Ford the automobileer,*" the featurewriter wrote in 1900,

"*Mr. Ford the automobileer began by giving his steed three or four sharp jerks with the lever at the righthand side of the seat; that is, he pulled the lever up and down sharply in order, as he said, to mix air with gasoline and drive the charge into the exploding cylinder. . . . Mr. Ford slipped a small electric switch handle and there followed a puff, puff, puff. . . . The puffing of the machine assumed a higher key. . . . She was flying along about eight miles an hour. The ruts in the road were deep, but the machine certainly went with a dreamlike smoothness. There was none of the bumping common even to a steamer. . . . By this time the boulevard had been reached, and the automobileer, letting a lever fall a little, let her out. Whiz! She picked up speed with infinite rapidity. As she ran on there was a clattering behind, the new noise of the automobile.*"

For twenty years or more,

ever since he'd left his father's farm when he was sixteen to get a job in a Detroit machineshop, Henry Ford had been nuts about machinery. First it was watches, then he designed a steamtractor, then he built a horseless carriage with an engine adapted from the Otto gas-engine he'd read about in *The World of Science*, then a mechanical buggy with a onecylinder fourcycle motor, that would run forward but not back;

at last, in ninetyeight, he felt he was far enough along to risk throwing up his job with the Detroit Edison Company, where he'd worked his way up from night fireman to chief engineer, to put all his time into working on a new gasoline engine,

(in the late eighties he'd met Edison at a meeting of electriclight employees in Atlantic City. He'd gone up to Edison after Edison had delivered an address and asked him if he thought gasoline was practical as a motor fuel. Edison had said yes. If Edison said it, it was true. Edison was the great admiration of Henry Ford's life);

and in driving his mechanical buggy, sitting there at the lever jauntily dressed in a tightbuttoned jacket and a high collar and a derby hat, back and forth over the level illpaved streets of Detroit,

scaring the big brewery horses and the skinny trotting horses and the sleekrumped pacers with the motor's loud explosions,

looking for men scatterbrained enough to invest money in a factory for building automobiles.

He was the eldest son of an Irish immigrant who during the Civil War had married the daughter of a prosperous Pennsylvania Dutch farmer and settled down to farming near Dearborn in Wayne County, Michigan;

like plenty of other Americans, young Henry grew up hating the endless sogging through the mud about the chores, the hauling and pitching manure, the kerosene lamps to clean, the irk and sweat and solitude of the farm.

He was a slender, active youngster, a good skater, clever with his hands; what he liked was to tend the machinery and let the others do the heavy work. His mother had told him not to drink, smoke, gamble, or go into debt, and he never did.

When he was in his early twenties his father tried to get him back from Detroit, where he was working as mechanic and repairman for the Drydock Engine Company that built engines for steamboats, by giving him forty acres of land.

Young Henry built himself an uptodate square white dwellinghouse with a false mansard roof and married and settled down on the farm.

but he let the hired men do the farming;

he bought himself a buzzsaw and rented a stationary engine and cut the timber off the woodlots.

He was a thrifty young man who never drank or smoked or gambled or coveted his neighbor's wife, but he couldn't stand living on the farm.

He moved to Detroit, and in the brick barn behind his house tinkered for years in his spare time with a mechanical buggy that would be light enough to run over the clayey wagonroads of Wayne County, Michigan.

By 1900 he had a practicable car to promote.

He was forty years old before the Ford Motor Company was started and production began to move.

Speed was the first thing the early automobile manufacturers went after. Races advertised the makes of cars.

Henry Ford himself hung up several records at the track at Grosse Pointe and on the ice on Lake St. Clair. In his 999 he did the mile in thirtynine and fourfifths seconds.

But it had always been his custom to hire others to do the heavy work. The speed he was busy with was speed in production, the records, records in efficient output. He hired Barney Oldfield, a stunt bicyclerider from Salt Lake City, to do the racing for him.

Henry Ford had ideas about other things than the designing of motors, carburetors, magnetos, jigs and fixtures, punches and dies; he had ideas about sales;

that the big money was in economical quantity production, quick turnover, cheap interchangeable easilyreplaced standardized parts;

it wasn't until 1909, after years of arguing with his partners, that Ford put out the first Model T.

Henry Ford was right.

That season he sold more than ten thousand tin lizzies, ten years later he was selling almost a million a year.

In these years the Taylor Plan was stirring up plantmanagers and manufacturers all over the country. Efficiency was the word. The same ingenuity that went into improving the performance of a machine could go into improving the performance of the workmen producing the machine.

In 1913 they established the assemblyline at Ford's. That season the profits were something like twentyfive million dollars, but they had trouble in keeping the men on the job, machinists didn't seem to like it at Ford's.

Henry Ford had ideas about other things than production.

He was the largest automobile manufacturer in the world; he paid high wages; maybe if the steady workers thought they were getting a cut (a very small cut) in the profits, it would give trained men an inducement to stick to their jobs,

wellpaid workers might save enough money to buy a tin lizzie; the first day Ford's announced that cleancut properlymarried American workers who wanted jobs had a chance to make five bucks a day (of course it turned out that there were strings to it; always there were strings to it)

such an enormous crowd waited outside the Highland Park plant

all through the zero January night

that there was a riot when the gates were opened; cops broke heads, jobhunters threw bricks; property, Henry Ford's own property, was destroyed. The company dicks had to turn on the firehose to beat back the crowd.

The American Plan; automotive prosperity seeping down from above;
it turned out there were strings to it.

But that five dollars a day

paid to good, clean American workmen

who didn't drink or smoke cigarettes or read or think,

and who didn't commit adultery

and whose wives didn't take in boarders,
made America once more the Yukon of the sweated workers of the world;
made all the tin lizzies and the automotive age, and incidentally,
made Henry Ford the automobileer, the admirer of Edison, the bird-lover,
the great American of his time.

But Henry Ford had ideas about other things besides assemblylines and the livinghabits of his employees. He was full of ideas. Instead of going to the city to make his fortune, here was a country boy who'd made his fortune by bringing the city out to the farm. The precepts he'd learned out of McGuffey's Reader, his mother's prejudices and preconceptions, he had preserved clean and unworn as freshprinted bills in the safe in a bank.

He wanted people to know about his ideas, so he bought the *Dearborn Independent* and started a campaign against cigarettesmoking.

When war broke out in Europe, he had ideas about that too. (Suspicion of armymen and soldiering were part of the Mid-West farm tradition, like thrift, stickativeness, temperance, and sharp practice in money matters.) Any intelligent American mechanic could see that if the Europeans hadn't been a lot of ignorant underpaid foreigners who drank, smoked, were loose about women, and wasteful in their methods of production, the war could never have happened.

When Rosika Schwimmer broke through the stockade of secretaries and servicemen who surrounded Henry Ford and suggested to him that he could stop the war,

he said sure they'd hire a ship and go over and get the boys out of the trenches by Christmas.

He hired a steamboat, the *Oscar II*, and filled it up with pacifists and socialworkers,
to go over to explain to the princelings of Europe
that what they were doing was vicious and silly.

It wasn't his fault that Poor Richard's commonsense no longer rules the world and that most of the pacifists were nuts,

goofy with headlines.

When William Jennings Bryan went over to Hoboken to see him off, somebody handed William Jennings Bryan a squirrel in a cage; William Jennings Bryan made a speech with the squirrel under his arm. Henry Ford threw American Beauty roses to the crowd. The band played *I Didn't Raise My Boy to Be a Soldier.* Practical jokers let loose more squirrels. An eloping couple was married by a platoon of ministers in the saloon, and Mr. Zero, the flophouse humanitarian, who reached the dock too late to sail,

dove into the North River and swam after the boat.

The *Oscar II* was described as a floating Chautauqua; Henry Ford said it felt like a Middle-Western village, but by the time they reached Christiansand in Norway, the reporters had kidded him so that he had gotten cold feet and gone to bed. The world was too crazy outside of Wayne County, Michigan. Mrs. Ford and the management sent an Episcopal dean after him who brought him home under wraps.

and the pacifists had to speechify without him.

Two years later Ford's was manufacturing munitions, Eagle boats; Henry Ford was planning oneman tanks, and oneman submarines like the one tried out in the Revolutionary War. He announced to the press that he'd turn over his war profits to the government,

but there's no record that he ever did.

One thing he brought back from his trip

was the Protocols of the Elders of Zion.

He started a campaign to enlighten the world in the *Dearborn Independent*; the Jews were why the world wasn't like Wayne County, Michigan, in the old horse-and-buggy days;

the Jews had started the war, Bolshevism, Darwinism, Marxism, Nietzsche, short skirts and lipstick. They were behind Wall Street and the international bankers, and the whiteslave traffic and the movies and the Supreme Court and ragtime and the illegal liquor business.

Henry Ford denounced the Jews and ran for Senator and sued the *Chicago Tribune* for libel,

and was the laughingstock of the kept metropolitan press;

but when the metropolitan bankers tried to horn in on his business

he thoroughly outsmarted them.

In 1918 he had borrowed on notes to buy out his minority stockholders for the picayune sum of seventyfive million dollars.

In February, 1920, he needed cash to pay off some of these notes that were coming due. A banker is supposed to have called on him and offered him every facility if the bankers' representative could be made a member of the board of directors. Henry Ford handed the banker his hat,

and went about raising money in his own way:

he shipped every car and part he had in his plant to his dealers and demanded immediate cash payment. Let the other fellow do the borrowing had always been a cardinal principle. He shut down production and canceled all orders from the supplyfirms. Many dealers were ruined, many supplyfirms failed, but when he reopened his plant,

he owned it absolutely,

the way a man owns an unmortgaged farm with the taxes paid up.

In 1922 there started the Ford boom for President (high wages, waterpower, industry scattered to the small towns) that was skillfully pricked behind the scenes by another crackerbarrel philosopher,

Calvin Coolidge;

but in 1922 Henry Ford sold one million three hundred and thirty-two thousand two hundred and nine tin lizzies; he was the richest man in the world.

Good roads had followed the narrow ruts made in the mud by the Model T. The great automotive boom was on. At Ford's production was improving all the time; less waste, more spotters, strawbosses, stool-pigeons (fifteen minutes for lunch, three minutes to go to the toilet, the Taylorized speedup everywhere, reachunder, adjustwasher, screwdown bolt, shove in cotterpin, reachunder, adjustwasher, screwdown bolt, reachunderadjustscrewdownreachunderadjust, until every ounce of life was sucked off into production and at night the workmen went home gray shaking husks).

Ford owned every detail on the process from the ore in the hills until the car rolled off the end of the assemblyline under its own power; the plants were rationalized to the last tenthousandth of an inch as measured by the Johansen scale;

in 1926 the production cycle was reduced to eightyone hours from the ore in the mine to the finished salable car proceeding under its own power,

but the Model T was obsolete.

New Era prosperity and the American Plan

(there were strings to it, always there were strings to it)

had killed Tin Lizzie.

Ford's was just one of many automobile plants.

When the stockmarket bubble burst,

Mr. Ford the crackerbarrel philosopher said jubilantly,

"I told you so.

Serves you right for gambling and getting in debt.

The country is sound."

But when the country on cracked shoes, in frayed trousers, belts tightened over hollow bellies,

idle hands cracked and chapped with the cold of that coldest March day of 1932,

started marching from Detroit to Dearborn, asking for work and the American Plan, all they could think of at Ford's was machineguns.

The country was sound, but they mowed the marchers down.

They shot four of them dead.

Henry Ford as an old man

is a passionate antiquarian

(lives besieged on his father's farm embedded in an estate of thousands of millionaire acres, protected by an army of servicemen, secretaries, secret agents, dicks under orders of an English exprizefighter, always afraid of the feet in broken shoes on the roads, afraid the gangs will kidnap his grandchildren,

that a crank will shoot him,

that Change and the idle hands out of work will break through the gates and the high fences;

protected by a private army against

the new America of starved children and hollow bellies and cracked shoes stamping on souplines,

that has swallowed up the old thrifty farmlands

of Wayne County, Michigan,

as if they had never been).

Henry Ford as an old man

is a passionate antiquarian.

He rebuilt his father's farmhouse and put it back exactly in the state he remembered it in as a boy. He built a village of museums for buggies, sleighs, coaches, old plows, waterwheels, obsolete models of motorcars. He scoured the country for fiddlers to play old-fashioned squaredances.

Even old taverns he bought and put back into their original shape, as well as Thomas Edison's early laboratories.

When he bought the Wayside Inn near Sudbury, Massachusetts, he had the new highway where the newmodel cars roared and slithered and hissed oilily past (*the new noise of the automobile*)

moved away from the door,

put back the old bad road,

so that everything might be

the way it used to be,

in the days of horses and buggies.

Catch-22
(1961)
Joseph Heller

The great comic entrepreneur in Heller's satirical epic of World War II is Milo Minderbinder, who claims (and appears to believe) that he is making almost everybody better off. (Minderbinder comes very close to expressing the normative standard that economists accept far more often than any other, Pareto efficiency. An action is Pareto-efficient if it makes at least one person

> *better off without making anyone else worse off.) So why do they complain so much? His schemes involve everything from stolen bedsheets to contracting out bombing raids against any nation's airfields to the highest bidder, sometimes using their own planes. But perhaps Minderbinder's signature accomplishment—condensed here from passages spread out over hundreds of pages in the novel—is figuring out how to make money buying eggs for seven cents apiece and selling them for five cents.*

Yossarian turned slowly to gaze at Milo with probing distrust. He saw a simple, sincere face that was incapable of subtlety or guile, an honest, frank face with disunited large eyes, rusty hair, black eyebrows and an unfortunate reddish-brown mustache. Milo had a long, thin nose with sniffing, damp nostrils heading sharply off to the right, always pointing away from where the rest of him was looking. It was the face of a man of hardened integrity who could no more consciously violate the moral principles on which his virtue rested than he could transform himself into a despicable toad. One of these moral principles was that it was never a sin to charge as much as the traffic would bear. He was capable of mighty paroxysms of righteous indignation, and he was indignant as could be when he learned that a C.I.D. man was in the area looking for him.

"He's not looking for you," Yossarian said, trying to placate him. "He's looking for someone up in the hospital who's been signing Washington Irving's name to the letters he's been censoring."

"I never signed Washington Irving's name to any letters," Milo declared.

"Of course not."

"But that's just a trick to get me to confess I've been making money in the black market." Milo hauled violently at a disheveled hunk of his off-colored mustache. "I don't like guys like that. Always snooping around people like us. Why doesn't the government get after ex-P.F.C. Wintergreen, if it wants to do some good? He's got no respect for rules and regulations and keeps cutting prices on me."

Milo's mustache was unfortunate because the separated halves never matched. They were like Milo's disunited eyes, which never looked at the same thing at the same time. Milo could see more things than most people, but he could see none of them too distinctly. In contrast to his reaction to news of the C.I.D. man, he learned with calm courage from Yossarian that Colonel Cathcart had raised the number of missions to fifty-five.

"We're at war," he said. "And there's no use complaining about the number of missions we have to fly. If the colonel says we have to fly fifty-five missions, we have to fly them."

"Well, I don't have to fly them," Yossarian vowed. "I'll go see Major Major."

"How can you? Major Major never sees anybody."

"Then I'll go back into the hospital."

"You just came out of the hospital ten days ago," Milo reminded him reprovingly. "You can't keep running into the hospital every time something happens you don't like. No, the best thing to do is fly the missions. It's our duty."

Milo had rigid scruples that would not even allow him to borrow a package of pitted dates from the mess hall that day of McWatt's stolen bedsheet, for the food at the mess hall was all still the property of the government.

"But I can borrow it from you," he explained to Yossarian, "since all this fruit is yours once you get it from me with Doctor Daneeka's letter. You can do whatever you want with it, even sell it at a high profit instead of giving it away free. Wouldn't you want to do that together?"

"No."

Milo gave up. "Then lend me one package of pitted dates," he requested. "I'll give it back to you. I swear I will, and there'll be a little something extra for you."

Milo proved good as his word and handed Yossarian a quarter of McWatt's yellow bedsheet when he returned with the unopened package of dates and with the grinning thief with the sweet tooth who had stolen the bedsheet from McWatt's tent. The piece of bedsheet now belonged to Yossarian. He had earned it while napping, although he did not understand how. Neither did McWatt.

"What's this?" cried McWatt, staring in mystification at the ripped half of his bedsheet.

"It's half of the bedsheet that was stolen from your tent this morning," Milo explained. "I'll bet you didn't even know it was stolen."

"Why should anyone want to steal half a bedsheet?" Yossarian asked.

Milo grew flustered. "You don't understand," he protested. "He stole the whole bedsheet, and I got it back with the package of pitted dates you invested. That's why the quarter of the bedsheet is yours. You made a very handsome return on your investment, particularly since you've gotten back every pitted date you gave me." Milo next addressed himself to McWatt. "Half the bedsheet is yours because it was all yours to begin with, and I really don't understand what you're complaining about, since you wouldn't have any of it if Captain Yossarian and I hadn't intervened in your behalf."

"Who's complaining?" McWatt exclaimed. "I'm just trying to figure out what I can do with half a bedsheet."

"There are lots of things you can do with half a bedsheet," Milo assured him. "The remaining quarter of the bedsheet I've set aside for myself as a reward for my enterprise, work and initiative. It's not for myself, you understand, but for the syndicate. That's something you might do with half the bedsheet. You can leave it in the syndicate and watch it grow."

"What syndicate?"

"The syndicate I'd like to form someday so that I can give you men the good food you deserve."

"You want to form a syndicate?"

"Yes, I do. No, a mart. Do you know what a mart is?"

"It's a place where you buy things, isn't it?"

"And sell things," corrected Milo.

"And sell things."

"All my life I've wanted a mart. You can do lots of things if you've got a mart. But you've got to have a mart."

"You want a mart?"

"And every man will have a share."

Yossarian was still puzzled, for it was a business matter, and there was much about business matters that always puzzled him.

"Let me try to explain it again," Milo offered with growing weariness and exasperation, jerking his thumb toward the thief with the sweet tooth, still grinning beside him. "I knew he wanted the dates more than the bedsheet. Since he doesn't understand a word of English, I made it a point to conduct the whole transaction in English."

"Why didn't you just hit him over the head and take the bedsheet away from him?" Yossarian asked.

Pressing his lips together with dignity, Milo shook his head. "That would have been most unjust," he scolded firmly. "Force is wrong, and two wrongs never make a right. It was much better my way. When I held the dates out to him and reached for the bedsheet, he probably thought I was offering to trade."

"What were you doing?"

"Actually, I was offering to trade, but since he doesn't understand English, I can always deny it."

"Suppose he gets angry and wants the dates?"

"Why, we'll just hit him over the head and take them away from him," Milo answered without hesitation. He looked from Yossarian to McWatt and back again. "I really can't see what everyone is complaining about. We're all much better off than before. Everybody is happy but this thief, and there's no sense worrying about him, since he doesn't even speak our language and deserves whatever he gets. Don't you understand?"

But Yossarian still didn't understand either how Milo could buy eggs in Malta for seven cents apiece and sell them at a profit in Pianosa for five cents.

Yossarian was riding beside Milo in the co-pilot's seat. "I don't understand why you buy eggs for seven cents apiece in Malta and sell them for five cents."

"I do it to make a profit."

"But how can you make a profit? You lose two cents an egg."

"But I make a profit of three and a quarter cents an egg by selling them for four and a quarter cents an egg to the people in Malta I buy them from for seven cents an egg. Of course, I don't make the profit. The syndicate makes the profit. And everybody has a share."

Yossarian felt he was beginning to understand. "And the people you sell the eggs to at four and a quarter cents apiece make a profit of two and three quarter cents apiece when they sell them back to you at seven cents apiece. Is that right? Why don't you sell the eggs directly to you and eliminate the people you buy them from?"

"Because I'm the people I buy them from," Milo explained. "I make a profit of three and a quarter cents apiece when I sell them to me and a profit of two and three quarter cents apiece when I buy them back from me. That's a total profit of six cents an egg. I lose only two cents an egg when I sell them to the mess halls at five cents apiece, and that's how I can make a profit buying eggs for seven cents apiece and selling them for five cents apiece. I pay only one cent apiece at the hen when I buy them in Sicily."

"In Malta," Yossarian corrected. "You buy your eggs in Malta, not Sicily."

Milo chortled proudly. "I don't buy eggs in Malta," he confessed, with an air of slight and clandestine amusement that was the only departure from industrious sobriety Yossarian had ever seen him make. "I buy them in Sicily for one cent apiece and transfer them to Malta secretly at four and a half cents apiece in order to get the price of eggs up to seven cents apiece when people come to Malta looking for them."

"Why do people come to Malta for eggs when they're so expensive there?"

"Because they've always done it that way."

"Why don't they look for eggs in Sicily?"

"Because they've never done it that way."

"Now I really don't understand. Why don't you sell your mess halls the eggs for seven cents apiece instead of for five cents apiece?"

"Because my mess halls would have no need for me then. Anyone can buy seven-cents-apiece eggs for seven cents apiece."

"Why don't they bypass you and buy the eggs directly from you in Malta at four and a quarter cents apiece?"

"Because I wouldn't sell it to them."

"Why wouldn't you sell it to them?"

"Because then there wouldn't be as much room for a profit. At least this way I can make a bit for myself as a middleman."

"Then you do make a profit for yourself," Yossarian declared.

"Of course I do. But it all goes to the syndicate. And everybody has a share. Don't you understand? It's exactly what happens with those plum tomatoes I sell to Colonel Cathcart."

"*Buy*," Yossarian corrected him. "You don't *sell* plum tomatoes to Colonel Cathcart and Colonel Korn. You *buy* plum tomatoes from them."

"No, *sell*," Milo corrected Yossarian. "I distribute my plum tomatoes in markets all over Pianosa under an assumed name so that Colonel Cathcart and Colonel Korn can buy them up from me under their assumed names at four cents apiece and sell them back to me the next day for the syndicate at five cents apiece. They make a profit of one cent apiece, I make a profit of three and a half cents apiece, and everybody comes out ahead."

"Everybody but the syndicate," said Yossarian with a snort. "The syndicate is paying five cents apiece for plum tomatoes that cost you only half a cent apiece. How does the syndicate benefit?"

"The syndicate benefits when I benefit," Milo explained, "because everybody has a share. And the syndicate gets Colonel Cathcart's and Colonel Korn's support so that they'll let me go out on trips like this one. You'll see how much profit that can mean in about fifteen minutes when we land in Palermo."

"Malta," Yossarian corrected him. "We're flying to Malta now, not Palermo."

"No, we're flying to Palermo," Milo answered. "There's an endive exporter in Palermo I have to see for a minute about a shipment of mushrooms to Bern that were damaged by mold."

"Milo, how do you do it?" Yossarian inquired with laughing amazement and admiration. "You fill out a flight plan for one place and then you go to another. Don't the people in the control towers ever raise hell?"

"They all belong to the syndicate." Milo said. "And they know that what's good for the syndicate is good for the country, because that's what makes Sammy run. The men in the control towers have a share, too, and that's why they always have to do whatever they can to help the syndicate."

"Do I have a share?"

"Everybody has a share."

"Does Orr have a share?"

"Everybody has a share."

"And Hungry Joe? He has a share, too?"

"Everybody has a share."

"Well, I'll be damned," mused Yossarian, deeply impressed with the idea of a share for the very first time.

Milo turned toward him with a faint glimmer of mischief. "I have a sure-fire plan for cheating the federal government out of six thousand dollars. We can make three thousand dollars apiece without any risk to either of us. Are you interested?"

"No."

Milo looked at Yossarian with profound emotion. "That's what I like about you," he exclaimed. "You're honest! You're the only one I know that I can really trust. That's why I wish you'd try to be of more help to me.

Banker
(1982)
Dick Francis

Entrepreneurs take profits where they find them—sometimes they even come on four legs.

Ursula Young, I was told, would put me right. "She's a bloodstock agent. Very sharp, very talkative, knows her stuff. She used to work on a stud farm, so you've got it every which way. She says she'll tell you anything you want, only if you want to see her in person this week it will have to be at Doncaster races on Saturday, she's too busy to spend the time else."

I went north to Doncaster by train and met the lady at the racecourse, where the last Flat meeting of the year was being held. She was waiting as arranged by the entrance to the Members' Club and wearing an identifying red velvet beret, and she swept me off to a secluded table in a bar where we wouldn't be interrupted.

She was fifty, tough, good-looking, dogmatic and inclined to treat me as a child. She also gave me a patient and invaluable lecture on the economics of owning a stallion.

"Stop me," she said to begin with, "if I say something you don't understand."

I nodded.

"All right. Say you own a horse that's won the Derby and you want to capitalize on your gold mine. You judge what you think you can get for the horse, then you divide that by forty and try to sell each of the forty shares at that price. Maybe you can, maybe you can't. It depends on the horse. With Troy, now, they were lining up. But if your winner isn't frightfully well bred or if it made little show *except* in the Derby you'll get a cool response and have to bring the price down. OK so far?"

"Um," I said. "Why only forty shares?"

She looked at me in amazement. "You don't know a *thing*, do you?"

"That's why I'm here."

"Well, a stallion covers forty mares in a season, and the season, incidentally, lasts roughly from February to June. The mares come to *him*, of course. He doesn't travel, he stays put at home. Forty is just about average; physically, I mean. Some can do more, but others get exhausted. So forty is the accepted number. Now, say you have a mare and you've worked out that if you mate her with a certain stallion you might get a top-class foal, you try to get one of those forty places. The places are called nominations. You apply for a nomination, either directly to the stud where the stallion is standing, or through an agent like me, or even by advertising in a breeders' newspaper. Follow?"

"Gasping," I nodded.

She smiled briefly. "People who invest in stallion shares sometimes have broodmares of their own they want to breed from." She paused. "Perhaps I should have explained more clearly that everyone who owns a share automatically has a nomination to the stallion every year."

"Ah," I said.

"Yes. So say you've got your share and consequently your nomination but you haven't a mare to send to the stallion, then you sell your nomination to someone who *has* a mare, in the ways I already described."

"I'm with you."

"After the first three years the nominations may vary in price and in fact are often auctioned, but of course for the first three years the price is fixed."

"Why of course?"

She signed and took a deep breath. "For three years no one knows whether the progeny on the whole are going to be winners or not. The gestation period is eleven months, and the first crop of foals don't race until they're two. If you work it out, that means that the stallion has stood for three seasons, and therefore covered a hundred and twenty mares, before the crunch."

"Right."

"So to fix the stallion fee for the first three years you divide the price of the stallion by one hundred and twenty, and that's it. That's the fee charged for the stallion to cover a mare. That's the sum you receive if you sell your nomination."

I blinked.

"That means," I said, "that if you sell your nomination for three years you have recovered the total amount of your original investment?"

"That's right."

"And after that . . . every time, every year you sell your nomination, it's clear profit?"

"Yes. But taxed, of course."

"And how long does that go on?"

She shrugged. "Ten to fifteen years. Depends on the stallion's potency."

"But that's . . ."

"Yes," she said. "One of the best investments on earth."

All My Sons
(1947)
Arthur Miller

Questions of business ethics are often newsworthy in times of war or peace; but the stakes—and perhaps ethical standards—are higher in times of war. Throughout history, most major wars have led to actual or alleged cases of profiteering; but those cases are rarely as dramatic and tragic as the story of a business's and family's survival presented here from Miller's first major play.

CHRIS: (*a broken whisper*) Then . . . you did it?

KELLER: (*the beginning of plea in his voice*) He never flew a P-40.

CHRIS: But the others.

KELLER: (*insistently*) She's out of her mind. (*He takes a step toward* CHRIS, *pleadingly*.)

CHRIS: (*unyielding*) Dad . . . you did it?

KELLER: He never flew a P-40, what's the matter with you?

CHRIS: (*still asking, and saying*) Then you did it. To the others.

KELLER: (*afraid of him, his deadly insistence*) What's the matter with you? (*Comes nervously closer to him, and, seeing wildness in his eyes)* What the hell is the matter with you?

CHRIS: (*quietly, incredulously*) How . . . how could you do that?

KELLER: (*Lost, he raises his fists.*) What's the matter with you?

CHRIS: (*his passion beginning to flow*) Dad . . . Dad, you killed twenty-one men.

KELLER: What, killed?

CHRIS: You killed them, you murdered them.

KELLER: (*as though throwing his whole nature open before* CHRIS) How could I kill anybody?

CHRIS: Dad! Dad!

KELLER: (*trying to hush him*) I didn't kill anybody!

CHRIS: Then explain it to me. What did you do? Explain it to me or I'll tear you to pieces! What did you do then? What did you do? Now tell me what you did. What did you do?

KELLER: (*horrified at his overwhelming fury*) Don't, Chris, don't . . .

CHRIS: I want to know what you did, now what did you do? You had a hundred and twenty-one cracked engine heads, now what did you do?

KELLER: If you're going to hang me then I . . .

CHRIS: I'm listening, God Almighty, I'm listening!

(Their movements now are those of subtle pursuit and escape.

KELLER *keeps a step out of* CHRIS'S *range, as he talks.)*

KELLER: You're a boy, what could I do! I'm in business, a man is in business; a hundred and twenty-one cracked, you're out of business; you got a process, the process don't work you're out of business; you don't know how to operate, your stuff is no good; they close you up, they tear up your contracts, what the hell's it to them? You lay forty years into a business and they knock you out in five minutes, what could I do, let them take forty years, let them take my life away? (*his voice cracking*) I never thought they'd install them. I swear to God. I thought they'd stop 'em before anybody took off.

CHRIS: Then why'd you ship them out?

KELLER: By the time they could spot them I thought I'd have the process going again, and I could show them they needed me and they'd let it go by. But weeks passed and I got no kick-back, so I was going to tell them.

CHRIS: Then why didn't you tell them?

KELLER: It was too late. The paper, it was all over the front page, twenty-one went down, it was too late. They came with handcuffs into the shop, what could I do? (*Weeping, he approaches* CHRIS.) Chris . . . Chris, I did it for you, it was a chance and I took it for you. I'm sixty-one years old, when would I have another chance to make something for you? Sixty-one years old you don't get another chance, do ya?

CHRIS: You even knew they wouldn't hold up in the air.

KELLER: I didn't say that . . .

CHRIS: But you were going to warn them not to use them . . .

KELLER: But that don't mean . . .

CHRIS: It means you knew they'd crash.

KELLER: It don't mean that.

CHRIS: Then you *thought* they'd crash.

KELLER: I was afraid maybe . . .

CHRIS: You were afraid maybe! Almighty God in heaven, what kind of a man are you? Kids were hanging in the air by those heads. You knew that!

KELLER: For you, a business for you!

CHRIS: (*with burning fury*) For me! Where do you live, where have you come from? For me!—I was dying every day and you were killing my boys and you did it for me? I was so proud you were helping us win and you did it for me? What the hell do you think I was thinking of, the goddam business? Is that as far as your mind can see, the business? What is that, the world—the business? What are you made of, dollar bills? What the hell do you mean, you did it for me? Don't you have a country? Don't you live in the world? What the hell are you? You're not even an animal, no animal kills his own, what are you? What must I do to you? I ought to tear the tongue out of your mouth, what must I do?

(He is weeping, and with his fist he begins to pound down upon his father's shoulder, and KELLER *stands there and weeps.)*

CHRIS: *(with each blow)* What? What! What! What! *(He stumbles away, covering his face as he weeps.)* What must I do, Jesus God, what must I do?

(He falls into a chair and cries. KELLER *raises a hand weakly, and comes toward him weeping, saying . . .)*

KELLER: Chris . . . My Chris . . .

CURTAIN FALLS

KELLER: What's the matter with you?

(CHRIS *remains silent.)*

KELLER: I want to talk to you.

CHRIS: I've got nothing to . . .

KELLER: *(He pushes him toward the steps of the porch.)* I want to talk to you!

CHRIS: Don't do that, Dad. I'm going to hurt you if you do that.

KELLER: *(quietly, with a break in his voice)* Go down.

CHRIS: *(after an instant)* There's nothing to say, so say it quick.

(CHRIS *comes down from the porch.* KELLER *then comes down, walks past him.)*

KELLER: Exactly what's the matter? Without the philosophy involved. What's the matter? You got too much money? Is that what bothers you?

CHRIS: *(with an edge of sarcasm)* It bothers me.

KELLER: Then what's the difficulty? When something bothers you you either get used to it or you get rid of it. If you can't get used to it then throw it away. You hear me? Take every cent and give it to charity, throw it in the sewer. Does that settle it? In the sewer, that's all.

(CHRIS *is silent.)*

KELLER: What's the matter, you think I'm kidding? I'm tellin' you what to do; if it's dirty then burn it. It's your money, that's not my money. I'm a dead man, I'm an old dead man, nothing's mine. Well talk to me!— What do you want to do!

CHRIS: *(trembling)* It's not what I want to do. It's what you want to do.

KELLER: What should I want to do?

(CHRIS *is silent.)*

KELLER: Jail? You want me to go to jail?

(CHRIS's *eyes filling with tears, he remains silent.)*

KELLER: *(himself near weeping)* What're you crying for? If you want me to go say so! don't cry! Is that where I belong?—Then tell me so! (*Slight pause.*) What's the matter, why can't you tell me? (*furiously*) You say everything else to me, say that! (*Slight pause.*) I'll tell you why you can't say it. Because you know I don't belong there. Because you know! (*He is moving around* CHRIS, *jerkily, with growing emphasis and passion, and a persistent tone of desperation.*) If my money's dirty there ain't a clean nickel in the United States. Who worked for nothin' in that war? When they work for nothin', I'll work for nothin'. Did they ship a gun or a truck outa Detroit before they got their price? Is that clean? Nothin's clean. It's dollars and cents, nickels and dimes; war and peace, it's nickels and dimes, what's clean? The whole goddam country is gotta go if I go! That's why you can't tell me.

CHRIS: That's exactly why.

KELLER: Then . . . why am *I* bad?

CHRIS: I don't call you bad. *I* know you're no worse than most, but I thought you were better. I never saw you as a man. I saw you as a father. (*almost breaking*) I can't look at you this way, and I can't look at myself!

(*He turns quickly and goes directly toward the porch. On this movement* ANN *goes quickly to* MOTHER, *snatching the letter from her hand, and starts for* CHRIS. MOTHER *instantly rushes to intercept her.*)

MOTHER: Give me that!

ANN: He's going to read it! (*She gets away from* MOTHER *and thrusts the letter into* CHRIS'S *hand as . . .*)

MOTHER: (*grasping for it in* CHRIS'S *hand*) Give it to me, Chris, give that to me!

CHRIS: (*Looking from her to* ANN, *holding the letter clenched in his fist. Looking from one to the other*) What . . . ?

ANN: Larry. He wrote that to me the day he died ...

KELLER: Larry?

MOTHER: Chris, it's not for you. Give it to me, please . . .

(*He unlocks her fingers from his wrist.*)

MOTHER: (*In terror she backs from him as he starts to read.*) Joe . . . go away . . .

KELLER: (*mystified, frightened*) Why'd she say, Larry, what . . . ?

MOTHER: (*She desperately pushes him toward the alley, glancing at* CHRIS.) Go to the street . . . ! (*He is resisting her, starting to speak; she leaves him and starts alone toward the driveway.*) Jim! Where's Jim . . . ! (*As she passes* CHRIS, *a little weeping laugh escapes him. She stops.*) Don't . . . (*pleading from her whole soul*) Don't tell him . . .

CHRIS: (*deadly, quiet, through his teeth to his father*) Three and one-half years . . . talking; talking. Now you tell me what you must do. . . . This is how he died, now tell me where you belong.

KELLER: (*backing, now in deadly fear*) Chris, a man can't be a Jesus in this world!

CHRIS: I know all about the world. I know the whole crap story. Now listen to this, and tell me what a man's got to be! (*Reads.*) "My Dear Ann: . . ." You listening? He wrote this the day he died. Listen, don't cry . . . listen! "My dear Ann: It is impossible to put down the things I feel. But I've got to tell you something. Yesterday they flew in a load of papers from the States and I read about Dad and your father being convicted. I can't express myself. I can't face the other men. . . . I can't bear to live any more. Last night I circled the base for twenty minutes before I could bring myself in. How could he have done that? Every day three or four men never return and he sits back there 'doing business.' I can't face anybody. . . . I don't know how to tell you what I feel. . . . I'm going out on a mission in a few minutes. They'll probably report me missing. If they do, I want you to know that you mustn't wait for me. I tell you, Ann, if I had him here now I could kill him."

(KELLER *grabs letter from* CHRIS *and reads. Pause.*)

CHRIS: (*after a long pause*) Now blame the world. Do you understand that letter?

KELLER: (*almost inaudibly, staring*) I think so. Get the car. I'll put on my jacket.

(*He turns and seems about to fall.* MOTHER *reaches out quickly to support him.*)

MOTHER: (*with a pleading, lost cry*) Joe . . .

KELLER: (*with complete self-disgust*) No, let me go; I want to go . . . I'm sorry, Kate.

MOTHER: You're so foolish; Larry was your son too, wasn't he? You know he'd never tell you to do this!

KELLER: (*indicating the letter*) What is this if it isn't telling me? Sure, he was my son. But I think to him they were all my sons. And I guess they were, kid . . . I guess they were. (*quietly to* CHRIS) I'll be down . . . in a minute. (*He turns and goes into the house.*)

MOTHER: He'll stay if you tell him to. Go to him!

CHRIS: Mother, he's got to go.

MOTHER: You both gone crazy! (*She presses* CHRIS *to go into the house.*) Tell him to sleep!

CHRIS: No, Mom.

MOTHER: God in heaven, what is accomplished if he goes?

CHRIS: I thought you read that!

MOTHER: The war is over, didn't you hear?—It's over!

CHRIS: Then what was Larry to you, a stone that fell into the water? It's *not* enough to be sorry. Larry didn't kill himself so you and Dad would be "sorry"!

MOTHER: What more can we be?

CHRIS: (*with all his power, beyond all restraint*) You can be better! Once and for all you can know now that the whole earth comes in through those fences; there's a universe outside and you're responsible to it, and if you're not you threw your son away, because that's why he died! He's got to go, and I'm . . .

(*A shot is heard from the house. They leap in shock.*)

CHRIS: Find Jim! (*He rushes into the house.*)

(ANN *runs off, toward Jim's house.* MOTHER *has not moved. Facing the house . . .*)

MOTHER: (*over and over*) Joe . . . Joe . . . Joe.

(CHRIS *comes out of the house.*)

CHRIS: (*apologetically*) Mother . . .

MOTHER: Sssh.

(CHRIS *comes to her, trying to speak. Weeping, she embraces him.*)

CHRIS: (*going to her arms*) I didn't mean that he . . . (CHRIS *breaks into a sob.*)

MOTHER: Sssh. Sssh . . . Don't, don't dear; you mustn't take it on yourself. Forget now. Live.

(*She moves from him, and as she mounts the porch he hears the growing sound of her weeping. She goes inside. Alone, he comes erect, moves away from the sound, does not turn to it, as the curtain falls.*)

CURTAIN

Markets, Prices, Supply, and Demand

In 1890 the English economist Alfred Marshall suggested that if a parrot were trained to answer "supply and demand" to every question it was asked, the parrot could be given a degree in economics. While even then that was an oversimplification, there is still a good deal of truth to Marshall's quip. In an economic system where buyers and sellers are, for the most part, free to buy and sell goods and services, including such basic commodities as food, clothing, housing, automobiles, and fuel, as well as luxury and entertainment goods items, markets are central.

Competitive markets automatically and impersonally gather signals about how much consumers are willing and able to buy at different prices, and how much producers are willing and able to sell at different prices. The market price for a good or service is the price where the amount buyers are willing and able to purchase is just equal to the amount sellers are willing and able to sell. At any higher price there will be more goods and services offered for sale than are purchased—a surplus—so prices will fall towards the market-clearing or equilibrium price. At any lower price, buyers will want to purchase more units of the product than are offered for sale—a shortage—so prices will rise towards the market price. This happens without any agency trying to figure out what people want and are willing to spend, and what producers will have to spend to produce and sell the product. Instead, we rely on individual buyers and sellers to make decisions in their own self-interest, with the understanding that if each buyer and seller makes good decisions, competing with other buyers and sellers, the overall system of production and distribution will be efficient, too. There is a legitimate role for government in keeping markets competitive, in preventing theft and fraud, and in enforcing regulations to keep food and drugs safe, but for the most part a market system is based on purchasing and production decisions made by individual buyers and sellers in the marketplace.

Literary authors frequently write about markets and prices, and occasionally they even write explicitly about supply and demand. Usually, though, when they write about market forces, they don't use the formal terminology—or jargon—of economics. For example, William Gilbert's "Up Goes the Price of Shoddy" illustrates how the demand for fashionable items, such as clothing, can shift dramatically as a result of changes in consumers' tastes and preferences. The excerpt from Frank Norris's Octopus, *on the other hand, is one of the shorter recorded lectures we have on supply and demand. In Tom Stoppard's* Arcadia, *Bernard and*

Valentine debate the true and market values of poetry and scientific discoveries, and whether such works are the result of automatic and impersonal forces or individual creativity and personality. From Emerson's Journals, *two short excerpts deal with the effects of market forces on human activities and how a person can make a name for himself as a good farmer, tradesman, or inventor.*

In John Steinbeck's East of Eden, *Cal makes a successful investment in the futures markets when the price of beans rises following the outbreak of World War I. His father, Adam, refuses to take any of the money made in this market because he serves on the local draft board sending young men to war. He tells Cal to give it back, and Cal responds with some very sophisticated arguments about the mutual gains from voluntary trade and the impersonal and automatic functioning of markets. He asks pointedly, "Give it back to who?"*

Washington Irving's "Poor-Devil Author" is a small town's favorite literary son who goes off to London to sell his magnum opus *and make his fame and fortune. Things don't work out as planned, but eventually he adapts and displays little patience for those who will not accept the verdict and workings of the marketplace. The passage from Ivan Doig's* Dancing at the Rascal Fair *shows sheep farmers making difficult decisions in the face of several years of low prices.*

Sebastian Junger's Perfect Storm *includes wonderful information on the market for fresh swordfish, and how that market has been affected by changing technologies, consumer demands, and government regulations made necessary by the overfishing of resources that, unlike cattle and other domesticated farm animals, cannot be owned and grown as private property.*

Amy Tan's Joy Luck Club *has a brief summary of what economists call the efficient market hypothesis—the idea that market prices for frequently traded goods and services will reflect any known factors that may cause the future price for the good or service to rise or fall. On the other hand,* The Pearl, *by John Steinbeck, is a story of love, fortune, and markets that are neither efficient nor competitive.*

The passage from The Robber Bride, *by Margaret Atwood, provides a history of a small retail store and how the store's owner reacts to changes in consumer tastes and incomes over a period of several decades. The passage also shows that the demand for workers in the store is derived from the customers' demand for the goods sold in the store.*

Songs of a Savoyard
(1890)
W. S. Gilbert

The noted economist Alfred Marshall explained that just as paper or cloth is cut by both blades of a pair of scissors, prices are determined both by factors that affect what producers supply and factors that influence what consumers demand. Here Marshall's contemporary, W. S. Gilbert, describes some of that process in rhyme.

There lived a King, as I've been told
In the wonder-working days of old,
When hearts were twice as good as gold,
　　And twenty times as mellow.
Good temper triumphed in his face,
And in his heart he found a place
For all the erring human race
　　And every wretched fellow.
When he had Rhenish wine to drink
It made him very sad to think
That some, at junket or at jink,
　　Must be content with toddy:
He wished all men as rich as he
(And he was rich as rich could be),
So to the top of every tree
　　Promoted everybody.

Ambassadors cropped up like hay,
Prime Ministers and such as they
Grew like asparagus in May,
　　And Dukes were three a penny:
Lord Chancellors were cheap as sprats,
And Bishops in their shovel hats
Were plentiful as tabby cats—
　　If possible, too many.
On every side Field-Marshals gleamed,
Small beer were Lords-Lieutenants deemed,
With Admirals the ocean teemed,
　　All round his wide dominions;
And Party Leaders you might meet

In twos and threes in every street
Maintaining, with no little heat,
Their various opinions.

That King, although no one denies,
His heart was of abnormal size,
Yet he'd have acted otherwise
If he had been acuter.

The end is easily foretold,
When every blessed thing you hold
Is made of silver, or of gold,
You long for simple pewter.
When you have nothing else to wear
But cloth of gold and satins rare,
For cloth of gold you cease to care—
Up goes the price of shoddy.

The Octopus: A Story of California (1901)

Frank Norris

Individuals decide what they will buy and produce, but in many ways market forces for goods and services operate automatically and impersonally. However, such is more clearly the case for competitive markets than the monopoly Norris depicted in The Octopus.

You are dealing with forces, young man, when you speak of Wheat and Railroads, not with men. There is the Wheat, the supply. It must be carried to feed the People. There is the demand. The Wheat is one force, the Railroad, another, and there is the law that governs them—supply and demand. Men have only little to do in the whole business. Complications may arise, conditions that bear hard on the individual—crush him maybe—*but the Wheat will be carried to feed the people* as inevitably as it will grow.

Arcadia
(1993)
Tom Stoppard

One of the many topics Stoppard addresses in Arcadia *is, as in the previous passage by Norris, the question of whether market forces—as well as social progress and scientific discoveries—are impersonal and automatic, or a matter of individual personalities and values.*

BERNARD: *(jeering)* Parameters! You can't stick Byron's head in your laptop! Genius isn't like your average grouse.

VALENTINE: *(casually)* Well, it's all trivial anyway.

BERNARD: What is?

VALENTINE: Who wrote what when . . .

BERNARD: Trivial?

VALENTINE: Personalities.

BERNARD: I'm sorry—did you say trivial?

VALENTINE: It's a technical term.

BERNARD: Not where I come from, it isn't.

VALENTINE: The questions you're asking don't matter, you see. It's like arguing who got there first with the calculus. The English say Newton, the Germans say Leibnitz. But it doesn't *matter*. Personalities. What matters is the calculus. Scientific progress. Knowledge.

BERNARD: Really? Why?

VALENTINE: Why what?

BERNARD: Why does scientific progress matter more than personalities?

VALENTINE: Is he serious?

HANNAH: No, he's trivial. Bernard—

VALENTINE: *(interrupting, to* BERNARD) Do yourself a favour, you're on a loser.

BERNARD: Oh, you're going to zap me with penicillin and pesticides. Spare me that and I'll spare you the bomb and aerosols. But don't confuse progress with perfectibility. A great poet is always timely. A great philosopher is an urgent need. There's no rush for Isaac Newton. We were quite happy with Aristotle's cosmos. Personally, I preferred it. Fifty-five crystal spheres geared to God's crankshaft is my idea of a satisfying universe. I can't think of anything more trivial than the speed of light. Quarks, quasars—big bangs, black holes—who gives a shit? How did you people con us out of all that status? All that money? And why are you so pleased with yourselves?

CHLOE: Are you against penicillin, Bernard?

BERNARD: Don't feed the animals. *(Back to* VALENTINE) I'd push the lot of you over a cliff myself. Except the one in the wheelchair, I think I'd lose the sympathy vote before people had time to think it through.

HANNAH: *(loudly)* What the hell do you mean, the dust-jacket?

BERNARD: *(ignoring her)* If knowledge isn't self-knowledge it isn't doing much, mate. Is the universe expanding? Is it contracting? Is it standing on one leg and singing "When Father Painted the Parlour"? Leave me out. I can expand my universe without you. "She walks in beauty, like the night of cloudless climes and starry skies, and all that's best of dark and bright meet in her aspect and her eyes." There you are, he wrote it after coming home from a party. *(With offensive politeness.)* What is it that you're doing with grouse, Valentine, I'd love to know?

*(*VALENTINE *stands up and it is suddenly apparent that he is shaking and close to tears.)*

VALENTINE: *(to* CHLOE) He's not against penicillin, and he knows I'm not against poetry.

JOURNALS (1853 & 1855)*

Ralph Waldo Emerson

Emerson apparently never wrote, and may or may not have said, that if someone invents a better mousetrap the world will beat a path to his or her door. But he often expressed the same sentiment. Emerson also often addressed broader issues concerning why some people and nations produce and earn more than others.

In Belgium and other countries, I have seen reports of model farms; they begun with downs or running sands,—it makes no difference what bottom, mere land to lay their basket of loam down upon;—then, they proceed from beach grass, or whatever, and rye and clover, manuring all the time, until they formed a soil fourteen inches deep. Well, so I conceive, it is in national genericulture, as in agriculture. You must manage to set up a national will . . . you must find a land like England, where temperate and sharp northern breezes blow, to keep that will alive and alert; markets on every possible side, because it is an island; the people tasked and kept at the top

* Emerson's *Journals* were written from 1819 to 1874. The years indicated here are for the years these entries were made in the journals.

of their condition by the continual activity of seafaring and the exciting nature of sea-risks, and the deep stimulus of gain: the land not large enough, the population not large enough, to glut the market and depress one another; but so proportioned is it to the size of Europe and of the world, that it keeps itself healthy and bright, and, like an immense manufactory, it yields, with perfect security and ease, incredible results.

Many things conduce to this. Over them all works a sort of *Anima mundi* or soul of the island,—the aggregation by time, experience, and demand and supply, of a great many personalities,—which fits them to each other, and enables them to keep step and time, cooperates as harmoniously and punctually as the parts of a human body.

I trust a good deal to common fame, as we all must. If a man has good corn, or wood, or boards, or pigs, to sell, or can make better chairs or knives, crucibles or church organs, than anybody else, you will find a broad hard-beaten road to his house, though it be in the woods. And if a man knows the law, people find it out, though he live in a pine shanty, and resort to him. And if a man can pipe or sing, so as to wrap the prisoned soul in an elysium; or can paint landscape, and convey into oils and ochres all the enchantments of Spring or Autumn; or can liberate or intoxicate all people who hear him with delicious songs and versus; 'tis certain that the secret cannot be kept: the first witness tells it to a second, and men go by fives and tens and fifties to his door. What a signal convenience is fame.

East of Eden
(1952)
John Steinbeck

In the following passage Cal exhibits a more sophisticated and technical understanding of how markets work than his father, Adam. Adam evaluates transactions on normative grounds of fairness and equity, basing his feelings partly on his own role in the national war effort, which plays an important role in Steinbeck's retelling of the story of Cain and Abel.

Cal asked, "How is the ice plant doing, Father?"

"Why, all right. Pays for itself and makes a little profit. Why?"

"I thought of a couple of things to make it really pay."

"Not today," said Adam quickly. "Monday, if you remember, but not today. You know," Adam said, "I don't remember when I've felt so good. I feel—well, you might call it fulfilled. Maybe it's only a good night's sleep and a good trip to the bathroom. And maybe it's because we're all together and at peace." He smiled at Aron. "We didn't know what we felt about you until you went away."

"I was homesick," Aron confessed. "The first few days I thought I'd die of it."

Abra came in with a little rush. Her cheeks were pink and she was happy. "Did you notice there's snow on Mount Toro?" she asked.

"Yes, I saw it," Adam said. "They say that means a good year to come. And we could use it."

"I just nibbled," said Abra. "I wanted to be hungry for here."

Lee apologized for the dinner like an old fool. He blamed the gas oven which didn't heat like a good wood stove. He blamed the new breed of turkeys which lacked a something turkeys used to have. But he laughed with them when they told him he was acting like an old woman fishing for compliments.

With the plum pudding Adam opened the champagne, and they treated it with ceremony. A courtliness settled over the table. They proposed toasts. Each one had his health drunk, and Adam made a little speech to Abra when he drank her health.

Her eyes were shining and under the table Aron held her hand. The wine dulled Cal's nervousness and he was not afraid about his present.

When Adam had finished his plum pudding he said, "I guess we never have had such a good Thanksgiving."

Cal reached in his jacket pocket, took out the red-ribboned package, and pushed it over in front of his father.

"What's this?" Adam asked.

"It's a present."

Adam was pleased. "Not even Christmas and we have presents. I wonder what it can be!"

"A handkerchief," said Abra.

Adam slipped off the grubby bow and unfolded the tissue paper. He stared down at the money.

Abra said, "What is it?" and stood up to look. Aron leaned forward. Lee, in the doorway, tried to keep the look of worry from his face. He darted a glance at Cal and saw the light of joy and triumph in his eyes.

Very slowly Adam moved his fingers and fanned the gold certificates. His voice seemed to come from far away. "What is it? What—" He stopped.

Cal swallowed. "It's—I made it—to give to you—to make up for losing the lettuce."

Adam raised his head slowly. "You made it? How?"

"Mr. Hamilton—we made it—on beans." He hurried on, "We bought futures at five cents and when the price jumped—It's for you, fifteen thousand dollars. It's for you."

Adam touched the new bills so that their edges came together, folded the tissue over them and turned the ends up. He looked helplessly at Lee. Cal caught a feeling—a feeling of calamity, of destruction in the air, and a weight of sickness overwhelmed him. He heard his father say, "You'll have to give it back."

Almost as remotely his own voice said, "Give it back? Give it back to who?"

"To the people you got it from."

"The British Purchasing Agency? They can't take it back. They're paying twelve and a half cents for beans all over the country."

"Then give it to the farmers you robbed."

"Robbed?" Cal cried. "Why, we paid them two cents a pound over the market. We didn't rob them." Cal felt suspended in space, and time seemed very slow.

His father took a long time to answer. There seemed to be long spaces between his words. "I send boys out," he said. "I sign my name and they go out. And some will die and some will lie helpless without arms and legs. Not one will come back untorn. Son, do you think I could take a profit on that?"

"I did it for you," Cal said. "I wanted you to have the money to make up your loss."

"I don't want the money, Cal. And the lettuce—I don't think I did that for a profit. It was a kind of game to see if I could get the lettuce there, and I lost. I don't want the money."

Cal looked straight ahead. He could feel the eyes of Lee and Aron and Abra crawling on his cheeks. He kept his eyes on his father's lips.

"I like the idea of a present," Adam went on. "I thank you for the thought—"

"I'll put it away. I'll keep it for you," Cal broke in.

"No. I won't want it ever. I would have been so happy if you could have given me—well, what your brother has—pride in the thing he's doing, gladness in his progress. Money, even clean money, doesn't stack up with that." His eyes widened a little and he said, "Have I made you angry, son? Don't be angry. If you want to give me a present—give me a good life. That would be something I could value."

Cal felt that he was choking. His forehead streamed with perspiration and he tasted salt on his tongue. He stood up suddenly and his chair fell over. He ran from the room, holding his breath.

Adam called after him, "Don't be angry, son."

They let him alone. He sat in his room, his elbows on his desk. He thought he would cry but he did not. He tried to let weeping start but tears could not pass the hot iron in his head.

The Poor-Devil Author (1824)

Washington Irving

In the literary marketplace, as in other arenas of life, many are called but few are chosen for greatness. Most people must be content to reign only in their youthful and sometimes small-town dreams, eventually settling down to lead decent and respectable, if unglamorous, lives. Rarely is that lesson learned so fully, or expressed so directly and humorously, as it is by Irving's poor-devil author.

I began life unluckily by being the wag and bright fellow at school; and I had the further misfortune of becoming the great genius of my native village. My father was a country attorney, and intended I should succeed him in business; but I had too much genius to study, and he was too fond of my genius to force it into the traces; so I fell into bad company, and took to bad habits. Do not mistake me. I mean that I fell into the company of village-literati, and village-blues, and took to writing village-poetry.

It was quite the fashion in the village to be literary. There was a little knot of choice spirits of us, who assembled frequently together, formed ourselves into a Literary, Scientific, and Philosophical Society, and fancied ourselves the most learned Philos in existence. Every one had a great character assigned him, suggested by some casual habit or affection. One heavy fellow drank an enormous quantity of tea, rolled in his arm-chair, talked sententiously, pronounced dogmatically, and was considered a second Dr. Johnson; another, who happened to be a curate, uttered coarse jokes, wrote doggerel rhymes, and was the Swift of our association. Thus we had also our Popes, and Goldsmiths and Addisons; and a blue-stocking lady, whose drawing-room we frequented, who corresponded about nothing with all the world, who wrote letters with the stiffness and formality of a printed book, was cried up as another Mrs. Montagu. I was, by common consent, the juvenile prodigy, the poetical youth, the great genius, the pride and hope of the village, through whom it was to become one day as celebrated as Stratford-on-Avon.

My father died, and left me his blessing and his business. His blessing brought no money into my pocket; and as to his business, it soon deserted me; for I was busy writing poetry, and could not attend to law, and my clients, though they had great respect for my talents, had no faith in a poetical attorney.

I lost my business, therefore, spent my money, and finished my poem. It was the *Pleasures of Melancholy*, and was cried up to the skies by the whole circle. The *Pleasures of Imagination*, the *Pleasures of Hope*, and the *Pleasures of Memory*, though each had placed its author in the first rank of poets, were blank prose in comparison. Our Mrs.

Montagu would cry over it from beginning to end. It was pronounced by all the members of the Literary, Scientific, and Philosophical Society the greatest poem of the age, and all anticipated the noise it would make in the great world. There was no doubt but the London book-sellers would be mad after it; and the only fear of my friends was, that I would make a sacrifice by selling it too cheap. Every time they talked the matter over, they increased the price. They reckoned up the great sums given for the poems of certain popular writers, and determined that mine was worth more than all put together, and ought to be paid for accordingly. For my part, I was modest in my expectations, and determined that I would be satisfied with a thousand guineas. So I put my poem in my pocket, and set off for London.

My journey was joyous. My heart was light as my purse, and my head was full of anticipations of fame and fortune. With what swelling pride did I cast my eyes upon old London from the heights of Highgate! I was like a general, looking down upon a place he expects to conquer. The great metropolis lay stretched before me, buried under a home-made cloud of murky smoke, that wrapped it from the brightness of a sunny day, and formed for it a kind of artificial bad weather. At the outskirts of the city, away to the west, the smoke gradually decreased until all was clear and sunny, and the view stretched uninterrupted to the blue line of the Kentish hills.

My eye turned fondly to where the mighty cupola of St. Paul's swelled dimly through this misty chaos, and I pictured to myself the solemn realm of learning that lies about its base. How soon should the *Pleasures of Melancholy* throw this world of booksellers and printers into a bustle of business and delight! How soon should I hear my name repeated by printers' devils throughout Paternoster Row, and Angel Court, and Ave-Maria Lane, until Amen Corner should echo back the sound!

Arrived in town, I repaired at once to the most fashionable publisher. Every new author patronizes him, of course. In fact, it has been determined in the village circle that he should be the fortunate man. I cannot tell you how vain-gloriously I walked the streets. My head was in the clouds. I felt the airs of heaven playing about it, and fancied it already encircled by a halo of literary glory. As I passed by the windows of book-shops, I anticipated the time when my work would be shining among the hot-pressed wonders of the day; and my face, scratched on copper, or cut on wood, figuring in fellowship with those of Scott, and Byron, and Moore.

When I applied at the publisher's house, there was something in the loftiness of my air, and the dinginess of my dress, that struck the clerks with reverence. They doubtless took me for some person of consequence; probably a digger of Greek roots, or a penetrator of pyramids. A proud man in a dirty shirt is always an imposing character in the world of letters; one must feel intellectually secure before he can venture to dress shabbily; none but a great genius, or a great scholar, dares to be dirty; so I was ushered at once to the sanctum sanctorum of this high-priest of Minerva.

The publishing of books is a very different affair nowadays from what it was in the time of Bernard Lintot. I found the publisher a fashionably dressed man, in an elegant drawing-room, furnished with sofas, and portraits of celebrated authors, and cases of splendidly bound books. He was writing letters at an elegant table. This was transacting business in style. The place seemed suited to the magnificent publications that issued from it. I rejoiced at the choice I had made of a publisher, for I always liked to encourage men of taste and spirit.

I stepped up to the table with the lofty poetical port I had been accustomed to maintain in our village circle; though I threw in it something of a patronizing air, such as one feels when about to make a man's fortune. The publisher paused with his pen in hand, and seemed waiting in mute suspense to know what was to be announced by so singular an apparition.

I put him at his ease in a moment, for I felt that I had but to come, see, and conquer. I made known my name, and the name of my poem; produced my precious roll of blotted manuscript; laid it on the table with an emphasis; and told him at once, to save time, and come directly to the point, the price was one thousand guineas.

I had given him no time to speak, nor did he seem so inclined. He continued looking at me for a moment with an air of whimsical perplexity; scanned me from head to foot; looked down at the manuscript, then up again at me, then pointed to a chair; and whistling softly to himself, went on writing his letter.

I sat for some time waiting his reply, supposing he was making up his mind; but he only paused occasionally to take a fresh dip of ink, to stroke his chin, or the tip of his nose, and then resumed his writing. It was evident his mind was intently occupied upon some other subject; but I had no idea that any other subject could be attended to, and my poem lie unnoticed on the table. I had supposed that everything would make way for the *Pleasures of Melancholy*.

My gorge at length rose within me. I took up my manuscript, thrust it into my pocket, and walked out of the room; making some noise as I went out, to let my departure be heard. The publisher, however, was too much buried in minor concerns to notice it. I was suffered to walk down-stairs without being called back. I sallied forth into the street, but no clerk was sent after me; nor did the publisher call after me from the drawing-room window. I have been told since that he considered me either a madman or a fool. I leave you to judge how much he was in the wrong in his opinion.

When I turned the corner, my crest fell. I cooled down in my pride and my expectations, and reduced my terms with the next bookseller to whom I applied. I had no better success, nor with a third, nor with a fourth. I then desired the booksellers to make an offer themselves; but the deuce an offer would they make. They told me poetry was a mere drug; everybody wrote poetry; the market was overstocked with it. And then they said, the title of my poem was not taking; that pleasures of all kinds were worn threadbare, nothing but horrors did nowadays, and even those were almost worn out. Tales of Pirates, Robbers, and bloody Turks, might answer tolerably well; but then they must come from some established, well-known name, or the public would not look at them.

At last I offered to leave my poem with a bookseller to read it, and judge for himself. "Why, really, my dear Mr. —, a—a—I forget your name," said he, casting his eye at my rusty coat and shabby gaiters; "really, sir, we are so pressed with business just now, and have so many manuscripts on hand to read, that we have not time to look at any new productions; but if you can call again in a week or two, or say the middle of next month, we may be able to look over your writings, and give you an answer. Don't forget, the month after next, good morning, sir; happy to see you any time you are passing this way." So saying, he bowed me out in the civilest way imaginable. In short, sir, instead of an eager competition to secure my poem, I could not even get it read! In the mean time I was harassed by letters from friends, wanting to know when the work was to appear; who was to be my publisher; and, above all things, warning me not to let it go too cheap.

There was but one alternative left. I determined to publish the poem myself; and to have my triumph over the booksellers when it should become the fashion of the day. I accordingly published the *Pleasures of Melancholy*,—and ruined myself. Excepting the copies sent to the reviews, and to my friends in the country, not one, I believe, even left the bookseller's warehouse. The printer's bill drained my purse; and the only notice that was taken of my work was contained in the advertisements paid for by myself.

I could have borne all this, and have attributed it, as usual, to the mismanagement of the publisher, or the want of taste in the public; and could have made the usual appeal to posterity; but my village friends would not let me rest in quiet. They were picturing me to themselves feasting with the great, communing with the literary, and in the high career of fortune and renown. Every little while, some one would call on me with a letter of introductions from the village circle, recommending him to my attentions, and requesting that I would make him known in society; with a hint, that an introduction to a celebrated literary nobleman would be extremely agreeable. I determined, therefore, to change my lodgings, drop my correspondence, and disappear altogether from the view of my village admirers. Besides, I was anxious to make one more poetic attempt. I was by no means disheartened by the failure of my first. I was evidently too didactic. The public was wise enough. It no longer read for instruction. "They want horrors, do they?" said I: "I'faith! then they shall have enough of them." So I looked out for some quiet, retired place, where I might be out of the reach of my friends, and have leisure to cook up some delectable dish of poetical "hell-broth."

❧

I see you are growing weary, so I will be brief with the residue of my literary career. I will not detain you with a detail of my various attempts to get astride of Pegasus; of the poems I have written which were never printed, the plays I have presented which were never performed, and the tracts I have published which were never purchased. It seemed as if booksellers, managers, and the very public, had entered into a conspiracy to starve me. Still I could not prevail upon myself to give up the trial, nor abandon those dreams of renown in which I had indulged. How should I be able to look the literary circle of my native village in the face, if I were so completely to falsify their predictions? For some time longer, therefore, I continued to write for fame, and was, of course, the most miserable dog in existence, besides being in continual risk of starvation. I accumulated loads of literary treasure on my shelves—loads which were to be treasures to posterity; but, alas! they put not a penny into my purse. What was all this wealth to my present necessities? I could not patch my elbows with an ode; nor satisfy my hunger with blank verse. "Shall a man fill his belly with the east wind?" says the proverb. He may as well do so as with poetry.

I have many a time strolled sorrowfully along, with a sad heart and an empty stomach, about five o'clock, and looked wistfully down the areas in the west end of the town, and seen through the kitchen-windows the fires gleaming, and the joints of meat turning on the spits and dripping with gravy, and the cook-maids beating up pudding, or trussing turkeys, and felt for the moment that if I could but have the run of one of those kitchens, Apollo and the Muses might have the hungry heights of Parnassus for me. Oh, sir! talk of meditations among the tombs,—they are nothing so melancholy as the meditations of a poor devil without penny in pouch, along a line of kitchen-windows towards dinnertime.

At length, when almost reduced to famine and despair, the ideal all at once entered my head, that perhaps I was not so clever a fellow as the village and myself had supposed. It was the salvation of me. The moment the idea popped into my brain it brought conviction and comfort with it. I awoke as from a dream. I gave up immortal fame to those who could live on air; took to writing for mere bread; and have ever since had a very tolerable life of it. There is no man of letters so much at his ease, sir, as he who has no character to gain or lose. I had to train myself to it a little, and to clip my wings short at first, or they would have carried me up into poetry in spite of myself. So I determined to begin by the opposite extreme, and abandoning the higher regions of the craft, I came plump down to the lowest and turned creeper.

"Creeper! and pray what is that?" said I.

"Oh, sir, I see you are ignorant of the language of the craft; a creeper is one who furnishes the newspapers with paragraphs at so much a line; and who goes about in quest of misfortunes; attends the Bow Street Office; the Courts of Justice, and every other den of mischief and iniquity. We are paid at the rate of a penny a line, and as we can sell the same paragraph to almost every paper, we sometimes pick up a very decent day's work. Now and then the Muse is unkind, or the day uncommonly quiet, and then we rather starve; and sometimes the unconscionable editors will clip our paragraphs when they are a little too rhetorical, and snip off twopence or threepence at a go. I have many a time had my pot of porter snipped off my dinner in this way, and have had to dine with dry lips. However, I cannot complain. I rose gradually in the lower ranks of the craft, and am now, I think, in the most comfortable region of literature."

"And pray," said I, "what may you be at present?"

"At present," said he, "I am a regular job-writer, and turn my hand to anything. I work up the writings of others at so much a sheet; turn off translations; write second-rate articles to fill up reviews and magazines; compile travels and voyages, and furnish theoretical criticisms for the newspapers. All this authorship, you perceive, is anonymous; it gives me no reputation except among the trade; where I am considered an author of all work, and am always sure of employ. That's the only reputation I want. I sleep soundly, without dread of duns or critics, and leave immortal fame to those that choose to fret and fight about it. Take my word for it, the only happy author in this world is he who is below the care of reputation."

Dancing at the Rascal Fair (1987)

Ivan Doig

Every year at harvest time, U.S. grain farmers decide whether to sell their grain at current prices or to store the grain in the hope that prices will rise. Cattle and sheep ranchers face the same question, with additional cost considerations related to feeding and tending their stock. These issues have been a basic part of American agriculture for centuries, with some years and decades far better for ranchers and farmers than others. The 1890s were a particularly bad time.

"By Jesus, the woollies do make a lovely sight," intoned Lucas. "If we could just sell them as scenery, ay?"

The time was September of 1896, a week before shipping the lambs, and Lucas and Rob and I were holding a Saturday war council on the west ridgeline of Breed Butte where we could meanwhile keep an eye on our grazing bands. By now Rob and Lucas's sheep had accumulated into two oversize bands, nearly twenty-five hundred altogether, as Rob kept back the ewe lambs each year since '93 rather than send them to market at pitiful prices. The band he and I owned in partnership I always insisted keeping at a regular thousand, as many as my hay would carry through a winter. So here they were in splendid gray scatter below us, six years of striving and effort, three and a half thousand prime ewes and a fat lamb beside each of them, and currently worth about as much as that many weeds.

"Next year is going to be a bit tight," Rob affirmed, which was getting to be an annual echo out of him.

"These tight years are starting to pinch harder than I'm comfortable with," he was informed by Lucas. Lucas's Jerusalem, Gros Ventre, was not prospering these days. Nowhere was prospering these days. I noticed how much older Lucas was looking, his beard gray now with patches of black. The years of '93 had put extra age on a lot of people in Montana. "So, Robbie lad, we have sheep galore. Now what in the pure holy hell are we going to do with them?"

"Prices can't stay down in the well forever," Rob maintained. "People still have to wear clothes, they still have to eat meat."

Lucas squinted at the neutral September sun. "But how soon can we count on them getting cold and hungry enough?"

"All right, all right, you've said the big question. But Lucas, we've got to hang onto as many sheep as we can until prices turn around. If we don't, we're throwing away these bands we've built up."

"Robbie," said Lucas levelly, "this year we've got to sell the ewe lambs along with the wether lambs. Even if we have to all but give the little buggers away with red bows on them, we've just got to—"

"I'll meet you halfway on that, how about," Rob put in with a smile.

"Halfway to what, bankruptcy?" retorted Lucas in as sharp a tone as I had ever heard from him.

I saw Rob swallow, the only sign of how tense a moment this was for him. Then he brought it out: "Halfway on selling the lambs, Lucas. I'm all for selling the ewe lambs, just as you say. But this year let's keep the wether lambs."

"Keep the wethers?" Lucas stared astounded at Rob. "What in the name of Christ for? Are you going to make history by teaching the wethers"—which was to say, the castrated male sheep whose sole role was mutton—"how to sprout tits and have lambs?"

"We'd keep them for their wool," Rob uttered as rapidly as he could say it. "Their wool crop next summer. Lucas, man, if we keep the wethers until they're yearlings they'll shear almost ten pounds of wool apiece. And if wool prices come back up to what they were—"

Lucas shook his head to halt Rob and brought up a stub to run vigorously along his beard. "I never listen to a proposition beyond the second *if*."

"Lucas, it's worth a try. It's got to be." If conviction counted, Rob right then would have had the three of us in bullion up to our elbows. "See now, the man McKinley is sure to be president, and that'll be like money in the bank for the sheep business." True, there was talk that McKinley could bring with him a tariff on Australian wool. If he did, prices for our fleeces then could climb right up. Pigs could fly if they had wings, too.

"Angus, what do you say to this new passion of Robbie's for wethers?"

"Maybe it's not entirely farfetched," I conceded, earning myself a mingled look from Rob.

Lucas still looked skeptical. "Here's the next thing you can enlighten me about, Robbie—how in holy hell do you handle that many sheep next summer? Tell me that, ay?" I knew it already was costing dear on them to hire herders for their two bands while Rob and I shared the herding of our one, and for them to add a third herder—

He was ready, our Rob. "I'll herd the wether band myself. Judith will have kittens about my doing it." And well she might, because with Rob herding in the mountains all summer she would need to manage everything else of the homestead, not to mention three daughters. "But she'll just have to have them, she married Breed Butte when she married me."

I regarded Rob for a waitful moment, Lucas glancing uncomfortably back and forth between us. Finally I said what was on my mind and Lucas's, even if it didn't seem to be within a hundred miles of Rob's:

"That leaves just one band of sheep unaccounted for."

"Yours and mine, of course," Rob spoke up brightly. "And there's where I have a proposition for you, Angus. If you'll take our band by yourself next summer, I'll give you half of my half."

I made sure: "On the wool and the lambs both?"

"Both."

Translated, half of Rob's half meant that I would receive three-fourths of any profit—wool and lambs both, the man had said it—on our band of sheep next year. And if wool went up as Rob was betting on . . . if lamb prices followed . . . Never listen to a proposition beyond the second *if*, ay, Lucas?

"Done." I snapped up Rob's offer, which would make me money while he made money for himself and Lucas on the wethers. "That is, if Lucas agrees to your end of it."

Lucas studied the two of us, and then the three-about-to-be-four bands of sheep below.

"There are so goddamn many ways to be a fool a man can't expect to avoid them all," he at last said, as much to the sheep as to us. "All right, all right, Robbie, keep the wethers. We'll see now if '97 is the year of years, ay?"

The Perfect Storm
(1997)
Sebastian Junger

The supply of a product is affected by production technologies, production and transportation costs, and the risks encountered in producing and selling it. Junger discusses all of these factors in his bestselling work on the swordfishing industry.

The *Andrea Gail* has a small refrigerator in the galley and twenty tons of ice in the hold. The ice keeps the baitfish and groceries from spoiling on the way out and the swordfish from spoiling on the way home. (In a pinch it can even be used to keep a dead crew member fresh: once a desperately alcoholic old fisherman died on the *Hannah Boden,* and Linda Greenlaw had to put him down the hole because the Coast Guard refused to fly him out.) Commercial fishing simply wouldn't be possible without ice. Without diesel engines, maybe; without loran, weather faxes, or hydraulic winches; but not without ice. There is simply no other way to get fresh fish to market. In the old days, Grand Banks fishermen used to run to Newfoundland to salt-dry their catch before heading home, but the coming of the railroads in the 1840s changed all that. Suddenly food could be moved faster than it would spoil, and ice companies sprang up practically overnight to accommodate the new market. They cut ice from ponds in the winter, packed it in sawdust and then sold it to schooners in the summer months. Properly-packed ice lasted so long—and was so valuable—that traders could ship it to India and still make a profit.

The market for fresh fish changed fishing forever. No longer could schooner captains return home at their leisure with a hold full of salt cod; now it was all one big race. Several full schooners pulling into port at once could saturate the market and ruin the efforts of anyone following. In the 1890s, one schooner had to dump 200 tons of halibut into Gloucester harbor because she'd been beaten into port by six other vessels. Overloaded schooners built like racing sloops dashed home through fall gales with every inch of canvas showing and their decks practically awash. Bad weather sank these elegant craft by the dozen, but a lot of people made a lot of money. And in cities like Boston and New York, people were suddenly eating fresh Atlantic cod.

Little has changed. Fishing boats still make the same mad dashes for shore they were making 150 years ago, and the smaller boats—the ones that don't have ice machines—are still buying it in bulk from Cape Pond Ice, located in a low brick building between Felicia Oil and Parisi Seafoods. In the old days, Cape Pond used to hire men to carve up a local pond with huge ice-saws, but now the ice is made in row upon row of 350-pound blocks, called "cans." The cans look like huge versions of the trays in people's refrigerators. They're extracted from freezers in the floor, skidded onto elevators, hoisted to the third floor, and dragged down a runway by men wielding huge steel hooks; the men work in a building-sized refrigerator and wear shirts that say, "Cape Pond Ice—The Coolest Guys Around." The ice blocks are shoved down a chute into a steel cutting drum, where they jump and rattle in terrible spasms until all 350 pounds have been eaten down to little chips and sprayed through a hose into the hold of a commercial boat outside.

Cape Pond is one of hundreds of businesses jammed into the Gloucester waterfront. Boats come into port, offload their catch, and then spend the next week making repairs and gearing up for the next trip. A good-sized wave can bury a sword boat underwater for a few seconds—"It just gets real dark in here," is how Linda Greenlaw describes the experience—and undoing the effects of a drubbing like that can take days, even weeks. (One boat came into port *twisted*.) Most boats are repaired at Gloucester Marine Railways, a haul-out place that's been in business since 1856. It consists of a massive wooden frame that rides steel rollers along two lengths of railroad track up out of the water. Six-hundred-ton boats are blocked up, lashed down, and hauled ashore by a double-shot of one-inch chain worked off a series of huge steel reduction gears. The gears were machined a hundred years ago and haven't been touched since. There are three railways in all, one in the Inner Harbor and two out on Rocky Neck. The harbor railway is the least robust of the three and terminates in a greasy little basement, which sports a pair of strangely Moorish-looking brick arches. The other two railways are surrounded by the famous galleries and piano bars of Rocky Neck. Tourists blithely wander past machinery that could rip their summer homes right off their foundations.

Almost as soon as the New World was discovered Europeans were fishing it. Twelve years after Columbus, a Frenchman named Jean Denys crossed the Atlantic, worked the Grand Banks off Newfoundland, and returned home with a hold full of cod. Within a few years there were so many Portuguese boats on the Banks that their king felt compelled to impose an import tax in order to protect the fishermen at home. Codfish ran so thick off Newfoundland, it was said, that they slowed ships down in the water.

Codfish weren't quite that plentiful, but they were certainly worth crossing the Atlantic for. And they were easily transported: Crews salted them aboard ship, dried them when they got home, and then sold them by the hundreds of thousands. The alternative was to go over with two crews, one to fish and another to preserve the catch on shore. The fish were split down the middle and then laid on racks, called flakes, to cure all summer in the Newfoundland air. Either way, the result was a rugged slab of protein that could be treated as indelicately as shoe leather and then soaked back to a palatable form. Soon European ships were shuttling back and forth across the North Atlantic in a hugely lucrative—if perilous—trade.

For the first fifty years the European powers were content to fish off Newfoundland and leave the coastlines alone. They were jagged, gloomy places that seemed to offer little more than a chance to impale one's ship. Then, in 1598, a French marquis named Troilus de Mesgouez pulled sixty convicts from French prisons and deposited them on a barren strip of sand called Sable Island, south of Nova Scotia. Left to shift for themselves, the men hunted wild cattle, constructed huts from shipwrecked vessels, rendered fish oil, and gradually killed one another off. By 1603, there were only eleven left alive, and these unfortunates were dragged back to France and presented to King Henri IV. They were clothed in animal skins and had beards halfway down their chests. Not only did the king pardon them their crimes, he gave them a bounty to make up for their suffering.

It was around this time that Cape Ann was first sighted by Europeans. In 1605, the great French explorer Samuel de Champlain was working his way south from Casco Bay, Maine, when he rounded the rock ledges of Thatcher's, Milk, and Salt islands and cast anchor off a sandy beach. The natives drew for him a map of the coastline to the south, and Champlain went on to explore the rest of New England before returning to Cape Ann the following year. This time he was clawing his way up the coast in some ugly fall weather when he sought shelter in a natural harbor he'd missed on his previous trip. He was greeted by a party of Abenaki Indians, some of whom wore the scraps of Portuguese clothing they had traded for a hundred years before, and they made a great show of hospitality before launching a surprise attack from the woods of Eastern Point. The Frenchmen easily fended them off and on the last day of September, 1606, with the Indians waving goodbye from the shore and the oaks and maples rusting into their fall colors, Champlain set sail again. Because of the sheltered coves and thick shellfish beds he called the place "Beauport"—The Good Harbor. Seventeen years later a group of Englishmen sailed into Beauport, eyed the local abundance of cod and cast their anchor. The year was 1623.

The ship was financed by the Dorchester Company, a group of London investors that wanted to start tapping the riches of the New World. Their idea was to establish a settlement on Cape Ann and use it to support a fleet of boats that would fish all spring and summer and return to Europe in the fall. The shore crew was charged with building a habitable colony and drying the catch as it came in. Unfortunately, luck was against the Dorchester men from the start. The first summer they caught a tremendous amount of fish, but the bottom dropped out of the cod market, and they didn't even make expenses. The next year prices returned to normal, but they caught almost no fish at all; and the third year violent gales damaged the boats and drove them back to England. The company was forced to liquidate their assets and bring their men home.

A few of the settlers refused to leave, though. They combined forces with a band of outcasts from the tyrannical Plymouth colony and formed the nucleus of a new colony at Gloucester. New England was an unforgiving land in those days, where only the desperate and the devout seemed to survive, and Gloucester wound up with more than its share of the former. Its most notorious citizen was the Reverend John Lyford, whose deeds were so un-Christian—he criticized the Church and groped a local servant girl—as to be deemed unprintable by a local historian; another was a "shipwrecked adventurer" named Fells who fled Plymouth to escape public whipping. His crime was that he'd had "unsanctioned relations" with a young woman.

Gloucester was a perfect place for loose cannons like Lyford and Fells. It was poor, remote, and the Puritan fathers didn't particularly care what went on up there. After a brief period of desertion, the town was re-settled in 1631, and almost immediately the inhabitants took to fishing. They had little choice, Cape Ann being one big rock, but in some ways that was a blessing. Farmers are easy to control because they're tied to their land, but fishermen are not so easy to control. A twenty-year-old off a three-month trip to the Banks has precious little reason to heed the bourgeois mores of the town. Gloucester developed a reputation for tolerance, if not outright debauchery, that drew people from all over the Bay Colony. The town began to thrive.

Other communities also had a healthy streak of godlessness in them, but it was generally relegated to the outskirts of town. (Wellfleet, for example, reserved an island across the harbor for its young men. In due time a brothel, a tavern, and a whale lookout were built there—just about everything a young fisherman needed.) Gloucester had no such buffer, though; everything happened right on the waterfront. Young women avoided certain streets, town constables were on the lookout for errant fishermen, and orchard-owners rigged guns up to trip-wires to protect their apple trees. Some Gloucester fishermen, apparently, didn't even respect the Sabbath: "Cape Cod captains went wild-eyed in an agony of inner conflict," recorded a Cape Cod historian named Josef Berger, "as they read the Scriptures to their crews while some godless Gloucester craft lay in plain sight . . . hauling up a full share of mackerel or cod."

If the fishermen lived hard, it was no doubt because they died hard as well. In the industry's heyday, Gloucester was losing a couple of hundred men every year to the sea, four percent of the town's population. Since 1650, an estimated ten thousand Gloucestermen have died at sea, far more Gloucestermen than died in all the country's wars. Sometimes a storm would hit the Grand Banks and half a dozen ships would go down, a hundred men lost overnight. On more than one occasion, Newfoundlanders woke up to find their beaches strewn with bodies.

The Grand Banks are so dangerous because they happen to sit on one of the worst storm tracks in the world. Low pressure systems form over the Great Lakes or Cape Hatteras and follow the jet stream out to sea, crossing right over the fishing grounds in the process. In the old days, there wasn't much the boats could do but put out extra anchor cable and try to ride it out. As dangerous as the Grand Banks were, though, Georges Bank—only 180 miles east of Cape Cod—was even worse. There was something so ominous about Georges that fishing captains refused to go near it for three hundred years. Currents ran in strange vortexes on Georges, and the tide was said to run off so fast that ocean bottom was left exposed for gulls to feed on. Men talked of strange dreams and visions they had there, and the uneasy feeling that dire forces were assembling themselves.

Unfortunately, Georges was also home to one of the greatest concentrations of marine life in the world, and it was only a matter of time before someone tried to fish it. In 1827, a Gloucester skipper named John Fletcher Wonson hove-to off Georges, threw out a fishing line, and pulled up a halibut. The ease with which the fish had been caught stuck in his mind, and three years later he went back to Georges expressly to fish. Nothing particularly awful happened, and soon ships were going back and forth to Georges without a second thought. It was only a one-day trip from Gloucester, and the superstitions about the place started to fade. That was when Georges turned deadly.

Because the fishing grounds were so small and close to shore, dozens of schooners might be anchored within sight of each other on a fair day. If a storm came on gradually, the fleet had time to weigh anchor and disperse into deeper water; but a sudden storm could pile ship upon ship until they all went down in a mass of tangled spars and rigging. Men would be stationed at the bow of each boat to cut their anchor cables if another boat were bearing down on them, but that was usually a death sentence in itself. The chances of sailing clear of the shoal water were horribly small.

One of the worst of these catastrophes happened in 1862, when a winter gale bore down on seventy schooners that were working a closely-packed school of cod. Without warning the sky turned black and the snow began to drive down almost horizontally. One fisherman described what ensued:

> My shipmates showed no sign of fear; they were now all on deck and the skipper was keeping a sharp lookout. Somewhere about nine o'clock, the skipper sang out, "There's a vessel adrift right ahead of us! Stand by with your hatchet, but don't cut until you hear the word!" All eyes were bent now on the drifting craft. On she came, directly at us. A moment more and the signal to cut must be given. With the swiftness of a gull, she passed by, so near that I could have leaped aboard. The hopeless, terror-stricken faces of the crew we saw but a moment, as the doomed craft sped on her course, She struck one of the fleet a short distance astern, and we saw the waters close over both vessels almost instantly.

The engine, an eight-cylinder, 365-horsepower turbocharged diesel, is slightly more powerful than the largest tractor-trailor rigs on the highway. The engine was refurbished in 1989 because the boat flooded at dock after a discharge pipe froze, cracking the weld. The engine drives a propellor shaft that runs through a cut-out in the aft bulkhead of the compartment and through the fish hold to the stern of the boat. Most boats have a gasket that seals the prop as it passes through the bulkhead, but the *Andrea Gail* does not. This is a weak point; flooding in the fish hold could conceivably slosh forward and kill the engine, crippling the boat.

The machinery room sits just forward of the engine and is crammed with tools, spare parts, lumber, old clothes, a backup generator, and three bilge pumps. The job of the pumps is to lift water out of the hold faster than it comes in; in the old days crews would be at the hand-pumps for days at a stretch, and ships went down when the storms outlasted the men. The tools are stored in metal lock-boxes on the floor and include just about everything you'd need to rebuild the engine—vice grips, pry bar, hammer, crescent wrenches, pipe wrenches, socket wrenches, allen wrenches, files, hacksaw, channel-lock pliers, bolt cutters, ball peen hammer. Spare parts are packed in cardboard boxes and stacked on wooden shelves: Starter motor, cooling pump, alternator, hydraulic hoses and fittings, v-belts, jumper wires, fuses, hose clamps, gasket material, nuts and bolts, sheet metal, silicone rubber, plywood, screw gun, duct tape, lube oil, hydraulic oil, transmission oil, and fuel filters.

Boats try at all costs to avoid going into Newfoundland for repairs. Not only does it waste valuable time, but it costs obscene amounts of money—one infamous repair bill amounted to $50,000 for what should've been a $3,500 job. (The machinists had reportedly run their lathes at 46 rpms rather than 400 in order to rack up overtime.) As a result, sword boat captains help each other out on the high seas whenever they can; they lend engine parts, offer technical advice, donate food or fuel. The competition between a dozen boats rushing a perishable commodity to market fortunately doesn't kill an inherent sense of concern for each other. This may seem terrifically noble, but it's not—or at least not entirely. It's also self-interested. Each captain knows he may be the next one with the frozen injector or the leaking hydraulics.

Diesel fuel on the *Andrea Gail* is carried in a pair of 2,000-gallon tanks along either side of the engine room, and in two 1,750-gallon tanks at the stern. There are also thirty plastic drums lashed to the whaleback with another 1,650 gallons of fuel. Each one has *AG* painted on them in white lettering. Two thousand gallons of fresh water are stored in two forepeak tanks, and another 500 gallons or so are stored in drums up on deck, along with the oil. There's also a "water-maker" that purifies saltwater by forcing it through a membrane at 800 pounds per square inch. The membrane is so fine that it even filters out bacteria and viruses. The boat butcher—

who is constantly covered in fish guts—gets to shower every day. The rest of the crew showers every two or three.

The fish hold is gained by a single steel ladder that drops steeply down from a hatch in the middle of the deck. During storms, the hatch is covered and lashed down so that big seas can't pry it off—although they still manage to. The hold is divided by plywood penboards that keep the load from shifting; a shifted load can put a boat over on her side and keep her there until she sinks. There's an industrial freezer in the stern where the food is stored, and then another compartment called the lazarette. The lazarette is where the steering mechanism is housed; like the engine room, it's not sealed off from the rest of the boat.

Breaking waves have lifted a 2,700-ton breakwater, *en masse,* and deposited it inside the harbor at Wick, Scotland. They have blasted open a steel door 195 feet above sea level at Unst Light in the Shetland Islands. They have heaved a half-ton boulder 91 feet into the air at Tillamook Rock, Oregon.

There is some evidence that average wave heights are slowly rising, and that freak waves of eighty or ninety feet are becoming more common. Wave heights off the coast of England have risen an average of 25 percent over the past couple of decades, which converts to a twenty-foot increase in the highest waves over the next half-century. One cause may be the tightening of environmental laws, which has reduced the amount of oil flushed into the oceans by oil tankers. Oil spreads across water in a film several molecules thick and inhibits the generation of capillary waves, which in turn prevent the wind from getting a "grip" on the sea. Plankton releases a chemical that has the same effect, and plankton levels in the North Atlantic have dropped dramatically. Another explanation is that the recent warming trend—some call it the greenhouse effect—has made storms more frequent and severe. Waves have destroyed docks and buildings in Newfoundland, for example, that haven't been damaged for decades.

As a result, stresses on ships have been rising. The standard practice is to build ships to withstand what is called a 25-year stress—the most violent condition the ship is likely to experience in 25 years. The wave that flooded the wheelhouse of the *Queen Mary,* ninety feet up, must have nearly exceeded her 25-year stress. North Sea oil platforms are built to accommodate a 111-foot wave beneath their decks, which is calculated to be a one-hundred-year stress. Unfortunately, the 25-year stress is just a statistical concept that offers no guarantee about what will happen next year, or next week. A ship could encounter several 25-year waves in a month or never encounter any at all. Naval architects simply decide what level of stress she's likely to encounter in her lifetime and then hope for the best. It's economically and structurally impractical to construct every boat to hundred-year specifications.

Inevitably, then, ships encounter waves that exceed their stress rating. In the dry terminology of naval architecture, these are called "non-negotiable waves." Mariners call them "rogue waves" or "freak seas." Typically they are very steep and have an equally steep trough in front of them—a "hole in the ocean" as some witnesses have described it. Ships cannot get their bows up fast enough, and the ensuing wave breaks their back. Maritime history is full of encounters with such waves. When Sir Ernest Shackleton was forced to cross the South Polar Sea in a 22-foot open life boat, he saw a wave so big that he mistook its foaming crest for a moonlit-cloud. He only had time to yell, "Hang on, boys, it's got us!" before the wave broke over his boat. Miraculously, they didn't sink. In February 1883, the 320-foot steamship *Glamorgan* was swept bow-to-stern by an enormous wave that ripped the wheelhouse right off the deck, taking all the ship's officers with it. She later sank. In 1966, the 44,000-ton *Michelangelo,* an Italian steamship carrying 775 passengers, encountered a single massive wave in an otherwise unremarkable sea. Her bow fell into a trough and the wave stove in her bow, flooded her wheelhouse, and killed a crewman and two passengers. In 1976, the oil tanker *Cretan Star* radioed, "... vessel was struck by a huge wave that went over the deck ...," and was never heard from again. The only sign of her fate was a four-mile oil slick off Bombay.

The Joy Luck Club
(1989)
Amy Tan

In markets that are very competitive and highly organized, with many people and organizations closely following and predicting price changes, all of the known information that affects a price may already be reflected in the current price. If so, future price changes will only reflect factors that are unknown, which are as likely to increase as decrease the price. Some economists have claimed that prices for publicly traded stocks on the major stock exchanges are good examples of this "efficient market hypothesis," which implies that someone picking stocks purely at random will do as well as the predictions of top stock analysts at large brokerage firms. That claim, though disputed by other economists, is accepted here in Amy Tan's most popular novel.

The Joy Luck aunties are all wearing slacks, bright print blouses, and different versions of sturdy walking shoes. We are all seated around the dining room table under a lamp that looks like a Spanish candelabra. Uncle George puts on his bifocals and starts the meeting by reading the minutes:

"Our capital account is $24,825, or about $6,206 a couple, $3,103 per person. We sold Subaru for a loss at six and three-quarters. We bought a hundred shares of Smith International at seven. Our thanks to Lindo and Tin Jong for the goodies. The red bean soup was especially delicious. The March meeting had to be canceled until further notice. We were sorry to have to bid a fond farewell to our dear friend Suyuan and extended our sympathy to the Canning Woo family. Respectfully submitted, George Hsu, president and secretary."

That's it. I keep thinking the others will start talking about my mother, the wonderful friendship they shared, and why I am here in her spirit, to be the fourth corner and carry on the idea my mother came up with on a hot day in Kweilin.

But everybody just nods to approve the minutes. Even my father's head bobs up and down routinely. And it seems to me my mother's life has been shelved for new business.

Auntie An-mei heaves herself up from the table and moves slowly to the kitchen to prepare the food. And Auntie Lin, my mother's best friend, moves to the turquoise sofa, crosses her arms, and watches the men still seated at the table. Auntie Ying, who seems to shrink even more every time I see her, reaches into her knitting bag and pulls out the start of a tiny blue sweater.

The Joy Luck uncles begin to talk about stocks they are interested in buying. Uncle Jack, who is Auntie Ying's younger brother, is very keen on a company that mines gold in Canada.

"It's a great hedge on inflation," he says with authority. He speaks the best English, almost accentless. I think my mother's English was the worst, but she always thought her Chinese was the best. She spoke Mandarin slightly blurred with a Shanghai dialect.

"Weren't we going to play mah jong tonight?" I whisper loudly to Auntie Ying, who's slightly deaf.

"Later," she says, "after midnight."

"Ladies, are you at this meeting or not?" says Uncle George.

After everybody votes unanimously for the Canada gold stock, I go into the kitchen to ask Auntie An-mei why the Joy Luck Club started investing in stocks.

"We used to play mah jong, winner take all. But the same people were always winning, the same people always losing," she says. She is stuffing wonton, one chopstick jab of gingery meat dabbed onto a thin skin and then a single fluid turn with her hand that seals the skin into the shape of a tiny nurse's cap. "You can't have luck when someone else has skill. So long time ago, we decided to invest in the stock market. There's no skill in that. Even your mother agreed."

Auntie An-mei takes count of the tray in front of her. She's already made five rows of eight wonton each. "Forty wonton, eight people, ten each, five row more," she says aloud to herself, and then continues stuffing. "We got smart. Now we can all win and lose equally. We can have stock market luck. And we can play mah jong for fun, just for a few dollars, winner take all. Losers take home leftovers! So everyone can have some joy. Smart-hanh?"

The Pearl
(1947)
John Steinbeck

If there are relatively few buyers or sellers of a product and they are able to successfully collude, they will act as monopolists rather than competitors, to the detriment of their suppliers or customers. Fortunately, it is difficult to establish such cartels, and even more difficult to maintain them—even if the cartels are not illegal, as they are for intranational dealings in many countries, including the United States. The best current example of an international cartel, the economic power of which has waxed and waned over recent decades, is OPEC. Steinbeck's short novel, written before OPEC's ascendancy, shows a cartel that, at least for a time, has become far too powerful. There are also descriptions of how one person's spending becomes income for someone else, starting a chain-reaction of spending and income in what economists call a "multiplier effect." Steinbeck also endorses on both positive and normative grounds economists' standard assumption that wants for material goods and services are essentially unlimited.

The brush houses of the fishing people were back from the beach on the right-hand side of the town, and the canoes were drawn up in front of this area.

Kino and Juana came slowly down to the beach and to Kino's canoe, which was the one thing of value he owned in the world. It was very old. Kino's grandfather had brought it from Nayarit, and he had given it to Kino's father, and so it had come to Kino. It was at once property and source of food, for a man with a boat can guarantee a woman that she will eat something. It is the bulwark against starvation. And every year Kino refinished his canoe with the hard shell-like plaster by the secret method that had also come to him from his father. Now he came to the canoe and touched the bow tenderly as he always did. He laid his diving rock and his basket and the two ropes in the sand by the canoe. And he folded his blanket and laid it in the bow.

Kino, in his pride and youth and strength, could remain down over two minutes without strain, so that he worked deliberately, selecting the largest shells. Because they were disturbed, the oyster shells were tightly closed. A little to the right a hummock of rubbly rock stuck up, covered with young oysters not ready to take. Kino moved next to the hummock, and then, beside it, under a little overhang, he saw a very large oyster lying by itself, not covered with its clinging brothers. The shell was partly open, for the overhang protected this ancient oyster, and in the lip-like muscle Kino saw a ghostly gleam, and then the shell closed down. His heart beat out a heavy rhythm and the melody of the maybe pearl shrilled in his ears. Slowly he forced the oyster loose and held it tightly against his breast. He kicked his foot free from the rock loop, and his body rose to the surface and his black hair gleamed in the sunlight. He reached over the side of the canoe and laid the oyster in the bottom.

Then Juana steadied the boat while he climbed in. His eyes were shining with excitement, but in decency he pulled up his rock, and then he pulled up his basket of oysters and lifted them in. Juana sensed his excitement, and she pretended to look away. It is not good to want a thing too much. It sometimes drives the luck away. You must want it just enough, and you must be very tactful with God or the gods. But Juana stopped breathing. Very deliberately Kino opened his short strong knife. He looked speculatively at the basket. Perhaps it would be better to open *the* oyster last. He took a small oyster from the basket, cut the muscle, searched the folds of flesh, and threw it in the water. Then he seemed to see the great oyster for the first time. He squatted in the bottom of the canoe, picked up the shell and examined it. The flutes were shining black to brown, and only a few small barnacles adhered to the shell. Now Kino was reluctant to open it. What he had seen, he knew, might be a reflection, a piece of flat shell accidentally drifted in or a complete illusion. In this Gulf of uncertain light there were more illusions than realities.

But Juana's eyes were on him and she could not wait. She put her hand on Coyotito's covered head. "Open it," she said softly.

Kino deftly slipped his knife into the edge of the shell. Through the knife he could feel the muscle tighten hard. He worked the blade lever-wise and the closing muscle parted and the shell fell apart. The lip-like flesh writhed up and then subsided. Kino lifted the flesh, and there it lay, the great pearl, perfect as the moon. It captured the light and refined it and gave it back in silver incandescence. It was as large as a sea-gull's egg. It was the greatest pearl in the world.

Juana caught her breath and moaned a little. And to Kino the secret melody of the maybe pearl broke clear and beautiful, rich and warm and lovely, glowing and gloating and triumphant. In the surface of the great pearl he could see dream forms.

He picked the pearl from the dying flesh and held it in his palm, and he turned it over and saw that its curve was perfect.

A town is a thing like a colonial animal. A town has a nervous system and a head and shoulders and feet. A town is a thing separate from all other towns, so that there are no two towns alike. And a town has a whole emotion. How news travels through a town is a mystery not easily to be solved. News seems to move faster than small boys can scramble and dart to tell it, faster than women can call it over the fences.

Before Kino and Juana and the other fishers had come to Kino's brush house, the nerves of the town were pulsing and vibrating with the news—Kino had found the Pearl of the World. Before panting little boys could strangle out the words, their mothers knew it. The news swept on past the brush houses, and it washed in a foaming wave into the town of stone and plaster. It came to the priest walking in his garden, and it put a thoughtful look in his eyes and a memory of certain repairs necessary to the church. He wondered what the pearl would be worth. And he wondered whether he had baptized Kino's baby, or married him for that matter. The news came to the shopkeepers, and they looked at men's clothing that had not sold so well.

The news came to the doctor where he sat with a woman whose illness was age, though neither she nor the doctor would admit it. And when it was made plain who Kino was, the doctor grew stern and judicious at the same time. "He is a client of mine," the doctor said. "I am treating his child for a scorpion sting." And the doctor's eyes rolled up a little in their fat hammocks and he thought of Paris. He remembered the room he had lived in there as a great and luxurious place, and he remembered the hard-faced woman who had lived with him as a beautiful and kind girl, although she had been none of these three. The doctor looked past his aged patient and saw himself sitting in a restaurant in Paris and a waiter was just opening a bottle of wine.

The news came early to the beggars in front of the church, and it made them giggle a little with pleasure, for they knew that there is no almsgiver in the world like a poor man who is suddenly lucky.

Kino had found the Pearl of the World. In the town, in little offices, sat the men who bought pearls from the fishers. They waited in their chairs until the pearls came in, and then they cackled and fought and shouted and threatened until they reached the lowest price the fisherman would stand. But there was a price below which they dared not go, for it had happened that a fisherman in despair had given his pearls to the church. And when the buying was over, these buyers sat alone and their fingers played restlessly with the pearls, and they wished they owned the pearls. For there were not many buyers really—there was only one, and he kept these agents in separate offices to give a semblance of competition. The news came to these men, and their eyes squinted and their fingertips burned a little, and each one thought how the patron could not live forever and someone had to take his place. And each one thought how with some capital he could get a new start.

All manner of people grew interested in Kino—people with little things to sell and people with favors to ask. Kino had found the Pearl of the World. The essence of pearl mixed with essence of men and a curious dark residue was precipitated. Every man suddenly became related to Kino's pearl, and Kino's pearl went into the dreams, the speculations, the schemes, the plans, the futures, the wishes, the needs, the lusts, the hungers, of everyone, and only one person stood in the way and that was Kino, so that he became curiously every man's enemy. The news stirred up something infinitely black and evil in the town; the black distillate was like the scorpion, or like hunger in the smell of food, or like loneliness when love is withheld. The poison sacs of the town began to manufacture venom, and the town swelled and puffed with the pressure of it.

But Kino and Juana did not know these things. Because they were happy and excited they thought everyone shared their joy. Juan Tomas and Apolonia did, and they were the world too. In the afternoon, when the sun had gone over the mountains of the Peninsula to sink in the outward sea, Kino squatted in his house with Juana beside him. And the brush house was crowded with neighbors. Kino held the great pearl in his hand, and it was warm and alive in his hand. And the music of the pearl had merged with the music of the family so that one beautified the other. The neighbors looked at the pearl in Kino's hand and they wondered how such luck could come to any man.

And Juan Tomas, who squatted on Kino's right hand because he was his brother, asked, "What will you do now that you have become a rich man?"

Kino looked into his pearl, and Juana cast her eyelashes down and arranged her shawl to cover her face so that her excitement could not be seen. And in the incandescence of the pearl the pictures formed of the things Kino's mind had considered in the past and had given up as impossible. In the pearl he saw Juana and Coyotito and himself standing and kneeling at the high altar, and they were being married now that they could pay. He spoke softly, "We will be married—in the church."

In the pearl he saw how they were dressed—Juana in a shawl stiff with newness and a new skirt, and from under the long skirt Kino could see that she wore shoes. It was in the pearl—the picture glowing there. He himself was dressed in new white clothes, and he carried a new hat—not of straw but of fine black felt—and he too wore shoes—not sandals but shoes that laced. But Coyotito—he was the one—he wore a blue sailor suit from the United States and a little yachting cap such as Kino had seen once when a pleasure boat put into the estuary. All of these things Kino saw in the lucent pearl and he said, "We will have new clothes."

And the music of the pearl rose like a chorus of trumpets in his ears.

Then to the lovely gray surface of the pearl came the little things Kino wanted: a harpoon to take the place of one lost a year ago, a new harpoon of iron with a ring in the end of the shaft; and—his mind could hardly make a leap—a rifle—but why not, since he was so rich. And Kino saw Kino in the pearl, Kino holding a Winchester carbine. It was the wildest daydreaming and very pleasant. His lips moved hesitantly over this—"A rifle," he said. "Perhaps a rifle."

It was the rifle that broke down the barriers. This was an impossibility, and if he could think of having a rifle whole horizons were burst and he could rush on. For it is said that humans are never satisfied, that you give them one thing and they want something more. And this is said in disparagement, whereas it is one of the greatest talents the species has and one that has made it superior to animals that are satisfied with what they have.

❧

"Kino," he said softly, "thou art named after a great man—and a great Father of the Church." He made it sound like a benediction. "Thy namesake tamed the desert and sweetened the minds of thy people, didst thou know that? It is in the books."

Kino looked quickly down at Coyotito's head, where he hung on Juana's hip. Some day, his mind said, that boy would know what things were in the books and what things were not. The music had gone out of Kino's head, but now, thinly, slowly, the melody of the morning, the music of evil, of the enemy sounded, but it was faint and weak. And Kino looked at his neighbors to see who might have brought this song in.

But the priest was speaking again. "It has come to me that thou hast found a great fortune, a great pearl."

Kino opened his hand and held it out, and the priest gasped a little at the size and beauty of the pearl. And then he said, "I hope thou wilt remember to give thanks, my son, to Him who has given thee this treasure, and to pray for guidance in the future."

Kino nodded dumbly, and it was Juana who spoke softly. "We will, Father. And we will be married now. Kino has said so." She looked at the neighbors for confirmation, and they nodded their heads solemnly.

The priest said, "It is pleasant to see that your first thoughts are good thoughts. God bless you, my children," He turned and left quietly, and the people let him through.

But Kino's hand had closed tightly on the pearl again, and he was glancing about suspiciously, for the evil song was in his ears, shrilling against the music of the pearl.

❧

It is wonderful the way a little town keeps track of itself and all of its units. If every single man and woman, child and baby, acts and conducts itself in a known pattern and breaks no walls and differs with no one and experiments in no way and is not sick and does not endanger the ease and peace of mind or steady unbroken flow of the town, then that unit can disappear and never be heard of. But let one man step out of the regular thought or the known and trusted pattern, and the nerves of the townspeople ring with nervousness and communication travels over the nerve lines of the town. Then every unit communicates to the whole.

Thus, in La Paz, it was known in the early morning through the whole town that Kino was going to sell his pearl that day. It was known among the neighbors in the brush huts, among the pearl fishermen; it was known among the Chinese grocery-store owners; it was known in the church, for the altar boys whispered about it. Word of it crept in among the nuns; the beggars in front of the church spoke of it, for they would be there to take the tithe of the first fruits of the luck. The little boys knew about it with excitement, but most of all the pearl buyers knew about it, and when the day had come, in the offices of the pearl buyers, each man sat alone with his little black velvet tray, and each man rolled the pearls about with his fingertips and considered his part in the picture.

It was supposed that the pearl buyers were individuals acting alone, bidding against one another for the pearls the fishermen brought in. And once it had been so. But this was a wasteful method, for often, in the excitement of bidding for a fine pearl, too great a price had been paid to the fishermen. This was extravagant and not to be countenanced. Now there was only one pearl buyer with many hands, and the men who sat in their offices and waited for Kino knew what price they would offer, how high they would bid, and what method each one would use. And although these men would not profit beyond their salaries, there was excitement among the pearl buyers, for there was excitement in the hunt, and if it be a man's function to break down a price, then he must take joy and satisfaction in breaking it as far down as possible. For every man in the world functions to the best of his ability, and no one does less than his best, no matter what he may think about it. Quite apart from any reward they might get, from any word of praise, from any promotion, a pearl buyer was a pearl buyer, and the best and happiest pearl buyer was he who bought for the lowest prices.

The sun was hot yellow that morning, and it drew the moisture from the estuary and from the Gulf and hung it in shimmering scarves in the air so that the air vibrated and vision was insubstantial. A vision hung in the air to the north of the city—the vision of a mountain that was over two hundred miles away, and the high slopes of this mountain were swaddled with pines and a great stone peak arose above the timber line.

And the morning of this day the canoes lay lined up on the beach; the fishermen did not go out to dive for pearls, for there would be too much happening, too many things to see when Kino went to sell the great pearl.

The gathering procession was solemn, for they sensed the importance of this day, and any children who showed a tendency to scuffle, to scream, to cry out, to steal hats and rumple hair, were hissed to silence by their elders. So important was this day that an old man came to see, riding on the stalwart shoulders of his nephew. The procession left the brush huts and entered the stone and plaster city where the streets were a little wider and there were narrow pavements beside the buildings. And as before, the beggars joined them as they passed the church; the grocers looked out at them as they went by; the little saloons lost their customers and the owners closed up shop and went along. And the sun beat down on the streets of the city and even tiny stones threw shadows on the ground.

The news of the approach of the procession ran ahead of it, and in their little dark offices the pearl buyers stiffened and grew alert. They got out papers so that they could be at work when Kino appeared, and they put their pearls in the desks, for it is not good to let an inferior pearl be seen beside a beauty. And word of the loveliness of Kino's pearl had come to them. The pearl buyers' offices were clustered together in one narrow street, and they were barred at the windows, and wooden slats cut out the light so that only a soft gloom entered the offices.

A stout slow man sat in an office waiting. His face was fatherly and benign, and his eyes twinkled with friendship. He was a caller of good mornings, a ceremonious shaker of hands, a jolly man who knew all jokes and yet who hovered close to sadness, for in the midst of a laugh he could remember the death of your aunt, and his eyes could become wet with sorrow for your loss. This morning he had placed a flower in a vase on his desk, a single scarlet hibiscus, and the vase sat beside the black velvet-lined pearl tray in front of him. He was shaved close to the blue roots of his beard, and his hands were clean and his nails polished. His door stood open to the morning, and he hummed under his breath while his right hand practiced legerdemain. He rolled a coin back and forth over his knuckles and made it appear and disappear, made it spin and sparkle. The coin winked into sight and as quickly slipped out of sight, and the man did not even watch his own performance. The fingers did it all mechanically, precisely, while the man hummed to himself and peered out the door. Then he heard the tramp of feet of the approaching crowd, and the fingers of his right hand worked faster and faster until, as the figure of Kino filled the doorway, the coin flashed and disappeared.

"Good morning, my friend," the stout man said. "What can I do for you?"

Kino stared into the dimness of the little office, for his eyes were squeezed from the outside glare. But the buyer's eyes had become as steady and cruel and unwinking as a hawk's eyes, while the rest of his face smiled in greeting. And secretly, behind his desk, his right hand practiced with the coin.

"I have a pearl," said Kino. And Juan Tomas stood beside him and snorted a little at the understatement. The neighbors peered around the doorway, and a line of little boys clambered on the window bars and looked through. Several little boys, on their hands and knees, watched the scene around Kino's legs.

"You have a pearl," the dealer said. "Sometimes a man brings in a dozen. Well, let us see your pearl. We will value it and give you the best price." And his fingers worked furiously with the coin.

Now Kino instinctively knew his own dramatic effects. Slowly he brought out the leather bag, slowly took from it the soft and dirty piece of deerskin, and then he let the great pearl roll into the black velvet tray, and instantly his eyes went to the buyer's face. But there was no sign, no movement, the face did not change, but the secret hand behind the desk missed in its precision. The coin stumbled over a knuckle and slipped silently into the dealer's lap. And the fingers behind the desk curled into a fist. When the right hand came out of hiding, the forefinger touched the great pearl, rolled it on the black velvet; thumb and forefinger picked it up and brought it near to the dealer's eyes and twirled it in the air.

Kino held his breath, and the neighbors held their breath, and the whispering went back through the crowd. "He is inspecting it—No price has been mentioned yet—They have not come to a price."

Now the dealer's hand had become a personality. The hand tossed the great pearl back in the tray, the forefinger poked and insulted it, and on the dealer's face there came a sad and contemptuous smile.

"I am sorry, my friend," he said, and his shoulders rose a little to indicate that the misfortune was no fault of his.

"It is a pearl of great value," Kino said.

The dealer's fingers spurned the pearl so that it bounded and rebounded softly from the side of the velvet tray.

"You have heard of fool's gold," the dealer said. "This pearl is like fool's gold. It is too large. Who would buy it? There is no market for such things. It is a curiosity only. I am sorry. You thought it was a thing of value, and it is only a curiosity."

Now Kino's face was perplexed and worried. "It is the Pearl of the World," he cried. "No one has ever seen such a pearl."

"On the contrary," said the dealer, "it is large and clumsy. As a curiosity it has interest; some museum might perhaps take it to place in a collection of seashells. I can give you, say, a thousand pesos."

Kino's face grew dark and dangerous. "It is worth fifty thousand," he said. "You know it. You want to cheat me."

And the dealer heard a little grumble go through the crowd as they heard his price. And the dealer felt a little tremor of fear.

"Do not blame me," he said quickly. "I am only an appraiser. Ask the others. Go to their offices and show your pearl—or better let them come here, so that you can see there is no collusion. Boy," he called. And when his servant looked through the real door, "Boy, go to such a one, and such another one and such a third one. Ask them to step in here and do not tell them why. Just say that I will be pleased to see them." And his right hand went behind the desk and pulled another coin from his pocket, and the coin rolled back and forth over the knuckles.

Kino's neighbors whispered together. They had been afraid of something like this. The pearl was large, but it had a strange color. They had been suspicious of it from the first. And after all, a thousand pesos was not to be thrown away. It was comparative wealth to a man who was not wealthy. And suppose Kino took a thousand pesos. Only yesterday he had nothing.

But Kino had grown tight and hard. He felt the creeping of fate, the circling of wolves, the hover of vultures. He felt the evil coagulating about him, and he was helpless to protect himself. He heard in his ears the evil music. And on the black velvet the great pearl glistened, so that the dealer could not keep his eyes from it.

The crowd in the doorway wavered and broke and let the three pearl dealers through. The crowd was silent now, fearing to miss a word, to fail to see a gesture or an expression. Kino was silent and watchful. He felt a little tugging at his back, and he turned and looked in Juana's eyes, and when he looked away he had renewed strength.

The dealers did not glance at one another nor at the pearl. The man behind the desk said, "I have put a value on this pearl. The owner here does not think it fair. I will ask you to examine this—this thing and make an offer. Notice," he said to Kino, "I have not mentioned what I have offered."

The first dealer, dry and stringy, seemed now to see the pearl for the first time. He took it up, rolled it quickly between thumb and forefinger, and then cast it contemptuously back into the tray.

"Do not include me in the discussion," he said dryly. "I will make no offer at all. I do not want it. This is not a pearl—it is a monstrosity." His thin lips curled.

Now the second dealer, a little man with a shy soft voice, took up the pearl, and he examined it carefully. He took a glass from his pocket and inspected it under magnification. Then he laughed softly.

"Better pearls are made of paste," he said. "I know these things. This is soft and chalky, it will lose its color and die in a few months. Look—." He offered the glass to Kino, showed him how to use it, and Kino, who had never seen a pearl's surface magnified, was shocked at the strange-looking surface.

The third dealer took the pearl from Kino's hands. "One of my clients likes such things," he said. "I will offer five hundred pesos, and perhaps I can sell it to my client for six hundred."

Kino reached quickly and snatched the pearl from his hand. He wrapped it in the deerskin and thrust it inside his shirt.

The man behind the desk said, "I'm a fool, I know, but my first offer stands. I still offer one thousand. What are you doing?" he asked, as Kino thrust the pearl out of sight.

"I am cheated," Kino cried fiercely. "My pearl is not for sale here. I will go, perhaps even to the capital."

Now the dealers glanced quickly at one another. They knew they had played too hard; they knew they would be disciplined for their failure, and the man at the desk said quickly, "I might go to fifteen hundred."

But Kino was pushing his way through the crowd. The hum of talk came to him dimly, his rage blood pounded in his ears, and he burst through and strode away. Juana followed, trotting after him.

When the evening came, the neighbors in the brush houses sat eating their corncakes and beans, and they discussed the great theme of the morning. They did not know, it seemed a fine pearl to them, but they had never seen such a pearl before, and surely the dealers knew more about the value of pearls than they. "And mark this," they said. "Those dealers did not discuss these things. Each of the three knew the pearl was valueless."

"But suppose they had arranged it before?"

"If that is so, then all of us have been cheated all of our lives."

Perhaps, some argued, perhaps it would have been better if Kino took the one thousand five hundred pesos. That is a great deal of money, more than he has ever seen. Maybe Kino is being a pigheaded fool. Suppose he should really go to the capital and find no buyer for his pearl. He would never live that down.

And now, said other fearful ones, now that he had defied them, those buyers will not want to deal with him at all. Maybe Kino has cut off his own head and destroyed himself.

And others said, Kino is a brave man, and a fierce man; he is right. From his courage we may all profit. These were proud of Kino.

The Robber Bride
(1993)
Margaret Atwood

Prices change over time because of changes in supply, demand, or both. That creates new opportunities for some people and firms, and challenges and problems for others, as both consumers and producers react to the new mix of prices by buying and producing more of some things and less of others.

The place where Charis works is called Radiance. It sells crystals of all kinds, big and small, made into pendants and earrings or just raw, and seashells; and essential oils imported from Egypt and southern France, and incense from India, and organic body creams and bath gels from California and England, and sachets of bark and herbs and dried flowers, from France mainly, and Tarot cards in six different patterns, and Afghan and Thai jewellery, and tapes of New Age music with a lot of harp and flute sounds in them, and CDs of seashores, waterfalls, and loon calls, and books on Native Indian spirituality and Health Secrets of the Aztecs, and mother-of-pearl inlaid chopsticks and lacquered bowls from Japan, and tiny carvings of Chinese jade, and recycled handmade-paper greeting cards with arrangements of dried weeds stuck onto them, and packets of wild rice, and non-caffeine teas from eight different countries, and necklaces of cowries, dried plant seeds, polished stones, and carved wooden beads.

Charis remembers this place from the sixties. It was called The Blown Mind Shoppe then, and had hash pipes and psychedelic posters and roach clips and tie-dyed undershirts and dashikis. In the seventies it was called Okkult, and had books on demonology, as well as on women's ancient religions and Wicca and the lost kingdoms of Atlantis and Mu, and some unappealing bone artefacts, and smelly—and in Charis's opinion, fraudulent—bundles of ground-up animal parts. There was a stuffed alligator in its window then, and for a while it even sold fright wigs and horror makeup kits, with fake blood and glue-on scars. That was a low point for it, although popular with the punk set.

It changed again in the early eighties. That was when Shanita took over, when it was still Okkult. She quickly got rid of the stuffed alligator and the bones and the demonology books—why borrow trouble, she says, and she didn't want any run-ins with the animal-rights folks, or any Christian weirdos spray-painting the window. It was her idea to start up the crystals, and to change the name to Radiance.

It was the name that attracted Charis. First she was just a customer: she came in for the herbal teas. But then the sales position came open, and since she was tired of her job filing reports at the Ministry of Natural Resources—too impersonal, too much pressure, and besides she wasn't very good at it—she applied. Shanita hired her because she had the right look, or so Shanita told her.

"You won't bug the customers," said Shanita. "They don't like to be pushed. They like to just sort of float around in here, know what I mean?"

Charis did. She likes to float around in Radiance herself. She likes the way it smells, and she likes the things in it. Sometimes she does a trade, taking goods—at a discount price—instead of pay, much to Augusta's disgust. *More of that junk?* she says. She does not see how many more Japanese lacquered bowls and tapes of loon calls Charis really needs. Charis says it isn't a matter of need, material need that is. It's a matter of spiritual need. Right now she has her eye on a truly lovely amethyst geode, from Nova Scotia. She will keep it in her bedroom, to ward off bad dreams.

She can picture Augusta's response to this geode. *Mom! What's this hunk of rock doing in your bed?* She can picture Tony's interested skepticism—*Does it really work?*—and Roz's maternal indulgence—*Honey, if it makes you happy I'm all for it!* This has been her problem all her life: picturing other people's responses. She's too good at it. She can picture the response of anyone—other people's reactions, their emotions, their criticisms, their demands—but somehow they don't reciprocate. Maybe they can't. Maybe they lack the gift, if it is one.

❧

She reaches Radiance at ten to ten, early for once, and lets herself in with her key, and puts on the mauve-and-aqua smock that Shanita designed for them so the customers will know they aren't customers themselves.

Shanita is already there. "Hi, Charis, how're you doing?" she calls out, from the stockroom at the back. It's Shanita who does all the ordering. She has a knack for it; she goes to crafts fairs and takes trips to little-known corners, and finds things, wonderful things that no other store in town has. She seems to know in advance what people will want.

Charis admires Shanita a lot. Shanita is smart and practical, as well as being psychic. Also she's strong, and also she's one of the most beautiful women Charis has ever seen. Though she isn't young—she must be well over forty. She refuses to tell her age—the one time Charis asked her, she only laughed, and said age was in the mind and in her mind she was two thousand—but she's getting a white streak in her hair. That's another thing Charis admires: Shanita doesn't dye.

The hair itself is black, neither curly nor frizzy but wavy, thick and shining and luscious, like pulled taffy or lava. Like hot black glass. Shanita coils it, and winds it here and there on her head: sometimes on top, sometimes on one side. Or else she lets it hang down her back in one thick curl. She has wide cheekbones, a trim high-bridged nose, full lips, and large darkly fringed eyes, which are a startling shade that shifts from brown to green, depending on what colour she's wearing. Her skin is smooth and unwrinkled, of indeterminate colour, neither black nor brown nor yellow. A deep beige; but beige is a bland word. Nor is it chestnut, nor burnt sienna, nor umber. It's some other word.

People coming into the store frequently ask Shanita where she's from. "Right here," she says, smiling her ultra-bright smile. "I was born right in this very city!" She's nice about it to their faces, but it's a question that bothers her a lot.

"I think they mean, where were your parents from," says Charis, because that's what Canadians usually mean when they ask that question.

"That's not what they mean," says Shanita. "What they mean is, when am I leaving."

Charis cannot see why anyone would want Shanita to leave, but when she says so, Shanita laughs. "You," she says, "have led one damn sheltered life." Then she tells Charis about the rudeness of white street-car conductors towards her. "*Move to the back*, they tell me, like I was dirt!"

"Streetcar conductors are *all* rude! They say *Move to the back* to everybody, they're rude to *me*!" says Charis, intending to console Shanita—although she's being slightly dishonest, it's only some streetcar conductors, and she herself hardly ever takes the streetcar—and Shanita throws her a glance of contempt, for being unable to acknowledge the racism of almost everybody, almost everybody white, and then Charis feels bad. Sometimes she thinks of Shanita as a dauntless explorer, hacking her way through the jungle. The jungle consists of people like Charis.

So she stops herself from being too curious, from asking too much about Shanita, about her background, about where she's *from*. Shanita teases her, though; she throws out hints, changes her story. Sometimes she's part Chinese and part black, with a West Indian grandmother; she can do the accent, so maybe there's something to it. That might be the grandmother who used to eat dirt; but there are other grandmothers too, one from the States and one from Halifax, and one from Pakistan and one from New Mexico, and even one from Scotland. Maybe they are step-grandmothers, or maybe Shanita moved around a lot. Charis can't sort them out: Shanita has more grandmothers than anyone she knows. But sometimes she's part Ojibway, or else part Mayan, and one day she was even part Tibetan. She can be whatever she feels like, because who can tell?

Whereas Charis is stuck with being white. A white rabbit. Being white is getting more and more exhausting. There are so many bad waves attached to it, left over from the past but spreading through the present, like the killing rays from atomic waste dumps. There's so much to expiate! It gives her anemia just to think about it. In her next life she's going to be a mixture, a blend, a vigorous hybrid, like Shanita. Then no one will have anything on her.

❧

The store doesn't open till eleven, so Charis helps take stock. Shanita goes through the shelves, counting, and Charis writes down the numbers on a clipboard. It's a good thing she found her reading glasses.

"We'll have to bring down the prices," says Shanita, frowning. "Stuff is not moving. We'll have to do a sale."

"Before Christmas?" says Charis, astonished.

"It's the Recession," says Shanita, pursing her lips. "That's reality. This time of year, we usually have to re-order for Christmas, right? Now, just look at all this!"

Charis peers: the shelves are upsettingly full. "You know what's moving?" says Shanita. "This thing."

Charis is familiar with it, because she's sold a lot of them lately. It's a little pamphlet-like book, a cookbook, done on grey recycled paper with black-and-white line drawings, a do-it-yourself home publishing effort: *Pot Luck: Penny-Pinching Soups & Stews*. It doesn't appeal to her, personally. Penny-pinching as a concept she finds very blocking. There's something hard and grinding about it, and *pinching* is a hurtful word. True, she saves candle ends and pieces of wool, but that's because she wants to, she wants to create things with them, that's an act of love towards the earth.

"I need more stuff like this," says Shanita. "Fact is, I'm thinking of changing the store. Changing the name, the concept, everything."

Charis's heart sinks. "What would you change it to?" she asks.

"I was thinking, Scrimpers," says Shanita.

"Scrimpers?" says Charis.

"You know. Like the old five-and-dime, all cheap stuff," says Shanita. "Only more creative. It could work! A few years ago, you could trade on the impulse buy. Mad money, you know? Folks were flinging it around. But the only way you make it through a recession is by getting people to buy stuff about how not to buy stuff, if you know what I mean."

"But Radiance is so lovely!" cries Charis unhappily.

"I know," says Shanita. "It was a lot of fun while it lasted. But *lovely* is luxury goods. How many of these dinky toys you think people are going to buy, right now? Maybe some, but only if we keep the price down. In these times you cut your losses, you cut your overheads, you do what you have to. This is a lifeboat, you know? It's my lifeboat, it's my life. I have worked damn hard, I know which way the wind is blowing, and I do not intend to go down with the sinking ship."

She's defensive. She looks at Charis, her gaze level—her eyes are green today—and Charis realizes that she herself is an overhead. If things get much worse, Shanita will cut her, and run the store by herself, and Charis will be out of a job.

H. Substitution and Income Effects, Elasticity

From Jon Krakauer's Into Thin Air, *a brief passage illustrates the idea of the price elasticity of demand. When the price of a good or service increases—holding constant such things as other prices, incomes, and consumer tastes and preferences—the amount consumers buy will fall. But for some products the amount purchased will fall a great deal (economists call this elastic demand) and for other products the amount purchased will only fall a little (inelastic demand). Two of the major factors that determine whether demand is elastic or inelastic are the number of close substitutes available to consumers when the price of one good rises or falls (in Krakauer's example, climbing Mt. Everest from either China or Nepal) and the proportion of a consumer's budget that is spent on the product. In the case of climbing Mt. Everest, until recently the fees charged by the governments of Nepal and China were a relatively small part of the overall costs of such an expedition.*

In an epistle from Alexander Pope's Imitations of Horace, *and also in the original poem by Horace, we have an example of what economists call the income effect. A soldier's demand for safety initially decreases when he loses his little purse of gold. He is so upset and desperate that in the next battle he leads the charge, not caring whether he lives or dies. Things change again when he receives a large reward for his bravery, however, much to the displeasure of the soldier's commander in the subsequent battle.*

Into Thin Air

Jon Krakauer

(1997)

Licenses for climbing expeditions on Mt. Everest are only a small part of the costs of such activities—for most people the largest costs concern the long periods of time they must spend away from their families and jobs, not to mention the risk of death and injury. Nevertheless, because there are approaches to Everest from more than one country, expeditions try to minimize their direct financial costs by avoiding high license fees.

For a great many climbers, the record shows, stealing time away from the daily grind has not been an insurmountable obstacle, nor has the hefty outlay of cash. Over the past half decade, the traffic on all of the Seven Summits, but especially Everest, has multiplied at an astonishing rate. And to meet the demand, the number of commercial enterprises peddling guided ascents of the Seven Summits, especially Everest, has multiplied correspondingly. In the spring of 1996, thirty distinct expeditions were on the flanks of Everest, at least ten of them organized as money-making ventures.

The government of Nepal recognized that the throngs flocking to Everest created serious problems in terms of safety, aesthetics, and impact to the environment. While grappling with the issue, Nepalese ministers came up with a solution that seemed to hold the dual promise of limiting the crowds while increasing the flow of hard currency into the impoverished national coffers: raise the fee for climbing permits. In 1991 the Ministry of Tourism charged $2,300 for a permit that allowed a team of any size to attempt Everest. In 1992 the fee was increased to $10,000 for a team of up to nine climbers, with another $1,200 to be paid for each additional climber.

But climbers continued to swarm to Everest despite the higher fees. In the spring of 1993, on the fortieth anniversary of the first ascent, a record fifteen expeditions, comprising 294 climbers, attempted to scale the peak from the Nepalese side. That autumn the ministry raised the permit fee yet again—to a staggering $50,000 for as many as five climbers, plus $10,000 for each additional climber, up to a maximum of seven. Additionally, the government decreed that no more than four expeditions would be allowed on the Nepalese flanks each season.

What the Nepalese ministers didn't take into consideration, however, was that China charged only $15,000 to allow a team of any size to climb the mountain from Tibet and placed no limit on the number of expeditions each season. The flood of Everesters therefore shifted from Nepal to Tibet, leaving hundreds of Sherpas out of work. The ensuing hue and cry persuaded Nepal, in the spring of 1996, to abruptly cancel the four-expedition limit. And while they were at it, the government ministers jacked up the permit fee once again—this time to $70,000 for up to seven climbers, plus another $10,000 for each additional climber. Judging from the fact that sixteen of the thirty expeditions on Everest last spring were climbing on the Nepalese side of the mountain, the high cost of obtaining a permit doesn't seem to have been a significant deterrent.

Imitations of Horace (1737)

Alexander Pope

As income and wealth rises, demand for safety usually increases, too. Pope describes this process with reference to its effect on soldiers.

In Anna's Wars, a Soldier poor and old,
Had dearly earn'd a little purse of Gold:
Tir'd with a tedious March, one luckless night,
He slept, poor Dog! and lost it, to a doit.
This put the Man in such a desp'rate Mind,
Between Revenge, and Grief, and Hunger join'd,
Against the Foe, himself, and all Mankind,
He leapt the Trenches, scal'd a Castle-Wall,
Tore down a Standard, took the Fort and all.
"Prodigious well!" his great Commander cry'd,
Gave him much Praise, and some Reward beside.
Next pleas'd his Excellence a Town to batter;
(Its Name I know not, and it's no great matter)
"Go on, my Friend (he cry'd) see yonder Walls!
"Advance and conquer! go where Glory calls!
"More Honours, more Rewards, attend the Brave"—
Don't you remember what Reply he gave?
"D'ye think me, noble Gen'ral, such a Sot?
"Let him take Castles who has ne'er a Groat."

I. Public Goods, Externalities, and the Coase Theorem

While private markets can efficiently allocate resources to the production and consumption of most goods and services, including basic necessities and extravagant luxuries, there are special characteristics associated with some goods and services that lead to market failures. Economists call the first class of such products public goods, to distinguish them from the private goods that are routinely traded in the marketplace.

When you buy and use a private good, for example, a hamburger, you have the right to exclude anyone else from using that product. The person who sells the hamburger to you is also able to keep you from consuming it until you have paid for it. When you do consume it, or give it to someone else to consume, it is gone—nobody else can consume it. With public goods, that is not the case: more than one person can use the product at the same time without reducing the amount available to others (economists call this the non-rival principle), and there is also no effective way to keep someone from consuming a purely public good, even if they have not paid for it. National defense is the classic example of a pure public good, because protecting one person from attack by missiles, bombs, or armies means that you are also protecting other people at the same time—even people who don't pay taxes. Mosquito fogging and spraying programs are another example—in many ways mosquitoes are just a different kind of invading air force, more annoying than lethal.

A second class of market failures is called externalities or spillovers. These problems arise when some of the costs or benefits associated with the production or consumption of a product affect parties other than the producers and consumers of the product. Pollution is the classic example of a spillover (or external) cost. Vaccinations against highly infectious diseases are an example of a spillover (or external) benefit. Children killed by drunk drivers are another example of spillover costs, and the increase in neighbors' property values when someone landscapes or paints the outside of their home is another example of a spillover benefit.

In Travels with Charley, *John Steinbeck describes a good that has some characteristics of both public and private goods—the redwood forests. While people and companies can buy and own these trees, and sell the lumber as a private good, the scenic qualities of a redwood forest have the characteristics of a public good: many people can look at the forest without using it up, and it is difficult to keep people from going to the forest to look at the trees, whether they pay an admission fee or not.*

With a public good such as national defense, the government must decide how many resources to allocate to this purpose, and then raise the money to pay for it with taxes. National parks are one way of doing the same thing with redwood forests and other kinds of scenic areas. But another way, discussed by Steinbeck, is for private individuals and organizations to purchase the forests so they will not be used for lumber. Since the 1940s, Ducks Unlimited has used this sort of approach to maintain and restore wetlands used by ducks and other migratory birds.

The Nobel laureate economist Ronald Coase explored the conditions that would lead to private corrections of public-good and externality problems. Basically, when the costs and benefits are clear and direct and the number of parties affected is relatively small, negotiations and transactions are relatively easy and inexpensive to conduct, and so private corrections are far more likely to occur. This idea has come to be known as the Coase theorem. Long before Coase's work, however, Francois Rabelais offered a hilarious example of the Coase theorem at work in a Paris tavern. Charles Dickens painted a stark picture of a more sweeping externality problem in Coketown, which was recently echoed in Arundhati Roy's description of pollution in India. Jon Krakauer describes both private and government policies to reduce pollution and trash on Mt. Everest.

Travels With Charley: In Search of America (1962)

John Steinbeck

The economic rationale for many public parks is that spectacular scenery can be simultaneously enjoyed by many people without reducing the scenery available for other people to see, at least until the parks become crowded. In some cases, however, individuals contribute funds to private organizations to purchase woodlands, wetlands, and wildlife breeding and feeding areas.

The redwoods, once seen, leave a mark or create a vision that stays with you always. No one has ever successfully painted or photographed a redwood tree. The feeling they produce is not transferable. From them comes silence and awe. It's not only their unbelievable stature, nor the color which seems to shift and vary under your eyes, no, they are not like any trees we know, they are ambassadors from another time. They have the mystery of ferns that disappeared a million years ago into the coal of the carboniferous era. They carry their own light and shade. The vainest, most slap-happy and irreverent of men, in the presence of redwoods, goes under a spell of wonder and respect. Respect—that's the word. One feels the need to bow to unquestioned sovereigns. I have known these great ones since my earliest childhood, have lived among them, camped and slept against their warm monster bodies, and no amount of association has bred contempt in me. And the feeling is not limited to me.

A number of years ago, a newcomer, a stranger, moved to my country near Monterey. His senses must have been blunted and atrophied with money and the getting of it. He bought a grove of sempervirens in a deep valley near the coast, and then, as was his right by ownership, he cut them down and sold the lumber, and left on the ground the wreckage of his slaughter. Shock and numb outrage filled the town. This was not only murder but sacrilege. We looked on that man with loathing, and he was marked to the day of his death.

Of course, many of the ancient groves have been lumbered off, but many of the stately monuments remain and will remain, for a good and interesting reason. States and governments could not buy and protect these holy trees. This being so, clubs, organizations, even individuals, bought them and dedicated them to the future. I don't know any other similar case. Such is the impact of the sequoias on the human mind.

Gargantua and Pantagruel (1534)

François Rabelais

There is often pleasure in "people watching," because it is interesting to observe those who are attractive, stylishly dressed, amusing, or eccentric. But these external benefits are usually not so high that it makes sense for those who are being observed to charge for their services, especially when one factors in the costs of pricing and collecting fees. This problem is dramatized in Rabelais' story, in which a dispute is eventually adjudicated by a stock character in much classic literature, the wise fool.

At Paris, in the Roast-meat Cookery of the Petit Chastelet, before the Cook-Shop of one of the Roast-meat Sellers of that Lane, a certain hungry Porter was eating his Bread, after he had by Parcels kept it a while above the Reek and Steam of a fat Goose on the Spit, turning at a great Fire, and found it so besmoaked with the Vapour, to be savoury; which the Cook observing, took no notice, till after having ravined his Penny Loaf, whereof no Morsel had been unsmoakified, he was about discamping and going away; but by your leave, as the Fellow thought to have departed thence shot-free, the Master-Cook laid hold upon him by the Gorget, demanded payment for the Smoak of his Roast-meat. The Porter answered, that he had sustained no loss at all; that by what he had done there was no Diminution made of the Flesh, that he had taken nothing of his, and that therefore he was not indebted to him in any thing: As for the Smoak in question, that, although he had not been there, it would howsoever have been evaporated: Besides that, before that time it had never been seen nor heard, that Roast-meat Smoak was sold upon the Streets of Paris. The Cook hereto replied, That he was not obliged nor any way bound to feed and nourish for nought a Porter whom he had never seen before with the Smoak of his Roast-meat; and thereupon swore, that if he would not forthwith content and satisfie him with present Payment for the Repast which he had thereby got, that he would take his crooked Staves from off his Back; which instead of having Loads thereafter laid upon them, should serve for Fuel to his Kitchen Fires. Whilst he was going about so to do, and to have pulled them to him by one of the bottom Rungs, which he had caught in his Hand, the sturdy Porter got out of his Gripes, drew forth the knotty Cudgel, and stood to his own Defence. The Altercation waxed hot in Words, which moved the gaping Holydons of the sottish Parisians to run from all parts thereabouts to see what the issue would be of that babbling Strife and Contention. In the interim of this Dispute, to very good purpose Seiny Jhon the Fool and Citizen of Paris, happened to be there, whom the Cook perceiving, said to the Porter, Wilt thou refer and submit unto the noble Seiny Jhon, the Decision of the Difference and Controversie which is betwixt us? Yes, by the blood of a Goose, answered the Porter, I am content. Seiny Jhon the Fool, finding that the Cook and Porter had compromised the Determination of their Variance and Debate to the Discretion of his Award and Arbitriment; after that the Reasons on either side whereupon was grounded the mutual fierceness of their brawling Jar had been to the full displayed and laid open before him, commanded the Porter to draw out of the Fab of his Belt a piece of Money, if he had it. Whereupon the Porter immediately without delay, in Reverence to the Authority of such a Judicious Umpire, put the tenth part of a Silver Phillip into his Hand. The little Phillip Seiny Jhon took, then set it on his left Shoulder, to try by feeling if it was a sufficient weight; after that, laying it on the palm of his Hand he made it ring and tingle, to understand by the Ear if it was of a good Alloy in the Metal whereof it was composed: Thereafter he put it to the Ball or Apple of his left Eye, to explore by the sight if it was well stamped and marked; all which being done, in a profound Silence of the whole doltish People, who were there Spectators of this Pageantry, to the great hope of the Cooks, and despair of the Porters Prevalency in the Suit that was in agitation, he finally caused the Porter to make it sound several times upon the Stall of the Cooks Shop. Then with a Presidential Majesty holding his Bable (Scepter-like) in his Hand, muffling his Head with a Hood of Martern Skins, each side whereof had the resemblance of an Ape's Face, sprucified up with Ears of pasted Paper, and having about his Neck a bucked Ruff, raised, furrowed, and ridged, with Ponting Sticks of the shape and fashion of small Organ-Pipes; he first, with all the force of his Lungs, coughed two or three times, and then with an audible Voice pronounced this following Sentence, The Court declareth, That the Porter, who ate his Bread at the Smoak of the Roast, hath civilly paid the Cook with the Sound of his Money: And the said Court Ordaineth, That every one return to his own Home, and attend his proper Business, without Cost and Charges, and for a Cause. This Verdict, Award and Arbitriment of the Parisian Fool, did appear so equitable, yea, so admirable to the aforesaid Doctors, that they very much doubted, if the Matter had been brought before the Sessions for Justice of the said Place, or that the Judges of the Rota at Rome had been Umpires therein; or yet that the Areopagites themselves had been the Deciders thereof, if by any one part, or all of them together, it had been so judicially sententiated and awarded. Therefore advise, if you will be counseled by a Fool.

Hard Times
(1854)
Charles Dickens

Pollution is the classic example of a major external cost that is not paid by producers or consumers of the goods and services that engender the pollution during the production, consumption, or disposal of the products. Because pollution affects so many people, private remedies are not practical, and the government must establish effective ways to reduce it. The rapid spread of new production technologies in the early decades of the Industrial Revolution far outpaced government's ability to deal with these problems, as noted here by Charles Dickens. Then again, for political, economic, and technical reasons, these are difficult problems to address. More than a century after Dickens wrote about Coketown, the Cuyahoga River in Cleveland caught fire. Since then, a wide range of policies have been developed to limit and reduce pollution, many featuring market-based incentive programs that are typically far more cost-effective than across-the-board regulations that establish particular pollution clean-up procedures or require producers to meet predetermined pollution reduction targets.

It was a town of red brick, or of brick that would have been red if the smoke and ashes had allowed it; but, as matters stood it was a town of unnatural red and black, like the painted face of a savage. It was a town of machinery and tall chimneys, out of which interminable serpents of smoke trailed themselves for ever and ever, and never got uncoiled. It had a black canal in it, and a river that ran purple with ill-smelling dye, and vast piles of building full of windows where there was a rattling and a trembling all day long, and where the piston of the steam engine worked monotonously up and down, like the head of an elephant in a state of melancholy madness. It contained several large streets all very like one another, and many small streets still more like one another, inhabited by people equally like one another, who all went in and out at the same hours, with the same sound upon the same pavements, to do the same work, and to whom every day was the same as yesterday and tomorrow, and every year the counterpart of the last and the next.

These attributes of Coketown were in the main inseparable from the work by which it was sustained. Against them were to be set off comforts of life which found their way all over the world, and elegancies of life which made, we will not ask how much of the fine lady, who could scarcely bear to hear the place mentioned. The rest of its features were voluntary, and they were these.

You saw nothing in Coketown but what was severely workful. If the members of a religious persuasion built a chapel there—as the members of eighteen religious persuasions had done—they made it a pious warehouse of red brick, with sometimes (but this only in highly ornamented examples) a bell in a birdcage on the top of it. The solitary exception was the New Church, a stuccoed edifice with a square steeple over the door, terminating in four short pinnacles like florid wooden legs. All the public inscriptions in the town were painted alike, in severe characters of black and white. The jail might have been the infirmary, the infirmary might have been the jail, the town-hall might have been either, or both, or anything else, for anything that appeared to the contrary in the graces of their construction. Fact, fact, fact, everywhere in the material aspect of the town; fact, fact, fact, everywhere in the immaterial. The M'Choakumchild school was all fact, and the school of design was all fact, and the relations between master and man were all fact, and everything was fact between the lying-in hospital and the cemetery, and what you couldn't state in figures, or show to be purchasable in the cheapest market and saleable in the dearest, was not, and never should be, world without end. Amen.

Into Thin Air

Jon Krakauer

(1997)

On Mount Everest, there are now both private and public efforts to restore and preserve the natural appearance of the mountain.

I had heard many stories about how Everest had been turned into a garbage dump by the ever-increasing hordes, and commercial expeditions were reputed to be the primary culprits. Although in the 1970s and '80s Base Camp was indeed a big rubbish heap, in recent years it had been turned into a fairly tidy place—certainly the cleanest human settlement I'd seen since leaving Namche Bazaar. And the commercial expeditions actually deserved much of the credit for the cleanup.

Bringing clients back to Everest year after year, the guides had a stake in this that one-time visitors did not. As part of their expedition in 1990, Rob Hall and Gary Baff spearheaded an effort that removed five tons of garbage from Base Camp. Hall and some of his fellow guides also began working with government ministries in Kathmandu to formulate policies that encouraged climbers to keep the mountain clean. By 1996, in addition to their permit fee, expeditions were required to post a $4,000 bond that would be refunded only if a predetermined amount of trash were carried back to Namche and Kathmandu. Even the barrels collecting the excrement from our toilets had to be removed and hauled away.

The previous winter, as he had done in winters past, Hall had consulted with the leaders of all the expeditions planning to climb Everest in the spring, and together they'd agreed on one team among them who would be responsible for establishing and maintaining a route through the Icefall. For its trouble, the designated team was to be paid $2,200 from each of the other expeditions on the mountain. In recent years this cooperative approach had been met with wide, if not universal, acceptance, but it wasn't always so.

The first time one expedition thought to charge another to travel through the ice was in 1988, when a lavishly funded American team announced that any expedition that intended to follow the route they'd engineered up the Icefall would have to fork over $2,000. Some of the other teams on the mountain that year, failing to understand that Everest was no longer merely a mountain but a commodity as well, were incensed. And the greatest hue and cry came from Rob Hall, who was leading a small, impecunious New Zealand team.

Hall carped that the Americans were "violating the spirit of the hills" and practicing a shameful form of alpine extortion, but Jim Frush, the unsentimental attorney who was the leader of the American group, remained unmoved. Hall eventually agreed through clenched teeth to send Frush a check and was granted passage through the Icefall. (Frush later reported that Hall never made good on his IOU.)

Within two years, however, Hall did an about-face and came to see the logic of treating the Icefall as a toll road. Indeed, from 1993 through '95 he volunteered to put in the route and collect the toll himself. In the spring of 1996 he elected not to assume responsibility for the Icefall, but he was happy to pay the leader of a rival commercial expedition—a Scottish Everest veteran named Mal Duff—to take over the job. Long before we'd even arrived at Base Camp, a team of Sherpas employed by Duff had blazed a zigzag path through the seracs, stringing out more than a mile of rope and installing some sixty aluminum ladders over the broken surface of the glacier. The ladders belonged to an enterprising Sherpa from the village of Gotak Shep who turned a nice profit by renting them out each season.

The God of Small Things (1997)

Arundhati Roy

Environmental choices and trade-offs are especially difficult problems to deal with in less-developed nations, in part because the demand for cleaner air and water only seems to increase as income levels rise.

Years later, when Rahel returned to the river, it greeted her with a ghastly skull's smile, with holes where teeth had been, and a limp hand raised from a hospital bed.

Both things had happened.

It had shrunk. And she had grown.

Downriver, a saltwater barrage had been built, in exchange for votes from the influential paddy-farmer lobby. The barrage regulated the inflow of salt water from the backwaters that opened into the Arabian Sea. So now they had two harvests a year instead of one. More rice, for the price of a river.

Despite the fact that it was June, and raining, the river was no more than a swollen drain now. A thin ribbon of thick water that lapped wearily at the mud banks on either side, sequined with the occasional silver slant of a dead fish. It was choked with a succulent weed, whose furred brown roots waved like thin tentacles underwater. Bronze-winged lily-trotters walked across it. Splay-footed, cautious.

Once it had had the power to evoke fear. To change lives. But now its teeth were drawn, its spirit spent. It was just a slow, sludging green ribbon lawn that ferried fetid garbage to the sea. Bright plastic bags blew across its viscous, weedy surface like subtropical flying-flowers.

The stone steps that had once led bathers right down to the water, and Fisher People to the fish, were entirely exposed and led from nowhere to nowhere, like an absurd corbelled monument that commemorated nothing. Ferns pushed through the cracks.

On the other side of the river, the steep mud banks changed abruptly into low mud walls of shanty hutments. Children hung their bottoms over the edge and defecated directly onto the squelchy, sucking mud of the exposed riverbed. The smaller ones left their dribbling mustard streaks to find their own way down. Eventually, by evening, the river would rouse itself to accept the day's offerings and sludge off to the sea, leaving wavy lines of thick white scum in its wake. Upstream, clean mothers washed clothes and pots in unadulterated factory effluents. People bathed. Severed torsos soaping themselves, arranged like dark busts on a thin, rocking, ribbon lawn.

On warm days the smell of shit lifted off the river and hovered over Ayemenem like a hat.

Further inland, and still across, a five-star hotel chain had bought the Heart of Darkness.

The History House (where map-breath'd ancestors with tough toe-nails once whispered) could no longer be approached from the river. It had turned its back on Ayemenem. The hotel guests were ferried across the backwaters, straight from Cochin. They arrived by speedboat, opening up a *V* of foam on the water, leaving behind a rainbow film of gasoline.

The view from the hotel was beautiful, but here too the water was thick and toxic. *No Swimming* signs had been put up in stylish calligraphy. They had built a tall wall to screen off the slum and prevent it from encroaching on Kari Saipu's estate. There wasn't much they could do about the smell.

J.

Government Regulation and the Legal and Social Framework for Markets

Property rights have, at times, been enforced by private citizens using force and weapons to protect what is theirs—usually in frontier or mining communities too remote to have access to impartial courts and law enforcement agencies. But when "civilization" arrives, the rule of law is reinstated for the enforcement and interpretation of deeds and other kinds of contracts. More generally, government laws, regulations, and enforcement agencies are necessary to establish the broader social context for a market economy—for example, to limit markets in light of constitutional and social commitments to basic human and political rights, or because of unreasonable risks and costs proscribed goods present to unsuspecting consumers or others. On these grounds, markets for slaves, narcotics, and votes on election day have now been prohibited in most of the world. The U.S. government also establishes safety regulations to reduce health and injury risks for consumers and workers (though not without controversy, since these regulations are costly to meet and enforce).

In determining how much economic regulation there should be, economists rely on the idea that, judged strictly in financial terms, a regulation should be adopted only if the additional benefits exceed or at least equal the additional costs. In many cases, laws and regulations do not meet that test. Rather, their passage and continued existence can usually be chalked up to political rather than economic reasons.

The first reading below, from Shakespeare's The Merchant of Venice, *deals with the broad and narrow details of enforcing contracts and establishing property rights and claims of ownership. Upton Sinclair's graphic descriptions of meat-packing plants in* The Jungle *helped to bring government regulations to the food processing industry, and still proves the adage that it is better not to know how sausage is made. Aleksandr Solzhenitsyn's* The Cancer Ward *describes some of the problems that develop when the government completely takes over the provision of a good that has many private benefits to producers and consumers: health care.*

The Merchant of Venice (1598)

William Shakespeare

Almost anything can be bought and sold in market transactions, often in formal exchanges involving legal contracts. This is especially true in commercial societies such as Shakespeare's Renaissance Venice, in which there was "no power to alter a decree" on the enforcement of contracts, for fear of setting a precedent that would allow all other contracts to be ignored. Fortunately for Antonio, a wise judge appears who understands all of the ramifications of the contract even after appeals to mercy and common sense have failed. On the other hand, many modern commentators have questioned the justice of some of the penalties the judge imposes on Shylock.

A Court of Justice; on a platform at the back a great chair of state with three lower chairs on either side; before these a table for clerks, lawyers' desks, etc. ANTONIO *(guarded)*, BASSANIO, GRATIANO, SOLANIO, *officers, clerks, attendants, and a concourse of people. The* DUKE *in white and six Magnificoes in red enter in state and take their seats*

DUKE: What, is Antonio here?
ANTONIO: Ready, so please your grace.
DUKE: I am sorry for thee—thou art come to answer
A stony adversary, an inhuman wretch
Uncapable of pity, void and empty
From any dram of mercy.
ANTONIO: I have heard,
Your Grace hath ta'en great pains to qualify
His rigorous course; but since he stands obdurate,
And that no lawful means can carry me
Out of his envy's reach, I do oppose
My patience to his fury, and am armed
To suffer with a quietness of spirit
The very tyranny and rage of his.
DUKE: Go one, and call the Jew into the court.
SALANIO: He is ready at the door, he comes, my
lord.

DUKE: Make room, and let him stand before our face. . . .

The crowd parts, and SHYLOCK *confronts the* DUKE; *he bows low.*

Shylock, the world thinks, and I think so too,
That thou but leadest this fashion of thy malice
To the last hour of act, and then 'tis thought
Thou'lt show thy mercy and remorse more strange
Than is thy strange apparent cruelty;
And where thou now exacts the penalty,
Which is a pound of this poor merchant's flesh,
Thou wilt not only loose the forfeiture,
But touched with human gentleness and love,
Forgive a moiety of the principal;
Glancing an eye of pity on his losses,
That have of late so huddled on his back;
Enow to press a royal merchant down,
And pluck commiseration of his state
From brassy bosoms and rough hearts of flint,
From stubborn Turks and Tartars, never trained
To offices of tender courtesy . . .
We all expect a gentle answer, Jew.

SHYLOCK: I have possessed your Grace of what I purpose,
And by our holy Sabbath have I sworn
To have the due and forfeit of my bond.
If you deny it, let the danger light
Upon your charter and your city's freedom!
You'll ask me why I rather choose to have
A weight of carrion flesh than to receive
Three thousand ducats: I'll not answer that!
But say it is my humour, is it answered?
What if my house be troubled with a rat,
And I be pleased to give ten thousand ducats
To have it baned? what, are you answered yet?
Some men there are love not a gaping pig,
Some that are mad if they behold a cat,
And others when the bag-pipe sings i'th' nose
Cannot contain their urine: for affection,
Mistress of passion, sways it to the mood
Of what it likes or loathes. Now, for your answer:
As there is no firm reason to be rendred,
Why he cannot abide a gaping pig;

Why he, a harmless necessary cat;
Why he, a woollen bag-pipe; but of force
Must yield to such inevitable shame,
As to offend, himself being offended;
So can I give no reason, nor I will not,
More than a lodged hate and a certain loathing
I bear Antonio, that I follow thus
A losing suit against him! Are you answered?

BASSANIO: This is no answer, thou unfeeling man,
To excuse the current of thy cruelty!

SHYLOCK: I am not bound to please thee with my answers!

BASSANIO: Do all men kill the things they do not love?

SHYLOCK: Hates any man the thing he would not kill?

BASSANIO: Every offence is not a hate at first!

SHYLOCK: What, wouldst thou have a serpent sting thee twice?

ANTONIO: I pray you, think you question with the Jew
You may as well go stand upon the beach
And bid the main flood bate his usual height,
You may as well use question with the wolf
Why he hath made the ewe bleat for the lamb;
You may as well forbid the mountain pines
To wag their high tops and to make no noise,
When they are fretten with the gusts of heaven;
You may as well do anything most hard,
As seek to soften that—than which what's harder?—
His Jewish heart. Therefore, I do beseech you,
Make no more offers, use no farther means,
But with all brief and plain conveniency
Let me have judgment and the Jew his will!

BASSANIO: For thy three thousand ducats here is six.

SHYLOCK: If every ducat in six thousand ducats
Were in six parts and every part a ducat,
I would not draw them, I would have my bond!

DUKE: How shalt thou hope for mercy, rendring none?

SHYLOCK: What judgment shall I dread, doing no wrong?
You have among you many a purchased slave,
Which, like your asses and your dogs and mules,
You use in abject and in slavish parts,
Because you bought them—shall I say to you,
Let them be free, marry them to your heirs?
Why sweat they under burthens? let their beds

Be made as soft as yours, and let their palates
Be seasoned with such viands? You will answer
"The slaves are ours." So do I answer you . . .
The pound of flesh, which I demand of him,
Is dearly bought, 'tis mine, and I will have it:
If you deny me, fie upon your law!
There is no force in the decrees of Venice . . .
I stand for judgment. Answer—shall I have it?

DUKE: Upon my power, I may dismiss this court,
Unless Bellario, a learned doctor,
Whom I have sent for to determine this,
Come here to-day.

SALANIO: My lord, here stays without
A messenger with letters from the doctor,
New come from Padua.

DUKE: Bring us the letters; call the messenger.

BASSANIO: Good cheer, Antonio! what man, courage yet:
The Jew shall have my flesh, blood, bones, and all,
Ere thou shalt lose for me one drop of blood.

SHYLOCK *takes a knife from his girdle and kneels to whet it*

ANTONIO: I am a tainted wether of the flock,
Meetest for death. The weakest kind of fruit
Drops earliest to the ground, and so let me;
You cannot better be employed, Bassanio,
Than to live still, and write mine epitaph.

NERISSA *enters, dressed as a lawyer's clerk.*

DUKE: Come you from Padua, from Bellario?

NERISSA: [*bows*] From both, my lord. Bellario greets your grace.

She presents a letter; the DUKE *opens and reads it*

BASSANIO: Why dost thou whet thy knife so earnestly?

SHYLOCK: To cut the forfeiture from that bankrupt there.

GRATIANO: Not on thy sole, but on thy soul, harsh Jew,
Thou mak'st thy knife keen: but no metal can,
No, not the hangman's axe, bear half the keenness
Of thy sharp envy: can no prayers pierce thee?

SHYLOCK: No, none that thou hast wit enough to make.

GRATIANO: Oh, be thou damned, inexorable dog,
And for thy life let justice be accused!
Thou almost mak'st me waver in my faith,
To hold opinion with Pythagoras
That souls of animals infuse themselves

Into the trunks of men: thy currish spirit
Governed a Wolf, who hanged for human slaughter,
Even from the gallows did his fell soul fleet,
And whilst thou layest in thy unhallowed dam,
Infused itself in thee; for thy desires
Are wolvish, bloody, starved, and ravenous.

SHYLOCK: Till thou canst rail the seal from off my bond,
Thou but offend'st thy lungs to speak so loud:
Repair thy wit, good youth, or it will fall
To cureless ruin. . . . I stand here for law.

DUKE: This letter from Bellario doth commend
A young and learned doctor to our court:
Where is he?

NERISSA: He attendeth here hard by
To know your answer, whether you'll admit him.

DUKE: With all my heart: some three or four of you,
Go give him courteous conduct to this place.

Attendants bow and depart

Meantime, the court shall hear Bellario's letter. . . .

He reads out the letter

"Your grace shall understand that at the receipt of your letter I am very sick, but in the instant that your messenger came, in loving visitation was with me a young doctor of Rome, his name is Balthazar: I acquainted him with the cause in controversy between the Jew and Antonio the merchant, we turned o'er many books together, he is furnished with my opinion, which bettered with his own learning, the greatness whereof I cannot enough commend, comes with him at my importunity to fill up your grace's request in my stead. I beseech you, let his lack of years be no impediment to let him lack a reverend estimation, for I never knew so young a body with so old a head: I leave him to your gracious acceptance, whose trial shall better publish his commendation."
You hear the learned Bellario, what he writes.

PORTIA *enters, dressed as a doctor of civil law, with a book in her hand*

And here, I take it, is the Doctor come. . . .
Give me your hand. Come you from old Bellario?

PORTIA: I did, my lord.

DUKE: You are welcome. Take your place . . .

An attendant ushers PORTIA *to a desk near the* DUKE

Are you acquainted with the difference
That holds this present question in the court?

PORTIA: I am informed thoroughly of the cause.
Which is the merchant here, and which the Jew?

DUKE: Antonio and old Shylock, both stand forth.

PORTIA: Is your name Shylock?

SHYLOCK: Shylock is my name.

PORTIA: Of a strange nature is the suit you follow,
Yet in such rule that the Venetian law
Cannot impugn you as you do proceed. . . .
You stand within his danger, do you not?

ANTONIO: Ay, so he says.

PORTIA: Do you confess the bond?

ANTONIO: I do.

PORTIA: Then must the Jew be merciful.

SHYLOCK: On what compulsion must I? Tell me that.

PORTIA: The quality of mercy is not strained,
It droppeth as the gentle rain from heaven
Upon the place beneath: it is twice blessed,
It blesseth him that gives, and him that takes,
'Tis mightiest in the mightiest, it becomes
The throned monarch better than his crown,
His sceptre shows the force of temporal power,
The attribute to awe and majesty,
Wherein doth sit the dread and fear of kings:
But mercy is above this sceptred sway,
It is enthroned in the hearts of kings,
It is an attribute to God himself;
And earthly power doth then show likest God's,
When mercy seasons justice: therefore, Jew,
Though justice be thy plea, consider this,
That in the course of justice none of us
Should see salvation: we do pray for mercy,
And that same prayer doth teach us all to render
The deeds of mercy. . . . I have spoke thus much,
To mitigate the justice of thy plea,
Which if thou follow, this strict court of Venice
Must needs give sentence 'gainst the merchant there.

SHYLOCK: My deeds upon my head! I crave the law,
The penalty and forfeit of my bond.

PORTIA: Is he not able to discharge the money?

BASSANIO: Yes, here I tender it for him in the court,
Yea, twice the sum. If that will not suffice,
I will be bound to pay it ten times o'er,
On forfeit of my hands, my head, my heart.
If this will not suffice, it must appear
That malice bears down truth. . . .

He kneels with hands uplifted

And I beseech you,
Wrest once the law to your authority—
To do a great right, do a little wrong,
And curb this cruel devil on his will.

PORTIA: It must not be. There is no power in Venice
Can alter a decree established:
'Twill be recorded for a precedent,
And many an error, by the same example
Will rush into the state. It cannot be.

SHYLOCK: A Daniel come to judgment: yea, a Daniel!

He kisses the hem of her robe

O wise young judge, how I do honor thee!

PORTIA: I pray you, let me look upon the bond.

SHYLOCK: *[swiftly snatching a paper from his bosom].* Here 'tis, most reverend Doctor, here it is.

PORTIA: *[taking the paper].* Shylock, there's thrice thy money offered thee.

SHYLOCK: An oath, an oath, I have an oath in heaven.
Shall I lay perjury upon my soul?
No, not for Venice.

PORTIA: [*perusing the paper*]. Why, this bond is forfeit,
And lawfully by this the Jew may claim
A pound of flesh, to be by him cut off
Nearest the merchant's heart . . . Be merciful,
Take thrice thy money, bid me tear the bond.

SHYLOCK: When it is paid according to the tenour. . . .
It doth appear you are a worthy judge,
You know the law, your exposition
Hath been most sound: I charge you by the law,
Whereof you are a well-deserving pillar,
Proceed to judgment: by my soul I swear,
There is no power in the tongue of man
To alter me. I stay here on my bond.

ANTONIO: Most heartily I do beseech the court
To give the judgment.

PORTIA: Why then, thus it is.
You must prepare your bosom for his knife.

SHYLOCK: O noble judge! O excellent young man!

PORTIA: For the intent and purpose of the law
Hath full relation to the penalty,
Which here appeareth due upon the bond.

SHYLOCK: 'Tis very true: O wise and upright judge!
How much more elder art thou than thy looks!

PORTIA: Therefore, lay bare your bosom.

SHYLOCK: Ay, his breast,
So says the bond, doth it not, noble judge?
"Nearest his heart," those are the very words.

PORTIA: It is so. Are there balance here to weigh
The flesh?

SHYLOCK: I have them ready.

He opens his cloak and takes them out

PORTIA: Have by some surgeon, Shylock, on your charge,
To stop his wounds, lest he do bleed to death.

SHYLOCK: Is it so nominated in the bond?

He takes it and examines it closely

PORTIA: It is not so expressed, but what of that?
'Twere good you do so much for charity.

SHYLOCK: I cannot find it, 'tis not in the bond.

He gives it back to PORTIA

PORTIA: You merchant, have you anything to say?

ANTONIO: But little; I am armed and well prepared.
Give me your hand, Bassanio, fare you well!
Grieve not that I am fall'n to this for you;
For herein Fortune shows herself more kind
Than is her custom: it is still her use,
To let the wretched man outlive his wealth,
To view with hollow eye and wrinkled brow
An age of poverty; from which ling'ring penance
Of such misery doth she cut me off....

They embrace

Commend me to your honorable wife,
Tell her the process of Antonio's end,
Say how I loved you, speak me fair in death;
And when the tale is told, bid her be judge

Whether Bassanio had not once a love . . .
Repent but you that you shall lose your friend,
And he repents not, that he pays your debt . . . .
For if the Jew do cut but deep enough,
I'll pay it instantly with all my heart.

BASSANIO: Antonio, I am married to a wife
Which is as dear to me as life itself,
But life itself, my wife, and all the world,
Are not with me esteemed above thy life.
I would lose all, ay, sacrifice them all
Here to this devil, to deliver you.

PORTIA: Your wife would give you little thanks for that,
If she were by, to hear you make the offer.

GRATIANO: I have a wife, whom, I protest, I love—
I would she were in heaven, so she could
Entreat some power to change this currish Jew.

NERISSA: 'Tis well you offer it behind her back,
The wish would make else an unquiet house.

SHYLOCK: These be the Christian husbands! I have a daughter—
Would any of the stock of Barrabas
Had been her husband, rather than a Christian. . . .
[*aloud*] We trifle time, I pray thee pursue sentence.

PORTIA: A pound of that same merchant's flesh is thine,
The court awards it, and the law doth give it.

SHYLOCK: Most rightful judge!

PORTIA: And you must cut this flesh from off his breast,
The law allows it, and the court awards it.

SHYLOCK: Most learned judge—A sentence—come, prepare.

He advances with knife drawn

PORTIA: Tarry a little, there is something else.
This bond doth give thee here no jot of blood—
The words expressly are "a pound of flesh":
Take then thy bond, take thou thy pound of flesh,
But, in the cutting it, if thou dost shed
One drop of Christian blood, thy lands and goods
Are by the laws of Venice confiscate
Unto the state of Venice.

GRATIANO: O upright judge!—mark, Jew—O learned judge!

SHYLOCK: Is that the law?

PORTIA: [*opens her book*]. Thyself shalt see the act:
For, as thou urgest justice, be assured

Thou shalt have justice more than thou desir'st.

GRATIANO: O learned judge!—mark, Jew—a learned judge!

SHYLOCK: I take this offer then—pay the bond thrice,
And let the Christian go.

BASSANIO: Here is the money.

PORTIA: Soft!
The Jew shall have all justice—soft, no haste—
He shall have nothing but the penalty.

GRATIANO: O Jew! an upright judge, a learned judge!

PORTIA: Therefore, prepare thee to cut off the flesh.
Shed thou no blood, nor cut thou less nor more
But just a pound of flesh: if thou tak'st more
Or less than a just pound, be it but so much
As makes it light or heavy in the substance,
Or the division of the twentieth part
Of one poor scruple, nay, if the scale do turn
But in the estimation of a hair,
Thou diest and all thy goods are confiscate.

GRATIANO: A second Daniel, a Daniel, Jew!
Now, infidel, I have you on the hip.

PORTIA: Why doth the Jew pause? take thy forfeiture.

SHYLOCK: Give me my principal, and let me go.

BASSANIO: I have it ready for thee, here it is.

PORTIA: He hath refused it in the open court,
He shall have merely justice and his bond.

GRATIANO: A Daniel, still say I, a second Daniel!
I thank thee, Jew, for teaching me that word.

SHYLOCK: Shall I not have barely my principal?

PORTIA: Thou shalt have nothing but the forfeiture
To be so taken at thy peril, Jew.

SHYLOCK: Why then the devil give him good of it!
I'll stay no longer question.

He turns to go

PORTIA: Tarry, Jew.
The law hath yet another hold on you. . . .

She reads from her book

It is enacted in the laws of Venice,
If it be proved against an alien,
That by direct or indirect attempts
He seek the life of any citizen,
The party 'gainst the which he doth contrive

Shall seize one half his goods, the other half
Comes to the privy coffer of the state,
And the offender's life lies in the mercy
Of the duke only, 'gainst all other voice. . . .

She closes the book

In which predicament, I say, thou stand'st,
For it appears by manifest proceeding,
That indirectly and directly too
Thou hast contrived against the very life
Of the defendant; and thou hast incurred
The danger formerly by me rehearsed. . . .
Down, therefore, and beg mercy of the duke.

GRATIANO Beg that thou mayst have leave to hang thyself,
And yet thy wealth being forfeit to the state,
Thou hast not left the value of a cord,
Therefore thou must be hanged at the state's charge.

DUKE: That thou shalt see the difference of our spirit,
I pardon thee thy life before thou ask it:
For half thy wealth, it is Antionio's—
The other half comes to the general state,
Which humbleness may drive unto a fine.

PORTIA: Ay, for the state, not for Antonio.

SHYLOCK: Nay, take my life and all, pardon not that.
You take my house, when you do take the prop
That doth sustain my house; you take my life,
When you do take the means whereby I live.

PORTIA: What mercy can you render him, Antonio?

GRATIANO: A halter gratis—nothing else, for God's sake.

ANTONIO: So please my lord the duke and all the court
To quit the fine for one half of his goods,
I am content; so he will let me have
The other half in use, to render it
Upon his death unto the gentleman
That lately stole his daughter. . . .

BASSANIO: Most worthy gentleman, I and my friend
Have by your wisdom been this day acquitted
Of grievous penalties, in lieu whereof,
Three thousand ducats, due unto the Jew,
We freely cope your courteous pains withal.

ANTONIO: And stand indebted, over and above,
In love and service to you evermore.

PORTIA: He is well paid that is well satisfied,
And I, delivering you, am satisfied,
And therein do account myself well paid.
My mind was never yet more mercenary. . . .

passing them with a bow

I pray you, know me when we meet again.

THE JUNGLE (1906)

Upton Sinclair

Many countries adopt regulation and inspection programs to improve the safety and quality of food supplies. For centuries people lived (or sometimes got sick or even died) inspecting their own food. As food processing became more elaborate and complex, however, and as consumers became wealthier, the demand for government inspection programs to prevent unhealthy and undesirable practices increased. In the United States, many such reforms were spurred on by Sinclair's famous novel.

With one member trimming beef in a cannery, and another working in a sausage factory, the family had a first-hand knowledge of the great majority of Packingtown swindles. For it was the custom, as they found, whenever meat was so spoiled that it could not be used for anything else, either to can it or else to chop it up into sausage. With what had been told them by Jonas, who had worked in the pickle-rooms, they could now study the whole of the spoiled-meat industry on the inside, and read a new and grim meaning into that old Packingtown jest,—that they use everything of the pig except the squeal.

Jonas had told them how the meat that was taken out of pickle would often be found sour, and how they would rub it up with soda to take away the smell, and sell it to be eaten on free-lunch counters; also of all the miracles of chemistry which they performed, giving to any sort of meat, fresh or salted, whole or chopped, any color and any flavor and any odor they chose. In the pickling of hams they had an ingenious apparatus, by which they saved time and increased the capacity of the plant—a machine consisting of a hollow needle attached to a pump; by plunging this needle into the meat and working with his foot, a man could fill a ham with pickle in a few seconds. And yet, in spite of this, there would be hams found spoiled, some of them with an odor so bad that a man could hardly bear to be in the room with them. To pump into these the packers had a second and much stronger pickle which destroyed the odor—a process known to the workers as "giving them thirty per cent." Also, after the hams had been smoked, there would be found some that had gone to the bad. Formerly these had been sold as "Number Three Grade," but later on some ingenious person had hit upon a new device, and now they would extract the bone, about which the bad part generally lay, and insert in the hole a white-hot iron. After this invention there was no longer Number One, Two, and Three Grade—there was only Number One Grade. The packers were always originating such schemes—they had what they called "boneless hams," which were all the odds and ends of pork stuffed into casings; and "California hams," which were the shoulders, with big knuckle-joints, and nearly all the meat cut out; and fancy "skinned hams," which were made of the oldest hogs, whose skins were so heavy and coarse that no one would buy them—that is, until they had been cooked and chopped fine and labeled "head cheese"!

It was only when the whole ham was spoiled that it came into the department of Elzbieta. Cut up by the two-thousand-revolutions-a-minute flyers, and mixed with half a ton of other meat, no odor that ever was in a ham could make any difference. There was never the least attention paid to what was cut up for sausage; there would come all the way back from Europe old sausage that had been rejected, and that was mouldy and white—it would be dosed with borax and glycerine, and dumped into the hoppers, and made over again for home consumption. There would be meat that had tumbled out on the floor, in the dirt and sawdust, where the workers had tramped and spit uncounted billions of consumption germs. There would be meat stored in great piles in rooms; and the water from leaky roofs would drip over it, and thousands of rats would race about on it. It was too dark in these storage places to see well, but a man could run his hand over these piles of meat and sweep off handfuls of the dried dung of rats. These rats were nuisances, and the packers would put poisoned bread out for them; they would die, and then rats, bread, and meat would go into the hoppers together. This is no fairy story and no joke; the meat would be shovelled into carts, and the man who did the shovelling would not trouble to lift out a rat even when he saw one—there were things that went into the sausage in comparison with which a poisoned rat was a tidbit. There was no place for the men to wash their hands before they ate their dinner, and so they made a practice of washing them in the water that was to be ladled into the sausage. There were the butt-ends of smoked meat, and the scraps of corned beef, and all the odds and ends of the waste of the plants, that would be dumped into old barrels in the cellar and left there. Under the system of rigid economy which the packers enforced, there were some jobs that it only paid to do once in a long time, and among these was the cleaning out of the waste-barrels. Every spring they did it; and in the barrels would be dirt and rust and old nails and stale water—and cart load after cart load of it would be taken up and dumped into the hoppers with fresh meat, and sent out to the public's breakfast. Some of it they would make into "smoked" sausage—but as the smoking took time, and was therefore expensive, they would call upon their chemistry department, and preserve it with borax and color it with gelatine to make it brown. All of their sausage came out of the same bowl, but when they came to wrap it they would stamp some of it "special," and for this they would charge two cents more a pound.

The Cancer Ward (1968)

Aleksandr Solzhenitsyn

Changing technology and increased specialization in the practice of medicine have resulted in dramatic improvements in life expectancies and the quality of life in many nations, but as always something is also lost through that specialization. In the former Soviet Union and other nations that adopted systems of nationalized health care, many of the problems of specialization were made even worse, even while some of the potential benefits of medical breakthroughs were also lost. Private insurance creates some of the same problems, and some of the policies suggested here, such as having patients pay for at least some of the services they receive in initial examinations and routine levels of treatment, are now widely used in many insurance programs.

"The family doctor is the most comforting figure in our lives, but he has been cut down and foreshortened. Without him, the family cannot exist in a modern society. Just as a mother knows the tastes of each one in the family, so he knows each one's needs. It's no shame to go to the family doctor with any trivial complaint that you wouldn't take to the clinic, where you have to take a number, wait in line, and face a doctor who treats nine patients an hour. And it's from the trivial complaints that all the neglected illnesses arise. How many grown people, right now, at this very minute, are tossing about blindly, wishing they could find the kind of doctor and the kind of person to whom they could express their most deeply concealed, even shameful, fears? This search for a doctor is the kind of thing you don't always discuss even with your friends, and you certainly don't advertise for one in the newspapers; it is essentially as intimate as a search for a mate. Sometimes it's easier to find a wife than to find a doctor nowadays who is prepared to give you as much time as you need and understands you completely, all of you."

Lyudmila Afanasyevna frowned. Abstractions. While her head was crowded with symptoms, and the symptoms arranged themselves in the worst array.

"All right, but how many of these family doctors would be needed? They just can't be fitted into our system of universal, free, public health services."

"Universal and public—yes, they could. Free, no," Oreshchenkov confidently asserted.

"But the fact that it is free is our greatest achievement."

"Is it such a great achievement? What do you mean by 'free'? The doctors don't work without pay. It's just that the patient doesn't pay them, they're paid out of the public budget. The public budget comes from those same patients. Treatment isn't free, it's just depersonalized. If the cost of it were left with the patient, he'd turn the ten rubles over and over in his hands. But when he really needed help, he'd come to the doctor five times over."

"But he wouldn't be able to afford it."

"He'd say to hell with new window curtains and a second pair of shoes, what good are they if he isn't in good health? Is it better the way it is now? You'd pay anything for careful and sympathetic attention from the doctor, but everywhere there's a schedule, a quota the doctors have to meet; next! And as for those of our clinics that charge fees, the pace there is even worse. And what do patients come for? For a certificate to be absent from work, for sick leave, for certification for invalids' pensions; and the doctor's job is to catch the frauds. Doctor and patient as enemies—is that medicine? Take medicines. In the twenties all medicines were free. Do you remember?"

"Really? I guess they were. One forgets."

"Surely you can't have forgotten. Everything was free. But they had to change back to charging for medicines. Why?"

"Was it too expensive for the government?" Dontsova said with an effort, and blinked a long time.

"Not only. Mostly, it was inefficient. The patient took every medicine he could get, since it was free, and then threw out half of it. Mind you, I don't say all treatment should be paid for by the patient. But the first visit should. After a patient has been ordered to enter a hospital, where complicated apparatus is needed, it would be only right for it to be free. But even there, consider your own hospital: Why do two surgeons operate, while three stand around watching? Because salaries have been allocated for them, why worry? But if the fees came from the patients, not one patient would go to them, and your Khalmukhamedov would run off in a trice. Or Pantekhina. One way or another, Lyudochka, the doctor has to depend on the impression he makes on the patients. On his popularity. And in our setup he doesn't depend on the patients."

"Thank God he doesn't depend on all of them! On troublemakers like Paulina Zavodchikova . . ."

"He should depend on her, too."

"Oh, no! What a humiliation that would be!"

"Is it better to be dependent on the chief doctor? Why is it more honest to collect a salary from the cashier, like a bureaucrat?"

K. Principal-Agent Problems

Another type of market failure often develops when people hire or elect other people to represent them in a wide variety of situations involving economic resources, including financial payments. For example, professional actors, athletes, and other artists and entertainers often hire agents to help find work and negotiate contracts. But these agents often represent many other people, and may not work as diligently for some clients as the clients would like. By the same token, firms hire workers to do certain jobs, and then have to monitor the effort and quality of the work done by their employees. Shareholders elect members of a company's board of directors, who then appoint the top managers of the corporation. Shareholders have to try to determine whether the directors and the top executives are really trying to maximize the value of the company's stock, or are rather taking too much in salary and other payments from the company. Union members face similar concerns with the officers they elect to represent them in contract negotiations, grievance procedures, and other union business. Citizens and voters face the same issue with the political leaders they elect and the government employees hired to represent the public interest. In all of these cases, there is at least the potential for a conflict of interest, largely based on the old adage that nobody spends somebody else's money as carefully as they spend their own, or works as hard for someone else as they work for themselves.

Different kinds of financial payments and bonuses and other kinds of incentive programs can be used to try to bring the agents' interests into closer alignment with the principals' interests. For example, a substantial part of payments to corporate board members and top executives may be based on a company's level of profits or stock price, or perhaps a comparison of the firm's profits and stock performance with other companies in the same industry. In recent decades, profit-sharing programs have become an increasingly popular way to give workers in a company, especially top executives, a greater stake in a company's performance. Nevertheless, principal-agent problems continue to present serious problems in many sectors of both the economic and political arenas.

Victor Hugo described this kind of problem, in a rather surprising context, in Les Miserables. *When Monsieur Madeleine (Jean Valjean) becomes the owner of a small factory and the mayor of the city in which the factory is located, he hires an elderly woman to oversee the woman's workshop at the factory and rarely visits it himself. As Hugo put it succinctly, "The best men are often compelled to delegate their authority." The overseer is a spinster, Madame*

Victurnien, who is recommended by the curé but who unfortunately is also the "guardian of everybody's virtue," "dry, rough, sour, sharp, crabbed, almost venomous"—in a word, a "bigot."

Monsieur Madeleine gives the overseer a fund for almsgiving and aid to the work-women, and requires no accounting on how these funds are spent. Following her own interests rather than Madeleine's, the overseer uses some of the funds to follow one of the workers, Fantine, who is behaving suspiciously and has become the subject of daily gossip at the factory. Madame Victurnien follows Fantine when she visits her illegitimate daughter, Cosette, at the Thénardier's Inn in Montfermeil. Fantine is fired by the overseer, receiving a severance pay of fifty francs from the "kind" mayor, but with no future prospects for respectable employment. The mayor never sees Fantine in person—until she is dying.

Les Miserables
Victor Hugo
(1862)

In literary works, the principal-agent problem is often represented as a form of hypocrisy, either comically, as in Moliere's Tartuffe, *or tragically, as here.*

Madame Victurnien Spends Thirty Francs on Morality

When Fantine realised how she was living, she had a moment of joy. To live honestly by her own labour; what a heavenly boon! The taste for labour returned to her, in truth. She bought a mirror, delighted herself with the sight of her youth, her fine hair and her fine teeth, forgot many things, thought of nothing save Cosette and the possibilities of the future, and was almost happy. She hired a small room and furnished it on the credit of her future labour; a remnant of her habits of disorder.

Not being able to say that she was married, she took good care, as we have already intimated, not to speak of her little girl.

At first, as we have seen, she paid the Thénardiers punctually. As she only knew how to sign her name she was obliged to write through a public letter-writer.

She wrote often; that was noticed. They began to whisper in the women's workshop that Fantine "wrote letters," and that "she had airs." For prying into any human affairs, none are equal to those whom it does not concern. "Why does this gentleman never come till dusk?" "Why does Mr. So-and-so never hang his key on the nail on Thursday?" "Why does he always take the by-streets?" "Why does madame always leave her carriage before getting to the house?" "Why does she send to buy a quire of writing-paper when she has her portfolio full of it?" etc. etc. There are persons who, to solve these enigmas, which are moreover perfectly immaterial to them, spend more money, waste more time, and give themselves more trouble than would suffice for ten good deeds; and that gratuitously, and for the pleasure of it, without being paid for their curiosity in any other way than by curiosity. They will follow this man or that woman whole days, stand guard for hours at the corners of the street, under the entrance of a passage-way, at night, in the cold and in the rain, bribe messengers, get hack-drivers and lackeys drunk, fee a chambermaid, or buy a porter. For what? For nothing. Pure craving to see, to know, and to find out. Pure itching for scandal. And often these secrets made known, these mysteries published, these enigmas brought into the light of day, lead to catastrophes, to duels, to failures, to the ruin of families, and make lives wretched, to the great joy of those who have "discovered all" without any interest, and from pure instinct. A sad thing.

Some people are malicious from the mere necessity of talking. Their conversation, tattling in the drawing-room, gossip in the antechamber, is like those fireplaces that use up wood rapidly; they need a great deal of fuel; the fuel is their neighbour.

So Fantine was watched.

Beyond this, more than one was jealous of her fair hair and of her white teeth.

It was reported that in the shop, with all the rest about her, she often turned aside to wipe away a tear. Those were moments when she thought of her child; perhaps also of the man whom she had loved.

It is a mournful task to break the sombre attachments of the past.

It was ascertained that she wrote, at least twice a month, and always to the same address, and that she prepaid the postage. They succeeded in learning the address: *Monsieur, Monsieur Thénardier, inn-keeper Montfermeil.* The public letter-writer, a simple old fellow, who could not fill his stomach with red-wine without emptying his pocket of his secrets, was made to reveal this at a drinking-house. In short, it became known that Fantine had a child. "She must be that sort of woman." And there was one old gossip who went to Montfermeil, talked with the Thénardiers, and said on her return: "For my thirty-five francs, I have found out all about it. I have seen the child!"

The busybody who did this was a beldame, called Madame Victurnien, keeper and guardian of everybody's virtue. Madame Victurnien was fifty-six years old, and wore a mask of old age over her mask of ugliness. Her voice trembled, and she was capricious. It seemed strange, but this woman had been young. In her youth, in '93, she married a monk who had escaped from the cloister in a red cap, and passed from the Bernardines to the Jacobins. She was dry, rough, sour, sharp, crabbed, almost venomous; never forgetting her monk, whose widow she was, and who had ruled and curbed her harshly. She was a nettle bruised by a frock. At the restoration she became a bigot, and so energetically, that the priests had pardoned her monk episode. She had a little property, which she had bequeathed to a religious community with great flourish. She was in very good standing at the bishop's palace in Arras. This Madame Victurnien then went to Montfermeil, and returned saying: "I have seen the child."

All this took time; Fantine had been more than a year at the factory, when one morning the overseer of the workshop handed her, on behalf of the mayor, fifty francs, saying that she was no longer wanted in the shop, and enjoining her, on behalf of the mayor, to leave the city.

This was the very same month in which the Thénardiers, after having asked twelve francs instead of six, had demanded fifteen francs instead of twelve. Fantine was thunderstruck. She could not leave the city; she was in debt for her lodging and her furniture. Fifty francs were not enough to clear off that debt. She faltered out some suppliant words. The overseer gave her to understand that she must leave the shop instantly. Fantine was moreover only a moderate worker. Overwhelmed with shame even more than with despair, she left the shop, and returned to her room. Her fault then was now known to all!

She felt no strength to say a word. She was advised to see the mayor; she dared not. The mayor gave her fifty francs, because he was kind, and sent her away, because he was just. She bowed to that decree.

Success of Madame Victurnien

The monk's widow was then good for something.

Monsieur Madeleine had known nothing of all this. These are combinations of events of which life is full. It was Monsieur Madeleine's habit scarcely ever to enter the women's workshop.

He had placed at the head of this shop an old spinster whom the curé had recommended to him, and he had entire confidence in this overseer, a very respectable person, firm, just, upright, full of that charity which consists in giving, but not having to the same extent that charity which consists in understanding and pardoning. Monsieur Madeleine left everything to her. The best men are often compelled to delegate their authority. It was in the exercise of this full power, and with the conviction that she was doing right, that the overseer had framed the indictment, tried, condemned, and executed Fantine.

As to the fifty francs, she had given them from a fund that Monsieur Madeleine had entrusted her with for alms-giving and aid to work-women, and of which she rendered no account.

Fantine offered herself as a servant in the neighbourhood; she went from one house to another. Nobody wanted her. She could not leave the city. The second-hand dealer to whom she was in debt for her furniture, and such furniture! had said to her: "If you go away, I will have you arrested as a thief." The landlord, whom she owed for rent, had said to her: "You are young and pretty, you can pay." She divided the fifty francs between the landlord and the dealer, returned to the latter three-quarters of his goods, kept only what was necessary, and found herself without work, without position, having nothing but her bed, and owing still about a hundred francs.

She began to make coarse shirts for the soldiers of the garrison, and earned twelve sous a day. Her daughter cost her ten. It was at this time that she began to get behindhand with the Thénardiers.

However, an old woman, who lit her candle for her when she came home at night, taught her the art of living in misery. Behind living on a little, lies the art of living on nothing. They are two rooms; the first is obscure, the second is utterly dark.

Fantine learned how to do entirely without fire in winter, how to give up a bird that eats a farthing's worth of millet every other day, how to make a coverlid of her petticoat, and a petticoat of her coverlid, how to save her candle in taking her meals by the light of an opposite window. Few know how much certain feeble beings, who have grown old in privation and honesty, can extract from a sou. This finally becomes a talent. Fantine acquired this sublime talent and took heart a little.

During these times, she said to a neighbour: "Bah! I say to myself: by sleeping but five hours and working all the rest at my sewing, I shall always succeed in nearly earning bread. And then, when one is sad, one eats less. Well! what with sufferings, troubles, a little bread on the one hand, anxiety on the other, all that will keep me alive."

In this distress, to have had her little daughter would have been a strange happiness. She thought of having her come. But what? to make her share her privation? and then, she owed the Thénardiers? How could she pay them? and the journey; how pay for that?

The old woman, who had given her what might be called lessons in indigent life, was a pious woman, Marguerite by name, a devotee of genuine devotion, poor, and charitable to the poor, and also to the rich, knowing how to write just enough to sign *Margeritte*, and believing in God, which is science.

There are many of these virtues in low places; some day they will be on high. This life has a morrow.

At first, Fantine was so much ashamed that she did not dare to go out.

When she was in the street, she imagined that people turned behind her and pointed at her; everybody looked at her and no one greeted her; the sharp and cold disdain of the passers-by penetrated her, body and soul, like a north wind.

In small cities an unfortunate woman seems to be laid bare to the sarcasm and the curiosity of all. In Paris, at least, nobody knows you, and that obscurity is a covering. Oh! how she longed to go to Paris! impossible.

She must indeed become accustomed to disrespect as she had to poverty. Little by little she learned her part. After two or three months she shook off her shame and went out as if there were nothing in the way. "It is all one to me," said she.

She went and came, holding her head up and wearing a bitter smile, and felt that she was becoming shameless.

Madame Victurnien sometimes saw her pass her window, noticed the distress of "that creature," thanks to her "put back to her place," and congratulated herself.

L. Government Failure and the Economics of Public Choice

While there are some special cases in which market failures require government intervention, even in a competitive market economy, government is also subject to systematic kinds of failures. The most pervasive factor consists of special-interest issues, in which the benefits of a given policy are concentrated enough that a relatively small group of people or organizations will receive substantial returns and thus lobby actively for the programs; the costs, meanwhile, are so diffuse that the individual taxpayers who fund the program have too little at stake to become informed about the programs and lobby against them, or even to vote against the elected officials who support them.

These problems have been recognized for centuries, but over the past fifty years a branch of economics known as "public choice" has been developed by Nobel laureate James Buchanan, Gordon Tullock, and many others. This work is largely based on the deceptively simple approach of predicting how voters, elected officials, and government employees will act if they follow their personal interests rather than a broader notion of the general good. Many of the insights that have been developed are surprising, and sometimes disturbing and controversial. For example, the approach helps to explain why people so often choose not to vote, and why they often know little or nothing about most candidates and referendums when they do vote. The reasons are depressingly simple: voting takes time and other resources, as does learning about candidates and propositions on the ballot, while the personal benefits of voting are quite limited (unless a voter derives pleasure or fulfills a personal sense of duty by voting), because it is extremely rare for national, state, or urban elections to be decided by only one vote. Candidates recognize this, and in many cases try to position themselves to attract the "median voter"—who usually possesses a limited amount of information, based largely on media reports and commercials, about election issues—so that they will be elected. The result is that mainstream candidates resemble each other fairly closely on most issues, to the point that many voters come to feel that it makes no great difference which party or candidate wins the election, which further compounds the problem of apathetic and uninformed voters and nonvoters. Moreover, a disproportionate share of those who do vote are "single-issue" voters who have an overriding economic or personal interest in one issue.

For economists and political scientists who try to address these problems, the challenge is to design political institutions that minimize the challenges posed by special interests and to bring the interests of public officials more closely into alignment with the overall public interest.

For example, it has been suggested that electing some senators and representatives on a national rather than statewide basis might help to blunt special-interest programs that favor particular states or regions of the country. Encouraging more people to vote and educating voters to recognize special-interest problems so that they vote against such proposals or the candidates who support them may also help.

In the two literary passages below, from Henry Adams's Democracy *and Joseph Heller's* Good As Gold, *the idea that elected officials and government consultants may pursue their self-interest rather than the public interest is pervasive. More generally, Washington is seen as a place where most people are interested in power, money, and popularity—with a little sex thrown in for good measure.*

Democracy: An American Novel (1880)

Henry Adams

Initially published anonymously, Adams's novel was one of the first major literary works to suggest that the American political experiment was not always or uniquely blessed with a consistently public-spirited sense of democracy. Instead, the political process is shown to be dispiritingly similar to how business is conducted in other walks of life. In the passages below, the widow Mrs. Lee determines to give up her residence in the commercial hub of New York City in the hope that she can restore her sense of civic duty in the seat of national political power, Washington D.C. There she receives—and rejects—a proposal of marriage from Senator Ratcliffe.

For reasons which many persons thought ridiculous, Mrs. Lightfoot Lee decided to pass the winter in Washington. She was in excellent health, but she said that the climate would do her good. In New York she had troops of friends, but she suddenly became eager to see again the very small number of those who lived on the Potomac. It was only to her closest intimates that she honestly acknowledged herself to be tortured by *ennui*. Since her husband's death, five years before, she had lost her taste for New York society; she had felt no interest in the price of stocks, and very little in the men who dealt in them; she had become serious. What was it all worth, this wilderness of men and women as monotonous as the brown-stone houses they lived in? In her despair she had resorted to desperate measures. She had read philosophy in the original German, and the more she read, the more she was disheartened that so much culture should lead to nothing—nothing. After talking of Herbert Spencer for an entire evening with a very literary transcendental commission-merchant, she could not see that her time had been better employed than when in former days she had passed it in flirting with a very agreeable young stock-broker; indeed, there was an evident proof to the contrary, for the flirtation might lead to something—had, in fact, led to marriage; while the philosophy could lead to nothing, unless it were perhaps to another evening of the same kind, because transcendental philosophers are mostly elderly men, usually married, and, when engaged in business, somewhat apt to be sleepy towards evening. Nevertheless Mrs. Lee did her best to turn her study to practical use. She plunged into philanthropy, visited prisons, inspected hospitals, read the literature of pauperism and crime, saturated herself with the statistics of vice, until her mind had nearly lost sight of virtue. At last it rose in rebellion against her, and she came to the limit of her strength. This path, too, seemed to lead nowhere. She declared that she had lost the sense of duty, and that, so far as concerned her, all the paupers and criminals in New York might henceforward rise in their majesty and manage every railway on the continent. Why should she care? What was the city to her? She could find nothing in it that seemed to demand salvation. What gave peculiar sanctity to numbers? Why were a million people, who all resembled each other, any way more interesting than one person? What aspiration could she help to put into the mind of this great million-armed monster that would make it worth her love or respect? Religion? A thousand powerful churches were doing their best, and she could see no chance for a new faith of which she was to be the inspired prophet. Ambition? High popular ideals? Passion for whatever is lofty and pure? The very words irritated her. Was she not herself devoured by ambition, and was she not now eating her heart out because she could find no one object worth a sacrifice?

Was it ambition—real ambition—or was it mere restlessness that made Mrs. Lightfoot Lee so bitter against New York and Philadelphia, Baltimore and Boston, American life in general and all life in particular? What did she want? Not social position, for she herself was an eminently respectable Philadelphian by birth; her father a famous clergyman; and her husband had been equally irreproachable, a descendant of one branch of the Virginia Lees, which had drifted to New York in search of fortune, and had found it, or enough of it to keep the young man there. His widow had her own place in society which no one disputed. Though not brighter than her neighbors, the world persisted in classing her among clever women; she had wealth, or at least enough of it to give her all that money can give by way of pleasure to a sensible woman in an American city; she had her house and her carriage; she dressed well; her table was good, and her furniture was never allowed to fall behind the latest standard of decorative art. She had travelled in Europe, and after several visits, covering some years of time, had returned home, carrying in one hand, as it were, a green-gray landscape, a remarkably pleasing specimen of Corot, and in the other some bales of Persian and Syrian rugs and embroideries, Japanese bronzes and porcelain. With this she declared Europe to be exhausted, and she frankly avowed that she was American to the tips of her fingers; she neither knew nor greatly cared whether America or Europe were best to live in; she had no violent love for either, and she had no objection to abusing both; but she meant to get all that American life had to offer, good or bad, and to drink it down to the dregs, fully determined that whatever there was in it she would have, and that whatever could be made out of it she would manufacture. "I know," said she, "that America produces petroleum and pigs; I have seen both on the steamers; and I am told it produces silver and gold. There is choice enough for any woman."

Yet, as has been already said, Mrs. Lee's first experience was not a success. She soon declared that New York might represent the petroleum or the pigs, but the gold of life was not to be discovered there by her eyes. Not but that there was variety enough; a variety of people, occupations, aims, and thoughts; but that all these, after growing to a certain height, stopped short. They found nothing to hold them up. She knew, more or less intimately, a dozen men whose fortunes ranged between one million and forty millions. What did they do with their money? What could they do with it that was different from what other men did? After all, it is absurd to spend more money than is enough to satisfy all one's wants; it is vulgar to live in two houses in the same street, and to drive six horses abreast. Yet, after setting aside a certain income sufficient for all one's wants, what was to be done with the rest? To let it accumulate was to own one's failure; Mrs. Lee's great grievance was that it did accumulate, without changing or improving the quality of its owners. To spend it in charity and public works was doubtless praiseworthy, but was it wise? Mrs. Lee had read enough political economy and pauper reports to be nearly convinced that public work should be public duty, and that great benefactions do harm as well as good. And even supposing it spent on these objects, how could it do more than increase and perpetuate that same kind of human nature which was her great grievance? Her New York friends could not meet this question except by falling back upon their native commonplaces, which she recklessly trampled upon, averring that, much as she admired the genius of the famous traveller, Mr. Gulliver, she never had been able, since she became a widow, to accept the Brobdingnagian doctrine that he who made two blades of grass grow where only one grew before deserved better of mankind than the whole race of politicians. She would not find fault with the philosopher had he required that the grass should be of an improved quality; "but," she said, "I cannot honestly pretend that I should be pleased to see two New York men where I now see one; the idea is too ridiculous; more than one and a half would be fatal to me."

Then came her Boston friends, who suggested that higher education was precisely what she wanted; she should throw herself into a crusade for universities and art-schools. Mrs. Lee turned upon them with a sweet smile; "Do you know," said she, "that we have in New York already the richest university in America, and that its only trouble has always been that it can get no scholars even by paying for them?

Do you want me to go out into the streets and waylay boys? If the heathen refuse to be converted, can you give me power over the stake and the sword to compel them to come in? And suppose you can? Suppose I march all the boys in Fifth Avenue down to the university and have them all properly taught Greek and Latin, English literature, ethics, and German philosophy. What then? You do it in Boston. Now tell me honestly what comes of it. I suppose you have there a brilliant society; numbers of poets, scholars, philosophers, statesmen, all up and down Beacon Street. Your evenings must be sparkling. Your press must scintillate. How is it that we New Yorkers never hear of it? We don't go much into your society; but when we do, it doesn't seem so very much better than our own. You are just like the rest of us. You grow six inches high, and then you stop. Why will not somebody grow to be a tree and cast a shadow?"

The average member of New York society, although not unused to this contemptuous kind of treatment from his leaders, retaliated in his blind, common-sense way. "What does the woman want?" he said. "Is her head turned with the Tuileries and Marlborough House? Does she think herself made for a throne? Why does she not lecture for women's rights? Why not go on the stage? If she cannot be contented like other people, what need is there for abusing us just because she feels herself no taller than we are? What does she expect to get from her sharp tongue? What does she know, anyway?"

Mrs. Lee certainly knew very little. She had read voraciously and promiscuously one subject after another. Ruskin and Taine had danced merrily through her mind, hand in hand with Darwin and Stuart Mill, Gustave Droz and Algernon Swinburne. She had even labored over the literature of her own country. She was perhaps the only woman in New York who knew something of American history. Certainly she could not have repeated the list of Presidents in their order, but she knew that the Constitution divided the government into Executive, Legislative, and Judiciary; she was aware that the President, the Speaker, and the Chief Justice were important personages, and instinctively she wondered whether they might not solve her problem; whether they were the shade trees which she saw in her dreams.

Here, then, was the explanation of her restlessness, discontent, ambition,—call it what you will. It was the feeling of a passenger on an ocean steamer whose mind will not give him rest until he has been in the engine-room and talked with the engineer. She wanted to see with her own eyes the action of primary forces; to touch with her own hand the massive machinery of society; to measure with her own mind the capacity of the motive power. She was bent upon getting to the heart of the great American mystery of democracy and government. She cared little where her pursuit might lead her, for she put no extravagant value upon life, having already, as she said, exhausted at least two lives, and being fairly hardened to insensibility in the process. "To lose a husband and a baby," said she, "and keep one's courage and reason, one must become very hard or very soft. I am now pure steel. You may beat my heart with a trip-hammer and it will beat the trip-hammer back again."

Perhaps after exhausting the political world she might try again elsewhere; she did not pretend to say where she might then go, or what she should do; but at present she meant to see what amusement there might be in politics. Her friends asked what kind of amusement she expected to find among the illiterate swarm of ordinary people who in Washington represented constituencies so dreary that in comparison New York was a New Jerusalem, and Broad Street a grove of Academe. She replied that if Washington society were so bad as this, she should have gained all she wanted, for it would be a pleasure to return,—precisely the feeling she longed for. In her own mind, however, she frowned on the idea of seeking for men. What she wished to see, she thought, was the clash of interests, the interests of forty millions of people and a whole continent, centering at Washington; guided, restrained, controlled, or unrestrained and uncontrollable, by men of ordinary mould; the tremendous forces of government and the machinery of society, at work. What she wanted was POWER.

Perhaps the force of the engine was a little confused in her mind with that of the engineer, the power with the men who wielded it. Perhaps the human interest of politics was after all what really attracted her, and, however strongly she might deny it, the passion for exercising power, for its own sake, might dazzle and mislead a woman who had exhausted all the ordinary feminine resources. But why speculate about her motives? The stage was before her, the curtain was rising, the actors were ready to enter; she had only to go quietly on among the supernumeraries and see how the play was acted and the stage effects were produced; how the great tragedians mouthed, and the stage-manager swore.

❧

"Is there no form of pledge I can give you? no sacrifice I can make? You dislike politics. Shall I leave political life? I will do anything rather than lose you. I can probably control the appointment of Minister to England. The President would rather have me there than here. Suppose I were to abandon politics and take the English mission. Would that sacrifice not affect you? You might pass four years in London where there would be no politics, and where your social position would be the best in the world; and this would lead to the Presidency almost as surely as the other. . . ."

"Mr. Ratcliffe! I have listened to you with a great deal more patience and respect than you deserve. For one long hour I have degraded myself by discussing with you the question whether I should marry a man who by his own confession has betrayed the highest trusts that could be placed in him, who has taken money for his votes as a Senator, and who is now in public office by means of a successful fraud of his own, when in justice he should be in a State's prison. I will have no more of this.

Understand, once for all, that there is an impassable gulf between your life and mine. I do not doubt that you will make yourself President, but whatever or wherever you are, never speak to me or recognize me again!"

He glared a moment into her face with a sort of blind rage, and seemed about to say more, when she swept past him, and before he realized it, he was alone.

Good As Gold
(1979)
Joseph Heller

Heller's novel shows a Washington not fundamentally changed from the place depicted one hundred years earlier by Henry Adams, although the scale of the bureaucracy has expanded at a mind-boggling rate. Academics have also become a larger part of the scene, but they prove to be not so different from ordinary businesspeople and politicians—except that they are perhaps more naïve.

Everything in Ralph Newsome's office in Washington had a bright shine but the seat of his pants. Gold had been greeted at the elevators by a young girl with a pretty face who turned him over to a stunning woman near thirty with straight black hair and a sheer, very expensive dress that clung bewitchingly to her incredibly supple figure, who conducted him at length to Ralph's secretary, a sunny, flirtatious woman of arresting sensual warmth who won his heart instantly with her seductive cordiality and caressing handshake. Everything in view gleamed with a polished intensity that made electric lighting, on these premises, seem superfluous.

Ralph had aged hardly at all. He was tall and straight, with languid movements, freckles, and reddish-brown hair parted on the side. What Gold remembered most clearly about Ralph was that he never needed a haircut or ever looked as though he'd had one. He wore a tapered, monogrammed shirt and his trousers looked freshly pressed. He was still, somehow, the only graduate of Princeton University Gold—or anyone Gold knew—had ever met.

"I hope you had fun last night," Ralph opened innocently. "This town is just bursting with good-looking women who will do almost anything for a good time."

Gold curtly answered, "I was tired when I got in. I wanted a rest."

This was a lie. Rather, he had spent the evening roaming dismally from one public room of his hotel to another, hoping in vain that someone might recognize him and take him somewhere else to girls as lovely as any one of the three who'd just welcomed him.

"Gosh, Bruce, I'm happy to see you again," Ralph said. "It's just like old times again, isn't it?" Gold was silent. It was not at all like old times. "The President will be pleased I'm seeing you today, if he ever finds out. You sure do boggle his mind. He has a framed copy of your review of his *My Year in the White House* under the glass top of his desk in the Oval Office so he can reread it all day long during vital conversations on agriculture, housing, money, starvation, health, education, and welfare, and other matters in which he has no interest." Ralph was in earnest. "I'm told he already has a blowup of your proverb 'Nothing Succeeds as Planned' on a wall of his breakfast room right beside a quotation from Pliny. It's a daily reminder not to attempt to do too much."

Gold was guarded in his reply. "I'm glad," he said and hesitated. "There's still much about his book I don't understand."

"That's one of the things he likes best about your review. He was afraid you might see through him."

"See through him?" Gold shifted his feet uneasily.

"Well, we all knew he really didn't have much to write about his one year in the White House, especially since he was so busy writing about it. He probably wants you here as soon as you can make the necessary arrangements, although he probably doesn't want you making any yet. That much is definite."

"Working as what?" asked Gold.

"As anything you want, Bruce. You can have your choice of anything that's open that we're willing to let you have. At the moment, there's nothing."

"Ralph, you aren't really telling me anything. Realistically, how far can I go?"

"To the top," answered Ralph. "You might even start there. Sometimes we have openings at the top and none at the bottom. I think we can bypass spokesman and senior official and start you higher, unless we can't. You're much too famous to be used anonymously, although not many people know who you are. Got anything else in the works?"

"I'm doing a book for Pomoroy and Lieberman and there's a short piece on education I have in mind."

"How I envy you," Ralph murmured. Gold eyed him with hostility. "What's the book about?"

The question gripped Gold by the throat. "About people in America, Ralph, about Jewish people."

"I gather you're in favor. I would rush that one out while there's still time."

"Still time for what?"

"Still time to risk it. The article on education should help. We'll be organizing another Presidential Commission on education soon and you'll be appointed." Ralph buzzed his intercom. "Dusty, darling, bring in our file on Dr. Gold, will you?"

"Sure thing, honey." The beautiful woman gave Ralph a folder containing a pad on which was written absolutely nothing. "Here you are, sweetheart."

"Thanks, love."

"She's gorgeous," said Gold, when she left. "And Dusty is an exciting nickname."

"That's her real name. Her nickname is Sweets."

"You didn't call her Sweets."

"In a government office?" Ralph chided benevolently. "Now, let's see where we are." Ralph addressed himself to the blank pad and wrote *spokesman, source,* and *senior official.* "We considered beginning you as a press aide, but one of the first things the boys from the press would want to know would be where does someone like you come off being a press aide. Would you like to work as a secretary?"

"It's a far cry from what I had in mind," said Gold stiffly. "I can't type."

"Oh, not *that* kind of secretary," Ralph laughed. "I mean—" he groped—"what do you call it? The Cabinet. You wouldn't have to type or take shorthand. You'd have girls like Dusty and Rusty and Misty to do that for you. Would you like to be in the Cabinet?"

Gold was more than mollified. "Ralph, is that really possible?"

"I don't see why not," was Ralph's reply. "Although you might have to start as an under."

"An under?"

"An under is a little bit over a deputy and assistant, I think, but not yet an associate. Unless it's the other way around. Nobody seemed sure any more."

"Could I really begin as an undersecretary?"

"In Washington, Bruce, you rise quickly and can't fall very far. How would you like to be Secretary of Labor?"

Gold, on firmer ground now, hesitated deliberately before evincing repugnance. "I think not."

"I can't say I blame you. How about Secretary of the Interior?"

"That sounds rather dark."

"I believe they work with coal mines. Transportation?"

Gold made a face. "That smacks of labor."

"Commerce?"

"It sounds a little bit like peddling."

"You're showing excellent judgment. What about Ambassador to the U.N.?"

"Don't make me laugh."

"What do you think about Secretary of the Treasury?"

Gold pricked up his ears. "What do you think?"

"It has more tone."

"What would I have to do?"

"I think I could find out. Harris Rosenblatt would know. Most of them are very rich and seem to care about money."

"I care about money."

"But they know about it."

Gold declined with regret. "I'm not sure I'd be comfortable. I'm supposed to be something of a pacifist and a radical reformer."

"But a conservative radical reformer, Bruce," Ralph reminded.

"That's true."

"Imagine what a blessing it might be to have you in the Department of Defense."

Gold had an inspiration. "How about Secretary of Defense?"

"That's good, Bruce. Especially for a pacifist."

"But I'm only a pacifist in times of peace."

"We'll put it down." Ralph added to his list. "And then there's head of the FBI or CIA to consider."

"Would I have to carry a gun?"

Ralph didn't believe so and wrote those down too. "These are all good, Bruce. Someone with your flair for publicity could probably get your name in the newspapers almost as often as the Secretary of State."

"What about Secretary of State?" asked Gold.

"That's a thought," said Ralph.

"Wouldn't I have to know anything?"

"Absolutely not," Ralph answered, and appeared astounded that Gold even should ask. "In government, Bruce, experience doesn't count and knowledge isn't important. If there's one lesson of value to be learned from the past, Bruce, it's to grab what you want when the chance comes to get it."

Gold asked with distress, "Is that good for the world?"

"Nothing's good for the world, Bruce. I thought you knew that. You've more or less said the same in that last piece of yours. Now, Bruce," Ralph continued awkwardly, "I have to be honest. You might have to get a better wife."

"Than Belle?" Gold was elated.

"I'm sorry." Ralph was solemn. "Belle would be okay for Labor or Agriculture. But not for Secretary of State or Defense."

"Belle and I have not been close," Gold confided.

"In that case I'm happy," said Ralph. "Try someone tall this time, Bruce. You're rather short, you know. It would add to your stature if you had a tall wife."

"Wouldn't a tall wife make me look smaller?" inquired Gold.

"No," said Ralph. "You would make *her* look taller. And that would add more to your stature and make her look smaller. Andrea Conover would be perfect."

"I'm seeing her tonight. Is she tall enough?"

"Oh, easily. And her father is a dying career diplomat with tons of money and the best connections. Propose."

"Tonight?" Gold demurred with a laugh. "I haven't seen her for seven years."

"So what?" Ralph laughed back in encouragement. "You can always get a divorce. Andrea's doing a great job with the Oversight Committee on Government

Expenditures. She's the reason we can't make personal phone calls any more. You know, Bruce—" Gold rose when Ralph did—"these are really our golden years, that period when men like us are appealing to all classes of women between sixteen and sixty-five. I hope you're making the most of them. A lot of them go for your kind."

"My kind?" Whatever currents of euphoria had been coursing through Gold's veins congealed.

"Yes," said Ralph.

"What do you mean by my kind?" Gold asked Ralph.

"The kind of person you are, Bruce. Why?"

"As opposed to what other kinds, Ralph?"

"The kinds of person you aren't, Bruce. Why do you ask?"

"Oh, never mind," said Gold and then decided to take the inky plunge. "Lieberman thinks you're anti-Semitic."

Ralph was stunned. "Me?" His voice was hurt and astonished. "Bruce, I would feel just awful if I thought I ever did or said a single thing to give you that impression."

Ralph was sincere and Gold was contrite. "You haven't, Ralph. I'm sorry I brought it up."

"Thank you, Bruce." Ralph was placated, and his handsome face fairly shone with grace when he grinned. "Why, I copied your papers at Columbia. You practically put me through graduate school. It's just that I really don't feel Lieberman is an especially nice person."

"He isn't." Gold laughed. "And I've known him all my life."

The strain gone, Ralph said, "Let me take these notes to Dusty and have her type them up. We've really covered a lot of ground today, haven't we?"

Gold was not certain, but never in his lifetime had he felt more sanguine about his prospects. He glanced out the window at official Washington and caught a glimpse of heaven. Through the doorway, a view of the open office space was a soothing pastoral, with vistas of modular desks dozing tranquilly under indirect fluorescent lighting that never flickered; there were shoulder-high partitions of translucent glass, other offices across the way as imposing as Ralph's, and the dreamlike stirrings of contented people at work who were in every respect impeccable. The woman all were sunny and chic—not a single one was overweight—the men wore jackets and ties, and every trouser leg was properly creased. If there was a worm at the core in this Garden of Eden, it escaped the cynical inspection of Gold, who could find detritus and incipient decay everywhere. Gold could look through a grapefruit and tell if it was pink.

"You'll like it here, won't you?" said Ralph, reading his mind.

M. Labor Markets, Unions, and Human Capital

The labor market is where the great majority of families earn most of their income, with wages and salaries today accounting for about three-fourths of all the income earned in the United States. (The other kinds of income people receive for the resources they own are rent, interest, and profits.) People with education, training, and skills in areas that are highly marketable—in other words valued by employers because they help produce goods and services that are strongly demanded by consumers—can earn very high wages and salaries, especially if that training and ability is something few other workers have to offer (think of Michael Jordan in his prime, for example, or an executive who saves a Fortune 500 firm from impending bankruptcy, and whose name will consequently become widely known in the business world).

Literary authors have always discussed work and wages. Some have stressed the Horatio Alger ideals of hard work, study (that is, human capital), and getting ahead, as represented here not by Horatio Alger, but by Benjamin Franklin's Autobiography *and a brief passage from F. Scott Fitzgerald's* Great Gatsby.

The passages by David Sedaris, Jon Krakauer, and Sebastian Junger deal with real and fictional examples of current labor markets and workers' experiences in those markets. George Orwell's description of British coal mining in the 1930s, from The Road to Wigan Pier, *is somewhat dated due to increased mechanization and extensive safety reforms undertaken by coal companies and government regulatory agencies; but coal mining is still a hot, dirty, and dangerous occupation, compared to most jobs. Percy Bysshe Shelly's short poem, "Song to the Men of England," reflects the Marxian idea that value is created not by the market forces of supply and demand, but by the amount of labor that goes into a product, with no allowances made for payments to the "embodied labor" of capital resources, interest payments for financial capital, or payments to entrepreneurs for risk-taking.*

The last two readings, from John Steinbeck's In Dubious Battle *and Erskine Caldwell's* God's Little Acre, *exemplify a common theme in American literature from 1890 through the 1930s: the labor union strike. These decades were a tumultuous—and therefore highly dramatic—period in U.S. labor history, featuring court injunctions against union organizers, "yellow dog" contracts, and violent clashes between workers, detective agencies, and the police. Stability came with federal legislation passed in the 1930s, especially the Wagner Act of 1935. From that point on, to be recognized as the bargaining agent for a group of workers, unions had to win an election, not a strike, and the National Labor Relations Board took on the task of conducting the election and limiting what both unions and firms could do in presenting their cases to workers. This institutional change calmed things down considerably, although there was a rash of strikes immediately after World War II, when wage and price controls and restrictions on strikes that had been imposed during the war were lifted. Since the 1950s strike activity has fallen sharply, with more work time lost to coffee breaks than strikes, and more than 90 percent of labor contracts renegotiated without a strike or lockout. With the continuing decline in the percentage of the labor force represented by unions, and firms since the 1980s turning more often to the practice of hiring permanent replacement workers during strikes, union-initiated work stoppages have become increasingly rare. The most publicized examples over the past decade have usually featured public-sector unions, such as teachers' unions, and occasionally unions for professional athletes.*

AUTOBIOGRAPHY
Benjamin Franklin
(1791)

Franklin and John Adams deferred to Thomas Jefferson as the better (and better-placed) writer of the Declaration of Independence. But in other genres Franklin's writing was the best of the colonial period. His abilities are most famously demonstrated in the Poor Richard's Almanacs *and his* Autobiography, *which was first published in French shortly after his death. The personal and social value of ambition, character, education, curiosity, wit, and dedication to one's work are Franklin's primary themes in this early statement and example of the American dream come true. Remarkably, the* Autobiography *was an immediate (and enduring) success, despite the fact that it ends before the last decades of Franklin's life, when he was involved in many of the projects for which he is now most renowned.*

My elder brothers were all put apprentices to different trades. I was put to the grammar-school at eight years of age, my father intending to devote me, as the tithe of his sons, to the service of the Church. My early readiness in learning to read (which must have been very early, as I do not remember when I could not read), and the opinion of all his friends, that I should certainly make a good scholar, encouraged him in this purpose of his. My uncle Benjamin, too, approved of it, and proposed to give me all his short-hand volumes of sermons, I suppose as a stock to set up with, if I would learn his character. I continued, however, at the grammar-school not quite one year, though in that time I had risen gradually from the middle of the class of that year to be the head of it, and farther was removed into the next class above it, in order to go with that into the third at the end of the year. But my father, in the meantime, from a view of the expense of a college education, which having so large a family he could not well afford, and the mean living many so educated were afterwards able to obtain,—reasons that he gave to his friends in my hearing,—altered his first intention, took me from the grammar-school, and sent me to a school for writing and arithmetic, kept by a then famous man, Mr. George Brownell, very successful in his profession generally, and that by mild, encouraging methods. Under him I acquired fair writing pretty soon, but I failed in the arithmetic, and made no progress in it. At ten years old I was taken home to assist my father in his business, which was that of a tallow-chandler and sope-boiler; a business he was not bred to, but had assumed on his arrival in New England, and on finding his dying trade would not maintain his family, being in little request. Accordingly, I was employed in cutting wick for the candles, filling the dipping mold and the molds for cast candles, attending the shop, going on errands, etc.

I disliked the trade, and had a strong inclination for the sea, but my father declared against it; however, living near the water, I was much in and about it, learnt early to swim well, and to manage boats; and when in a boat or canoe with other boys, I was commonly allowed to govern, especially in any case of difficulty; and upon other occasions I was generally a leader among the boys, and sometimes led them into scrapes, of which I will mention one instance, as it shows an early projecting public spirit, tho' not then justly conducted.

There was a salt-marsh that bounded part of the mill-pond, on the edge of which, at high water, we used to stand to fish for minnows. By much trampling, we had made it a mere quagmire. My proposal was to build a wharf there fit for us to stand upon, and I showed my comrades a large heap of stones, which were intended for a new house near the marsh, and which would very well suit our purpose. Accordingly, in the evening, when the workmen were gone, I assembled a number of my play-fellows, and working with them diligently like so many emmets, sometimes two or three to a stone, we brought them all away and built our little wharf. The next morning the workmen were surprised at missing the stones, which were found in our wharf. Inquiry was made after the removers; we were discovered and complained of; several of us were corrected by our fathers; and, though I pleaded the usefulness of the work, mine convinced me that nothing was useful which was not honest.

I think you may like to know something of his person or character. He had an excellent constitution of body, was a middle stature, but well set, and very strong; he was ingenious, could draw prettily, was skilled a little in music, and had a clear, pleasing voice, so that when he played psalm tunes on his violin and sung withal, as he sometimes did in an evening after the business of the day was over, it was extremely agreeable to hear. He had a mechanical genius too, and, on occasion, was very handy in the use of other tradesmen's tools; but his great excellence lay in a sound understanding and solid judgment in prudential matters, both in private and publick affairs. In the latter, indeed, he was never employed, the numerous family he had to educate and the straitness of his circumstances keeping him close to his trade; but I remember well his being frequently visited by leading people, who consulted him for his opinion in affairs of the town or of the church he belonged to, and showed a good deal of respect for his judgment and advice: he was also much consulted by private persons about their affairs when any difficulty occurred, and frequently chosen an arbitrator between contending parties. At his table he liked to have, as often as he could, some sensible friend or neighbor to converse with, and always took care to start some ingenious or useful topic for discourse, which might tend to improve the minds of his children. By this means he turned our attention to what was good, just, and prudent in the conduct of life, and little or no notice was ever taken of what related to the victuals on the table, whether it was well or ill dressed, in or out of season, of good or bad flavor, preferable or inferior to this or that other thing of the kind, so that I was bro't up in such a perfect inattention to those matters as to be quite indifferent what kind of food was set before me, and so unobservant of it that to this day if I am asked I can scarcely tell a few hours after dinner what I dined upon. This has been a convenience to me in traveling, where my companions have been sometimes very unhappy for want of a suitable gratification of their more delicate, because better instructed, tastes and appetites.

My mother had likewise an excellent constitution: she suckled all her ten children. I never knew either my father or mother to have any sickness but that of which they dy'd, he at eighty-nine, and she at eighty-five years of age. They lie buried together at Boston, where I some years since placed a marble over their grave. . . .

❧

To return: I continued thus employed in my father's business for two years, that is, till I was twelve years old; and my brother John, who was bred to that business, having left my father, married, and set up for himself at Rhode Island, there was all appearance that I was destined to supply his place, and become a tallow-chandler. But my dislike to the trade continuing, my father was under apprehensions that if he did not find one for me more agreeable, I should break away and get to sea, as his son Josiah had done, to his great vexation. He therefore sometimes took me to walk with him, and see joiners, bricklayers, turners, braziers, etc., at their work, that he might observe my inclination and endeavour to fix it on some trade or other on land. It has ever since been a pleasure to me to see good workmen handle their tools; and it has been useful to me, having learnt so much by it as to be able to do little jobs myself in my house when a workman could not readily be got, and to construct little machines for my experiments, while the intention of making the experiment was fresh and warm in my mind. My father at last fixed upon the cutler's trade, and my uncle Benjamin's son Samuel, who was bred to that business in London, being about that time established in Boston, I was sent to be with him some time on liking. But his expectations of a fee with me displeasing my father, I was taken home again.

From a child I was fond of reading, and all the money that came into my hands was ever laid out in books. Pleased with the *Pilgrim's Progress*, my first collection was of John Bunyan's works in separate little volumes. I afterward sold them to enable me to buy R. Burton's *Historical Collections*; they were small chapmen's books, and cheap, forty or fifty in all. My father's little library consisted chiefly of books in polemic divinity, most of which I read, and have since often regretted that, at a time when I had such a thirst for knowledge, more proper books had not fallen in my way, since it was now resolved I should not be a clergyman. Plutarch's *Lives* there was in which I read abundantly, and I still think that time spent to great advantage. There was also a book of De Foe's, called an *Essay on Projects*, and another of Dr. Mather's called *Essays to do Good*, which perhaps gave me a turn of thinking that had an influence on some of the principal future events of my life.

This bookish inclination at length determined my father to make me a printer, though he had already one son (James) of that profession. In 1717 my brother James returned from England with a press and letters to set up his business in Boston. I liked it much better than that of my father, but still had a hankering for the sea. To prevent the apprehended effect of such an inclination, my father was impatient to have me bound to my brother. I stood out some time, but at last was persuaded, and signed the indentures when I was yet but twelve years old. I was to serve as an apprentice till I was twenty-one years of age, only I was to be allowed journeyman's wages during the last year. In a little time I made great proficiency in the business, and became a useful hand to my brother. I now had access to better books. An acquaintance with the apprentices of booksellers enabled me sometimes to borrow a small one, which I was careful to return soon and clean. Often I sat up in my room reading the greatest part of the night, when the book was borrowed in the evening and to be returned early in the morning, lest it should be missed or wanted.

And after some time an ingenious tradesman, Mr. Matthew Adams, who had a pretty collection of books, and who frequented our printing-house, took notice of me, invited me to his library, and very kindly lent me such books as I chose to read. I now took a fancy to poetry, and made some little pieces; my brother, thinking it might turn to account, encouraged me, and put me on composing occasional ballads. One was called *The Lighthouse Tragedy*, and contained an account of the drowning of Captain Worthilake, with his two daughters; the other was a sailor's song, on the taking of *Teach* (or Blackbeard) the pirate. They were wretched stuff, in the Grub-street-ballad style; and when they were printed he sent me about the town to sell them. The first sold wonderfully; the event, being recent, having made a great noise. This flattered my vanity; but my father discouraged me by ridiculing my performances, and telling me verse-makers were generally beggars. So I escaped being a poet, most probably a very bad one; but as prose writing has been of great use to me in the course of my life, and was a principal means of my advancement, I shall tell you how, in such a situation, I acquired what little ability I have in that way.

There was another bookish lad in the town, John Collins by name, with whom I was intimately acquainted. We sometimes disputed, and very fond we were of argument, and very desirous of confuting one another, which disputatious turn, by the way, is apt to become a very bad habit, making people often extremely disagreeable in company by the contradiction that is necessary to bring it into practice; and thence, besides souring and spoiling the conversation, is productive of disgusts and, perhaps, enmities where you may have occasion for friendship. I had caught it by reading my father's books of dispute about religion. Persons of good sense, I have since observed, seldom fall into it, except lawyers, university men, and men of all sorts that have been bred at Edinborough.

A question was once, somehow or other, started between Collins and me, of the propriety of educating the female sex in learning, and their abilities for study. He was of opinion that it was improper, and that they were naturally unequal to it. I took the contrary side, perhaps a little for dispute's sake. He was naturally more eloquent, had a ready plenty of words, and sometimes, as I thought, bore me down more by his fluency than by the strength of his reasons. As we parted without settling the point, and were not to see one another again for some time, I sat down to put my arguments in writing which I copied fair and sent to him. He answered, and I replied. Three of four letters of a side had passed, when my father happened to find my papers and read them. Without entering into the discussion, he took occasion to talk to me about the manner of my writing; observed that, though I had the advantage of my antagonist in correct spelling and pointing (which I ow'd to the printing-house), I fell far short in elegance of expression, in method and in perspicuity, of which he convinced me by several instances. I saw the justice of his remarks, and thence grew more attentive to the manner in writing, and determined to endeavor at improvement.

About this time I met with an odd volume of the *Spectator*. It was the third. I had never before seen any of them. I bought it, read it over and over, and was much delighted with it. I thought the writing excellent, and wished, if possible, to imitate it. With this view I took some of the papers, and, making short hints of the sentiment in each sentence, laid them by a few days, and then, without looking at the book, try'd to compleat the papers again, by expressing each hinted sentiment at length, and as fully as it had been expressed before, in any suitable words that should come to hand. Then I compared my *Spectator* with the original, discovered some of my faults, and corrected them. But I found I wanted a stock of words, or a readiness in recollecting and using them, which I thought I should have acquired before that time if I had gone on making verses; since the continual occasion for words of the same import, but of different length, to suit the measure, or of different sound for the rhyme, would have laid me under a constant necessity of searching for variety, and also have tended to fix that variety in my mind, and make me master of it. Therefore I took some of the tales and turned them into verse.

The Great Gatsby
(1925)
F. Scott Fitzgerald

After Gatsby is killed Fitzgerald introduces his family from the West to show that Gatsby had pursued the American dream from his youth through school and the military only to lose it by being "subtly unadaptable to Eastern life." Gatsby came close enough to his dreams of love (and the wealth he learned Daisy demanded) to believe he could not fail to grasp them, not realizing that they were already lost. Still, although Gatsby dies in disgrace, because of his dreams he is, as the narrator says, the only character in this story who seems partially redeemed.

"Look here, this is a book he had when he was a boy. It just shows you."

He opened it at the back cover and turned it around for me to see. On the last fly-leaf was printed the word SCHEDULE, and the date September 12, 1906. And underneath:

Rise from bed .... *6:00* A.M.

Dumbbell exercise and wall-scaling .... *6:15-6:30* "

Study electricity, etc. .... *7:15-8:15* "

Work .... *8:30-4:30* P.M.

Baseball and sports .... *4:30-5:00* "

Practice elocution, poise and how to attain it . *5:00-6:00* "

Study needed inventions .... *7:00-9:00* "

GENERAL RESOLVES

No wasting time at Shafters or [a name, indecipherable]

No more smoking or chewing.

Bath every other day

Read one improving book or magazine per week

Save $5.00 [crossed out] *$3.00 per week*

Be better to parents

"I come across this book by accident," said the old man. "It just shows you, don't it?"

"It just shows you."

"Jimmy was bound to get ahead. He always had some resolves like this or something. Do you notice what he's got about improving his mind? He was always great for that. He told me I et like a hog once, and I beat him for it."

He was reluctant to close the book, reading each item aloud and then looking eagerly at me. I think he rather expected me to copy down the list for my own use.

A little before three the Lutheran minister arrived from Flushing, and I began to look involuntarily out the windows for other cars. So did Gatsby's father. And as the time passed and the servants came in and stood waiting in the hall, his eyes began to blink anxiously, and he spoke of the rain in a worried, uncertain way. The minister glanced several times at his watch, so I took him aside and asked him to wait for half an hour. But it wasn't any use. Nobody came.

Something For Everyone (1997)

David Sedaris

Many people who fail in the workplace fail because of self-inflicted wounds. Drug use, laziness, unreliability, limited ambition, poor self-confidence, failure to develop marketable skills, and more generally a failure to understand or develop any close or permanent attachment to employment and the labor force—all of these factors play a role in that failure. These attributes are the opposite of those depicted in the previous passages from Franklin and Fitzgerald, but as Sedaris shows, they too have their literary uses.

The day after graduating from college, I found fifty dollars in the foyer of my Chicago apartment building. The single bill had been folded into eighths and was packed with cocaine. It occurred to me then that if I played my cards right, I might never have to find a job. People lost things all the time. They left class rings on the sinks of public bathrooms and dropped gem-studded earrings at the doors of the opera house. My job was to keep my eyes open and find these things. I didn't want to become one of those coots who combed the beaches of Lake Michigan with a metal detector, but if I paid attention and used my head, I might never have to work again.

The following afternoon, hung over from cocaine, I found twelve cents and an unopened tin of breath mints. Figuring in my previous fifty dollars, that amounted to an average of twenty-five dollars and six cents per day, which was still a decent wage.

The next morning I discovered two pennies and a comb matted with short curly hairs. The day after that I found a peanut. It was then that I started to worry.

I have known people who can quit one job and find another in less time than it takes to quarter a fryer. Regardless of their experience, these people exude charm and confidence. The charm is something they were either born with or had beaten into them at an early age, but what gives them their confidence is the knowledge that someone like me has also filed an application. Mine is a history of almosts. I can type, but only with one finger, and have never touched a computer except to clean it. I never learned to drive, which eliminates delivery work and narrows my prospects to jobs located on or near the bus line. I can sort of hammer things together but have an ingrained fear of electric saws, riding lawn mowers, and any motorized equipment louder or more violent than a vacuum cleaner. Yes, I have experience in sales, but it is limited to marijuana, a product that sells itself. I lack the size and bulk to be a guard, and the aggression necessary for store detectives, crossing guards, and elementary schoolteachers. Years ago I had waited on tables, but it was the sort of restaurant where customers considered the phrase "Have a good day" to be an acceptable tip. On more than one occasion I had found it necessary to physically scrape the cook off the floor and scramble the eggs myself, but this hardly qualified me as a chef.

It wouldn't have worked to include the job on my resume and list it as a reference, as the manager never answered the telephone, fearful that it might be someone phoning in a take-out order. The waiters in Chicago tended to apply with a modeling portfolio in one hand and a gym bag in the other, and it seemed useless to compete. If my shirt was pressed, it was more or less guaranteed that my fly was down.

When luck was with me I tended to stumble into jobs, none of which were the type to hand out tax statements at the end of the year. People gave me money and I spent it. As a result, I seemed to have fallen through some sort of crack. You needed certain things to secure a real job, and the longer you went without them, the harder it was to convince people of your worth. Why *can't* you work a cash register or operate a forklift? How is it you've reached the age of thirty and still have no verifiable employment record? Why are you sweating so, and what force compels you to obsessively activate your cigarette lighter throughout the course of this interview?

These questions were never spoken but rather were implied every time a manager turned my application face down on his desk.

I leafed through the Art Institute's outdated employment notebook, and page by page it mocked my newly acquired diploma. Most of the listings called for someone who could paint a mural or enamel a map of Normandy onto a medallion the size of a quarter. I had no business applying for any of these jobs or even attending the Art Institute in the first place, but that's the beauty of an art school: as long as you can pay the tuition, they will never, even in the gentlest way, suggest that you have no talent. I was ready to pack it in when I came across the number of a woman who wanted her apartment painted. Bingo. I had plenty of experience there. If anything, I was considered too meticulous a painter. As long as she supplied the ladder and I could carry the paint on the bus, I figured I was set.

The woman began by telling me she had always painted the apartment herself. "But I'm old now. It hurts my hands to massage my husband's feet, let alone lift a heavy brush over my head. Yes, sir, I'm old. Withered and weak as a kitten. I'm an old, old woman." She spoke as if this were something that had come upon her with no prior notice. "All the sudden my back gives out, I'm short of breath, and some days I can't see more than two feet in front of my face."

This was sounding better all the time. I'd learned to be wary of people forced to pay others for a job they used to do themselves. As a rule they tended to be hypercritical, but with her, I didn't think there would be any problem. It sounded as if she couldn't see anything well enough to complain about it. I could probably just open the paint can, broadcast the fumes, and call it a day. We made arrangements for me to visit her home the following morning, and I hung up the phone cheering.

The apartment was located in a high-rise building on Lake Shore Drive. I knocked and the door was answered by a trim, energetic woman holding a tennis racket. Her hair was white, but except for a few spidery lines beneath her eyes, her face was smooth and unwrinkled. I asked to speak to her mother, and she chuckled, poking me in the ribs with the handle of her racket.

"Oh, I am just so happy to see a young person." She grabbed my hand. "Look what we've got here, Abe: a young fella. Why, he's practically a toddler!"

Her husband bounded into the room. Muscular and tanned, he wore a nylon fitness suit complete with a headband and sparkling sneakers. "Ahh, a youngster!"

"He's a graduate," the woman said, squatting to perform a knee bend. "A kid, thinks he's ready to paint our sarcophagus. He's looking at us thinking he's discovered a pair of fossils he can maybe sell to the museum. Oh, we're old all right. Out to pasture. Long in the tooth."

"Built the great Pyramids with my own two hands," the husband added. "Used to swap ideas with Plato and ride a chariot through the cobbled streets of Rome."

"Face it, baby," his wife said. "We're ancient. A couple of has-beens."

"Oh, no," I said. "You're not old. Why, neither one of you looks a day over fifty. Look at you, so trim and fit, you're in much better shape than I am. I'm sure you've got plenty of time left."

"Yeah, right." The woman hopped onto an exercycle. "Time to forget our own names, time to lose control of our bowels, time to stoop and blather and drool onto our bibs. We've got all the time in the world. Days were when I'd throw on a rucksack and head out for a good two-, three-week hike, but now, forget it. I'm too old."

"She's older than the hills she used to climb," her husband said.

"Oh, look who's talking, Father Time himself."

"I'm an old geezer and I'll admit it," the man said. "Still, though, I'm what you call an 'up person'."

"That's right," she cackled. "Washed up and used up!"

I understood then that this was their act: the Squabbling Old Folks, appearing interminably.

"I guess if you're going to be painting the place, I might as well scrape these tired old bones together and give you a tour," the woman said. She guided me through their home, where every room was furnished with a piece of exercise equipment. A NordicTrack stood parked beside a rowing machine, both facing the living-room television. In the bedroom they kept a set of barbells and colorful mats upon which to practice aerobics. Swimsuits hung drip-drying in the bathroom, and athletic shoes neatly lined the floors of every closet. Except for a few smudges near the guest-room punching bag, the walls were spotless. The doors and baseboards were in fine shape, not a chip or scratch on them. They led me beneath the chin-up bar and into the study, which was decorated floor to ceiling with photographs documenting their various adventures. Here they were riding a tandem bicycle through the streets of Peking or trading beads in a dusty Peruvian marketplace. The pictures spanned the course of forty years spent kneeling in kayaks and pitching tents on the peaks of snow-covered mountains, hiking muddy trails and taking the waters of frigid streams.

"Look what we've got here," the woman said. "There's old Methuselah staggering up Mount Rainier. First one to make it all the way to the top with a walker."

"And here's the missus in Egypt," her husband said, pointing to a framed photograph of a mummy.

I tried to turn the subject back to painting, but they wouldn't hear of it.

"Stay for lunch, why don't you," the woman said. "I'll just hook Old Crusty up to his feeding tubes and throw us together a couple of sandwiches."

"A sandwich!" the man cried. "How are you planning to manage the bread? Those chops of yours can't take on anything harder than applesauce."

"Well, I can still chew *you* out," she said. "And they don't come any harder than that."

I drew up an estimate and phoned the next day, knowing in my heart that it was a waste of time.

"It's our young person," I heard her yell to her husband in the background. "Listen, doll, it seems we've decided not to have the place painted after all. Not much point in it, seeing as we'll probably be packed off to the nursing home before you get your ladder set up."

It was my role to contradict her. Instead, I said, "You're probably right. As feebleminded as you are, I guess it's about time to make plans for a structured environment."

"Hey now," she snapped. "No need to get ugly."

During episodes of unemployment I find it rewarding to sleep as much as possible—anywhere from twelve to fourteen hours a day is a good starting point. Sleep spares you humiliation and saves money at the same time: nothing to eat, nothing to buy, just lie back and dream your life away. I'd wake up in the afternoon, watch my stories on TV, and then head over to the sofa for a few more hours of shut-eye. It became my habit to pick up a newspaper just after five o'clock and spend some time searching the want ads, wondering who might qualify for any of the advertised positions: vault verifier, pre-press salesman, audit technical reviewer. Show me the child who dreams of being a sausage-casing inspector. What sort of person is going to raise his clenched fist in victory after reading "New Concept=Big $! High energy=Return + Comm. Fax résumé." Fax résumé for what?

I called responding to a quadriplegic looking for a part-time aide. He answered on the fifteenth ring shouting, "For the love of God, Mother, can't a man have five minutes of privacy?"

At the supermarket I dropped a five-dollar bill and turned around just in time to watch someone stuff it in his pocket. My luck was reversing itself.

"Why the hell don't you go back to school and take some *real* classes?" my father said. "Learn to program computers, that's what the Stravides boy did. He'd gone to college and studied show tunes or folklore, some damned thing—went back to school for programming and now he's heading up the shipping department over at Flexy-Wygaart, whole damned department! Computers, that's where the action is!"

Aside from the fact I had no interest in computers, it seemed a betrayal to graduate from one school only to enter another. That would be admitting I'd borrowed ten thousand dollars and learned absolutely nothing of value, and I was not ready to face that fact.

INTO THIN AIR
(1997)
Jon Krakauer

Labor markets develop even in exotic locales and for exotic occupations. The guides and support crews that accompany expeditions up Mt. Everest are one example. The jobs pay very well—compared to other jobs in the area—because the skill requirements are demanding and the risks high, but there is stiff competition for the limited number of jobs that are available. Some observers have questioned whether the Sherpas and the society in which they live are really better off because of these jobs. Krakauer takes the standard point of view in economics that such evaluations are best made by the individuals who voluntarily accept the risks associated with these jobs.

For better and worse, over the past two decades the economy and culture of the Khumbu has become increasingly and irrevocably tied to the seasonal influx of trekkers and climbers, some 15,000 of whom visit the region annually. Sherpas who learn technical climbing skills and work high on the peaks—especially those who have summitted Everest—enjoy great esteem in their communities. Those who become climbing stars, alas, also stand a fair chance of losing their lives: ever since 1922, when seven Sherpas were killed in an avalanche during the second British expedition, a disproportionate number of Sherpas have died on Everest—fifty-three all told. Indeed, they account for more than a third of all Everest fatalities.

Despite the hazards, there is stiff competition among Sherpas for the twelve to eighteen staff positions on the typical Everest expedition. The most sought-after jobs are the half dozen openings for skilled climbing Sherpas, who can expect to earn $1,400 to $2,500 for two months of hazardous work—attractive pay in a nation mired in grinding poverty and with an annual per capita income of around $160.

To handle the growing traffic from Western climbers and trekkers, new lodges and teahouses are springing up across the Khumbu region, but the new construction is especially evident in Namche Bazaar. On the trail to Namche I passed countless porters headed up from the lowland forests, carrying freshly cut wood beams that weighed in excess of one hundred pounds—crushing physical toil, for which they were paid about three dollars a day.

Longtime visitors to the Khumbu are saddened by the boom in tourism and the change it has wrought on what early Western climbers regarded as an earthly paradise, a real-life Shangri-La. Entire valleys have been denuded of trees to meet the increased demand for firewood. Teens hanging out in Namche *carrom* parlors are more likely to be wearing jeans and Chicago Bulls T-shirts than quaint traditional robes. Families are apt to spend their evenings huddled around video players viewing the latest Schwarzenegger opus.

The transformation of the Khumbu culture is certainly not all for the best, but I didn't hear many Sherpas bemoaning the changes. Hard currency from trekkers and climbers, as well as grants from international relief organizations supported by trekkers and climbers, have funded schools and medical clinics, reduced infant mortality, built footbridges, and brought hydroelectric power to Namche and other villages. It seems more than a little patronizing for Westerners to lament the loss of the good old days when life in the Khumbu was so much simpler and more picturesque. Most of the people who live in this rugged country seem to have no desire to be severed from the modern world or the untidy flow of human progress. The last thing Sherpas want is to be preserved as specimens in an anthropological museum.

The Perfect Storm (1997)

Sebastian Junger

Jobs with high degrees of financial and physical risk are also found in the United States and other industrialized nations. Those risks result in higher wages and more fringe benefits compared to the wages and benefits associated with other jobs open to people with similar levels of education, training, and experience. In the passage below, Junger offers a summary of the wage structure on commercial fishing boats, which in some ways is reminiscent of how prize money was divided among crews in the British (and other) navies well into the nineteenth century. Patrick O'Brian briefly describes that system in one of the volumes of his Aubrey/Maturin series.

They'd been at sea a month and taken fifteen tons of swordfish. Prices fluctuate so wildly, though, that a sword boat crew often has no idea how well they've done until after the fish have been sold. And even then there's room for error: boat owners have been known to negotiate a lower price with the buyer and then recover part of their loss in secret. That way they don't share the entire profit with their crew. Be that as it may, the *Andrea Gail* sold her catch to O'Hara Seafoods for $136,812, plus another $4,770 for a small amount of tuna. Bob Brown, the owner, first took out for fuel, fishing tackle, bait, a new mainline, wharfage, ice, and a hundred other odds and ends that added up to over $35,000. That was deducted from the gross, and Brown took home half of what was left: roughly $53,000. The collected crew expenses—food, gloves, shore help—were paid on credit and then deducted from the other $53,000, and the remainder was divided up among the crew: Almost $20,000 to Captain Billy Tyne, $6,453 to Pierre and Murphy, $5,495 to Moran, and $4,537 each to Shatford and Kosco. The shares were calculated by seniority and if Shatford and Kosco didn't like it, they were free to find another boat.

The week on shore started hard. That first night, before the fish had even been looked at, Brown cut each crew member a check for two hundred dollars, and by dawn it was all pretty much spent. Bobby crawled into bed with Chris around one or two in the morning and crawled out again four hours later to help take out the catch. His younger brother Brian—built like a lumberjack and filled with one desire, to fish like his brothers—showed up to help, along with another brother, Rusty. Bob Brown was there, and even some of the women showed up. The fish were hoisted out of the hold, swung up onto the dock, and then wheeled into the chill recesses of Rose's. Next they hauled twenty tons of ice out of the hold, scrubbed the decks, and stowed the gear away. It was an eight- or nine-hour day. At the end of the afternoon Brown showed up with checks for half the money they were owed—the rest would be paid after the dealer had actually sold the fish—and the crew went across the street to a bar called Pratty's. The partying, if possible, reached heights not attained the night before. "Most of them are single kids with no better thing to do than spend a lot of dough," says Charlie Reed, former captain of the boat. "They're highrollers for a couple of days. Then they go back out to sea."

High-rollers or not, the crew is still supposed to show up at the dock every morning for work. Inevitably, something has broken on the trip—a line gets wound around the drive shaft and must be dove on, the antennas get snapped off, the radios go dead. Depending on the problem, it can take anywhere from an afternoon to several days to fix. Then the engine has to be overhauled: change the belts and filters, check the oil, fill the hydraulics, clean the injectors, clean the plugs, test the generators. Finally, there's the endless task of maintaining the deck gear. Blocks have to be greased, ropes have to be spliced, chains and cables have to be replaced, rust spots have to be ground down and painted. One ill-kept piece of gear can kill a man. Charlie Reed saw a hoisting block fall on someone and shear his arm right off; another crew member had forgotten to tighten a shackle.

Murph and Sully drive to the Cape Ann Market out on Route 127 and begin stalking up and down the aisles throwing food into their carts by the armful. They grab fifty loaves of bread, enough to fill two carts. They take a hundred pounds of potatoes, thirty pounds of onions, twenty-five gallons of milk, eighty-dollar racks of steak. Every time they fill a cart they push it to the back of the store and get another one. The herd of carts starts to grow—ten, fifteen, twenty carts—and people stare nervously and get out of the way. Murph and Sully grab anything they want and lots of it: ice cream sandwiches, Hostess cupcakes, bacon and eggs, creamy peanut butter, porterhouse steaks, chocolate-coated cereal, spaghetti, lasagna, frozen pizza. They get top-of-the-line food and the only thing they don't get is fish. Finally they get thirty cartons of cigarettes—enough to fill a whole cart—and round their carts up like so many stainless steel cattle. The store opens two cash registers especially for them, and it takes half an hour to ring them through. The total nearly cleans Sully out; he pays while Murph backs the truck up to a loading dock, and they heave the food on and then drive it down to Rose's wharf. Bag by bag, they carry four thousand dollars' worth of groceries down into the fish hold of the *Andrea Gail.*

A few modern swordfishing boats still fish Georges Bank, but most make the long trip to the Grand. They're out for longer but come back with more fish—the old trade-off. It takes a week to reach the Grand Banks on a modern sword boat. You drive east-northeast around the clock until you're twelve hundred miles out of Gloucester and four hundred miles out of Newfoundland. From there it's easier to get to the Azores than back to the Crow's Nest. Like Georges, the Grand Banks are shallow enough to allow sunlight to penetrate all the way to the bottom. An infusion of cold water called the Labrador Current crosses the shoals and creates the perfect environment for plankton; small fish collect to feed on the plankton, and big fish collect to feed on the small fish. Soon the whole food chain's there, right up to the seventy-foot sword boats.

The trips in and out are basically the parts of the month that swordfishermen sleep. In port they're too busy cramming as much life as they can into five or six days, and on the fishing grounds they're too busy working. They work twenty hours a day for two or three weeks straight and then fall into their bunks for the long steam back. The trips entail more than just eating and sleeping, though. Fishing gear, like deck gear, takes a terrific amount of abuse and must be repaired constantly. The crew doesn't want to waste a day's fishing because their gear's messed up, so they tend to it on the way out: they sharpen hooks, tie gangions, tie ball drops, set up the leader cart, check the radio buoys. At the Hague Line—where they enter Canadian waters—they must stow the gear in accordance with international law, and are briefly without anything to do. They sleep, talk, watch T.V., and read; there are high school dropouts who go through half a dozen books on the Grand Banks.

Around eight or nine at night the crew squeeze into the galley and shovel down whatever the cook has put together. (Murph is the cook on the *Andrea Gail;* he's paid extra and stands watch while the other men eat.) At dinner the crew talk about what men everywhere talk about—women, lack of women, kids, sports, horseracing, money, lack of money, work. They talk a lot about work; they talk about it the way men in prison talk about time. Work is what's keeping them from going home, and they all want to go home. The more fish they catch, the sooner the trip's over, which is a simple equation that turns them all into amateur marine biologists. After dinner someone takes his turn at the dishes, and Billy goes back up to the wheelhouse so Murph can eat. No one likes washing dishes, so guys sometimes trade the duty for a pack of cigarettes. The longer the trip, the cheaper labor gets, until a $50,000-a-year fisherman is washing dishes for a single smoke. Dinner, at the end of such a trip, might be a bowl of croutons with salad dressing.

Everyone on the crew stands watch twice a day. The shifts are two hours long and involve little more than watching the radar and occasionally punching numbers into the autopilot. If the gear is out, the night watches might have to jog back onto the mainline to keep from drifting too far away. The *Andrea Gail* has a padded chair in her wheelhouse, but it's set back from the helm so that no one can fall asleep on watch. The radar and loran are bolted to the ceiling, along with the VHF and single sideband, and the video plotter and autopilot are on the control panel to the left. There are nine Lexan windows and a pistol-grip spotlight that protrudes from the ceiling. The wheel is the size of a bicycle tire and positioned at the very center of the helm, about waist high. There's no reason to touch the wheel unless the boat has been taken off autopilot, and there's almost no reason to take the boat off autopilot. From time to time the helmsman checks the engine room, but otherwise he just stares out at sea. Strangely, the sea doesn't get tedious to look at—wave trains converge and crisscross in patterns that have never happened before and will never happen again. It can take hours to tear one's eyes away.

Billy Tyne's been out to the Grand Banks dozens of times before, and he's also fished off the Carolinas, Florida, and deep into the Caribbean. He grew up on Gloucester Avenue, near where Route 128 crosses the Annisquam River, and married a teenaged girl who lived a few blocks away. Billy was exceptional for downtown Gloucester in that he didn't fish and his family was relatively well-off. He ran a Mexican import business for a while, worked for a vault manufacturer, sold waterbeds. His older brother was killed at age twenty-one by a landmine in Vietnam, and perhaps Billy drew the conclusion that life was not something to be pissed away in a bar. He enrolled in school, set his sights on being a psychologist, and started counselling drug-addicted teenagers. He was searching for something, trying out different lives, but nothing seemed to fit. He dropped out of school and started working again, but by then he had a wife and two daughters to support. His wife, Jodi, had been urging him to give fishing a try because she had a cousin whose husband made a lot of money at it. You never know, she told him, you just might like it.

The Road to Wigan Pier (1937)

George Orwell

Coal mining is still a dangerous and physically demanding occupation, but it is considerably more mechanized and regulated today than it was during the Great Depression, when Orwell wrote this vivid description. Remarkably, Orwell himself notes that the conditions he describes are considerably better than the situation in the mines just a short time earlier. The high risk and cost of mining coal is a key reason why today there is far more reliance on petroleum and other energy sources, and far less reliance on coal.

The first impression of all, overmastering everything else for a while, is the frightful, deafening din from the conveyor belt which carries the coal away. You cannot see very far, because the fog of coal dust throws back the beam of your lamp, but you can see on either side of you the line of half-naked kneeling men, one to every four or five yards, driving their shovels under the fallen coal and flinging it swiftly over their left shoulders. They are feeding it on to the conveyor belt, a moving rubber belt a couple of feet wide which runs a yard or two behind them. Down this belt a glittering river of coal races constantly. In a big mine it is carrying away several tons of coal every minute. It bears it off to some place in the main roads where it is shot into tubs holding half a ton, and thence dragged to the cages and hoisted to the outer air.

It is impossible to watch the "fillers" at work without feeling a pang of envy for their toughness. It is a dreadful job that they do, an almost superhuman job by the standards of an ordinary person. For they are not only shifting monstrous quantities of coal, they are also doing it in a position that doubles or trebles the work. They have got to remain kneeling all the while—they could hardly rise from their knees without hitting the ceiling—and you can easily see by trying it what a tremendous effort this means. Shovelling is comparatively easy when you are standing up, because you can use your knee and thigh to drive the shovel along; kneeling down, the whole of the strain is thrown upon your arm and belly muscles. And the other conditions do not exactly make things easier. There is the heat—it varies, but in some mines it is suffocating—and the coal dust that stuffs up your throat and nostrils and collects along your eyelids, and the unending rattle of the conveyor belt, which in that confined space is rather like the rattle of a machine gun. But the fillers look and work as though they were made of iron. They really do look like iron—hammered iron statues—under the smooth coat of coal dust which clings to them from head to foot. It is only when you see miners down the mine and naked that you realize what splendid men they are. Most of them are small (big men are at a disadvantage in that job) but nearly all of them have the most noble bodies; wide shoulders tapering to slender supple waists, and small pronounced buttocks and sinewy thighs, with not an ounce of waste flesh anywhere. In the hotter mines they wear only a pair of thin drawers, clogs, and knee-pads; in the hottest mines of all, only the clogs and knee-pads. You can hardly tell by the look of them whether they are young or old. They may be any age up to sixty or even sixty-five, but when they are black and naked they all look alike. No one could do their work who had not a young man's body, and a figure fit for a guardsman at that; just a few pounds of extra flesh on the waist-line, and the constant bending would be impossible. You can never forget that spectacle once you have seen it—the line of bowed, kneeling figures, sooty black all over, driving their huge shovels under the coal with stupendous force and speed. They are on the job for seven and a half hours, theoretically without a break, for there is no time "off." Actually they snatch a quarter of an hour or so at some time during the shift to eat the food they have brought with them, usually a hunk of bread and dripping and a bottle of cold tea. The first time I was watching the "fillers" at work I put my hand upon some dreadful slimy thing among the coal dust. It was a chewed quid of tobacco. Nearly all the miners chew tobacco, which is said to be good against thirst.

Probably you have to go down several coal-mines before you can get much grasp of the processes that are going on round you. This is chiefly because the mere effort of getting from place to place makes it difficult to notice anything else. In some ways it is even disappointing, or at least is unlike what you have expected. You get into the cage, which is a steel box about as wide as a telephone box and two or three times as long. It holds ten men, but they pack like pilchards in a tin, and a tall man cannot stand upright in it. The steel door shuts upon you, and somebody working the winding gear above drops you into the void. You have the usual momentary qualm in your belly and a bursting sensation in the ears, but not much sensation of movement till you get near the bottom, when the cage slows down so abruptly that you could swear it is going upwards again. In the middle of the run the cage probably touches sixty miles an hour; in some of the deeper mines it touches even more. When you crawl out at the bottom you are perhaps four hundred yards under ground. That is to say you have a tolerable-sized mountain on top of you; hundreds of yards of solid rock, bones of extinct beasts, subsoil, flints, roots of growing things, green grass, and cows grazing on it—all this suspended over your head and held back only by wooden props as thick as the calf of your leg. But because of the speed at which the cage has brought you down, the complete blackness through which you have travelled, you hardly feel yourself deeper down than you would at the bottom of the Piccadilly Tube.

What *is* surprising, on the other hand, is the immense horizontal distances that have to be travelled underground. Before I had been down a mine I had vaguely imagined the miner stepping out of the cage and getting to work on a ledge of coal a few yards away. I had not realized that before he even gets to his work he may have to creep through passages as long as from London Bridge to Oxford Circus. In the beginning, of course, a mine shaft is sunk somewhere near a seam of coal. But as that seam is worked out and fresh seams are followed up, the workings get further and further from the pit bottom. If it is a mile from the pit bottom to the coal face, that is probably an average distance; three miles is a fairly normal one; there are even said to be a few mines where it is as much as five miles. But these distances bear no relation to distances above ground. For in all that mile or three miles as it may be, there is hardly anywhere outside the main road, and not many places even there, where a man can stand upright.

You do not notice the effect of this till you have gone a few hundred yards. You start off, stooping slightly, down the dim-lit gallery, eight or ten feet wide and about five high, with the walls built up with slabs of shale, like the stone walls in Derbyshire. Every yard or two there are wooden props holding up the beams and girders; some of the girders have buckled into fantastic curves under which you have to duck. Usually it is bad going underfoot—thick dust or jagged chunks of shale, and in some mines where there is water it is mucky as a farmyard. Also there is the track for the coal tubs, like a miniature railway track with sleepers a foot or two apart, which is tiresome to walk on. Everything is grey with shale dust; there is a dusty fiery smell which seems to be the same in all mines. You see mysterious machines of which you never learn the purpose, and bundles of tools slung together on wires, and sometimes mice darting away from the beam of the lamps. They are surprisingly common, especially in mines where there are or have been horses. It would be interesting to know how they got there in the first place; probably by falling down the shaft—for they say a mouse can fall any distance uninjured, owing to its surface area being so large relative to its weight. You press yourself against the wall to make way for lines of tubs jolting slowly towards the shaft, drawn by an endless steel cable operated from the surface. You creep through sacking curtains and thick wooden doors which, when they are opened, let out fierce blasts of air. These doors are an important part of the ventilation system. The exhausted air is sucked out of one shaft by means of fans, and the fresh air enters the other of its own accord. But if left to itself the air will take the shortest way round, leaving the deeper workings unventilated; so all short cuts have to be partitioned off.

At the start to walk stooping is rather a joke, but it is a joke that soon wears off. I am handicapped by being exceptionally tall, but when the roof falls to four feet or less it is a tough job for anybody except a dwarf or a child. You have not only got to bend double, you have also got to keep your head up all the while so as to see the beams and girders and dodge them when they come. You have, therefore, a constant crick in the neck, but this is nothing to the pain in your knees and thighs. After half a mile it becomes (I am not exaggerating) an unbearable agony. You begin to wonder whether you will ever get to the end—still more, how on earth you are going to get back. Your pace grows slower and slower. You come to a stretch of a couple of hundred yards where it is all exceptionally low and you have to work yourself along in a squatting position. Then suddenly the roof opens out to a mysterious height—scene of an old fall of rock probably—and for twenty whole yards you can stand upright. The relief is overwhelming. But after this there is another low stretch of a hundred yards and then a succession of beams which you have to crawl under. You go down on all fours; even this is a relief after the squatting business. But when you come to the end of the beams and try to get up again, you find that your knees have temporarily struck work and refuse to lift you. You call a halt, ignominiously, and say that you would like to rest for a minute or two. Your guide (a miner) is sympathetic. He knows that your muscles are not the same as his. "Only another four hundred yards," he says encouragingly; you feel that he might as well say another four hundred miles. But finally you do somehow creep as far as the coal face. You have gone a mile and taken the best part of an hour; a miner would do it in not much more than twenty minutes. Having got there, you have to sprawl in the coal dust and get your strength back for several minutes before you can even watch the work in progress with any kind of intelligence.

Coming back is worse than going, not only because you are already tired out but because the journey back to the shaft is probably slightly uphill. You get through the low places at the speed of a tortoise, and you have no shame now about calling a halt when your knees give way. Even the lamp you are carrying becomes a nuisance and probably when you stumble you drop it; whereupon, if it is a Davy lamp, it goes out. Ducking the beams becomes more and more of an effort, and sometimes you forget to duck. You try walking head down as the miners do, and then you bang your backbone. Even the miners bang their backbones fairly often. This is the reason why in very hot mines, where it is necessary to go about half naked, most of the miners have what they call "buttons down the back"—that is, a permanent scab on each vertebra. When the track is downhill the miners sometimes fit their clogs, which are hollow underneath, on to the trolley rails and slide down. In mines where the "travelling" is very bad all the miners carry sticks about two and a half feet long, hollowed out below the handle. In normal places you keep your hand on top of the stick and in the low places you slide your hand down into the hollow. These sticks are a great help, and the wooden crash-helmets—a comparatively recent invention—are a godsend. They look like a French or Italian steel helmet, but they are made of some kind of pith and very light, and so strong that you can take a violent blow on the head without feeling it. When finally you get back to the surface you have been perhaps three hours underground and travelled two miles, and you are more exhausted than you would be by a twenty-five-mile walk above ground. For a week afterwards your thighs are so stiff that coming downstairs is quite a difficult feat; you have to work your way down in a peculiar sidelong manner, without bending the knees. Your miner friends notice the stiffness of your walk and chaff you about it. ("How'd ta like to work down pit, eh?" etc.) Yet even a miner who has been long away from work—from illness, for instance—when he comes back to the pit, suffers badly for the first few days.

It may seem that I am exaggerating, though no one who has been down an old-fashioned pit (most of the pits in England are old-fashioned) and actually gone as far as the coal face, is likely to say so. But what I want to emphasize is this. Here is this frightful business of crawling to and fro, which to any normal person is a hard day's work in itself; and it is not part of the miner's work at all, it is merely an extra, like the City man's daily ride in the Tube. The miner does that journey to and fro, and sandwiched in between there are seven and a half hours of savage work. I have never travelled much more than a mile to the coal face; but often it is three miles, in which case I and most people other than coal-miners would never get there at all. This is the kind of point that one is always liable to miss. When you think of a coal-mine you think of depth, heat, darkness, blackened figures hacking at walls of coal; you don't think, necessarily, of those miles of creeping to and fro. There is the question of time, also. A miner's working shift of seven and a half hours does not sound very long, but one has got to add on to it at least an hour a day for "travelling," more often two hours and sometimes three. Of course, the "travelling" is not technically work and the miner is not paid for it; but it is as like work as makes no difference. It is easy to say that miners don't mind all this. Certainly, it is not the same for them as it would be for you or me. They have done it since childhood, they have the right muscles hardened, and they can move to and fro underground with a startling and rather horrible agility. A miner puts his head down and *runs*, with a long swinging stride, through places where I can only stagger. At the workings you see them on all fours, skipping round the pit props almost like dogs. But it is quite a mistake to think that they enjoy it. I have talked about this to scores of miners and they all admit that the "travelling" is hard work; in any case when you hear them discussing a pit among themselves the "travelling" is always one of the things they discuss. It is said that a shift always returns from work faster than it goes; nevertheless the miners all say that it is the coming away, after a hard day's work, that is especially irksome. It is part of their work and they are equal to it, but certainly it is an effort. It is comparable, perhaps, to climbing a smallish mountain before and after your day's work.

When you have been down two or three pits you begin to get some grasp of the processes that are going on underground. (I ought to say, by the way, that I know nothing whatever about the technical side of mining: I am merely describing what I have seen.) Coal lies in thin seams between enormous layers of rock, so that essentially the process of getting it out is like scooping the central layer from a Neapolitan ice. In the old days the miners used to cut straight into the coal with pick and crowbar—a very slow job because coal, when lying in its virgin state, is almost as hard as rock. Nowadays the preliminary work is done by an electrically-driven coal-cutter, which in principle is an immensely tough and powerful band-saw, running horizontally instead of vertically, with teeth a couple of inches long and half an inch or an inch thick. It can move backwards or forwards on its own power, and the men operating it can rotate it this way and that. Incidentally it makes one of the most awful noises I have ever heard, and sends forth clouds of coal dust which make it impossible to see more than two or three feet and almost impossible to breathe. The machine travels along the coal face cutting into the base of the coal and undermining it to the depth of five feet or five feet and a half; after this it is comparatively easy to extract the coal to the depth to which it has been undermined. Where it is "difficult getting," however, it has also to be loosened with explosives. A man with an electric drill, like a rather smaller version of the drills used in street-mending, bores holes at intervals in the coal, inserts blasting powder, plugs it with clay, goes round the corner if there is one handy (he is supposed to retire to twenty-five yards distance) and touches off the charge with an electric current. This is not intended to bring the coal out, only to loosen it. Occasionally, of course, the charge is too powerful, and then it not only brings the coal out but brings the roof down as well.

After the blasting has been done the "fillers" can tumble the coal out, break it up, and shovel it on to the conveyor belt. It comes out at first in monstrous boulders which may weigh anything up to twenty tons. The conveyor belt shoots it on to tubs, and the tubs are shoved into the main road and hitched on to an endlessly revolving steel cable which drags them to the cage. Then they are hoisted, and at the surface the coal is sorted by being run over screens, and if necessary is washed as well. As far as possible the "dirt"—the shale, that is—is used for making the roads below. All that cannot be used is sent to the surface and dumped; hence the monstrous "dirt-heaps," like hideous gray mountains, which are the characteristic scenery of the coal areas. When the coal has been extracted to the depth to which the machine has cut, the coal face has advanced by five feet. Fresh props are put in to hold up the newly exposed roof, and during the next shift the conveyor belt is taken to pieces, moved five feet forward, and re-assembled. As far as possible the three operations of cutting, blasting, and extraction are done in three separate shifts, the cutting in the afternoon, the blasting at night (there is a law, not always kept, that forbids its being done when there are other men working near by), and the "filling" in the morning shift, which lasts from six in the morning until half past one.

Even when you watch the process of coal-extraction you probably only watch it for a short time, and it is not until you begin making a few calculations that you realize what a stupendous task the "fillers" are performing. Normally each man has to clear a space four or five yards wide. The cutter has undermined the coal to the depth of five feet, so that if the seam of coal is three or four feet high, each man has to cut out, break up, and load on to the belt something between seven and twelve cubic yards of coal. This is to say, taking a cubic yard as weighing twenty-seven hundred-weight, that each man is shifting coal at a speed approaching two tons an hour. I have just enough experience of pick and shovel work to be able to grasp what this means. When I am digging trenches in my garden, if I shift two tons of earth during the afternoon, I feel that I have earned my tea. But earth is tractable stuff compared with coal, and I don't have to work kneeling down, a thousand feet underground, in suffocating heat and swallowing coal dust with every breath I take; nor do I have to walk a mile bent double before I begin. The miner's job would be as much beyond my power as it would be to perform on the flying trapeze or to win the Grand National. I am not a manual labourer and please God I never shall be one, but there are some kinds of manual work that I could do if I had to. At a pinch I could be a tolerable road-sweeper or an inefficient gardener or even a tenth-rate farm hand. But by no conceivable amount of effort or training could I become a coal miner; the work would kill me in a few weeks.

Watching coal-miners at work, you realize momentarily what different universes different people inhabit. Down there where coal is dug it is a sort of world apart which one can quite easily go through life without ever hearing about. Probably a majority of people would even prefer not to hear about it. Yet it is the absolutely necessary counterpart of our world above. Practically everything we do, from eating an ice to crossing the Atlantic, and from baking a loaf to writing a novel, involves the use of coal, directly or indirectly. For all the arts of peace coal is needed; if war breaks out it is needed all the more. In time of revolution the miner must go on working or the revolution must stop, for revolution as much as reaction needs coal. Whatever may be happening on the surface, the hacking and shovelling have got to continue without a pause, or at any rate without pausing for more than a few weeks at the most. In order that Hitler may march the goosestep, that the Pope may denounce Bolshevism, that the cricket crowds may assemble at Lord's, that the Nancy poets may scratch one another's backs, coal has got to be forthcoming. But on the whole we are not aware of it; we all know that we "must have coal," but we seldom or never remember what coal-getting involves. Here am I, sitting writing in front of my comfortable coal fire. It is April but I still need a fire. Once a fortnight the coal cart drives up to the door and men in leather jerkins carry the coal indoors in stout sacks smelling of tar and shoot it clanking into the coal-hole under the stairs. It is only very rarely, when I make a definite mental effort, that I connect this coal with that far-off labour in the mines. It is just "coal"—something that I have got to have; black stuff that arrives mysteriously from nowhere in particular, like manna except that you have to pay for it. You could quite easily drive a car right across the north of England and never once remember that hundreds of feet below the road you are on the miners are hacking at the coal. Yet in a sense it is the miners who are driving your car forward. Their lamp-lit world down there is as necessary to the daylight world above as the root is to the flower.

It is not long since conditions in the mines were worse than they are now. There are still living a few very old women who in their youth have worked underground, with a harness round their waists and a chain that passed between their legs, crawling on all fours and dragging tubs of coal. They used to go on doing this even when they were pregnant. And even now, if coal could not be produced without pregnant women dragging it to and fro, I fancy we should let them do it rather than deprive ourselves of coal.

"Song to the Men of England" (1819)

Percy Bysshe Shelley

Written at a time of considerable unrest in British labor markets—many men had recently been discharged from military service after the Napoleonic wars and unemployment levels had consequently risen—Shelly hoped that this poem would become a hymn for the fledgling labor movements of the time (which it did) and perhaps even spark a social revolution (which it did not). Shelly originally intended to write a series of poems for workers, but he abandoned the project.

I

Men of England, wherefore plough
For the lords who lay ye low?
Wherefore weave with toil and care
The rich robes your tyrants wear?

II

Wherefore feed, and clothe, and save,
From the cradle to the grave,
Those ungrateful drones who would
Drain your sweat—nay, drink your blood?

III

Wherefore, Bees of England, forge
Many a weapon, chain, and scourge,
That these stingless drones may spoil
The forced produce of your toil?

IV

Have ye leisure, comfort, calm,
Shelter, food, love's gentle balm?
Or what is it ye buy so dear
With your pain and with your fear?

V

The seed ye sow, another reaps;
The wealth ye find, another keeps;
The robes ye weave, another wears;
The arms ye forge, another bears.

VI

Sow seed,—but let no tyrant reap;
Find wealth,—let no imposter heap;
Weave robes,—let not the idle wear;
Forge arms,—in your defence to bear.

VII

Shrink to your cellars, holes, and cells;
In halls ye deck, another dwells.
Why shake the chains ye wrought? Ye see
The steel ye tempered glance on ye.

VIII

With plough and spade, and hoe and loom,
Trace your grave, and build your tomb,
And weave your winding-sheet, till fair
England be your sepulchre.

In Dubious Battle (1936)

John Steinbeck

When a union had to win a strike to be recognized as the bargaining agent for a group of workers, and when national levels of union membership depended largely on winning big, highly publicized strikes against employers, the stakes involved in strikes were much higher than they have been under the system established by the Wagner Act of 1935. As a result, the incentives facing both union organizers and employers were much different, as were the frequency and level of violence associated with major strikes.

Jim went to the kitchen and filled his bowl again.

Mac said, "Here's the layout. Torgas is a little valley, and it's mostly apple orchards. Most of it's owned by a few men. Of course there's some little places, but there's not very many of them. Now when the apples are ripe the crop tramps come in and pick them. And from there they go on over the ridge and south, and pick the cotton. If we can start the fun in the apples, maybe it will just naturally spread over into the cotton. Now these few guys that own most of the Torgas Valley waited until most of the crop tramps were already there. They spent most of their money getting there, of course. They always do. And then the owners announced their price cut. Suppose the tramps are mad? What can they do? They've got to work picking apples to get out even."

Jim's dinner was neglected. With his spoon he stirred the meat and potatoes around and around. He learned forward. "So then we try to get the men to strike? Is that it?"

"Sure. Maybe it's all ready to bust and we just give it a little tiny push. We organize the men, and then we picket the orchards."

Jim said, "Suppose the owners raise the wages to get their apples picked?"

Mac pushed away his finished second bowl. "Well, we'd find another job to do somewhere else soon enough. Hell, we don't want only temporary pay raises, even though we're glad to see a few poor bastards better off. We got to take the long view. A strike that's settled too quickly won't teach the men how to organize, how to work together. A tough strike is good. We want the men to find out how strong they are when they work together."

"Well, suppose," Jim insisted, "suppose the owners do meet the demands?"

"I don't think they will. There's the bulk of power in the hands of a few men. That always makes 'em cocky. Now we start our strike, and Torgas County gets itself an ordinance that makes congregation unlawful. Now what happens? We congregate the men. A bunch of sheriff's men try to push them around, and that starts a fight. There's nothing like a fight to cement the men together. Well, then the owners start a vigilantes committee, bunch of fool shoe clerks, or my friends the American Legion boys trying to pretend they aren't middle-aged, cinching in their belts to hide their pot-bellies—there I go again. Well, the vigilantes start shooting. If they knock over some of the tramps we have a public funeral; and after that, we get some real action. Maybe they have to call out the troops." He was breathing hard in excitement. "Jesus, man! The troops win, all right! But every time a guardsman jabs a fruit tramp with a bayonet a thousand men all over the country come on our side. Christ Almighty! If we can only get the troops called out." He settled back on his cot. "Aw, I'm looking ahead too much. Our job's just to push along our little baby strike, if we can. But God damn it, Jim, if we could get the National Guard called out, now with the crops coming ready, we'd have the whole district organized by spring."

Jim had been crouching on his bed, his eyes shining and his jaws set. Now and then his fingers went nervously to his throat. Mac continued, "The damn fools think they can settle strikes with soldiers." He laughed. "Here I go again—talking like a soap-boxer. I get all worked up, and that's not so good. We got to think good. Oh say, Jim, have you got some blue jeans?"

"No. This suit's all the clothes I own."

"Well, we'll have to go out and buy you some in a second-hand store, then. You're going to pick apples, boy. And you're going to sleep in jungles. And you're going to do Party work after you've done ten hours in the orchard. Here's the work you wanted."

Jim said, "Thanks, Mac. My old man always had to fight alone. He got licked every time."

Mac came and stood over him. "Get those three letters finished, Jim, and then we'll go out and buy you some jeans."

God's Little Acre (1933)

Erskine Caldwell

Many American literary works set in the period between 1890 and 1935 depict violent and even deadly labor strikes.

Will had turned and was pointing out the window towards the darkened cotton mill. There was no light in the huge building, but arc lights under the trees threw a thin coating of yellow glow over the ivy-covered walls.

"When's the mill going to start up again?" Pluto asked.

"Never," Will said disgustedly. "Never. Unless we start it ourselves."

"What's the matter? Why won't it run?"

Will learned forward in his chair.

"We're going in there some day ourselves and turn the power on," he said slowly. "If the company doesn't start up soon, that's what we're going to do. They cut the pay down to a dollar-ten eighteen months ago, and when we raised hell about it, they shut off the power and drove us out. But they still charge rent for these God damn privies we have to live in. You know why we're going to run it ourselves now, don't you?"

"But some of the other mills in the Valley are running," Pluto said. "We passed five or six lighted mills when we drove over from Augusta tonight. Maybe they'll start this one again soon."

"Like so much hell they will, at a dollar-ten. They are running the other mills because they starved the loomweavers into going back to work. That was before the Red Cross started passing out sacks of flour. They had to go back to work and take a dollar-ten, or starve. But, by God, we don't have to do it in Scottsville. As long as we can get a sack of flour once in a while we can hold out. And the State is giving out yeast now. Mix a cake of yeast in a glass of water and drink it, and you feel pretty good for a while. They started giving out yeast because everybody in the Valley has got pellagra these days from too much starving. The mill can't get us back until they shorten the hours, or cut out the stretchout, or go back to the old pay. I'll be damned if I work nine hours a day for a dollar-ten, when those rich sons-of-bitches who own the mill ride up and down the Valley in five thousand dollar automobiles."

Will had got warmed to the subject, and once started, he could not stop. He told Pluto something of their plans for taking over the mill from the owners and running it themselves. The mill workers in Scottsville had been out of work for a year and a half already, he said, and they were becoming desperate for food and clothing. During that length of time the workers had reached an understanding among themselves that bound every man, woman, and child in the company town to a stand not to give in to the mill. The mill had tried to evict them from their homes for nonpayment of rent, but the local had got an injunction from a judge in Aiken that restrained the mill from turning the workers out of the company houses. With that, Will said, they were prepared to stand for their demands just as long as the mill stood in Scottsville.

❧

"Where you going, Will?" the man asked, stopping and looking at them and at Pluto's car.

"Just over to Georgia for a day or two, Harry."

Will felt like a traitor, running off like that. He waited for Rosamond to go down the walk first.

"Are you sure you're not leaving for good, Will?" the man asked suspiciously.

"I'll be back in town in a few days, Harry. And when I get back, you'll know it."

"All right, but don't forget to come back. If everybody leaves, pretty soon the company is going to rush a crew of operators in here and start up without us. We've all got to stay here and hold out. If the mill ever once got started without us, we wouldn't have a chance in the world. You know that, Will."

Will went down the walk and got in front of Rosamond. He walked down the street with the other man, talking to him in a low voice. They stopped several yards away and began arguing. Will would talk a little while, tapping the other man on the chest with his forefinger; the other man would nod his head and glance down at the ivy-walled mill below. They turned and walked a little further, both talking at the same time. When they stopped again, the other man began talking to Will, tapping him on the chest with his forefinger. Will nodded his head, shook it violently, nodded again.

"We can't let anybody go in there and wreck the machinery," Will said. "Nobody wants to see that done."

"That's just what I've been trying to tell you, Will. What we want to do is to go in there and turn the power on. When the company comes and sees what's happening, they'll either try to drive us out, or else get down to business."

"Now listen, Harry," Will said, "when that power is turned on, nobody on God's earth is going to shut it off. It's going to stay turned on. If they try to turn it off, then we'll—well, God damn it, Harry, the power is going to stay turned on."

"I've always been in favor of turning it on and never shutting it off. That's what I've tried to tell the local, but what can you tell that son-of-a-bitch A.F.L.? Nothing! They're drawing pay to keep us from working. When we start to work, the money will stop coming in here to pay them. Well, God damn it, Will, we're nothing but suckers to listen to them talk about arbitration. Let the mill run three shifts, maybe four shifts, when we turn the power on, but keep it running all the time. We can turn out as much print cloth as the company can, maybe a lot more. But all of us will be working then, anyway. We can speed up after everybody gets back on the job. What we're after now is turning on the power. And if they try to shut off the power, then we'll get in there and—well, God damn it, Will, the power ain't going to be shut off once we turn it on. Now, God damn it, Will, I've never been in favor of wrecking anything. You know that, and so does everybody else. That son-of-a-bitch A.F.L. started that talk when they heard we were thinking about turning the power on. All I'm after is running the mill."

"That's what I've been saying at every local meeting since the shutdown," Will said. "The local is all hopped-up with the A.F.L. They've been saying nothing is going to get us our jobs back except by arbitrating. I've never been in favor of that. You can't talk to the company and get nothing but a one-sided answer. They're not going to say a thing but 'a dollar-ten.' You know that as well as I do. And how in the hell can a man pay rent on these stinking privies we live in out of a dollar-ten? You tell me how it can be done, and I'll be the first to vote for arbitrating. No, sir. It just can't be done."

"Well, I'm in favor of going in there and turning on the power. That's what I've been saying all the time. I've never said anything else, and I never will."

"Try to get that meeting called for Friday night," he shouted. "By God, we'll show the A.F.L. and the company what we mean by turning the power on."

Darling Jill raced down the unpaved street and turned the corner recklessly. They were off in a cloud of dust that blew up and sifted thickly through the hot air to settle on the trees and front porches of the yellow company houses.

They sped along the hot concrete toward Augusta, passing an almost endless cluster of company houses. They passed through the other company towns, slowing down in the restricted zones and looking out at the humming mills. They could see the men and girls through the open windows and they could almost hear the hum of the moving machinery behind the ivy-covered walls. Along the streets there were few people to be seen. There were not nearly so many as there were on the streets of Scottsville.

"Hurry up and let's get to Augusta," Will said. "I want to get out of the Valley as soon as this car can take me out. I'm damn tired of looking at spinning mills and company houses every minute of the day and night."

He knew he was not tired of looking at them, or of living with them; it was the sight of so many open mills that irritated him.

"Will was shot yesterday morning."

"Shot? What with—corn?"

"Killed with a pistol, Pa," Darling Jill said. "We buried Will this afternoon in the Valley. He's dead now, and covered with earth."

Ty Ty was speechless for a moment. He leaned against the car, searching each face before him. When he saw Rosamond's face, he knew it was true.

"Now, you don't mean Will Thompson," Ty Ty said. "Not our Will! Say it ain't so!"

"It is so, Pa. Will is dead now, and covered with earth over there in Horse Creek Valley."

"Trouble at the mill then, I'll bet a pretty. Or else over a female."

Rosamond got out and ran to the house. The others got out slowly and looked strangely at the buildings in the twilight. Pluto did not know whether to remain where he was or whether to go home immediately.

Ty Ty sent Darling Jill into the house to cook supper without loss of time.

"You stay here and tell me what happened to Will Thompson," he told Griselda. "I can't let our Will pass on without knowing all about it. Will was one of the family."

They left Pluto sitting on the runningboard of his car, and walked across the yard to the front steps. Ty Ty sat down and waited to hear what Griselda had to tell him about Will. She was still crying a little.

"Did they shoot him for breaking into company property, Griselda?"

"Yes, Pa. All the men in Scottsville went into the mill and tried to start it. Will was the one who turned the power on."

"Oh, so that's what he was talking about when he said he was going to turn the power on? Well, I never did fully understand what he had in mind when he said that. And our Will turned the power on!"

"Some company police from the Piedmont shot him when he turned it on."

Ty was silent for several minutes. He gazed out through the gray dusk, seeing through it to the boundaries of his land. He could see each mound of earth that had been excavated, each deep round hole they had dug. And far beyond them all he could see the cleared field beyond the woods where God's little acre lay. For some reason he wished then to bring it closer to the house where he might be near it all the time. He felt guilty of something—maybe it was sacrilege or desecration—whatever it was, he knew he had not played fair with God. Now he wished to bring God's little acre back to its rightful place beside the house where he could see it all the time. He had very little in the world to live for anyway, and when men died, he could find consolation only in his love of God. He brought God's little acre back from the far side of the farm and placed it under him. He promised himself to keep it there until he died.

Ty Ty had no eulogy for Will Thompson. Will would never help them dig for gold. He laughed at them when Ty Ty asked him to help. He said it was foolish to try to find gold where there was no gold. Ty Ty knew there was gold in the ground, and he had always been a little angry with Will for laughing at his efforts to find it. Will had always seemed to be more interested in getting back to Horse Creek Valley than he was in staying there and helping Ty Ty.

"Sometimes I wished Will would stay here and help us, and sometimes I was glad he didn't. He was a fool about cotton mills, I reckon, and couldn't pretend to be a farmer. Maybe God made two kinds of us, after all. It looks like now, though I used to never think so, that God made a man to work the ground and a man to work the machinery. I reckon I was a fool to try to make Will Thompson take an interest in the land. He was always saying something about spinning and weaving, and about how pretty the girls and how hungry the men were in the Valley. I couldn't always make out what he was talking about, but sometimes I could just about feel something inside that told me all the things he said were true. He used to sit here and tell me how strong men were in the Valley when they were young and how weak they were when they grew up breathing cotton lint into their lungs and dying with blood on their lips. And Will used to say how pretty the girls were when they were young and how ugly they were when they were old and starving with pellagra. But he didn't like the land, anyway. He was one of the people of Horse Creek Valley."

N.
Discrimination

Racial, ethnic, and gender discrimination is as old as humanity. It can occur even in competitive markets, despite the fact that in that setting discrimination is not only a waste of resources, but also imposes costs on those who want to discriminate—whether they are employers, co-workers, or customers—as well as those who are discriminated against. In the long run, a particularly serious consequence of discrimination is that members of groups who are discriminated against may have fewer financial incentives to invest in education and training, and so enter the labor market with fewer chances to pursue professional, managerial, and technical careers.

Discrimination knows few, if any, geographical or temporal boundaries. The excerpt from Arundhati Roy's God of Small Things *describes ethnic discrimination in India, while the passage from John Steinbeck's* Travels with Charley *deals with a famous episode of racial discrimination in the United States. Both of these novels are set in the twentieth century.*

The famous passage from Mark Twain's Adventures of Huckleberry Finn *is set before the American Civil War and shows the final stages of this young boy's difficult journey in rejecting a special case of statistical discrimination—treating one racial group as slaves in some parts of the nation. Statistical discrimination occurs when people are treated and judged as members of a group rather than as individuals. After intense soul-searching, Huckleberry Finn comes to see and accept Jim as a good person and a good friend, even though that entails breaking the law, a law that Huckleberry (and many of his contemporaries) did not recognize to be immoral.*

The God of Small Things
(1996)
Arundhati Roy

Roy provides a striking story of what happens when an "untouchable" succeeds in breaking down both economic and personal barriers in the face of incredibly high costs and risks.

Her co-passenger's madness comforted Rahel. It drew her closer into New York's deranged womb. Away from the other, more terrible thing that haunted her.

. . . It *was* Velutha.

That much Rahel was sure of. She'd seen him. He'd seen her. She'd have known him anywhere, any time. And if he hadn't been wearing a shirt, she would have recognized him from behind. She knew his back. She'd been carried on it. More times than she could count. It had a light-brown birthmark, shaped like a pointed dry leaf. He said it was a Lucky Leaf, that made the Monsoons come on time. A brown leaf on a black back. An autumn leaf at night.

A lucky leaf that wasn't lucky enough.

Velutha wasn't supposed to be a carpenter.

He was called Velutha—which means White in Malayalam—because he was so black. His father, Vellya Paapen, was a Paravan. A toddy tapper. He had a glass eye. He had been shaping a block of granite with a hammer when a chip flew into his left eye and sliced right through it.

As a young boy, Velutha would come with Vellya Paapen to the back entrance of the Ayemenem House to deliver the coconuts they had plucked from the trees in the compound. Pappachi would not allow Paravans into the house. Nobody would. They were not allowed to touch anything that Touchables touched. Caste Hindus and Caste Christians. Mammachi told Estha and Rahel that she could remember a time, in her girlhood, when Paravans were expected to crawl backwards with a broom, sweeping away their footprints so that Brahmins or Syrian Christians would not defile themselves by accidentally stepping into a Paravan's footprint. In Mammachi's time, Paravans, like other Untouchables, were not allowed to walk on public roads, not allowed to cover their upper bodies, not allowed to carry umbrellas. They had to put their hands over their mouths when they spoke, to divert their polluted breath away from those whom they addressed.

When the British came to Malabar, a number of Paravans, Pelayas and Pulayas (among them Velutha's grandfather, Kelan) converted to Christianity and joined the Anglican Church to escape the scourge of Untouchability. As added incentive they were given a little food and money. They were known as the Rice-Christians. It didn't take them long to realize that they had jumped from the frying pan into the fire. They were made to have separate churches, with separate services, and separate priests. As a special favor they were even given their own separate Pariah Bishop. After independence they found they were not entitled to any government benefits like job reservations or bank loans at low interest rates, because officially, on paper, they were Christians, and therefore casteless. It was a little like having to sweep away your footprints without a broom. Or worse, not being *allowed* to leave footprints at all.

It was Mammachi, on vacation from Delhi and Imperial Entomology, who first noticed little Velutha's remarkable facility with his hands. Velutha was eleven then, about three years younger than Ammu. He was like a little magician. He could make intricate toys—tiny windmills, rattles, minute jewel boxes out of dried palm reeds; he could carve perfect boats out of tapioca stems and figurines on cashew nuts. He would bring them for Ammu, holding them out on his palm (as he had been taught) so she wouldn't have to touch him to take them. Though he was younger than she was, he called her Ammukutty—Little Ammu. Mammachi persuaded Vella Paapen to send him to the Untouchables' School that her father-in-law Pennyan Kunju had founded.

Velutha was fourteen when Johann Klein, a German carpenter from a carpenter's guild in Bavaria, came to Kottayam and spent three years with the Christian Mission Society, conducting a workshop with local carpenters. Every afternoon, after school, Velutha caught a bus to Kottayam where he worked with Klein till dusk. By the time he was sixteen, Velutha had finished high school and was an accomplished carpenter. He had his own set of carpentry tools and a distinctly German design sensibility. He built Mammachi a Bauhaus dining table with twelve dining chairs in rosewood and a traditional Bavarian chaise lounge in lighter jackwood. For Baby Kochamma's annual Nativity plays he made her a stack of wireframed angels' wings that fitted onto children's backs like knapsacks, cardboard clouds for the Angel Gabriel to appear between, and a manger for Christ to be born in. When her garden cherub's silver arc dried up inexplicably, it was Dr. Velutha who fixed its bladder for her.

Apart from his carpentry skills, Velutha had a way with machines. Mammachi (with impenetrable Touchable logic) often said that if only he hadn't been a Paravan, he might have become an engineer. He mended radios, clocks, water pumps. He looked after the plumbing and all the electrical gadgets in the house.

When Mammachi decided to enclose the back verandah, it was Velutha who designed and built the sliding-folding door that later became all the rage in Ayemenem.

Velutha knew more about the machines in the factory than anyone else.

When Chacko resigned his job in Madras and returned to Ayemenem with a Bharat bottle-sealing machine, it was Velutha who re-assembled it and set it up. It was Velutha who maintained the new canning machine and the automatic pineapple slicer. Velutha who oiled the water pump and the small diesel generator. Velutha who built the aluminum sheet-lined, easy-to-clean cutting surfaces, and the ground-level furnaces for boiling fruit.

Velutha's father, Vellya Paapen, however, was an Old-World Paravan. He had seen the Crawling Backwards Days and his gratitude to Mammachi and her family for all that they had done for him was as wide and deep as a river in spate. When he had his accident with the stone chip, Mammachi organized and paid for his glass eye. He hadn't worked off his debt yet, and though he knew he wasn't expected to, that he wouldn't ever be able to, he felt that his eye was not his own. His gratitude widened his smile and bent his back.

Vellya Paapen feared for his younger son. He couldn't say what it was that frightened him. It was nothing that he had said. Or done. It was not *what* he said, but the *way* he said it. Not *what* he did, but the *way* he did it.

Perhaps it was just a lack of hesitation. An unwarranted assurance. In the way he walked. The way he held his head. The quiet way he offered suggestions without being asked. Or the quiet way in which he disregarded suggestions without appearing to rebel.

While these were qualities that were perfectly acceptable, perhaps even desirable, in Touchables, Vellya Paapen thought that in a Paravan they could (and would, and indeed, *should*) be construed as insolence.

Vellya Paapen tried to caution Velutha. But since he couldn't put his finger on what it was that bothered him, Velutha misunderstood his muddled concern. To him it appeared as though his father grudged him his brief training and his natural skills. Vellya Paapen's good intentions quickly degenerated into nagging and bickering and a general air of unpleasantness between father and son. Much to his mother's dismay, Velutha began to avoid going home. He worked late. He caught fish in the river and cooked it on an open fire. He slept outdoors, on the banks of the river.

Then one day he disappeared. For four years nobody knew where he was. There was a rumor that he was working on a building site for the Department of Welfare and Housing in Trivandrum. And more recently, the inevitable rumor that he had become a Naxalite. That he had been to prison. Somebody said they had seen him in Quilon.

There was no way of reaching him when his mother, Chella, died of tuberculosis. Then Kuttappen, his older brother, fell off a coconut tree and damaged his spine. He was paralyzed and unable to work. Velutha heard of the accident a whole year after it happened.

It had been five months since he returned to Ayemenem. He never talked about where he had been, or what he had done.

Mammachi rehired Velutha as the factory carpenter and put him in charge of general maintenance. It caused a great deal of resentment among the other Touchable factory workers because, according to them, Paravans were not *meant* to be carpenters. And certainly, prodigal Paravans were not meant to be rehired.

To keep the others happy, and since she knew that nobody else would hire him as a carpenter, Mammachi paid Velutha less than she would a Touchable carpenter but more than she would a Paravan. Mammachi didn't encourage him to enter the house (except when she needed something mended or installed). She thought that he ought to be grateful that he was allowed on the factory premises at all, and allowed to touch things that Touchables touched. She said that it was a big step for a Paravan.

When he returned to Ayemenem after his years away from home, Velutha still had about him the same quickness. The sureness. And Vellya Paapen feared for him now more than ever. But this time he held his peace. He said nothing.

At least not until the Terror took hold of him. Not until he saw, night after night, a little boat being rowed across the river. Not until he saw it return at dawn. Not until he saw what his Untouchable son had touched. More than touched.

Entered.

Loved.

Travels With Charley: In Search of America (1961)

John Steinbeck

Attempts to racially integrate public schools in many parts of the United States in the 1950s and 1960s resulted in mob violence and organized expressions of racial hatred. As Steinbeck was nearing the end of his drive across the country, the most infamous episode was unfolding in New Orleans. Steinbeck felt compelled to observe and record the mob scene, writing about the effects of discrimination on both those who discriminate and those who are discriminated against. He also discussed the idea of equality of opportunity and suggested an ingenious empirical test of claims concerning "separate but equal" that is similar to the broader ethical proposals later put forward by the philosopher John Rawls.

In Salinas in California, where I was born and grew and went to school gathering the impressions that formed me, there was only one Negro family. The name was Cooper and the father and mother were there when I was born, but they had three sons, one a little older than I, one my age, and one a year younger, so that in grade school and high school there was always a Cooper in the grade ahead, one in my class, and one in the class below. In a word, I was bracketed with Coopers. The father, universally called Mr. Cooper, ran a little trucking business—ran it well and made a good living. His wife was a warm and friendly woman who was good for a piece of gingerbread any time we wanted to put the hustle on her.

If there was any color prejudice in Salinas I never heard or felt a breath of it. The Coopers were respected, and their self-respect was in no way forced. Ulysses, the oldest, was one of the best pole-vaulters our town ever developed, a tall, quiet boy. I remember the lean grace of his movements in a track suit and I remember envying his smooth and perfect timing. He died in his third year in high school and I was one of his pallbearers, and I think I was guilty of the sin of pride at being chosen. The second son, Ignatius, my classmate, was not my favorite, I discover now, because he was far and away the best student. In arithmetic and later in mathematics he topped our grades, and in Latin he not only was a better student but he didn't cheat. And who can like a classmate like that? The youngest Cooper—the baby—was all smiles. It's odd that I do not remember his first name. He was a musician from the start, and when I last saw him he was deep in composition which seemed, to my partially instructed ear, bold and original and good. But beyond this giftedness, the Cooper boys were my friends.

Now, these were the only Negroes I knew or had contact with in the days of my flypaper childhood, and you can see how little I was prepared for the great world. When I heard, for example, that Negroes were an inferior race, I thought the authority was misinformed. When I heard that Negroes were dirty I remembered Mrs. Cooper's shining kitchen. Lazy? The drone and clop of Mr. Cooper's horse-drawn dray in the street outside used to awaken us in the dawn. Dishonest? Mr. Cooper was one of the very few Salinians who never let a debt cross the fifteenth of the month.

I realize now that there was something else about the Coopers that set them apart from other Negroes I have seen and met since. Because they were not hurt or insulted, they were not defensive or combative. Because their dignity was intact, they had no need to be overbearing, and because Cooper boys had never heard that they were inferior, their minds could grow to their true limits.

That was my Negro experience until I was well grown, perhaps too far grown to reform the inflexible habits of childhood. Oh, I have seen plenty since and have felt the shattering waves of violence and despair and confusion. I have seen Negro children who really cannot learn, particularly those who in their gelatin plate of babyness have been told they were inferior. And, remembering the Coopers and how we felt about them, I think my main feeling is sorrow at the curtain of fear and anger drawn down between us. And I've just thought of an amusing possibility. If in Salinas anyone from a wiser and more sophisticated world had asked, "How would you like your sister to marry a Cooper?" I think we would have laughed. For it might have occurred to us that a Cooper might not have wanted to marry our sister, good friends though we all were.

Thus it remains that I am basically unfitted to take sides in the racial conflict. I must admit that cruelty and force exerted against weakness turn me sick with rage, but this would be equally true in the treatment of any weak by any strong.

Beyond my failings as a racist, I knew I was not wanted in the South. When people are engaged in something they are not proud of, they do not welcome witnesses. In fact, they come to believe the witness causes the trouble.

In all this discussion of the South I have been speaking only about the violence set loose by the desegregation movement—the children going to school, the young Negroes demanding the questionable privilege of lunch counters, buses, and toilets. But I am particularly interested in the school business, because it seems to me that the blight can disappear only when there are millions of Coopers.

Recently a dear Southern friend instructed me passionately in the theory of "equal but separate." "It just happens," he said, "that in my town there are three new Negro schools not equal but superior to the white schools. Now wouldn't you think they would be satisfied with that? And in the bus station the washrooms are exactly the same. What's your answer to that?"

I said, "Maybe it's a matter of ignorance. You could solve it and really put them in their places if you switched schools and toilets. The moment they realized that your schools weren't as good as theirs, they would realize their error."

And do you know what he said? He said, "You troublemaking son of a bitch." But he said it smiling.

While I was still in Texas, late in 1960, the incident most reported and pictured in the newspapers was the matriculation of a couple of tiny Negro children in a New Orleans school. Behind these small dark mites were the law's majesty and the law's power to enforce—both the scales and the sword were allied with the infants—while against them were three hundred years of fear and anger and terror of change in a changing world. I had seen photographs in the papers every day and motion pictures on the television screen. What made the newsmen love the story was a group of stout middle-aged women who, by some curious definition of the word "mother," gathered every day to scream invectives at children. Further, a small group of them had become so expert that they were known as Cheerleaders, and a crowd gathered every day to enjoy and to applaud their performance.

This strange drama seemed so improbable that I felt I had to see it. It had the same draw as a five-legged calf or a two-headed foetus at a sideshow, a distortion of normal life we have always found so interesting that we will pay to see it, perhaps to prove to ourselves that we have the proper number of legs or heads. In the New Orleans show, I felt all the amusement of the improbable abnormal, but also a kind of horror that it could be so.

. . . And so I . . . scudded on toward New Orleans, for I wanted to catch a show of the Cheerleaders.

Even I know better than to drive a car near trouble, particularly Rocinante, with New York license plates. Only yesterday a reporter had been beaten and his camera smashed, for even convinced voters are reluctant to have their moment of history recorded and preserved.

So, well on the edge of town I drove into a parking lot. The attendant came to my window. "Man, oh man, I thought you had a nigger in there. Man, oh man, it's a dog. I see that big old black face and I think it's a big old nigger."

"His face is blue-gray when he's clean," I said coldly.

"Well I see some blue-gray niggers and they wasn't clean. New York, eh?"

It seemed to me a chill like the morning air came into his voice. "Just driving through," I said. "I want to park for a couple of hours. Think you can get me a taxi?"

"Tell you what I bet. I bet you're going to see the Cheerleaders."

"That's right."

"Well, I hope you're not one of those trouble-makers or reporters."

"I just want to see it."

"Man, oh man, you going to see something. Ain't those Cheerleaders something? Man, oh man, you never heard nothing like it when they get going."

I locked Charley in Rocinante's house after giving the attendant a tour of the premises, a drink of whisky, and a dollar. "Be kind of careful about opening the door when I'm away," I said. "Charley takes his job pretty seriously. You might lose a hand." This was an outrageous lie, of course, but the man said, "Yes, sir. You don't catch me fooling around with no strange dog."

The taxi driver, a sallow, yellowish man, shriveled like a chickpea with the cold, said, "I wouldn't take you more than a couple of blocks near. I don't go to have my cab wrecked."

"Is it that bad?"

"It ain't is it. It's can it get. And it can get that bad."

"When do they get going?"

He looked at his watch. "Except it's cold, they been coming in since dawn. It's quarter to. You get along and you won't miss nothing except it's cold."

I had camouflaged myself in an old blue jacket and my British navy cap on the supposition that in a seaport no one ever looks at a sailor any more than a waiter is inspected in a restaurant. In his natural haunts a sailor has no face and certainly no plans beyond getting drunk and maybe in jail for fighting. At least that's the general feeling about sailors. I've tested it. The most that happens is a kindly voice of authority saying, "Why don't you go back to your ship, sailor? You wouldn't want to sit in the tank and miss your tide, now would you, sailor?" And the speaker wouldn't recognize you five minutes later. And the Lion and Unicorn on my cap made me even more anonymous. But I must warn anyone testing my theory, never try it away from a shipping port.

"Where you from?" the driver asked with a complete lack of interest.

"Liverpool."

"Limey, huh? Well, you'll be all right. It's the goddamn New York Jews cause all the trouble."

I found myself with a British inflection and by no means one of Liverpool. "Jews—what? How do they cause trouble?"

"Why, hell, mister. We know how to take care of this. Everybody's happy and getting along fine. Why, I *like* niggers. And then goddamn New York Jews come in and stir the niggers up. They just stay in New York there wouldn't be no trouble. Ought to take them out."

"You mean lynch them?"

"I don't mean nothing else, mister."

He let me out and I started to walk away. "Don't try to get too close, mister," he called after me. "Just you enjoy it but don't mix in."

"Thanks," I said, and killed the "awfully" that came to my tongue.

As I walked toward the school I was in a stream of people all white and all going in my direction. They walked intently like people going to a fire after it has been burning for some time. They beat their hands against their hips or hugged them under coats, and many men had scarves under their hats and covering their ears.

Across the street from the school the police had set up wooden barriers to keep the crowd back, and they paraded back and forth, ignoring the jokes called to them. The front of the school was deserted but along the curb United States marshals were spaced, not in uniform but wearing armbands to identify them. Their guns bulged decently under their coats but their eyes darted about nervously, inspecting faces. It seemed to me that they inspected me to see if I was a regular, and then abandoned me as unimportant.

It was apparent where the Cheerleaders were, because people shoved forward to try to get near them. They had a favored place at the barricade directly across from the school entrance, and in that area a concentration of police stamped their feet and slapped their hands together in unaccustomed gloves.

Suddenly I was pushed violently and a cry went up: "Here she comes. Let her through. . . . Come on, move back. Let her through. Where you been? You're late for school. Where you been, Nellie?"

The name was not Nellie. I forget what it was. But she shoved through the dense crowd quite near enough to me so that I could see her coat of imitation fleece and her gold earrings. She was not tall, but her body was ample and full-busted. I judge she was about fifty. She was heavily powdered, which made the line of her double chin look very dark.

She wore a ferocious smile and pushed her way through the milling people, holding a fistful of clippings high in her hand to keep them from being crushed. Since it was her left hand I looked particularly for a wedding ring, and saw that there was none. I slipped in behind her to get carried along by her wave, but the crush was dense and I was given a warning too. "Watch it, sailor. Everybody wants to hear."

Nellie was received with shouts of greeting. I don't know how many Cheerleaders there were. There was no fixed line between the Cheerleaders and the crowd behind them. What I could see was that a group was passing newspaper clippings back and forth and reading them aloud with little squeals of delight.

Now the crowd grew restless, as an audience does when the clock goes past curtain time. Men all around me looked at their watches. I looked at mine. It was three minutes to nine.

The show opened on time. Sound of sirens. Motorcycle cops. Then two big black cars filled with big men in blond felt hats pulled up in front of the school. The crowd seemed to hold its breath. Four big marshals got out of each car and from somewhere in the automobiles they extracted the littlest Negro girl you ever saw, dressed in shining starchy white, with new white shoes on feet so little they were almost round. Her face and little legs were very black against the white.

The big marshals stood her on the curb and a jangle of jeering shrieks went up from behind the barricades. The little girl did not look at the howling crowd but from the side the whites of her eyes showed like those of a frightened fawn. The men turned her around like a doll, and then the strange procession moved up the broad walk toward the school, and the child was even more a mite because the men were so big. Then the girl made a curious hop, and I think I know what it was. I think in her whole life she had not gone ten steps without skipping, but now in the middle of her first skip the weight bore her down and her little round feet took measured, reluctant steps between the tall guards. Slowly they climbed the steps and entered the school.

The papers had printed that the jibes and jeers were cruel and sometimes obscene, and so they were, but this was not the big show. The crowd was waiting for the white man who dared to bring his white child to school. And here he came along the guarded walk, a tall man dressed in light gray, leading his frightened child by the hand. His body was tensed as a strong leaf spring drawn to the breaking strain; his face was grave and gray, and his eyes were on the ground immediately ahead of him. The muscles of his cheeks stood out from clenched jaws, a man afraid who by his will held his fears in check as a great rider directs a panicked horse.

A shrill, grating voice rang out. The yelling was not in chorus. Each took a turn and at the end of each the crowd broke into howls and roars and whistles of applause. This is what they had come to see and hear.

No newspaper had printed the words these women shouted. It was indicated that they were indelicate, some even said obscene. On television the sound track was made to blur or had crowd noises cut in to cover. But now I heard the words, bestial and filthy and degenerate. In a long and unprotected life I have seen and heard the vomitings of demoniac humans before. Why then did these screams fill me with a shocked and sickened sorrow?

The words written down are dirty, carefully and selectedly filthy. But there was something far worse here than dirt, a kind of frightening witches' Sabbath. Here was no spontaneous cry of anger, of insane rage.

Perhaps that is what made me sick with weary nausea. Here was no principle good or bad, no direction. These blowzy women with their little hats and their clippings hungered for attention. They wanted to be admired. They simpered in happy, almost innocent triumph when they were applauded. Theirs was the demented cruelty of egocentric children, and somehow this made their insensate beastliness much more heartbreaking. These were not mothers, not even women. They were crazy actors playing to a crazy audience.

The crowd behind the barrier roared and cheered and pounded one another with joy. The nervous strolling police watched for any break over the barrier. Their lips were tight but a few of them smiled and quickly unsmiled. Across the street the U.S. marshals stood unmoving. The gray-clothed man's legs had speeded for a second, but he reined them down with his will and walked up the school pavement.

The crowd quieted and the next cheer lady had her turn. Her voice was the bellow of a bull, a deep and powerful shout with flat edges like a circus barker's voice. There is no need to set down her words. The pattern was the same; only the rhythm and tonal quality were different. Anyone who has been near the theater would know that these speeches were not spontaneous. They were tried and memorized and carefully rehearsed. This was theater. I watched the intent faces of the listening crowd and they were the faces of an audience. When there was applause, it was for a performer.

My body churned with weary nausea, but I could not let an illness blind me after I had come so far to look and to hear. And suddenly I knew something was wrong and distorted and out of drawing. I knew New Orleans, I have over the years had many friends there, thoughtful, gentle people, with a tradition of kindness and courtesy. I remembered Lyle Saxon, a huge man of soft laughter. How many days I have spent with Roark Bradford, who took Louisiana sounds and sights and created God and the Green Pastures to which He leadeth us. I looked in the crowd for such faces of such people and they were not there. I've seen this kind bellow for blood at a prize fight, have orgasms when a man is gored in the bull ring, stare with vicarious lust at a highway accident, stand patiently in line for the privilege of watching any pain or any agony. But where were the others—the ones who would be proud they were of a species with the gray man—the ones whose arms would ache to gather up the small, scared black mite?

I don't know where they were. Perhaps they felt as helpless as I did, but they left New Orleans misrepresented to the world. The crowd, no doubt, rushed home to see themselves on television, and what they saw went out all over the world, unchallenged by the other things I know are there.

Adventures of Huckleberry Finn (1885)

Mark Twain

Twain began to write his masterpiece shortly after taking a trip down the Mississippi River to New Orleans and seeing for himself how the Civil War and the end of legalized slavery had failed to change social and economic conditions for the former slaves. In what is widely regarded as the greatest American novel, Twain set out to make readers see Jim (and other former slaves) as a real person, as good and decent as any other character in the novel, and better than many.

After all this long journey, and after all we'd done for them scoundrels, here was it all come to nothing, everything all busted up and ruined, because they could have the heart to serve Jim such a trick as that, and make him a slave again all his life, and amongst strangers, too, for forty dirty dollars.

Once I said to myself it would be a thousand times better for Jim to be a slave at home where his family was, as long as he'd *got* to be a slave, and so I'd better write a letter to Tom Sawyer and tell him to tell Miss Watson where he was. But I soon give up that notion, for two things: she'd be mad and disgusted at his rascality and ungratefulness for leaving her, and so she'd sell him straight down the river again; and if she didn't, everybody naturally despises an ungrateful nigger, and they'd make Jim feel it all the time, and so he'd feel ornery and disgraced. And then think of *me!* It would get all around, that Huck Finn helped a nigger to get his freedom; and if I was to ever see anybody from that town again, I'd be ready to get down and lick his boots for shame. That's just the way: a person does a low-down thing, and then he don't want to take no consequences of it. Thinks as long as he can hide it, it ain't no disgrace. That was my fix exactly. The more I studied about this, the more my conscience went to grinding me, and the more wicked and low-down and ornery I got to feeling. And at last, when it hit me all of a sudden that here was the plain hand of Providence slapping me in the face and letting me know my wickedness was being watched all the time from up there in heaven, whilst I was stealing a poor old woman's nigger that hadn't ever done me no harm, and now was showing me that there's One that's always on the lookout, and ain't agoing to allow no such miserable doings to go on only just so far and no further, I almost dropped in my tracks I was so scared. Well, I tried the best I could to kinder soften it up somehow for myself, by saying I was brung up wicked, and so I warn't so much to blame; but something inside of me kept saying, "There was the Sunday school, you could a gone to it ; and if you'd a done it they'd a learnt you, there, that people that acts as I'd been acting about that nigger goes to everlasting fire."

It made me shiver. And I about made up my mind to pray; and see if I couldn't try to quit being the kind of boy I was, and be better. So I kneeled down. But the words wouldn't come. Why wouldn't they? It warn't no use to try to hide from Him. Nor from *me,* neither. I knowed very well why they wouldn't come. It was because my heart wasn't right; it was because I wasn't square; it was because I was playing double. I was letting *on* to give up sin, but away inside of me I was holding on to the biggest one of all. I was trying to make my mouth *say* I would do the right thing and the clean thing, and go and write to that nigger's owner and tell where he was; but deep down in me I knowed it was a lie—and He knowed it. You can't pray a lie—I found that out.

So I was full of trouble, full as I could be ; and didn't know what to do. At last I had an idea; and I says, I'll go and write the letter—and *then* see if I can pray. Why, it was astonishing, the way I felt as light as a feather, right straight off, and my troubles all gone. So I got a piece of paper and a pencil, all glad and excited, and set down and wrote:

> *Miss Watson your runaway nigger Jim is down here two mile below Pikesville and Mr. Phelps has got him and he will give him up for the reward if you send.*
>
> *Huck Finn*

I felt good and all washed clean of sin for the first time I had ever felt so in my life, and I knowed I could pray now. But I didn't do it straight off, but laid the paper down and set there thinking—thinking how good it was all this happened so, and how near I come to being lost and going to hell. And went on thinking. And got to thinking over our trip down the river; and I see Jim before me, all the time, in the day, and in the nighttime, sometimes moonlight, sometimes storms, and we a floating along, talking, and singing, and laughing. But somehow I couldn't seem to strike no places to harden me against him, but only the other kind. I'd see him standing my watch on top of his'n, stead of calling me, so I could go on sleeping; and see him how glad he was when I come back out of the fog; and when I come to him again in the swamp, up there where the feud was; and such-like times; and would always call me honey, and pet me, and do everything he could think of for me, and how good he always was; and at last I struck the time I saved him by telling the men we had small-pox aboard, and he was so grateful, and said I was the best friend old Jim ever had in the world, and the *only* one he's got now; and then I happened to look around, and see that paper.

It was a close place. I took it up, and held it in my hand. I was a trembling, because I'd got to decide, forever, betwixt two things, and I knowed it. I studied a minute, sort of holding my breath, and then says to myself:

"All right, then, I'll *go* to hell"—and tore it up.

Immigration

Ellis Island and the inscription at the base of the nearby Statue of Liberty have inspired many stories about families leaving the Old World—whether Europe, Asia, or another continent—to come to the New World in pursuit of their dream of economic freedom and prosperity. Both theoretical and empirical studies of immigration conducted by economists generally offer strong support for the popular notion that such dreams are often realized, and that the nation as a whole benefits from immigration.

Although there are some circumstances under which a large influx of immigrants who take (at least initially) low-wage jobs can further depress wages in those jobs, even in those cases the immigrants usually benefit the overall economy by increasing production and demand for goods and services. Over time, as their education, training, and language skills improve, and as they are assimilated into society, economic gains are even greater.

The passage below is Ivan Doig's sweeping account of Scottish immigrants coming to Montana in the nineteenth century from Dancing at the Rascal Fair.

Dancing at the Rascal Fair (1987)

Ivan Doig

Immigrants have always faced high risks and costs, accepting them either willingly or by necessity. Those concerns are undoubtedly most keenly felt at the start of the journey to a new country.

"Now then, whoever of you are for the *James Watt*, straight on to the queue there, New York at its other end, step to it please, thank you." And so we let ourselves be shooed from the sight of poor old horsemeat Ginger and went and stepped onto line with our fellow steerage ticketholders beside the bulk of the steamship. Our fellow Scotland-leavers, half a thousand at once, each and every of us now staring sidelong at this black iron island that was to carry us to America. One of the creels which had held the sugar was bobbing against the ship's side, while over our heads deckhands were going through the motions of some groaning chore I couldn't begin to figure.

"Now if this was fresh water, like," sang out one above the dirge of their task, "I'd wager ye a guinea this harbor'd right now taste sweet as treacle."

"But it's not, ye bleedin' daftie. The bleedin' Clyde is tide salt from the Tail of the Bank the full way up to bleedin' Glasgow, now en't it? And what to hell kind of concoction are ye going to get when ye mix sugar and salt?"

"Ask our bedamned cook," put in a third. "All the time he must be doing it, else why's our mess taste like what the China dog walked away from?" As emphasis he spat a throat gob over the side into the harbor water, and my stomach joined my other constituent parts in trepidation about this world-crossing journey of ours. A week and a half of the Atlantic and dubious food besides?

That steerage queue seemed eternal. Seagulls mocked the line of us with sharp cries. A mist verging on rain dimmed out the Renfrewshire hills beyond Greenock's uncountable roofs. Even you appeared a least little bit ill at ease with this wait, Rob, squinting now and again at the steamship as if calculating how it was that so much metal was able to float. And then the cocked head once more, as if pleased with your result. I started to say aloud that if Noah had taken this much time to load the ark, only the giraffes would have lasted through the deluge, but that was remindful of the waiting water and its fate for cart horses and others not amphibious.

Awful, what a person lets himself do to himself. There I stood on that Greenock dock, wanting more than anything else in this life not to put foot aboard that iron ship; and wanting just as desperately to do so and do it that instant. Oh, I knew what was wrestling in me. We had a book—*Crofutt's Trans-Atlantic Emigrants' Guide*—and my malady was right there in it, page one. Crofutt performed as our tutor that a shilling was worth 24 American cents, and how much postal stamps cost there in the big country, and that when it came midnight in old Scotland the clocks of Montana were striking just five of the afternoon. Crofutt told this, too, I can recite it yet today: *Do not emigrate in a fever, but consider the question in each and every aspect. The mother country must be left behind, the family ties, all old associations, broken. Be sure that you look at the dark side of the picture: the broad Atlantic, the dusty ride to the great West of America, the scorching sun, the cold winter—coldest ever you experienced!—and the hard work of the homestead. But if you finally, with your eyes open, decide to emigrate, do it nobly. Do it with no divided heart.*

Right advice, to keep your heart in one pure piece. But easier seen than followed.

I knew I oughtn't, but I turned and looked up the river, east up the great broad trough of the Clyde. East into yesterday. For it had been only the day before when the pair of us were hurled almost all the way across Scotland by train from Nethermuir into clamorsome Glasgow. A further train across the Clyde bridge and westward alongside mile upon brown mile of the river's tideflats and their smell. Then here came Greenock to us, Watt's city of steam, all its shipyards and docks, the chimney stalks of its sugar refineries, its sharp church spires and high, high above all its municipal tower of crisp new stone the color of pie crust. A more going town than our old Nethermuir could be in ten centuries, it took just that first look to tell us of Greenock. For night we bedded where the emigration agent had advised, the Model Lodging House, which may have been a model of something but lodging wasn't it; when morning at last came, off we set to ask our way to the Cumbrae Line's moorage, to the *James Watt*, and to be told in a Clydeside gabble it took the both of us to understand:

"The *Jemmy*, lads? Ye wan' tae gi doon tae the fit of Pa'rick."

And there at the foot of Patrick Street was the Albert Harbor, there was the green-funneled steam swimmer to America, there were the two of us.

For I can't but think of you then, Rob. The Rob you were. In all that we said to each other, before and thereafter, this step from our land to our new was flat fact with you. The Atlantic Ocean and the continent America all the way across to Montana stood as but the width of a cottage threshold, so far as you ever let on. No second guess, never a might-have-done instead out of you, none. A silence too total, I realize at last. You had family and a trade to scan back at and I had none of either, yet I was the one tossing puppy looks up the Clyde to yesterday. Man, man, what I would give to know. Under the stream of words by which you talked the two of us into our long step to America, what were your deep reasons? I am late about asking, yes. Years and years and years late. But when was such asking ever not? And by the time I learned there was so much within you that I did not know and you were learning the same of me, we had greater questions for each other.

A soft push on my shoulder. When I turned to your touch you were smiling hard, that Barclay special mix of entertainment and estimation. We had reached the head of the queue, another whiskery geezer in Cumbrae green uniform was trumpeting at us to find Steerage Number One, go forward toward the bow, descend those stairs the full way down, mind our footing and our heads . . .

You stayed where you stood, though, facing me instead of the steamship. You still had the smile on, but your voice was as serious as I ever had heard it.

"Truth now, Angus. Are we both for it?"

Standing looking at it has never been known to help. I filled myself with breath, the last I intended to draw of the air of the pinched old earth called Scotland. *With no divided heart.*

"Both," I made myself say. And up the *Jemmy's* gangplank we started.

Robert Burns Barclay, a single man, apprentice wheelwright, of Nethermuir, Forfarshire. That was Rob on the passenger list of the *James Watt*, 22nd of October of the year 1889. Angus Alexander McCaskill, single man, wheelworks clerk, of

Nethermuir, Forfarshire, myself. Both of us nineteen and green as the cheese of the moon and trying our double damnedest not to show it.

Not that we were alone in tint. Our steerage compartment within the *Jemmy* proved to be the forward one for single men—immediately the report went around that the single women were quartered farthest aft, and between them and us stood the married couples and a terrific populace of children—and while not everyone was young, our shipmates were all as new as we to voyaging. Berths loomed in unfamiliar tiers with a passageway not a yard wide between them, and the twenty of us bumped and backed and swirled like a herd of colts trying to establish ourselves.

I am tall, and the inside of the ship was not. Twice in those first minutes of steerage life I cracked myself.

"You'll be hammered down to my size by the time we reach the other shore," Rob came out with, and those around us hoohawed. I grinned the matter away but I did not like it, either the prospect of a hunched journey to America or the public comment about my altitude. But that was Rob for you.

Less did I like the location of Steerage Number One. So far below the open deck, down steep stair after stair into the iron gut of the ship. When you thought about it, and I did, this was like being a kitten in the bottom of a rainbarrel.

"Here I am, mates," recited a fresh voice, that of the steward. "Your shepherd while at sea. First business is three shillings from you each. That's for mattress to keep you company and tin to eat with and the finest saltwater soap you've ever scraped yourself with." Ocean soap and straw bed Rob and I had to buy along with everyone else, but on Crofutt's advice we'd brought our own trustworthy tinware. "Meals are served at midship next deck up, toilets you'll find in the deckhouses, and that's the circle of life at sea, mates," the steward rattled at us, and then he was gone.

As to our compartment companions, a bit of listening told that some were of a fifty embarking to settle in Manitoba, others of a fifty fixed upon Alberta for a future. The two heavenly climes were argued back and forth by their factions, with recitations of rainfall and crop yields and salubrious health effects and imminence of railroads, but no minds were changed, these being Scottish minds.

Eventually someone deigned to ask us neutral pair what our destination might be.

"Montana," Rob enlightened them as if it was Eden's best neighborhood. "I've an uncle there these seven years."

"What does the man do there," sang out an Alberta adherent, "besides boast of you as a nephew? Montana is nothing but mountains, like the name of it."

"He's the owner of a mine," Rob reported with casual grandness, and this drew us new looks from the compartment citizenry. Rob, though, was not one to quit just because he was ahead. "A silver mine at Helena, called the Great Maybe."

All of steerage except the two of us thought that deserved the biggest laugh there was, and for the next days we were known as the Maybe Miners. Well, they could laugh like parrots at a bag-piper. It was worth that and more, to have Lucas Barclay there in Montana ahead of us.

"Up?" offered Rob to me now, with a sympathetic toss of his head. Back to deck we climbed, to see how the *Jemmy's* departure was done.

As I look on it from now, I suppose the others aboard cannot but have wondered about the larky companion beside me at the deck rail, dispensing his presiding smile around the ship as if he had invented oceangoing. The bearing of a bank heir, but in a flat cap and rough clothes? A mien of careless independence, but with those workworn wheelwright's hands at the ends of his young arms? And ever, ever, that unmatchable even-toothed smile, as though he was about to say something bright even when he wasn't; Rob could hold that smile effortlessly the way a horse holds the bit between his teeth. You could be fooled in a hurry about Rob, though. It maybe can be said my mind lacks clench. Rob had a fist there in his head. The smile gave way to it here when he spotted a full family, tykes to grandfolks, among us America-goers.

"They all ought've come, Angus. By damn, but they ought've. Am I right?" He meant all the rest of his own family, his father and mother and three older brothers and young sister; and he meant it hotly. Rob had argued for America until the air of the Barclay household was blue with it, but there are times when not even a Barclay can budge Barclays. Just thinking about it still made him tense as a harp. "They ought've let the damned 'wright shop go, let old Nethermuir doze itself to death. They can never say I didn't tell them. You heard."

"I heard."

"Lucas is the only one of the bunch who's ever looked ahead beyond his nose. See now, Angus, I almost wish we'd been in America as long as Lucas. Think of all he must've seen and done, these years."

"You'd have toddled off there when you were the age of Adair, would you?" Adair was Rob's sister, just twelve or so, and a little replica of Rob or at least close enough; tease her as I did by greeting her in gruff hard-man style *Hello you, Dair Barclay*, and she always gave me right back, snappy as beans, *Hello yourself, old Angus McCaskill.*

"Adair's the one in the bunch who most ought've come," Rob persisted. "Just look around you, this ship is thick with children not a minute older than Adair." He had a point there. "She'd positively be thriving here. And she'd be on her way to the kind of life she deserves instead of that"—Rob pointed his chin up the Clyde, to the horizon we had come from—"back there. I tried for her."

"Your parents would be the first to say so."

"Parents are the world's strangest commodity, haven't you ever noticed—Angus, forgive that. My tongue got ahead of itself."

"It went right past my ears. What about a walk around deck, shall we?"

At high tide on the Clyde, when the steam tug arrived to tow this behemoth ship of ours to deep water at the Tail of the Bank, Rob turned to me and lifted his cap in mock congratulation.

"We're halfway there," he assured me.

"Only the wet part left, you're telling me."

He gave my shoulder a push. "McAngus, about this old water. You'll grow used to it, man. Half of Scotland has made this voyage by now."

I started to retort that I seemed to belong to the half without webfeet, but I was touched by this, Rob's concern for me, even though I'd hoped I was keeping my Atlantic apprehensions within me. The way they resounded around in there—*Are we both for it? Both*—I suppose it was a wonder the entire ship wasn't hearing them like the thump of a drum.

We watched Greenock vanish behind the turn of the Firth. "Poor old River Carrou," from Rob now. "This Clyde makes it look like a piddle, doesn't it?"

Littler than that, actually. We from an inland eastern town such as Nethermuir with its sea-seeking stream Carrou were born thinking that the fishing ports of our counties of Fife and Forfar and Kincardine and Aberdeen must be the rightful entrances to the ocean, so Rob and I came with the natural attitude that these emigration steamships of Greenock and Glasgow pittered out the back door of Scotland. The Firth of Clyde was showing us otherwise. Everywhere around us the water was wider than wide, arms of it delving constantly between the hills of the shore, abundant islands were stood here and there on the great gray breadth as casually as haycocks. Out and out the *Jemmy* steamed, past the last of the beetle-busy packet boats, and still the Clyde went on carving hilly shores. Ayr. Argyll. Arran. This west of Scotland perhaps all sounded like gargle, but it was as handsome a coast as could be fashioned. Moor and cliff and one entire ragged horizon of the Highlands mountains for emphasis, shore-tucked villages and the green exactness of fields for trim.

And each last inch of it everlastingly owned by those higher than Angus McCaskill and Rob Barclay, I reminded myself. Those whose names began with Lord. Those who had the banks and mills. Those whitehanded men of money. Those who watched from their fat fields as the emigrant ships steamed past with us.

Daylight lingered along with the shore. Rain came and went at edges of the Firth. You saw a far summit, its rock brows, and then didn't.

"Just damp underfoot, try to think of the old ocean as," Rob put in on me.

"I *am* trying, man. And I'd still just as soon walk to America."

"Or we could ride on each other's shoulders, what if?" Rob swept on. "No, McAngus, this steam yacht is the way to travel." Like the duke of dukes, he patted the deck rail of the *Jemmy* and proclaimed: "See now, this is proper style for going to America and Montana."

America. Montana. Those words with their ends open. Those words that were ever in the four corners of my mind, and I am sure Rob's, too, all the minutes since we had left Nethermuir. I hear that set of words yet, through all the time since, the pronouncement Rob gave them that day. America and Montana echoed and echoed in us, right through my mistrust of journeying on water, past Rob's breeze of manner, into the tunnels of our bones. For with the *Jemmy* underway out the Firth of Clyde we were threading our lives into the open beckon of those words. Like Lucas Barclay before us, now we were on our way to be Americans. To be—what did people call themselves in that far place Montana? Montanese? Montanians? Montaniards? Whatever that denomination was, now the two of us were going to be its next members, with full feathers on.

My first night in steerage I learned that I was not born to sleep on water. The berth was both too short and too narrow for me, so that I had to kink myself radically; curl up and wedge in at the same time. Try that if you ever want to be cruel to yourself. Too, steerage air was thick and unpleasant, like breathing through dirty flannel. Meanwhile Rob, who could snooze through the thunders of Judgment Day, was composing a nose song below me. But discomfort and bad air and snores were the least of my wakefulness, for in that first grief of a night—oh yes, and the *Jemmy* letting forth an iron groan whenever its bow met the waves some certain way—my mind rang with everything I did not want to think of. Casting myself from Nethermuir. The drowned horse Ginger. Walls of this moaning ship, so close. The coffin confines of my bedamned berth. The ocean, the ocean on all sides, including abovehead. *Dark Neptune's labyrinthine lanes | 'Neath these savage liquid plains.* I rose in heartrattling startlement once when I accidentally touched one hand against the other and felt wetness there. My own sweat.

I still maintain that if the Atlantic hadn't been made of water I could have gone to America at a steady trot. But it seems to be the case that fear can sniff the bothering places in us. Mine had been in McCaskills for some eighty years now. The bones of the story are this. With me on this voyage, into this unquiet night, came the fact that I was the first McCaskill since my father's grandfather to go upon the sea. That voyage of Alexander McCaskill was only a dozen miles, but the most famous dozen miles in Great Britain of the time, and he voyaged them over and over and over again. He was one of the stonemasons of Arbroath who worked with the great engineer Robert Stevenson to build the Bell Rock lighthouse. On the clearest of days I have seen that lighthouse from the Arbroath harbor and have heard the story of the years of workshops and cranes and winches and giant blocks of granite and sandstone, and to this moment I don't know how they could do what was done out there, build a hundred-foot tower of stone on a reef that vanished deep beneath every high tide. But there it winks at the world even today, impossible Bell Rock, standing in the North Sea announcing the Firth of Forth and Edinburgh beyond, and my great-grandfather's toolmarks are on its stones. The generations of us, we who are not a sea people, dangle from that one man who went to perform stonework in the worst of the waters around Scotland. Ever since him, Alexander has been the first or second name of a McCaskill in each of those generations. Ever since him, we have possessed a saga to measure ourselves against. I lay there in the sea-plowing *Jemmy* trying to think myself back into that other manhood, to leave myself, damp sackful of apprehension that I was, and to feel from the skin inward what it would have been like to be Alexander McCaskill of the Bell Rock those eighty years ago. *A boat is a hole in the water,* began my family's one scrap of our historic man, the solitary story from our McCaskill past that my father would ever tell. In some rare furlough from his brooding, perhaps Christmas or Hogmanay and enough drinks of lubrication, that silence-locked man my father would suddenly unloose the words. *But there was a time your great-grandfather was more glad than anything to see a boat, I'm here to tell you. Out there on the Bell Rock they were cutting down into the reef for the lighthouse's foundation, the other one and your great-grandfather, that day. When the tide began to come in they took up their tools and went across the reef to meet their boat. Stevenson was there ahead of them, as high as he could climb on the reef and standing looking out into the fog on the water. Your great-grandfather knew there was wrong as soon as he saw Stevenson. Stevenson the famous engineer of the Northern Lights, pale as the cat's milk. As he ought have been, for there was no boat on the reef and none in sight anywhere. The tide was coming fast, coming to cover all of the Bell Rock with water higher than this roof. Your great-grandfather saw Stevenson turn to speak to the men. "This I'll swear to, Alexander the Second," your great-grandfather always told me it just this way. "Mister Stevenson's mouth moved as if he was saying, but no words came out. The fear had dried his mouth so." Your great-grandfather and the men watched Stevenson go down on his knees and drink water like a dog from a pool in the rock. When he stood up to try to speak this time, somebody shouted out, "A boat! There, a boat!" The pilot boat, it was, bringing the week's mail to the workship. Your great-grandfather always ended saying, "I almost ran out onto the water to hail that boat, you can believe."*

"You ask was I afraid, Alexander the Second?" My father's voice became a strange, sad thunder when he told of my great-grandfather's reply to him. "*Every hour of those three Bell Rock years, and most of the minutes, drowning was on my mind. I was afraid enough, yes. But the job was there at the Bell Rock. It was to be done, afraid or no afraid.*"

The past. The past past, so to speak, back there beyond myself. What can we ever truly know of it, how can we account for what it passes to us, what it withholds? Employ my imagination to its utmost, I could not see myself doing what Alexander McCaskill did in his Bell Rock years, travel an extent of untrustable water each day to set Abroath stone onto reef stone. Feed me first to the flaming hounds of hell. Yet for all I knew, my ocean-defying great-grandfather was afraid of the dark or whimpered at the sight of a spider but any such perturbances were whited out by time. Only his brave Bell Rock accomplishment was left to sight. And here I lay, sweating steerage sweat, with a dread of water that had no logic newer than eighty years, no personal beginning, and evidently no end. It simply was in me, like life's underground river of blood. Ahead there, I hoped *far* ahead, when I myself became the past—would the weak places in me become hidden, too? Say I ever did become husband, father, eventual great-grandfather of Montana McCaskills. What were they going to comprehend of me as their firstcomer? Not this sweated night here in my midnight cage of steerage, not my mental staggers. No, for what solace it was, eventually all that could be known of Angus Alexander McCaskill was that I did manage to cross the Atlantic Ocean.

If I managed to cross it.

❧

Income Inequality, Poverty, and Income Redistribution Policies

After World War II, the United States was in the historically unprecedented position of having its industrial production base intact while that of Europe and Japan lay largely in ruins. During this period, manufacturing jobs filled mainly by high school graduates commanded high wages, and most adult women did not take jobs in the labor market. By the 1960s things were rapidly changing. Not only were the economies of Europe and Asia rebuilt and highly competitive, but the labor force was beginning to grow at an incredible rate as the baby boomers and more and more women—soon a majority of both married and unmarried adult females—began to take full-time jobs, to pursue careers, and to seek out post-secondary education and training. Technological innovations in communications, transportation, and computers began to change the way work was done, with the service industries employing a much greater proportion of the labor force. Meanwhile, living standards in other industrialized nations were rapidly converging with those in the United States.

The wage premium for college graduates—that is, the difference in wages between college graduates and those with less education—fell for a time in the 1970s, as the number of college graduates expanded due to demographic forces, and then rose sharply through the 1980s and 1990s. The distribution of income became less equal in virtually all industrialized nations during these decades, especially in the United States and United Kingdom. But these two countries also experienced sharply lower unemployment rates than did others.

Always a favorite topic of conversation at bars and political assemblies, questions about who makes how much and why began to make headlines in the financial press and other media outlets during the '80s and '90s, with the lifestyles of the rich and famous becoming a regular feature in the general print and electronic media, especially in the tabloids. Income distribution, poverty, and the government's role in redistributing income are longstanding and popular topics for literary authors, too. Seven passages are included in this section; the excerpt from Mark Twain's Connecticut Yankee in King Arthur's Court, *included in the later section on real versus nominal values, also deals with these issues.*

The famous speech from Shakespeare's Troilus and Cressida*—"take but degree away and hark, what discord follows"—was emphasized by E. M. W. Tillyard and other literary critics who have cast Shakespeare as a defender of a conservative and hierarchical social order. In a brief passage from his* Journals, *Ralph Waldo Emerson also accepts the necessity of high* *degrees of inequality as a way of encouraging enterprise and order and discouraging sloth.*

In The Road to Wigan Pier, *George Orwell describes the circumstances facing a family living "on the dole" in England, and the perverse incentives that many public assistance programs in Europe and the United States featured through much of the twentieth century because of the "means test" that, when low-income families earned some money in the labor market, reduced their public assistance by exactly that amount. Economists of all political persuasions have decried the incentive effects of such policies, which effectively impose a 100 percent tax rate on welfare recipients. Partly as a consequence of these critiques, in recent decades all the major political parties in the United States and the United Kingdom have actively pursued various kinds of welfare reform programs and policies.*

In a passage from The Octopus, *Frank Norris juxtaposes scenes of a starving widow and child with a lavish feast served at the opulent home of a railroad president. In* A Moveable Feast, *Ernest Hemingway recalls the poverty he experienced before becoming financially and artistically successful. Erskine Caldwell described the rural poverty of hardscrabble farming in* Tobacco Road. *These passages, especially those by Norris and Caldwell, represent the kind of writing that has led some economists to argue that there is a pervasive anti-market or even anti-economic bias in literature and drama. But economists and social scientists have published similar accounts of the effects and culture of poverty, and the literary depictions are by no means one-sided. For example, Kurt Vonnegut's short story "Harrison Bergeron" is a scathing, hilarious, and sobering satire of government policies aimed at achieving complete equality.*

Troilus and Cressida
(1609)
William Shakespeare

This passage presents a Renaissance version of the Great Chain of Being image of social and cosmological order in which there are clear differences in function, status, and income for people in different occupations and social stations. As Arthur Lovejoy noted in his 1966 intellectual history of this image, however, unlike most medieval versions that stressed a contemplative and essentially otherworldly life, during the Renaissance the image was often used to encourage an active life in which all people are called to imitate the creative works of God, as best they can. In recognizing and rewarding that creativity, a considerable degree of social and economic mobility was accepted during the Renaissance, both in theory and practice.

The heavens themselves, the planets, and this centre,
Observe degree, priority and place,

Insisture, course, proportion, season, form,
Office and custom, in all line of order:
And therefore is the glorious planet Sol
In noble eminence enthroned and sphered
Amidst the other, whose medicinable eye
Corrects the ill aspects of planets evil,
And posts like the commandment of a king,
Sans check to good and bad: but when the planets
In evil mixture to disorder wander,
What plagues and what portents, what mutiny,
What raging of the sea, shaking of earth,
Commotion in the winds, frights, changes, horrors,
Divert and crack, rend and deracinate
The unity and married calm of states
Quite from their fixture! Oh, when degree is shaked,
Which is the ladder to all high designs,
The enterprise is sick! How could communities,
Degrees in schools and brotherhoods in cities,
Peaceful commerce from dividable shores,
The primogenitive and due of birth,
Prerogative of age, crowns, sceptres, laurels,
But by degree, stand in authentic place?
Take but degree away, untune that string,
And hark, what discord follows! each thing meets
In mere oppugnancy: the bounded waters
Should lift their bosoms higher than the shores,
And make a sop of all this solid globe:
Strength should be lord to imbecility,
And the rude son strike his father dead:
Force should be right; or rather, right and wrong,
Between whose endless jar justice resides,
Should lose their names, and so should justice too.
Then every thing includes itself in power,
Power into will, will into appetite;
And appetite, a universal wolf,
So doubly seconded with will and power,
Must make perforce a universal prey,
And last eat up himself. Great Agamemnon,
This chaos, when degree is suffocate,

Follows the choking.
And this neglection of degree it is
That by a pace goes backward, with a purpose
It hath to climb.

JOURNALS (1851)

Ralph Waldo Emerson

Emerson identifies here some of the factors—risk, effort, faculty, and the overall order of the set of relative wages across different occupations—recognized by economists as creating differences in incomes, wages, and land values. Distinctions between primary and artificial values are not part of orthodox economics, but historically, different economic schools have proceeded—at least for a time—on the premise that factors such as land or labor are the primary or only true source of economic value.

The odious inequality must be borne. A superintendent at the mills must have two thousand dollars, whilst the most industrious operative has only four hundred. Because, order and faculty are rare and costly. Why should not the wheels of the loom say, "See me, I whirl and buzz with two hundred revolutions in a minute, whilst that great lazy water-wheel, down below there, only turns five times. I will not go faster than he."

I learned also that the valuations of Massachusetts, of Boston, of New York, are nowise reliable for direct comparison. As, for example, the saying that Boston could buy Maine and have $80,000,000 left. Because the values of Boston are artificial values, the values of luxuries, furniture, books, pictures, inflated prices of land and house lots and houses, etc., whilst the values of Maine are primary and necessary, and therefore permanent under any state of society.

This consideration of inflation goes into all farming value. The farmer gets two hundred, whilst the merchant gets two thousand dollars. . . . But the farmer's two hundred is far safer, and is more likely to remain to him . . . so that the two sums turn out at last to be equivalent.

The Road to Wigan Pier (1937)

George Orwell

Well-intentioned public policies often have unintended and perverse results. The means test for public assistance programs to low-income familes was, as administered in both the United Kingdom and the United States through much of the twentieth century, a classic example of this problem. Reducing assistance payments on a dollar-for-dollar basis whenever a family began to earn some income in the labor market created a prohibitively high tax rate—100 percent—with the rational and predictable consequence of reducing peoples' incentives to work, save, and invest in education and training.

It will be seen that the income of a family on the dole normally averages round about thirty shillings a week. One can write at least a quarter of this off as rent, which is to say that the average person, child or adult, has got to be fed, clothed, warmed, and otherwise cared-for for six or seven shillings a week. Enormous groups of people, probably at least a third of the whole population of the industrial areas, are living at this level. The Means Test is very strictly enforced, and you are liable to be refused relief at the slightest hint that you are getting money from another source. Dock-labourers, for instance, who are generally hired by the half-day, have to sign on at a Labour Exchange twice daily; if they fail to do so it is assumed that they have been working and their dole is reduced correspondingly. I have seen cases of evasion of the Means Test, but I should say that in the industrial towns, where there is still a certain amount of communal life and everyone has neighbours who know him, it is much harder than it would be in London. The usual method is for a young man who is actually living with his parents to get an accommodation address, so that supposedly he has a separate establishment and draws a separate allowance. But there is much spying and talebearing. One man I knew, for instance, was seen feeding his neighbour's chickens while the neighbour was away. It was reported to the authorities that he "had a job feeding chickens" and he had great difficulty in refuting this. The favourite joke in Wigan was about a man who was refused relief on the ground that he "had a job carting firewood." He had been seen, it was said, carting firewood at night. He had to explain that he was not carting firewood but doing a moonlight flit. The "firewood" was his furniture.

The most cruel and evil effect of the Means Test is the way in which it breaks up families. Old people, sometimes bedridden, are driven out of their homes by it. An old age pensioner, for instance, if a widower, would normally live with one or other of his children; his weekly ten shillings goes towards the household expenses, and probably he is not badly cared for. Under the Means Test, however, he counts as a "lodger" and if he stays at home his children's dole will be docked. So, perhaps at seventy or seventy-five years of age, he has to turn out into lodgings, handing his pension over to the lodging-house keeper and existing on the verge of starvation. I have seen several cases of this myself. It is happening all over England at this moment, thanks to the Means Test.

Nevertheless, in spite of the frightful extent of unemployment, it is a fact that poverty—extreme poverty—is less in evidence in the industrial North than it is in London. Everything is poorer and shabbier, there are fewer motorcars and fewer well-dressed people; but also there are fewer people who are obviously destitute. Even in a town the size of Liverpool or Manchester you are struck by the fewness of the beggars. London is a sort of whirlpool which draws derelict people towards it, and it is so vast that life there is solitary and anonymous. Until you break the law nobody will take any notice of you, and you can go to pieces as you could not possibly do in a place where you had neighbours who knew you. But in the industrial towns the old communal way of life has not yet broken up, tradition is still strong and almost everyone has a family—potentially, therefore, a home. In a town of 50,000 or 100,000 inhabitants there is no casual and as it were unaccounted-for population; nobody sleeping in the streets, for instance. Moreover, there is just this to be said for the unemployment regulations, that they do not discourage people from marrying. A man and wife on twenty-three shillings a week are not far from the starvation line, but they can make a home of sorts; they are vastly better off than a single man on fifteen shillings. The life of a single unemployed man is dreadful. He lives sometimes in a common lodging-house, more often in a "furnished" room for which he usually pays six shillings a week, finding himself as best he can on the other nine (say six shillings a week for food and three for clothes, tobacco, and amusements). Of course he cannot feed or look after himself properly, and a man who pays six shillings a week for his room is not encouraged to be indoors more than is necessary. So he spends his days loafing in the public library or any other place where he can keep warm. That—keeping warm—is almost the sole preoccupation of a single unemployed man in winter. In Wigan, a favourite refuge was the pictures, which are fantastically cheap there. You can always get a seat for fourpence, and at the matinee at some houses you can even get a seat for twopence. Even people on the verge of starvation will readily pay twopence to get out of the ghastly cold of a winter afternoon. In Sheffield I was taken to a public hall to listen to a lecture by a clergyman, and it was by a long way the silliest and worst-delivered lecture I have ever heard or ever expect to hear. I found it physically impossible to sit it out; indeed my feet carried me out, seemingly of their own accord, before it was halfway through. Yet the hall was thronged with unemployed men; they would have sat through far worse drivel for the sake of a warm place to shelter in.

At times I have seen unmarried men on the dole living in the extreme of misery. In one town I remember a whole colony of them who were squatting, more or less illicitly, in a derelict house which was practically falling down. They had collected a few scraps of furniture, presumably off refuse-tips, and I remember that their sole table was an old marble-topped wash-hand-stand. But this kind of thing is exceptional. A working-class bachelor is a rarity, and so long as a man is married unemployment makes comparatively little alteration in his way of life. His home is impoverished but it is still a home, and it is noticeable everywhere that the anomalous position created by unemployment—the man being out of work while the woman's work continues as before—has not altered the relative status of the sexes. In a working-class home it is the man who is the master and not, as in a middle-class home, the woman or the baby. Practically never, for instance, in a working-class home, will you see the man doing a stroke of the housework. Unemployment has not changed this convention, which on the face of it seems a little unfair. The man is idle from morning to night but the woman is as busy as ever—more so, indeed, because she has to manage with less money. Yet so far as my experience goes the women do not protest. I believe that they, as well as the men, feel that a man would lose his manhood if, merely because he was out of work, he developed into a "Mary Ann."

But there is no doubt about the deadening, debilitating effect of unemployment upon everybody, married or single, and upon men more than upon women. The best intellects will not stand up against it. Once or twice it has happened to me to meet unemployed men of genuine literary ability; there are others whom I haven't met but whose work I occasionally see in the magazines. Now and again, at long intervals, these men will produce an article or a short story which is quite obviously better than most of the stuff that gets whooped up by the blurb-reviewers. Why, then, do they make so little use of their talents? They all have the leisure in the world; why don't they sit down and write books? Because to write books you need not only comfort and solitude—and solitude is never easy to attain in a working-class home—you also need peace of mind. You can't settle to anything, you can't command the spirit of *hope* in which anything has got to be created, with that dull evil cloud of unemployment hanging over you. Still, an unemployed man who feels at home with books can at any rate occupy himself by reading. But what about the man who cannot read without discomfort? Take a miner, for instance, who has worked in the pit since childhood and has been trained to be a miner and nothing else. How the devil is he to fill up the empty days? It is absurd to say that he ought to be looking for work. There is no work to look for, and everybody knows it. You can't go on looking for work every day for seven years. There are allotments, which occupy the time and help to feed a family, but in a big town there are only allotments for a small proportion of the people. Then there are the occupational centres which were started a few years ago to help the unemployed. On the whole this movement has been a failure, but some of the centres are still flourishing. I have visited one or two of them. There are shelters where the men can keep warm and there are periodical classes in carpentering, boot-making, leather-work, handloom-weaving, basket-work, sea-grass work, etc., etc.; the idea being that the men can make furniture and so forth, not for sale but for their own homes, getting tools free and materials cheaply. Most of the Socialists I have talked to denounce this movement as they denounce the project—it is always being talked about but it never comes to anything—to give the unemployed small-holdings. They say that the occupational centres are simply a device to keep the unemployed quiet and give them the illusion that something is being done for them. Undoubtedly that *is* the underlying motive. Keep a man busy mending boots and he is less likely to read the *Daily Worker*. Also there is a nasty Y.M.C.A. atmosphere about these places which you can feel as soon as you go in. The unemployed men who frequent them are mostly of the cap-touching type—the type who tells you oilily that he is "Temperance" and votes Conservative. Yet even here you feel yourself torn both ways. For probably it is better that a man should waste his time even with such rubbish as sea-grass work than for years upon end he should do absolutely *nothing*.

The Octopus: A Story of California (1901)

Frank Norris

Norris's influential novel presented a stark picture of two nations: one wealthy and powerful, the other powerless and poor.

Presley entered the dining-room of the Gerard mansion with little Miss Gerard on his arm. The other guests had preceded them—Cedarquist with Mrs. Gerard; a pale-faced, languid young man (introduced to Presley as Julian Lambert) with Presley's cousin Beatrice, one of the twin daughters of Mr. and Mrs. Cedarquist; his brother Stephen, whose hair was straight as an Indian's, but of a pallid straw color, with Beatrice's sister; Gerard himself, taciturn, bearded, rotund, loud of breath, escorted Mrs. Cedarquist. Besides these, there were one or two other couples, whose names Presley did not remember.

The dining-room was superb in its appointments. On three sides of the room, to the height of some ten feet, ran a continuous picture, an oil painting, divided into long sections by narrow panels of black oak. The painting represented the personages in the *Roman de la Rose*, and was conceived in an atmosphere of the most delicate, most ephemeral allegory. One saw young chevaliers, blue-eyed, of elemental beauty and purity; women with crowns, gold girdles, and cloudy wimples; young girls, entrancing in their loveliness, wearing snow-white kerchiefs, their golden hair unbound and flowing, dressed in white samite, bearing armfuls of flowers; the whole procession defiling against a background of forest glades, venerable oaks, half-hidden fountains, and fields of asphodel and roses.

Otherwise, the room was simple. Against the side of the wall unoccupied by the picture stood a sideboard of gigantic size, that once had adorned the banquet hall of an Italian palace of the late Renaissance. It was black with age, and against its sombre surfaces glittered an array of heavy silver dishes and heavier cut-glass bowls and goblets.

The company sat down to the first course of raw Blue Point oysters, served upon little pyramids of shaved ice, and the two butlers at once began filling the glasses of the guests with cool Haut Sauterne.

Mrs. Gerard, who was very proud of her dinners, and never able to resist the temptation of commenting upon them to her guests, leaned across to Presley and Mrs. Cedarquist, murmuring, "Mr. Presley, do you find that Sauterne too cold? I always believe it is so *bourgeois* to keep such a delicate wine as Sauterne on the ice, and to ice Bordeaux or Burgundy—oh, it is nothing short of a crime."

"This is from your own vineyard, is it not?" asked Julian Lambert. "I think I recognize the bouquet."

He strove to maintain an attitude of *fin gourmet*, unable to refrain from comment upon the courses as they succeeded one another.

Little Honora Gerard turned to Presley:

"You know," she explained, "Papa has his own vineyards in southern France. He is so particular about his wines; turns up his nose at California wines. And I am to go there next summer. Ferrieres is the name of the place where our vineyards are, the dearest village!"

She was a beautiful little girl of a dainty porcelain type, her colouring low in tone. She wore no jewels, but her little undeveloped neck and shoulders, or an exquisite immaturity, rose from the tulle bodice of her first *décolleté* gown.

"Yes," she continued; "I'm to go to Europe for the first time. Won't it be gay? And I am to have my own *bonne*, and Mamma and I are to travel—so many places, Baden, Homburg, Spa, the Tyrol. Won't it be gay?"

Presley assented in meaningless words. He sipped his wine mechanically, looking about that marvellous room, with its subdued saffron lights, its glitter of glass and silver, its beautiful women in their elaborate toilets, its deft, correct servants; its array of tableware—cut glass, chased silver, and Dresden crockery. It was Wealth, in all its outward and visible forms, the signs of an opulence so great that it need never be husbanded. It was the home of a railway "Magnate," a Railroad King. For this, then, the farmers paid. It was for this that S. Behrman turned the screw, tightened the vise. It was for this that Dyke had been driven to outlawry and a jail. It was for this that Lyman Derrick had been bought, the Governor ruined and broken, Annixter shot down, Hooven killed.

The soup, *purée à la Derby*, was served, and at the same time, as *hors d'oeuvres*, ortolan patties, together with a tiny sandwich made of browned roast and thin slices of ham sprinkled over with Parmesan cheese. The wine, so Mrs. Gerard caused it to be understood, was Xeres, of the 1815 vintage.

Mrs. Hooven crossed the avenue. It was growing late. Without knowing it, she had come to a part of the city that experienced beggars shunned. There was nobody about. Block after block of residences stretched away on either hand, lighted, full of people. But the sidewalks were deserted.

"Mammy," whimpered Hilda, "I'm tired, carry me."

Using all her strength, Mrs. Hooven picked her up and moved on aimlessly.

Then again that terrible cry, the cry of the hungry child appealing to the helpless mother:

"Mammy, I'm hungry."

"Ach, Gott, leedle girl," exclaimed Mrs. Hooven, holding her close to her shoulder, the tears starting from her eyes. "Ach, leedle tochter. Doand, doand, doand. You praik my hairt. I cen't vind any subber. We got noddings to eat, noddings, noddings."

"When do we have those bread'n milk again, Mammy?"

"To-morrow—soon—py-and-py, Hilda. I doand know what pecome oaf us now, what pecome oaf my leedle babby."

She went on, holding Hilda against her shoulder with one arm as best she might, one hand steadying herself against the fence railings along the sidewalk. At last, a solitary pedestrian came into view, a young man in a top hat and overcoat, walking rapidly. Mrs. Hooven held out a quivering hand as he passed her.

"Say, say, den Meest'r, blease hellup a boor womun."

The other hurried on.

The fish course was *grenadins* of bass and small salmon, the latter stuffed, and cooked in white wine and mushroom liquor.

"I have read your poem, of course, Mr. Presley," observed Mrs. Gerard. "'The Toilers,' I mean. What a sermon you read us, you dreadful young man. I felt that I ought at once to 'sell all that I have and give to the poor.' Positively, it did stir me up. You must congratulate yourself upon making at least one convert. Just because of that poem Mrs. Cedarquist and I have started a movement to send a whole shipload of wheat to the starving people in India. Now, you horrid *réactionnaire*, are you satisfied?"

"I am very glad," murmured Presley.

"But I am afraid," observed Mrs. Cedarquist, "that we may be too late. They are dying so fast, those poor people. By the time our ship reaches India the famine may be all over."

"One need never be afraid of being 'too late' in the matter of helping the destitute," answered Presley. "Unfortunately, they are always a fixed quantity. 'The poor ye have always with you.'"

"How very clever that is," said Mrs. Gerard.

Mrs. Cedarquist tapped the table with her fan in mild applause.

"Brilliant, brilliant," she murmured, "epigrammatical."

"Honora," said Mrs. Gerard, turning to her daughter, at that moment in conversation with the languid Lambert, "Honora, *entends-tu, ma chérie, l'esprit de notre jeune Lamartine.*"

Mrs. Hooven went on, stumbling from street to street, holding Hilda to her breast. Famine gnawed incessantly at her stomach; walk though she might, turn upon her tracks up and down the streets, back to the avenue again, incessantly and relentlessly the torture dug into her vitals. She was hungry, hungry, and if the want of food harassed and rended her, full-grown woman that she was, what must it be in the poor, starved stomach of her little girl? Oh, for some helping hand now, oh, for one little mouthful, one little nibble! Food, food, all her wrecked body clamoured for nourishment; anything to numb those gnawing teeth—an abandoned loaf, hard, mouldered; a half-eaten fruit, yes, even the refuse of the gutter, even the garbage of the ash heap. On she went, peering into dark corners, into the areaways, anywhere, everywhere, watching the silent prowling of cats, the intent rovings of stray dogs. But she was growing weaker; the pains and cramps in her stomach returned. Hilda's weight bore her to the pavement. More than once a great giddiness, a certain wheeling faintness all but overcame her. Hilda, however, was asleep. To wake her would only mean to revive her to the consciousness of hunger; yet how to carry her further? Mrs. Hooven began to fear that she would fall with her child in her arms. The terror of a collapse upon those cold pavements glistening with fog-damp roused her; she must make an effort to get through the night. She rallied all her strength, and pausing a moment to shift the weight of her baby to the other arm, once more set off through the night. A little while later she found on the edge of the sidewalk the peeling of a banana. It had been trodden upon and it was muddy, but joyfully she caught it up.

"Hilda," she cried, "wake oop, leedle girl. See, loog den, dere's somedings to eat. Look den, hey? Dat's goot, ain't it? Zum bunaner."

But it could not be eaten. Decayed, dirty, all but rotting, the stomach turned from the refuse, nauseated.

"No, no," cried Hilda, "that's not good. I can't eat it. Oh, Mammy, please gif me those bread'n milk."

A Moveable Feast
(1964)
Ernest Hemingway

The poverty facing the young Hemingways in Paris was certainly sharp and severe, but clearly something different from the scenes in Norris or Caldwell. Here, poverty is viewed as a voluntary and self-imposed part of becoming a good writer, probably temporary, and willfully denied through strong doses of arrogance.

There was no quarter too poor to have at least one copy of a racing paper but you had to buy it early on a day like this. I found one in the rue Descartes at the corner of the Place Contrescarpe. The goats were going down the rue Descartes and I breathed the air in and walked back fast to climb the stairs and get my work done. I had been tempted to stay out and follow the goats down the early morning street. But before I started work again I looked at the paper. They were running at Enghien, the small, pretty and larcenous track that was the home of the outsider.

So that day after I had finished work we would go racing. Some money had come from the Toronto paper that I did newspaper work for and we wanted a long shot if we could find one. My wife had a horse one time at Auteuil named Chèvre d'Or that was a hundred and twenty to one and leading by twenty lengths when he fell at the last jump with enough savings on him to keep us six months. We tried never to think of that. We were ahead on that year until Chevre d'Or.

"Do we have enough money to really bet, Tatie?" my wife asked.

"No. We'll just figure to spend what we take. Is there something else you'd rather spend it for?"

"Well," she said.

"I know. It's been terribly hard and I've been tight and mean about money."

"No," she said. "But—"

I knew how severe I had been and how bad things had been. The one who is doing his work and getting satisfaction from it is not the one the poverty bothers. I thought of bathtubs and showers and toilets that flushed as things that inferior people to us had or that you enjoyed when you made trips, which we often made. There was always the public bathhouse down at the foot of the street by the river. My wife had never complained once about these things any more than she cried about Chèvre d'Or when he fell. She had cried for the horse, I remembered, but not for the money. I had been stupid when she needed a grey lamb jacket and had loved it once she had bought it. I had been stupid about other things too. It was all part of the fight against poverty that you never win except by not spending. Especially if you buy pictures instead of clothes. But then we did not think ever of ourselves as poor. We did not accept it. We thought we were superior people and other people that we looked down on and rightly mistrusted were rich. It had never seemed strange to me to wear sweatshirts for underwear to keep warm. It only seemed odd to the rich. We ate well and cheaply and drank well and cheaply and slept well and warm together and loved each other.

"I think we ought to go," my wife said. "We haven't been for such a long time. We'll take a lunch and some wine. I'll make good sandwiches."

"We'll go on the train and it's cheap that way. But let's not go if you don't think we should. Anything we'd do today would be fun. It's a wonderful day."

"I think we should go."

"You wouldn't rather spend it some other way?"

"No," she said arrogantly. She had the lovely high cheekbones for arrogance. "Who are we anyway?"

Tobacco Road
(1932)
Erskine Caldwell

The "vicious circle of poverty" refers to the idea that with low incomes people (or nations) cannot afford to save or invest, and then face low incomes in the future because they have not saved or invested. Over time, that cycle saps the will to work and save, especially during recessions or major changes in production and employment patterns. To break the circle often requires a dramatic and risky break from how things have been done in the past, which some people are not willing to undertake as long as they have any choice in the matter.

Jeeter remained seated on his heels by the chimney in the yard for half an hour after Ellie May had run away crying. He stared at the tracks left in the yard by the new automobile, amazed at the sharpness of the imprint of the tiretread. The tires of his own car, which was still standing in the yard between the house and the corn-crib, were worn smooth. When they rolled on the sand, they left no track, except two parallel bands of smoothed sand. He was wondering now what he could do about his tires. If he could pump them all up at the same time, he could haul a load of wood to Augusta and sell it. He might even get as much as a dollar for the load.

It was fifteen miles to the city, and after he had bought enough gasoline and oil for the trip there and back, there would not be much left of the dollar. A quarter, possibly, with which he could buy two or three jars of snuff and a peck of cotton-seed meal. Even a quarter would not buy enough corn meal for them to eat. He had already begun buying cotton-seed meal, because corn meal cost too much. Fifteen cents would buy enough cotton-seed meal to last them a whole week.

But Jeeter was not certain whether it was worth the trouble of hauling a load of wood. It would take him nearly half a day to load the car with blackjack, and half a day for the trip to Augusta. And then after he got there he might not be able to find anybody to buy it.

He still planned a crop for that year, though. He had by no means given up his plans to raise one. Ten or fifteen acres of cotton could be raised, if he could get the seed and guano. There was a mule over near Fuller he thought he could borrow, and he had a plow that would do; but it took money or an equal amount of credit to buy seed-cotton and guano. The merchants in Fuller had said they would not let him have anything on credit again, and it was useless to try to raise a loan in a bank in Augusta. He had tried to do that three or four times already, but the first thing they asked him was whom did he have to sign his notes, and what collateral had he to put up. Right there was where the deal fell through every time. Nobody would sign his notes, and he had nothing to put up for security. The men in the bank had told Jeeter to try a loan company.

The loan companies were the sharpest people he had ever had anything to do with. Once he had secured a two-hundred-dollar loan from one of them, but he swore it was the last time he would ever bind himself to such an agreement. To begin with, they came out to see him two or three times a week; some of them from the company's office would come out to the farm and try to tell him how to plant the cotton and how much guano to put in to the acre. Then on the first day of every month they came back to collect interest on the loan. He could never pay it, and they added the interest to the principal, and charged him interest on that, too.

By the time he sold his cotton in the fall, there was only seven dollars coming to him. The interest on the loan amounted to three per cent a month to start with, and at the end of ten months he had been charged thirty per cent, and on top of that another thirty per cent on the unpaid interest. Then to make sure that the loan was fully protected, Jeeter had to pay the sum of fifty dollars. He could never understand why he had to pay that, and the company did not undertake to explain it to him. When he had asked what the fifty dollars was meant to cover, he was told that it was merely the fee for making the loan. When the final settlement was made, Jeeter found that he had paid out more than three hundred dollars, and was receiving seven dollars for his share. Seven dollars for a year's labor did not seem to him a fair portion of the proceeds from the cotton, especially as he had done all the work, and had furnished the land and mule, too. He was even then still in debt, because he owed ten dollars for the hire of the mule he had used to raise the cotton. With Lov and Ada's help, he discovered that he had actually lost three dollars. The man who had rented him the mule insisted on being paid, and Jeeter had given him the seven dollars, and he was still trying to get the other three to pay the balance.

Jeeter swore that he would never again have anything to do with the rich people in Augusta. They had hounded him nearly every day, trying to tell him how he should cultivate the cotton, and in the end they came out and took it all away from him, leaving him three dollars in debt. He had done all the work, furnished the mule and the land, and yet the loan company had taken all the money the cotton brought, and made him lose three dollars. He told everybody he saw after that, that God was not working in a deal such as that one was. He told the men who represented the finance company the same thing, too.

"You rich folks in Augusta is just bleeding us poor people to death. You don't work none, but you get all the money us farmers make. Here I is working all the year myself, Dude plowing, and Ada and Ellie May helping to chop the cotton in summer and pick it in the fall, and what do I get out of it? Not a durn thing, except a debt of three dollars. It ain't right, I tell you. God ain't working on your side. He won't stand for such cheating much longer, neither. He ain't so liking of you rich people as you think He is. God, He likes the poor."

The men collecting for the loan company listened to Jeeter talk, and when he had finished, they laughed at him and got in their new automobile and drove back to Augusta.

That was one reason why Jeeter was not certain he could raise a crop that year. But he thought now that if he could get the seed and guano on credit from a man in Fuller, he would not be robbed. The people in Fuller were farmers, just as he was, or as he tried to be, and he did not believe they would cheat him. But every time he had said something about raising credit in Fuller, the merchants had waved him away and would not even listen to him.

"Ain't no use in talking no more, Jeeter," they had said. "There's farmers coming into Fuller every day from all over the country wanting the same thing. If there's one, there's a hundred been here. But we can't help you people none. Last year we let some of you farmers have seed-cotton and guano on credit, and when fall came there was durn little cotton made, and what there was didn't bring more than seven cents, middling grade. Ain't no sense in farming when things is like that. And we can't take no more chances. All of us has just got to wait until the rich give up the money they're holding back."

"But, praise God, me and my folks is starving out there on that tobacco road. We ain't got nothing to eat, and we ain't got nothing to sell that will bring money to get a meal and meat. You storekeepers won't let us have no more credit since Captain John left, and what is we going to do? I don't know what's going to happen to me and my folks if the rich don't stop bleeding us. They've got all the money, holding it in the banks, and they won't lend it out unless a man will cut off his arms and leave them there for security."

"The best thing you can do, Jeeter," they had said, "is to move your family up to Augusta, or across the river in South Carolina to Horsecreek Valley, where all the mills is, and go to work in one of them. That's the only thing left for you to do now. Ain't no other way."

"No! By God and by Jesus, no!" Jeeter had said. "That's one thing I ain't going to do! The Lord made the land, and He put me here to raise crops on it. I been doing that, and my daddy before me, for the past fifty years, and that's what's intended. Them durn cotton mills is for the women folks to work in. They ain't no place for a man to be, fooling away with little wheels and strings all day long. I say, it's a hell of a job for a man to spend his time winding strings on spools. No! We was put here on the land where cotton will grow, and it's my place to make it grow. I wouldn't fool with the mills if I could make as much as fifteen dollars a week in them. I'm staying on the land till my time comes to die."

"Have it your own way, Jeeter."

Harrison Bergeron (1961)

Kurt Vonnegut

What happens if people who are created unequal in terms of talents and abilities are all made equal "every which way" by Big Brother, personified here by the Handicapper General? It's not a pretty picture.

The year was 2081, and everybody was finally equal. They weren't only equal before God and the law. They were equal every which way. Nobody was smarter than anybody else. Nobody was better looking than anybody else. Nobody was stronger or quicker than anybody else. All this equality was due to the 211th, 212th, and 213th Amendments to the Constitution, and to the unceasing vigilance of agents of the United States Handicapper General.

Some things about living still weren't quite right, though. April, for instance, still drove people crazy by not being springtime. And it was in that clammy month that the H-G men took George and Hazel Bergeron's fourteen-year-old son, Harrison, away.

It was tragic, all right, but George and Hazel couldn't think about it very hard. Hazel had a perfectly average intelligence, which meant she couldn't think about anything except in short bursts. And George, while his intelligence was way above normal, had a little mental handicap radio in his ear. He was required by law to wear it all times. It was tuned to a government transmitter. Every twenty seconds or so, the transmitter would send out some sharp noise to keep people like George from taking unfair advantage of their brains.

George and Hazel were watching television. There were tears on Hazel's cheeks, but she'd forgotten for the moment what they were about.

On the television screen were ballerinas.

A buzzer sounded in George's head. His thoughts fled in panic, like bandits from a burglar alarm.

"That was a real pretty dance, that dance they just did," said Hazel.

"Huh?" said George.

"That dance—it was nice," said Hazel.

"Yup," said George. He tried to think a little about the ballerinas. They weren't really very good—no better than anybody else would have been, anyway. They were burdened with sash-weights and bags of birdshot, and their faces were masked, so that no one, seeing a free and graceful gesture or a pretty face, would feel like something the cat drug in. George was toying with the vague notion that maybe dancers shouldn't be handicapped. But he didn't get very far with it before another noise in his ear radio scattered his thoughts.

George winced. So did two out of the eight ballerinas.

Hazel saw him wince. Having no mental handicap herself, she had to ask George what the latest sound had been.

"Sounded like somebody hitting a milk bottle with a ball peen hammer," said George.

"I'd think it would be real interesting, hearing all the different sounds," said Hazel, a little envious. "All the things they think up."

"Um," said George.

"Only, if I was Handicapper General, you know what I would do?" said Hazel. Hazel, as a matter of fact, bore a strong resemblance to the Handicapper General, a woman named Diana Moon Glampers. "If I was Diana Moon Glampers," said Hazel, "I'd have chimes on Sunday—just chimes. Kind of in honor of religion."

"I could think, if it was just chimes," said George.

"Well—maybe make 'em real loud," said Hazel. "I think I'd make a good Handicapper General."

"Good as anybody else," said George.

"Who knows better'n I do what normal is?" said Hazel.

"Right," said George. He began to think glimmeringly about his abnormal son who was now in jail, about Harrison, but a twenty-one-gun salute in his head stopped that.

"Boy!" said Hazel, "that was a doozy, wasn't it?"

It was such a doozy that George was white and trembling, and tears stood on the rims of his red eyes. Two of the eight ballerinas had collapsed to the studio floor, were holding their temples.

"All of a sudden you look so tired," said Hazel. "Why don't you stretch out on the sofa, so's you can rest your handicap bag on the pillows, honeybunch." She was referring to the forty-seven pounds of birdshot in a canvas bag, which was padlocked around George's neck. "Go on and rest the bag for a little while," she said. "I don't care if you're not equal to me for a while."

George weighed the bag with his hands. "I don't mind it," he said. "I don't notice it any more. It's just part of me."

"You been so tired lately—kind of worn out," said Hazel. "If there was just some way we could make a little hole in the bottom of the bag, and just take out a few of them lead balls. Just a few."

"Two years in prison and two thousand dollars fine for every ball I took out," said George. "I don't call that a bargain."

"If you could just take a few out when you came home from work," said Hazel. "I mean—you don't compete with anybody around here. You just set around."

"If I tried to get away with it," said George, "then other people'd get away with it—and pretty soon we'd be right back to the dark ages again, with everybody competing against everybody else. You wouldn't like that, would you?"

"I'd hate it," said Hazel.

"There you are," said George. "The minute people start cheating on laws, what do you think happens to society?"

If Hazel hadn't been able to come up with an answer to this question, George couldn't have supplied one. A siren was going off in his head.

"Reckon it'd fall all apart," said Hazel.

"What would?" said George blankly.

"Society," said Hazel uncertainly. "Wasn't that what you just said?"

"Who knows?" said George.

The television program was suddenly interrupted for a news bulletin. It wasn't clear at first as to what the bulletin was about, since the announcer, like all announcers, had a serious speech impediment. For about half a minute, and in a state of high excitement, the announcer tried to say, "Ladies and gentlemen—"

He finally gave up, handed the bulletin to a ballerina to read.

"That's all right—" Hazel said of the announcer, "he tried. That's the big thing. He tried to do the best he could with what God gave him. He should get a nice raise for trying so hard."

"Ladies and gentlemen—" said the ballerina, reading the bulletin. She must have been extraordinarily beautiful, because the mask she wore was hideous. And it was easy to see that she was the strongest and most graceful of all the dancers, for her handicap bags were as big as those worn by two-hundred-pound men.

And she had to apologize at once for her voice, which was a very unfair voice for a woman to use. Her voice was a warm, luminous, timeless melody. "Excuse me—" she said, and she began again, making her voice absolutely uncompetitive.

"Harrison Bergeron, age fourteen," she said in a grackle squawk, "has just escaped from jail, where he was held on suspicion of plotting to overthrow the government. He is a genius and an athlete, is under-handicapped, and should be regarded as extremely dangerous."

A police photograph of Harrison Bergeron was flashed on the screen—upside down, then sideways, upside down again, then right side up. The picture showed the full length of Harrison against a background calibrated in feet and inches. He was exactly seven feet tall.

The rest of Harrison's appearance was Halloween and hardware. Nobody had ever born heavier handicaps. He had outgrown hindrances faster than the H-G men could think them up. Instead of a little ear radio for a mental handicap, he wore a tremendous pair of earphones, and spectacles with thick wavy lenses. The spectacles were intended to make him not only half blind, but to give him whanging headaches besides.

Scrap metal was hung all over him. Ordinarily, there was a certain symmetry, a military neatness to the handicaps issued to strong people, but Harrison looked like a walking junkyard. In the race of life, Harrison carried three hundred pounds.

And to offset his good looks, the H-G men required that he wear at all times a red rubber ball for a nose, keep his eyebrows shaved off, and cover his even white teeth with black caps at snaggle-tooth random.

"If you see this boy," said the ballerina, "do not—I repeat, do not—try to reason with him."

There was a shriek of a door being torn from its hinges.

Screams and barking cries of consternation came from the television set. The photograph of Harrison Bergeron on the screen jumped again and again, as though dancing to the tune of an earthquake.

George Bergeron correctly identified the earthquake, and well he might have—for many was the time his own home had danced to the same crashing tune. "My God—" said George, "that must be Harrison!"

The realization was blasted from his mind instantly by the sound of an automobile collision in his head.

When George could open his eyes again, the photograph of Harrison was gone. A living, breathing Harrison filled the screen.

Clanking, clownish, and huge, Harrison stood in the center of the studio. The knob of the uprooted studio door was still in his hand. Ballerinas, technicians, musicians, and announcers cowered on their knees before him, expecting to die.

"I am the Emperor!" cried Harrison. "Do you hear? I am the Emperor! Everybody must do what I say at once!" He stamped his foot and the studio shook.

"Even as I stand here—" he bellowed, "crippled, hobbled, sickened—I am a greater ruler than any man who ever lived! Now watch me become what I *can* become!"

Harrison tore the straps of his handicap harness like wet tissue paper, tore straps guaranteed to support five thousand pounds.

Harrison's scrap-iron handicaps crashed to the floor.

Harrison thrust his thumbs under the bar of the padlock that secured his head harness. The bar snapped like celery. Harrison smashed his headphones and spectacles against the wall.

He flung away his rubber-ball nose, revealed a man that would have awed Thor, the god of thunder.

"I shall now select my Empress!" he said, looking down on the cowering people. "Let the first woman who dares rise to her feet claim her mate and her throne!"

A moment passed, and then a ballerina arose, swaying like a willow.

Harrison plucked the mental handicap from her ear, snapped off her physical handicaps with marvellous delicacy. Last of all, he removed her mask.

She was blindingly beautiful.

"Now—" said Harrison, taking her hand, "shall we show the people the meaning of the word dance? Music!" he commanded.

The musicians scrambled back into their chairs, and Harrison stripped them of their handicaps, too. "Play your best," he told them, "and I'll make you barons and dukes and earls."

The music began. It was normal at first—cheap, silly, false. But Harrison snatched two musicians from their chairs, waved them like batons as he sang the music as he wanted it played. He slammed them back into their chairs.

The music began again and was much improved.

Harrison and his Empress merely listened to the music for a while—listened gravely, as though synchronizing their heartbeats with it.

They shifted their weights to their toes.

Harrison placed his big hands on the girl's tiny waist, letting her sense the weightlessness that would soon be hers.

And then, in an explosion of joy and grace, into the air they sprang!

Not only were the laws of the land abandoned, but the law of gravity and the laws of motion as well.

They reeled, whirled, swiveled, flounced, capered, gamboled, and spun.

They leaped like deer on the moon.

The studio ceiling was thirty feet high, but each leap brought the dancers nearer to it.

It became their obvious intention to kiss the ceiling.

They kissed it.

And then, neutralizing gravity with love and pure will, they remained suspended in air inches below the ceiling, and they kissed each other for a long, long time.

It was then that Diana Moon Glampers, the Handicapper General, came into the studio with a double-barreled ten-gauge shotgun. She fired twice, and the

Emperor and the Empress were dead before they hit the floor.

Diana Moon Glampers loaded the gun again. She aimed it at the musicians and told them they had ten seconds to get their handicaps back on.

It was then that the Bergerons' television tube burned out.

Hazel turned to comment about the blackout to George. But George had gone out into the kitchen for a can of beer.

George came back in with the beer, paused while a handicap signal shook him up. And then he sat down again. "You been crying?" he said to Hazel.

"Yup," she said.

"What about?" he said.

"I forget," she said. "Something real sad on television."

"What was it?" he said.

"It's all kind of mixed up in my mind," said Hazel.

"Forget sad things," said George.

"I always do," said Hazel.

"That's my girl," said George. He winced. There was a sound of a rivetting gun in his head.

"Gee—I could tell that one was a doozy," said Hazel.

"You can say that again," said George.

"Gee—" said Hazel, "I could tell that one was a doozy."

Barter, Money, and Inflation

In most situations barter is a woefully inefficient way to conduct the ordinary business of life, since it requires people to lug stuff around to trade until they find someone who has what they want—and who also wants what they have to trade. A stable currency eliminates the need for this coincidence of wants. Because money can be used to purchase anything, it is accepted by everyone who has something to sell, no matter what they want to buy. Many things can be (and have been) used as money—rare shells and beads, cattle, precious metals, paper currencies, even cigarettes in POW camps during World War II—but whatever is used must be easy to recognize, carry, divide, and, what is most important, must remain scarce.

Unfortunately, the value of money can be eroded, gradually or rapidly, by inflation. If inflation becomes too severe, people will revert to barter. Rapid inflation occurs when the money supply is increased much faster than the production of goods and services. Wars, and their aftermaths, have led to many of the most famous episodes of rapid or hyperinflation, for example in America during the American Revolution (as in "not worth a Continental") and Civil War, and in Germany after World War I.

The British economist John Maynard Keynes opposed the Treaty of Versailles that ended World War I because he believed the reparations imposed on Germany were so severe that the German government would be forced to print money to pay its debts, leading to hyperinflation, social upheavals, and another world war. More recently, many of the transition economies of eastern and central Europe and the former Soviet Union experienced astronomical inflation until their fiscal and monetary policies were brought under control to support the development of their new economic systems.

In the literary passages in this section, Charles Frazier describes the effects of inflation in the Confederacy in Cold Mountain, *while Erich Maria Remarque recorded the post–World War I German hyperinflation in* The Black Obelisk. *In Goethe's* Faust, *as in the first reading from Milton's* Comus *on scarcity, the same kind of disreputable figure tries to mislead humans, this time through the creation of paper money. He believes it is only a matter of time until the government creates too much paper money; and Mephistopheles notes that the king's fool is wise to convert his paper money into land and other real assets. Gertrude Stein's short article on "Money" raises the fundamental question "Is money money?"—focusing on the difference between household and government spending, and foreshadowing the late Illinois*

Senator Everett Dirksen's quip that eventually millions and millions of dollars of public spending can add up to "real money."

Cold Mountain
(1997)
Charles Frazier

In times of financial crisis and high inflation, people rush—or are driven—to put their resources in real assets rather than money, which rapidly loses value and eventually may no longer be accepted as money at all.

The agreement Ada and Ruby reached on that first morning was this: Ruby would move to the cove and teach Ada how to run a farm. There would be very little money involved in her pay. They would take most of their meals together, but Ruby did not relish the idea of living with anyone else and decided she would move into the old hunting cabin. After they had eaten their first dinner of chicken and dumplings, Ruby went home and was able to wrap everything worth taking in a quilt. She had gathered the ends, slung it over her shoulder, and headed to Black Cove, never looking back.

The two women spent their first days together making an inventory of the place, listing the things that needed doing and their order of urgency. They walked together about the farm, Ruby looking around a lot, evaluating, talking constantly. The most urgent matter, she said, was to get a late-season garden into the ground. Ada followed along, writing it all down in a notebook that heretofore had received only her bits of poetry, her sentiments on life and the large issues of the day. Now she wrote entries such as these:

To be done immediately: Lay out a garden for cool season crops—turnips, onions, cabbage, lettuce, greens.

Cabbage seed, do we have any?

Soon: Patch shingles on barn roof; do we have a maul and froe?

Buy clay crocks for preserving tomatoes and beans.

Pick herbs and make from them worm boluses for the horse.

And on and on. So much to do, for apparently Ruby planned to require every yard of land do its duty.

The hayfields, Ruby said, had not been cut frequently enough, and the grass was in danger of being taken over by spurge and yarrow and ragweed, but it was not too far gone to save. The old cornfield, she declared, had profited from having been left to lie fallow for several years and was now ready for clearing and turning. The outbuildings were in fair shape, but the chicken population was too low. The root cellar in the can house was, in her estimation, a foot too shallow; she feared a bad cold spell might freeze potatoes stored there if they didn't dig it deeper. A martin colony, if they could establish one alongside the garden in gourd houses, would help keep crows away.

Ruby's recommendations extended in all directions, and she never seemed to stop. She had ideas concerning schedules for crop rotation among the various fields. Designs for constructing a tub mill so that once they had a corn crop they could grind their own meal and grits using waterpower from the creek and save having to give the miller his tithe. One evening before she set off in the dark to walk up to the cabin, her last words were, We need us some guineas. I'm not partial to their eggs for frying, but they'll do for baking needs. Even discarding the eggs, guineas are a comfort to have around and useful in a number of ways. They're good watchdogs, and they'll bug out a row of pole beans before you can turn around. All that aside from how pleasant they are to look at walking around the yard.

The next morning her first words were, Pigs. Do you have any loose in the woods?

Ada said, No, we always bought our hams.

—There's a world more to a hog than just the two hams, Ruby said. Take lard for example. We'll need plenty.

Despite the laxity of Monroe's tenure at Black Cove, there was nevertheless much more to work with than Ada had realized. On one of their first walks about the place, Ruby was delighted by the extensive apple orchards. They had been planted and maintained by the Blacks and were only now beginning to show the first marks of inattention. Despite lack of recent pruning, they were thick with maturing fruit.

—Come October, Ruby said, we'll get enough in trade for those apples to make our winter a sight easier than it would be otherwise.

She paused and thought a minute. You don't have a press, do you? she said. When Ada said she thought they might indeed, Ruby whooped in joy.

—Hard cider is worth considerably more in trade than apples, she said. All we'll have to do is make it.

Ruby was pleased too with the tobacco patch. In the spring, Monroe had given the hired man permission to plant a small field of tobacco for his own use. Despite most of a summer of neglect, the plants were surprisingly tall and full-leaved and worm-free, though weeds grew thick in the rows and the plants were badly in need of topping and suckering. Ruby believed the plants had thrived despite disregard because they must have been planted in full accordance with the signs. She calculated that with luck they might get a small crop and said that if they cured the leaves and soaked them in sorghum water and twisted them into plugs, they could trade off tobacco for seed and salt and leavening and other items they could not produce themselves.

Barter was very much on Ada's mind, since she did not understand it and yet found herself suddenly so untethered to the money economy. In the spirit of partnership and confidence, she had shared with Ruby the details of her shattered finances. When she told Ruby of the little money they had to work with, Ruby said, I've never held a money piece bigger than a dollar in my hand. What Ada came to understand was that though she might be greatly concerned at their lack of cash, Ruby's opinion was that they were about as well off without it. Ruby had always functioned at arm's length from the buying of things and viewed money with a great deal of suspicion even in the best of times, especially when she contrasted it in her mind with the solidity of hunting and gathering, planting and harvesting. At present, matters had pretty much borne out Ruby's darkest opinions. Scrip had gotten so cheapened in its value that it was hard to buy anything with it anyway. On their first trip together into town they had been stunned to have to give fifteen dollars for a pound of soda, five dollars for a paper of triple-ought needles, and ten for a quire of writing paper. Had they been able to afford it, a bolt of cloth would have cost fifty dollars. Ruby pointed out that cloth would cost them not a cent if they had sheep and set about shearing, carding, spinning, winding, dyeing, and weaving the wool into cloth for dresses and underdrawers. All Ada could think was that every step in the process that Ruby had so casually sketched out would be many days of hard work to come up with a few yards of material coarse as sacking. Money made things so much easier.

But even if they had it, shopkeepers really didn't want money since the value of it would likely drop before they could get shut of it. The general feeling was that paper money ought to be spent as soon as possible; otherwise it might easily become worth no more than an equal volume of chaff. Barter was surer. And that Ruby seemed to understand fully. She had a headful of designs as to how they might make Black Cove answer for itself in that regard.

In short order Ruby had devised a plan. She put it to Ada as a choice. The two things she had marked in her inventory of the place as being valuable and portable and inessential were the cabriolet and the piano. She believed she could trade either one for about all they would need to make it through the winter. Ada weighed them in her mind for two days. At one point she said, It would be a shame to reduce that fine dapple gelding to drawing a plow, and Ruby said, He'll be doing that whichever way you pick. He'll have to work out his feed like anybody else around here.

Four crows, Notchwing in the lead, drifted down into the cove and then flared when they saw the new scarecrow. They flew away squealing like shot pigs.

Ruby called it a favorable comment on Ada's construction.

—That hat in particular's a fine touch, she said.

—It came from France, Ada said,

—France? Ruby said. We've got hats here. A man up East Fork weaves straw hats and will swap them for butter and eggs. Hatter in town makes beaver and wool but generally wants money.

This business of carrying hats halfway around the world to sell made no sense to her. It marked a lack of seriousness in a person that they could think about such matters. There was not one thing in a place like France or New York or Charleston that Ruby wanted. And little she even needed that she couldn't make or grow or find on Cold Mountain. She held a deep distrust of travel, whether to Europe or anywhere else. Her view was that a world properly put together would yield inhabitants so suited to their lives in their assigned place that they would have neither need nor wish to travel. No stagecoach or railway or steamship would be required; all such vehicles would sit idle. Folks would, out of utter contentment, choose to stay home since the failure to do so was patently the root of many ills, current and historic. In such a stable world as she envisioned, some might live many happy years hearing the bay of a distant neighbor's dog and yet never venture out far enough from their own fields to see whether the yawp was from hound or setter, plain or pied.

Ada did not bother arguing, for she figured that her life was moving toward a place where travel and imported hats would figure small.

The Black Obelisk (1956)

Erich Maria Remarque

At the height of the German hyperinflation after World War I, workers demanded to be paid several times a day, immediately rushing to give the money to other family members who could run to the stores to buy food, clothing, or other products before prices were increased again and the money lost even more value. The personal and social costs of such arrangements are incredibly high and obviously bizarre even to those who find that they must endure them.

With anticipation I take a cigar out of the drawer. It is a black Brazilian. The salesman for the Württemberg Metal Works gave it to me this morning with the intention of foisting off on me later a consignment of bronze wreaths; so it is a good cigar. I look for a match, but as usual they have been mislaid. Fortunately a small fire is burning in the Dutch oven. I roll up a ten-mark bill, hold it in the flame and light the cigar with it. At the end of April there is no longer any real need for a fire in the oven; it is just a selling aid devised by my employer Georg Kroll. He believes that in time of sorrow when people have to hand out money they do it more willingly in a warm room than when they are cold. Sorrow in itself is a chilling of the soul, and if you add cold feet, it is hard to extract a decent price. Warmth has a thawing effect—even on the purse. Therefore our office is overheated, and our representatives have it dinned into them as an overriding principle never to attempt to close a sale in the cemetery when it is cold or rainy, but always in a warm room and, if possible, after a meal. Sorrow, cold, and hunger are bad business partners. I throw the remnant of the ten-mark bill into the oven and stand up.

Georg Kroll is barely forty, but his head is already as shiny as the bowling alley at Boll's Garden Restaurant. It has been shiny as long as I have known him, and that is over five years. It is so shiny that when we were in the trenches, where we belonged to the same regiment, a special order was issued that even at the quietest times Georg had to wear his steel helmet—such would have been the temptation, for even the kindliest of enemies, to find out by a shot whether or not his head was a giant billiard ball.

Georg takes the cigar out of my mouth. He examines it briefly and classifies it like a butterfly. "Booty from the metalworks."

He takes a beautifully clouded, golden-brown meerschaum cigar holder out of his pocket, fits the Brazilian into it and goes on smoking.

"I have nothing against your requisitioning the cigar," I say. "It is naked force, and that's all you noncoms know about life. But why the cigar holder?"

"In the war you used my spoon to eat pea soup whenever I could steal it from the canteen. And the spoon stayed in my dirty boot and was never washed."

Georg examines the ash of the Brazilian. It is snow white. "The war was four and a half years ago," he informs me. "At that time infinite misery made us human. Today the shameless lust for gain has made us robbers again. To keep this secret we use the varnish of convention. Ergo! Isn't there still another Brazilian? The metalworks never tries to bribe an employee with just one."

I take the second cigar out of the drawer and hand it to him. "You know everything! Intelligence, experience, and age seem to be good for something after all."

He grins and gives me in return a half-empty package of cigarettes. "Anything else been happening?" he asks.

"Not a thing. No customers. But I must urgently request a raise."

"What, again? You got one only yesterday!"

"Not yesterday. This morning at nine o'clock. A miserable ten thousand marks. However, it was still worth something at nine this morning. Now the new dollar exchange rate has been posted and instead of a new tie all I can buy is a bottle of cheap wine. But what I need is a tie."

"Where does the dollar stand now?"

"Thirty-six thousand marks at noon today. This morning it was thirty-three thousand."

Georg Kroll examines his cigar. "Thirty-six thousand! It's a rat race. Where will it end?"

"In a wholesale crash. Meanwhile we have to live. Did you get some money?"

"Only a small suitcaseful for today and tomorrow. Thousands, ten thousands, even a couple of packages of hundreds. Something like five pounds of paper money. The inflation is moving so fast that the Reichsbank can't print money rapidly enough to keep up with it. The new hundred-thousand bills were only issued two weeks ago—soon we'll need million-mark notes. When will we be in the billions?"

"If it goes on like this, in a couple of months."

"My God!" Georg signs. "Where are the fine peaceful times of 1922? Then the dollar only rose from two hundred fifty to ten thousand in a whole year. Not to mention 1921—when it went up a beggarly three hundred per cent."

I look out the window toward the street. Now Lisa is standing across the way in a printed silk dressing gown decorated with parrots. She has put a mirror on the window ledge and is brushing her mane.

"Look at that," I say bitterly. "She sows not neither does she reap, and our Father in Heaven supports her nevertheless. She didn't have that dressing gown yesterday. Yards of silk! And I can't scrape together the price of a tie."

Georg grins. "You're just an innocent victim of the times. But Lisa spreads her sails before the gale of the inflation. She is the fair Helen of the black marketeers. You can't get rich on tombstones. Why don't you go into the herring business or the stock market like your friend Willy?"

"Because I am a philosopher and a sentimentalist. I shall remain true to tombstones. Well, what about my raise? Even philosophers need to spend something on their wardrobes."

Georg shrugs his shoulders. "Can't you buy the tie tomorrow?"

"Tomorrow is Sunday. And I need it tomorrow."

Georg sighs and gets his bagful of money out of the vestibule. He reaches inside and throws me two packages. "Will that do?"

I see that they are mostly hundreds. "Hand over another pound of that wallpaper," I say. "This is not more than five thousand. Catholic profiteers put that much in the collection plate at Sunday mass and feel ashamed of being so stingy."

Georg scratches his bald skull, an atavistic gesture without meaning in his case. Then he hands me a third package. "Thank God tomorrow is Sunday," he says. "No dollar exchange rate. One day of the week the inflation stands still. God surely did not have that in mind when He created the Sabbath."

"How are we doing really?" I ask. "Are we ruined or in clover?"

Georg takes a long drag on the meerschaum holder. "I don't believe anyone in Germany knows that about himself. Not even the godlike Stinnes. People with savings are ruined, of course. So are all the factory workers and office workers. Also most of the small-business people, only they don't know it. The only ones who are making hay are the people with foreign exchange, stocks, or negotiable property. Does that answer your question?"

"Negotiable property!" I look out into the garden which serves as our warehouse. "We haven't much left. Mostly sandstone and poured concrete. Very little marble or granite. And what little we have your brother is selling at a loss. The best thing would be to sell nothing at all, wouldn't it?"

There is no need for Georg to answer.

Faust
(1790–1832)
Johann Goethe

Although policymakers can insure that a paper currency maintains its value, and in fact the U.S. dollar has not been backed by gold or other precious metals for more than forty years, paper money does present a greater risk of inflation because it is so easy, inexpensive, and sometimes tempting for governments to print more bills or add more zeroes. While most economists now accept currencies not backed by gold as a normal and desirable state of affairs—after all, why spend all that money to mine gold only to bury it again in the vaults of Fort Knox—a few economists and other writers still condemn it. In Faust, *Goethe, himself a former finance minister, suggested that paper currency came from an evil parentage, and would be systematically manipulated by government officials to support greater spending and to pay off public debt with money worth less than the money the government had borrowed earlier.*

LORD HIGH SENESCHAL: [*entering in haste*] Illustrious, in all my life I never
Had thought to tell of Fortune's fairest favour,
Such as entrances me with glee
Before thy face—most happy me.
For bill on bill is paid unbated,
The claws of usury are sated,
From hellish torment am I free;

In Heaven it cannot brighter be!

COMMANDER OF THE FORCES: [*following in haste*] Arrears of pay in part are cancelled,
And the whole army newly handselled.
The men-at-arms their heart recover,
And host and wenches are in clover.

EMPEROR: How breathe ye as your breasts were lightened!
How are the knitted brows now brightened!
Ye enter with what eager speed!

LORD HIGH TREASURER: [*joining the others*] These question, that have done the deed.

FAUST: The Chancellor's it is to expound the matter.

LORD HIGH CHANCELLOR: [*coming slowly forward*] Mine old age what abundant joy doth flatter!
Hear then and see the paper, big with fate,
That all our woe to weal transformed straight.

He reads.

"Hereby may all men surely know that would,
This paper for a thousand crowns is good.
A safe assured security lies stored
The Empire in, an untold buried hoard.
It is provided that this rich reserve,
Raised straightway, to redeem the bills shall serve."

EMPEROR: I augur malversation, monstrous fraud.
Who hath here forged the Emperor's hand un-awed?
Ye have not left unpunished such malfeasance?

LORD HIGH TREASURER: Bethink thee, but this night thyself thine hand
Didst set thereto. Thou as great Pan didst stand.
The Chancellor addressed thee in our presence:
"Accord thyself a festal gratification!
With a few quill-strokes give thy folk salvation!"
Thou wrotest; swift it was ere night had rolled
By thousand-artists copied thousandfold.
That all the boon might share we made no queries,
But stamped incontinently all the series.
Tens, Thirties, Fifties, Hundreds, all are there;
You cannot think how glad the people were!
Behold your city, half in death grown musty—
'Tis all alive, aswarm and pleasure-lusty.

Although thy name the world hath long o'erjoyed,
So lovingly it never yet was eyed.
Now is the Alphabet indeed redundant;
Each in this sign is blessed with bliss abundant.

EMPEROR: They're current with my folk as steering gold?
Them doth the Camp, the Court as quittance hold?
Sanction I must, though in amazement utter.

LORD HIGH TREASURER: The hope were vain to catch them as thy flutter.
Like lightning-flash they scattered in their flight.
The changers' booths stand open day and night.
There every bill is honoured, high and low,
With gold and silver . . . at a discount though.
Then off to butcher, baker, vintner flows all,
And half the world seems bent but on carousal,
The while in brand-new clothes the other struts—
The tailor stitches as the draper cuts.
To toast the Emperor wine flows like water;
They roast and boil and broil—the platters clatter.

MEPHISTOPHELES: Who on the terrace lonely strays doth spy
The fairst fair, pranked splendidly. One eye
With the proud peacock-fan she covers shyly,
And smirks, and looks for such a note full slyly,
And its good offices more swift and sure
Than wit or words Love's richest boon procure.
Who now with purse or pouch himself will harry?
A leaflet in the breast is light to carry.
There snugly with the billets-doux 'twill nestle.
His will the priest bear reverent in his missal.
The soldier, his agility to heighten,
The girdle round his loins will swiftly lighten.
I crave your Highness' pardon, if one tittle
I seem a work so lofty to belittle.

FAUST: The hoards of wealth untold, that torpid sleep
Within the Empire's borders buried deep,
Lie profitless. The thought's most ample measure
Is the most niggard bound of such a treasure.
Not Fancy's self, in her most daring flight,
Strain as she will, can soar to such a height;
Yet minds that worthy are to sound the soundless
A boundless trust accord unto the boundless.

MEPHISTOPHELES: Not gold or pears are half so handy as
Such paper. There a man knows what he has.
No need to truck or chaffer with such treasure—
On wine or love can one get drunk at pleasure.
Would you have cash, a changer is at hand.
If there it lack you dig it from the land.
Goblet and chain are straight by auction sold,
The paper then, redeemed with sterling gold,
The doubter shames that whets on us his wit.
Naught else the folk will have—they're used to it.
Henceforth thy Realm, for spender or for scraper,
Will have good store of jewels, gold and paper.

EMPEROR: To you the Realm this glorious weal doth owe.
Unto the service would we fit the guerdon.
To you entrusted be the realm below—
You are most meet to be the treasure's warden.
You know the ample, well-preserved hoard,
And when we dig, 'tis you shall give the word.
According ye now, ye Masters of our Treasure,
Fulfil the honours of your post with pleasure,
Wherein the Nether World, for endless weal,
Doth with the Upper World alliance seal.

LORD HIGH TREASURER: Between us shall not reign the leave division!
I'm fain to have as colleague the Magician.

Exit with FAUST.

EMPEROR: The court shall taste my bounty, great and small.
Confess how ye will use it, one and all.

PAGE: [*taking*] I'll lead a merry life.

ANOTHER: [*ditto*] I in a trice
Will buy my sweetheart chain and rings.

CHAMBERLAIN: [*accepting*] My throttle
Henceforth I'll wet with twice as good a bottle.

ANOTHER: [*ditto*] Already in my pocket itch the dice.

KNIGHT BANNERET: [*thoughtfully*] My land and tower from debt I'll liberate.

ANOTHER: [*ditto*] A treasure 'tis, with treasurers will I lay't.

EMPEROR: I hoped for heart and will to new endeavour.
Who knows ye though will lightly read ye ever.
Well do I see, though treasures on ye pour,
Ye still are, after, what ye were before.

FOOL: [*coming up*] Largesse you give, to me too be not chary.
EMPEROR: What, art alive again? Thou'lt drink it,
marry!
FOOL: The magic leaves! It passes my poor wit!
EMPEROR: Aye marry, for thou'lt make bad use of it.
FOOL: These others flutter down, what shall I do?
EMPEROR:. Why, pick them up, thy share they fell unto.

Exit.

FOOL: Five thousand crowns are mine? O happy season!
MEPHISTOPHELES: Thou two-legged wineskin! What, and art arisen?
FOOL: Betides me oft, but not to luck like this!
MEPHISTOPHELES: Upon my word, thou'rt all asweat with bliss!
FOOL: Look you now, can I indeed make money of it?
MEPHISTOPHELES: 'Twill buy what throat and belly most do covet.
FOOL: And this for cattle, land and house they'll take?
MEPHISTOPHELES: Aye truly, so thou offer, naught will lack.
FOOL: Castle, with wood, chase, fishing?
MEPHISTOPHELES: Take my word!
Marry, I'd like to see thee *Dread My Lord*!
FOOL: Upon mine own estate I'll sleep this night!

Exit.

MEPHISTOPHELES: [*solus*] Who still will doubt that this our fool hath wit?

Money
(1936)
Gertrude Stein

Stein poses two questions to the modern world and its large central governments: (1) How much money does it take before we are talking about "real money"? And (2) How can we get elected officials to spend public funds as if they were spending their own money?

Everybody now just has to make up their mind. Is money money or isn't money money. Everybody who earns it and spends it every day in order to live knows that money is money, anybody who votes it to be gathered in as taxes knows money is not money. That is what makes everybody go crazy.

Once upon a time there was a king and he was called Louis the fifteenth. He spent money as they are spending it now. He just spent it and spent it and one day somebody dared say something to the king about it. Oh, he said, after me the deluge, it would last out his time, and so what was the difference. When this king had begun his reign he was known as Louis the Well-beloved, when he died, nobody even stayed around to close his eyes.

But all the trouble really comes from this question is money money. Everybody who lives on it every day knows that money is money but the people who vote money, presidents and congress, do not think about money that way when they vote it. I remember when my nephew was a little boy he was out walking somewhere and he saw a lot of horses; he came home and he said, oh papa, I have just seen a million horses. A million, said his father, well anyway, said my nephew, I saw three. That came to be what we all used to say when anybody used numbers that they could not count well anyway a million or three. That is the whole point. When you earn money and spend money everyday anybody can know the difference between a million and three. But when you vote money away there really is not any difference between a million and three. And so everybody has to make up their mind is money money for everybody or is it not.

That is what everybody has to think about a lot or everybody is going to be awfully unhappy, because the time does come when the money voted comes suddenly to be money just like the money everybody earns every day and spends every day to live and when that time comes it makes everybody very unhappy. I do wish everybody would make up their mind about money being money.

It is awfully hard for anybody to think money is money when there is more of it than they can count. That is why there ought to be some kind of system that money should not be voted right away. When you spend money that you earn every day you naturally think several times before you spend more than you have, and you mostly do not. Now if there was some arrangement made that when one lot voted to spend money, that they would have to wait a long time, and another lot have to vote, before they vote again to have that money, in short, if there was any way to make a government handle money the way a father of a family has to handle money if there only was. The natural feeling of a father of a family is that when anybody asks him for money he says no. Any father of a family, any member of a family, knows all about that.

So until everybody who votes public money remembers how he feels as a father of a family, when he says no, when anybody in the family wants money, until that time comes, there is going to be a lot of trouble and some years later everybody is going to be very unhappy.

In Russia they tried to decide that money was not money, but now slowly and surely they are coming back to know that money is money.

Whether you like it or whether you do not money is money and that is all there is about it. Everybody knows it. When they earn it and spend what they earn they know it they really know that money is money and when they vote it they do not know it as money.

That is the trouble with everybody, it is awfully hard to really know what you know.

When you earn it and spend it you do know the difference between three dollars and a million dollars, but when you say it and vote it, it all sounds the same.

Of course it does, it would to anybody, and that is the reason they vote it and keep on voting it. So, now please, everybody, everybody, everybody, please, is money money, and if it is, it ought to be the same whether it is what a father of a family earns and spends or a government, if it isn't sooner or later there is disaster.

Real versus Nominal Values

In comparing prices over time or across nations, what is truly important is the real cost of goods and services, not simply the stated monetary prices. For example, something that cost $100 in the United States in 1950 was, in truth, far more expensive than something that cost $100 in 2000. As anyone born before say, 1980, knows from their own experience, because of all the inflation that has occurred since 1950, a dollar is worth far less now than it was then. A similar issue arises in comparing prices in different countries. If you know that a product costs 100 units of the local currency in one country, but 50 units of a different currency in a different country, you really don't know in which country the product is more expensive. You must first get a better idea of what other goods and services a unit of each currency will buy in each nation.

The title character in Mark Twain's Connecticut Yankee in King Arthur's Court *is driven to distraction and despair—much to readers' pleasure, of course—in trying to explain this idea to some workers from a neighboring country that uses a currency with the same name, but not the same real value. The workers are not particularly apt or receptive students, but then every professor of economics has taught at least one class like this. And in fact, responses such as these are especially likely to occur in sessions dealing with exchange rates and real versus nominal values.*

A Connecticut Yankee in King Arthur's Court

(1889)

Mark Twain

The real value of a dollar—or, as in Twain's novel, a "milray"—depends on what it will buy. When two neighboring countries both call their currency milrays, but a milray from one country buys more goods and services than a milray from the other country, real wages in the two countries—which are also paid in milrays— may very well be different, too. Comparing money

> *or nominal wages in the two countries on a milray-for-milray basis won't accurately reflect differences in the real standards of living in the two countries, even though this may not be universally understood.*

"In your country, brother, what is the wage of a master bailiff, master hind, carter, shepherd, swineherd?"

"Twenty-five milrays a day; that is to say, a quarter of a cent."

The smith's face beamed with joy. He said:

"With us they are allowed the double of it! And what may a mechanic get—carpenter, dauber, mason, painter, blacksmith, wheelwright, and the like?"

"On the average, fifty milrays; half a cent a day."

"Ho-ho! With us they are allowed a hundred! With us any good mechanic is allowed a cent a day! I count out the tailor, but not the others—they are all allowed a cent a day, and in driving times they get more—yes, up to a hundred and ten and even fifteen milrays a day. I've paid a hundred and fifteen myself, within the week. 'Rah for protection—to Sheol with free trade!"

And his face shone upon the company like a sunburst. But I didn't scare at all. I rigged up my pile driver, and allowed myself fifteen minutes to drive him into the earth—drive him *all* in—drive him in till not even the curve of his skull should show above ground. Here is the way I started in on him. I asked:

"What do you pay a pound for salt?"

"A hundred milrays."

"We pay forty. What do you pay for beef and mutton—when you buy it?" That was a neat hit; it made the color come.

"It varieth somewhat, but not much; one may say seventy-five milrays the pound."

"*We* pay thirty-three. What do you pay for eggs?"

"Fifty milrays the dozen."

"We pay twenty. What do you pay for beer?"

"It costeth us eight and one half milrays the pint."

"We get it for four; twenty-five bottles for a cent. What do you pay for wheat?"

"At the rate of nine hundred milrays the bushel."

"We pay four hundred. What do you pay for a man's tow-linen suit?"

"Thirteen cents."

"We pay six. What do you pay for a stuff gown for the wife of the laborer or the mechanic?"

"We pay eight cents and four mills."

"Well, observe the difference: you pay eight cents and four mills, we pay only four cents." I prepared, now, to sock it to him. I said: "Look here, dear friend, *what's become of your high wages you were bragging so about, a few minutes ago?* And I looked around on the company with placid satisfaction, for I had slipped up on him gradually and tied him hand and foot, you see, without his ever noticing that he was being tied at all. "What's become of those noble high wages of yours? I seem to have knocked the stuffing all out of them, it appears to me."

But if you will believe me, he merely looked surprised, that is all! He didn't grasp the situation at all, didn't know he had walked into a trap, didn't discover that he was *in* a trap. I could have shot him, from sheer vexation. With cloudy eye and a struggling intellect, he fetched this out:

"Marry, I seem not to understand. It is *proved* that our wages be double thine; how then may it be that thou'st knocked therefrom the stuffing?—an I miscall not the wonderly word, this being the first time under grace and providence of God it hath been granted me to hear it."

Well, I was stunned; partly with this unlooked-for stupidity on his part, and partly because his fellows so manifestly sided with him and were of his mind—if you might call it mind. My position was simple enough, plain enough; how could it ever be simplified more? However, I must try:

"Why, look here, brother Dowley, don't you see? Your wages are merely higher than ours in *name*, not in *fact*."

"Hear him! They are the *double*—ye have confessed it yourself."

"Yes-yes, I don't deny that at all. But that's got nothing to do with it; the *amount* of the wages in mere coins, with meaningless names attached to them to know them by, has got nothing to do with it. The thing is, how much can you *buy* with your wages? That's the idea. While it is true that with you a good mechanic is allowed about three dollars and a half a year, and with us only about a dollar and seventy-five—"

"There—ye're confessing it again, ye're confessing it again!"

"Confound it, I've never denied it I tell you! What I say is this. With us *half* a dollar buys more than a *dollar* buys with you—and *therefore* it stands to reason and the commonest kind of common sense, that our wages are *higher* than yours."

He looked dazed, and said, despairingly:

"Verily, I cannot make it out. Ye've just *said* our are the higher, and with the same breath ye take it back."

"Oh, great Scott, isn't it possible to get such a simple thing through your head? Now look here—let me illustrate. We pay four cents for a woman's stuff gown, you pay eight cents four mills which is four mills more than *double*. What do you allow a laboring woman who works on a farm?"

"Two mills a day."

"Very good; we allow but half as much; we pay her only a tenth of a cent a day; and—"

"Again ye're conf—"

"Wait! Now, you see, the thing is very simple; this time you'll understand it. For instance, it takes your woman forty-two days to earn her gown, at two mills a day—

seven weeks' work; but ours earns hers in forty days—two days *short* of seven weeks. Your woman has a gown, and her whole seven weeks' wages are gone; ours has a gown, and two days' wages left, to buy something else with. There—*now* you understand it!"

He looked—well, he merely looked dubious, it's the most I can say; so did the others. I waited—to let the thing work. Dowley spoke at last—and betrayed the fact that he actually hadn't gotten away from his rooted and grounded superstitions yet. He said, with a trifle of hesitancy:

"But—but—ye cannot fail to grant that two mills a day is better than one."

Shucks! Well, of course I hated to give it up. So I chanced another flyer:

"Let us suppose a case. Suppose one of your journeymen goes out and buys the following articles:

"1 pound of salt;

1 dozen eggs;

1 dozen pints of beer;

1 bushel of wheat;

1 tow-linen suit;

5 pounds of beef;

5 pounds of mutton.

"The lot will cost him thirty-two cents. It takes him thirty-two working days to earn the money—five weeks and two days. Let him come to us and work thirty-two days at *half* the wages; he can buy all those things for a shade under fourteen and a half cents; they will cost him a shade under twenty-nine days' work, and he will have about half a week's wages over. Carry it through the year; he would save nearly a week's wages every two months, *your* man nothing; thus saving five or six weeks' wages in a year, your man not a cent. *Now* I reckon you understand that 'high wages' and 'low wages' are phrases that don't mean anything in the world until you find out which of them will *buy* the most!"

Unemployment and Fiscal Policy

Unemployment entails not only economic costs—lost production, idle resources, etc.—but also increased crime and other forms of social unrest. There are, of course, even higher personal costs to be paid by those who lose their sources of income.

While there is no economic law that suggests the economy has to experience occasional recessions, historically that is what has happened ever since accurate records of recessions and expansions started being collected in the 1930s (and, if economic historians are correct, in earlier decades and centuries as well), albeit with less frequency and severity during the past twenty years. Sometimes recessions are caused or made more severe by dramatic events, such as the oil embargo and OPEC crude oil production cuts of the 1970s, or the terrorist attacks of September 11, 2001. In other cases, higher interest rates or concerns over future profits and wages can lead businesses to cut back on investment spending, or households to cut back on consumption spending, or both.

The most extreme case of the U.S. and world economies falling into a period of lower output and higher rates of unemployment was, of course, the Great Depression of the 1930s. During that decade, at one point fully one fourth of the U.S. labor force—adults who are working or actively looking for work—was unemployed. John Maynard Keynes and many later economists argued that the government could use fiscal policies—the national government's overall level of spending and taxing—to promote full employment and stable prices. For example, if the main problem in the economy was too much unemployment, the government could increase its spending levels or cut taxes so that people and businesses would spend more, pumping up sales, production levels, and hiring.

Whether fiscal policies can be used effectively in periods of moderate unemployment or inflation is a considerably more controversial question among economists, because of concerns about the difficulty of enacting such policies on a timely basis, concerns that people and businesses may react to those policies in ways that will undermine their effectiveness, and the political unpopularity of fiscal policies that fight inflation—raising taxes and cutting government spending—versus the popularity of policies that lower unemployment.

Many literary works have been set during periods of recession or the Great Depression, most famously John Steinbeck's Grapes of Wrath. *More recently published works set in this period often discuss directly government fiscal policies and the ideas of contemporary economists such as Keynes. One example, excerpted here, is Ivan Doig's* Bucking the Sun.

Although the first passage in this section deals with a later and much milder recession, it is often noted that from the viewpoint of any individual who has lost his job, the economy is always in the midst of a depression. Poignantly and hilariously, Neil Simon's The Prisoner of Second Avenue *portrays the sometimes unbearable personal costs of unemployment. Simon also shows that, even for well-intentioned families, designing policies to help unemployed workers can be difficult, expensive, and controversial. The same kinds of questions and issues face government assistance policies: How much help is required, and how much will it cost? Is it better to give assistance in the form of cash, or support for only certain kinds of expenditures? Will the assistance be provided only once, for a limited period of time, or repeatedly? What can the people receiving assistance reasonably be expected to do to help themselves? How can assistance be provided without stigmatizing the recipients?*

Bucking the Sun
(1996)
Ivan Doig

The main objective of fiscal policy is to increase aggregate levels of spending in the national economy. Spending on virtually anything can satisfy that goal, but the massive expenditure programs of the WPA and other federal agencies during the Great Depression were often directed at building regional infrastructure—in Doig's novel, a massive dam. Another objective of the spending programs was, undoubtedly, to moderate social unrest.

"Got yourself a dam to build, Ownie, huh?"

"Not quite by myself. There'll be stuff that needs some main strength and ignorance, Bruce."

That hadn't come out as lightly as Owen wanted, but Bruce seemed to take it as teasing. "You're the expert. We're just here to fill in around the edges, aren't we, Neil?"

"Four bits an hour, up from nothing." Neil smiled around his words. "That'll be different."

"Yeah, helluva deal," Bruce backed that with an even bigger smile. "When did somebody come up with this wage idea, anyway? The Old Man never told us it existed."

"Uncle Sam is here now. You're going to see a lot that didn't exist before five minutes ago."

And if they don't hand out some moolah somehow, the sheriff was mulling with a hot towel over his face, reclining in the barber chair in Glasgow as on every Monday noon since he had been elected, *if Roosevelt and his brainbust bunch don't put people on these so-called public work jobs*—well, that was moot, they surely to Christ *were* signing every man who could stagger to a crew truck onto the Fort Peck payroll. How to make wages flow: pump them out of the government treasury. The idea on high was from some fruitcake Englishman professor named John Maynard Keynes, compensatory-spending-by-the-government-to-set-the-economy-in-motion, by way of Roosevelt's alphabet-soup agencies. Make the American eagle lay dollars into hands that had forgotten the feel of a nickel. The sheriff uneasily crossed his feet, one neat little boot of handtooled leather atop the other. He couldn't argue with the need to do something about the economic side of things, although he sorely would have liked to. Out there in the street this morning while the hiring was going on, the sheriff had kept an obvious eye on the crowd and even contributed a couple of minor offenders to it, telling them he'd bounce their butts right back into jail if they didn't hang on to these jobs on a platter, and he'd managed to stay impassive at the sight of Corps officers and civvie bureaucrats busy as bees; but the Fort Peck project rankled him. Some New Dealer's finger had come down on Valley County, Montana, on a place where the Missouri River seemed a little skinnier than elsewhere, and now there was going to be five years of dam building commotion. Yet the sheriff had to look only a couple of counties away, over by the North Dakota line, for the example of how things could go if something wasn't done about the Depression. When there was enough rain, the soil of the northeastern corner of Montana grew hard red wheat. When drought came, politics of that same coloration sprouted instead. In '28, Sheridan County had elected as its sheriff a Bolshevik, no less. Calling himself a Fusion candidate but amounting to Communist and proud of it, Lawrence Mott had lost office in the Roosevelt sweep of '32 but pretty damned narrowly. (As someone who prided himself on enough gray matter to run as a Democrat if that's what it took to reach office, Sheriff Kinnick could not savvy why Mott hadn't at least called himself a Roosevelt Communist.) Mott and his—what do you call a nest of Reds—cadre still had a Communist newspaper going, over there in the Sheridan County seat of Plentywood. *The Producers News*; you bet, they knew how to produce trouble, whenever they had half a chance. At least he, Carl Kinnick, did not have to put up with that kind of Red ruckus in his county, nor would he, even if it took—

Something approximating spring, at last, and as work at the dam site stirred in 1935's first days of thaw, so did the towns.

For a place barely past its first birthday, Wheeler showed atrocious age-spots where ashes and dishwater had been thrown all winter, wrinkles of ruts in every street and alley, and the general dishevelment of a veteran tramp. Its sibling downstream from the dam, Park Grove, had just wakened to the fact that whole neighborhoods were going to be eaten by the dredges, but the rest of the scatter of Fort Peck's shacky suburbs were starting to hear the sing of hammers again. The workforce, talk had it, was about to increase by another thousand wallets.

Second Friday of the month. Rosellen's day was rat-a-tat-tat at the oversize Blickensderfer typewriter, turning out paychecks. Every maxim of the Lewis & Clark Business School applied. Her chin up. Her spine straight as could be but not rigid. Her backside (which, seated or otherwise, was thoroughly admired by the male contingent of the Ad Building) snuggled against the back of the chair. Fingers downpoised into "tiger claws," as the L&CBS typing teacher sang out a dozen times every class. Steady rate of typing rather than fitful bursts. Kersplickety splick. Typewriter keyboard deliberately *qwerted* and *yoioped* by its inventor to slow down matters and prevent jamming, but Rosellen's fingers flew nonetheless. Dollar-sign number number decimal-point number number. Keynes crooning in the keys. The quick green wage jumps over the lazy Wall Street claque. Out the checks roll, deft translation by Rosellen's fingers of the Fort Peck Dam project into alphabet and dollars and cents, to be cashed at the New Deal Grocery or the Rondola Cafe or the Blue Eagle Tavern.

J. L. Hill, wages for his percussive tunnel work . . .

John B. Hinch, wages for dredgeline carpentry . . .

Charles S. Siderius, wages for resolution of land titles . . .

"The duded-up one is Plimpton, the newspaper guy," Jaarala whispered to Darius as people milled into Plentywood's clapboard Temple of Labor. Darius mentally marked the plumpish editor, in a pearl-gray suit and vest, there at the end of the front row. From issues slipped to him by Jaarala in the barracks, Darius knew that *The Producers News* was a wordslinging fiesta, even by radical standards. "He gets against somebody in that newspaper of his and he tears them a new asshole," Jaarala favorably critiqued Plimpton's journalism now. "Him and Mott have worked together a long time."

The crowd grew, and Jaarala kept on naming off the ones he knew, abundantly Scandinavian from the sound of it, as Darius tried to make himself at home in the Red Corner of Montana.

Clydesiders were said to spoon the politics of the left into themselves along with their oatmeal, and the young riveter Darius Duff hungrily sat up to that table. His first feast there was the rent strike, when the city streets boiled with marching people; Scotland had found its feet at last, Darius exulted. The columns from the factories and the shipyards poured into Glasgow, passing a column of soldiers embarking for the war in France. "Down your tools, boys!" shouted the civilian army to the uniformed one.

Then Darius, tall in the human swell, could see the lines of the tenement women who had fomented the strike, and the great crowd that packed the streets around the Sheriff's Court. Faces by the thousands and thousands, a maw of mouths and eyes for the powers that be to look out upon, festival and class war feeding each other as they disbelievingly watched.

Each new minute of the massing forces brought a bolt of excitement to Darius. By then he had been in attendance at a hundred meetings, a dozen committees, a thousand arguments over Georges Sorel's doctrine of the general strike ("to render the maintenance of socialism compatible with the minimum of brutality," Darius could reel off by heart) versus parliamentary gradualism ("Having been preyed on does not entitle one to prey back," Ramsay MacDonald kept scolding them from Westminster). And now here it was, exactly as Sorel, in the densest of the arguing Bibles of the left, had prophesied: mass belief, passion, mania, whatever you cared to term it, the ingredient that forged the early Christians against the Romans and that turned Paris upside down street by street in the French Revolution was working in this epic strike of 1915. Chapter and verse, the workers triumphing with the weight of their numbers.

The Prisoner of Second Avenue (1971)

Neil Simon

Mel is a middle-aged mid-level executive who loses his job during a recession. He adopts a conspiracy theory to explain his situation to himself and his wife, Edna, and eventually suffers a nervous breakdown. There is an old joke that says one of the three great lies in history is: "I'm from the government and I'm here to help you." In Mel's case it's not someone from the government offering help whom he must fear, but his brother and three sisters.

MEL: (*smirking, as though he has some secret*) You think it's just by accident I can't find any work? You think it's just the breaks? I'm having a bad streak of luck, is that what you think?

EDNA: I think it's the times, Mel. We are going through bad times.

MEL: You have no suspicion of the truth, do you? None at all?

EDNA: What truth? What truth are you talking about, Mel?

MEL: I'm talking about the *plot*, Edna. The *plot*.

(She looks at him for a long time.)

EDNA: What plot, Mel?

MEL (*He stares at her increduously, then laughs*): "What plot, Mel?" . . . I'm telling you about the plot and all you can say is, "What plot, Mel?"

EDNA: I don't know what plot you're talking about. You mentioned there's a plot and all I can think of to say is "What plot, Mel?"

MEL: What plot? Jeez!

(He turns away from her)

EDNA: (*exasperated*) What plot? WHAT PLOT??

MEL : (*He turns back toward her*) The-social-economical-and-political-plot-to-undermine-the-working-classes-in-this-country.

EDNA: Oh, that plot.

MEL: Yes, *that* plot! Instead of rushing downtown every morning, stay home and listen to the radio once in a while. Listen to the talk shows. Find out what's going on in this country. Ten minutes of WQXR and you'll want to move to Switzerland.

EDNA: If it depresses you, Mel, don't listen to the talk shows. Listen to some nice music.

MEL: Nice music . . . (*laughs*) Incredible. You're a child. You're an uninformed, ignorant little child . . . They've taken it over, Edna. Our music, our culture, it's not ours anymore, it's *theirs*.

EDNA: They have our music?

MEL: All of it. The arts, the media, every form of mass communication. *They got it, baby*!

EDNA: Don't get mad, Mel . . . Who?

MEL: *Who? . . . WHO?? . . .* Jesus God in heaven! *Who???*

EDNA: Mel, I've got to be in the office in twenty minutes. Please tell me who's taking over so I won't be late.

MEL: All right, sit down.

EDNA: I may not get a cab, Mel. Can't you tell me who's taking over standing up?

MEL: Are you going to sit down?

EDNA: Do I have to, Mel? Is it a long name?

MEL: *Sit down, for Christ sakes!* (EDNA *sits down, while* MEL *paces*) Now . . . Once you do away with the middle class—what have you got left?

EDNA (*She looks at him. It can't be that easy*) What's left? After you take away the middle class? (MEL *nods*) The lower class and the upper class?

(MEL *stares at her incredulously*)

MEL: I can't talk to you. You have no understanding at all. Go on. Go to work.

EDNA: You mean there's another class besides the lower, the middle and the upper?

MEL (*He walks to center of the room and looks around suspiciously.*) Come here.

(EDNA *looks at him*)

EDNA: I thought you wanted me to sit down.

MEL: Will you come here. Away from the walls.

(EDNA *gets up and goes over to him in the middle of the room*)

EDNA: If it's that secret, Mel, I don't think I want to know.

(*He grabs her by the wrist and pulls her to him*)

MEL: (*in a soft voice*) There *is* a plot, Edna. It's very complicated, very sophisticated, almost invisible . . . Maybe only a half a dozen people in this country really know about it.

EDNA: And they told it on the radio?

MEL: Yes.

EDNA: Then everyone heard it.

MEL: Did you hear it?

EDNA: No.

MEL: Then everyone didn't hear it. How many people you think listen to the radio at ten o'clock in the morning? Everybody is working. But I heard it . . . And as sure as we're standing here in the middle of the room, there is a plot going on in this country today.

EDNA: Against whom?

MEL: Against me.

EDNA: The whole country?

MEL: Not me personally. Although I'm a victim of it. A plot to change the system. To destroy the status quo. It's not just me they're after, Edna. They're after you. They're after our kids, my sisters, every one of our friends. They're after the cops, they're after the hippies, they're after the government, they're after the anarchists, they're after Women's Lib, the fags, the blacks, the whole military complex. That's who they're after, Edna.

EDNA: Who? You mentioned everyone. There's no one left.

MEL: There's someone left. Oh, baby, there's someone left all right.

EDNA: Well, I'm sure there is . . . if you say so, Mel.

MEL: (*yells*) Don't patronize me. I know what I'm talking about. I am open to channels of information twenty-four hours a day.

(EDNA *is becoming increasingly alarmed at* MEL*'s obvious paranoiac behavior but doesn't quite know how to handle it yet*)

EDNA: Mel, Mel . . . Would you come here for a minute. Just sit with me for a minute. (*He sits down*) . . . Mel . . . You know I love you and believe in you completely. I always have . . . But I just want to say something, I hope you don't misunderstand this—

MEL: You think I'm paranoiac? You think I'm having some sort of mental, nervous breakdown because I'm out of work? Because of the pressure, the strain I've been under, because I sound like a deranged person because of the personal hell I have gone through these past seven weeks. Is that it?

EDNA: (*nods*) That's it. That's exactly it, Mel . . . I wouldn't have put it that strongly, but that's more or less it. Exactly.

MEL: Do you want proof, Edna? Do you want me to give you actual, indisputable proof?

EDNA: (*trying to be kinder now*) Of what, Mel?

MEL: That me, that Dave Polichek, that Mike Ambrozi, Hal Chesterman, twenty-three secretaries, six point seven of the working force in this country today is unemployed not because of a recession, not because of wages and high prices, but because of a well-organized, calculated, brilliantly executed *plot*! Do you want me to give you proof right here and now in this room?

EDNA: (*hesitates*) Well—all right . . . If you want, Mel.

MEL: I CAN'T GIVE YOU ANY PROOF!!! . . . *What kind of proof do I have*? I'm out of work, that's my proof . . . They won't let me work!

EDNA: Who is it, Mel? Tell me who's behind the plot? Is it the kids? The addicts? The Army? The Navy? The-Book-of-the-Month Club? WHO THE HELL IS IT, MEL?

MEL: It is the human race! . . . It is the sudden, irrevocable, deterioration of the spirit of man. It is man undermining himself, causing a self-willed, self-imposed, self-evident *self-destruction* . . . That's who it is.

EDNA: (*looks at him*) The human race? . . . The human race is responsible for the unemployment?

MEL: (*a little smirk*) Surprised, aren't you?

EDNA: (*nods, quite shaken*) I never would have guessed. I kept thinking it was somebody else.

MEL: (*glares at her*) Don't mock me. Don't patronize me and don't mock me.

EDNA: I'm not mocking you, Mel.

MEL: *You're mocking me*! . . . I know when I'm being mocked. I know what I'm talking about. You're working, you've got a job, you're not affected by any of this.

EDNA: I am so affected by it, Mel, you wouldn't believe it was possible…

MEL: You don't know the first thing I'm talking about . . . You don't know what it is to be in my place . . . You've never stood on line for two hours waiting for an unemployment check with a shirt and tie, trying to look like you don't need the money. And some fat old dame behind the counter screaming out so everyone can hear, "*Did you look for a job this week*?" . . . "Yes, I looked for a job" "*Did you turn down any work this week*?" "What the hell am I doing here if I turned down work this week?" . . . You never walked into your own building and had a ninety-one-year-old doorman with no teeth, asthma and beer on his breath giggle at you because he's working . . . You've never been on your own terrace and gotten hit with a bucket of ice-cold ice water . . . I haven't forgotten that son of a bitch! (*He goes to the terrace door, but not out on it, and yells up*) I haven't forgotten you, you son of a bitch!

EDNA: Mel, don't start in again. Please don't start in again.

MEL: I'm waiting for him. I'm just waiting for him. He's up there now, but one day he's gonna be down there and I'm gonna be up here and then we'll see. One cold, snowy day some son of a bitch in this building is gonna be buried under three feet of snow. They won't find him until the spring. (*Yells up again*) They won't find you until the spring, you son of a bitch!

EDNA: Mel, listen to me. Listen to me very carefully. I want you to see a doctor . . . I don't want to put it off any more, Mel, I want you to see a doctor as soon as possible. Today, Mel. Now.

MEL: (*disregarding her, he keeps talking through her speeches*) He thinks I don't know what he looks like . . . I know what he looks like, all right . . . I know what they *all* look like. I've got their faces engraved in my brain.

❧

HARRY: It hurts all of us. That's why we're here. To try to do something.

PAULINE: Harry, let her cry if she wants. She came all the way from Lakewood . . . Go on, Harry.

HARRY: Fact number one, Mel has had a nervous breakdown. Fact number two, besides a nervous breakdown, Mel doesn't have a job. That man is totally unemployed.

JESSIE: (*sniffles again*): You think that doesn't hurt me too?

PAULINE: Jessie, let him finish, you can cry on the way home.

HARRY: Fact—

PAULINE: Go on with the facts, Harry.

HARRY: Fact number three, besides a nervous breakdown and not having a job, the man is practically penniless . . . I don't want to pass any comments on how a man and a woman mishandled their money for twenty-seven years. It's none of my business how a man squandered a life's savings on bad investments for which he never asked my advice once, the kind of advice which has given me solvency, security, and a beautiful summer place in the country. Thank God, *I'll* never have a nervous breakdown . . . None of that is my business. My business is what are we going to do for Mel? How much are we going to give? Somebody make a suggestion. (*The silence is deafening. No one speaks. No one looks at each other. There is a lot of coffee drinking, but no offers of how much they're going to give . . . After what seems like an hour of silence,* HARRY *speaks again*) Well?

PEARL: You're a businessman, Harry. You make a suggestion. You tell us how much we should all give.

HARRY: (*thinks a moment*) Let me have some coffee. (PEARL *pours him a cup of coffee*) So let's face the facts . . . The man needs help. Who else can he turn to but us? This is my suggestion. We make Mel a loan. We all chip in X number of dollars a week, and then when he gets back on his feet, when he gets straightened out, gets a job again, then he can pay us all back. That's my suggestion. What do you all think?

(*There is a moment's silence.* PAULINE *whispers to* PEARL. PEARL *nods*)

PEARL: Pauline has a question.

HARRY: What's the question?

PAULINE: How much is X number of dollars?

HARRY: X is X. We have to figure out what X is. We'll talk and we'll decide.

PAULINE: I mean is it a big X or a little x?

HARRY: It's not even an X. It's a blank until we fill X in with a figure.

PAULINE: I'm not complaining. We have to do the right thing. But when you say it like that, "X number of dollars," it sounds like a lot of money . . . I have limited capital, you know.

JESSIE: Everybody has limited capital. Nobody has *un*limited capital. Pearl, do you have unlimited capital?

PEARL: I wish I did. I'd give Mel X number of dollars in a minute.

PAULINE: All I'm asking is, how much is X. I can't figure with letters, I have to know numbers.

JESSIE: Harry, don't say X any more. We're not business-women, we don't know about X. Say a number that we can understand.

HARRY: I can't say a number until I figure out A, how much does Mel need a week and B, how much are we willing to give. I can't even guess what X is until we figure out how much A and B comes to.

PEARL: All right, suppose we figure out what A is and what B is. And if we know that, then we'll figure what X is, right?

HARRY: Right.

PEARL: And now suppose everyone here agrees except one person. She thinks it's too much. She doesn't want to give X. She wants to give M or W, whatever. What do we do then?

HARRY: Forget X. Forget I ever said X. (*He rubs his head and drinks some more coffee*) Let's figure what Mel needs to get over his nervous breakdown . . . His biggest expense is the doctor, right? Edna says he's the best and he has to go five times a week.

PAULINE: Five times a week to the best doctor? I'm beginning to see what X is going to come to.

JESSIE: Maybe it's not even a nervous breakdown. Doctors can be wrong, too. Remember your pains last year, Pearl?

PEARL: It's true. They took out all my top teeth, then found out it was kidney stones.

HARRY: I can't believe what I'm listening to . . . You're a hundred and sixty years old between the three of you and not one of you makes any sense . . . If you'll all be quiet for a minute, I'll settle this thing.

PEARL: All right, we're quiet. Settle it, Harry.

HARRY: The most important thing is that Mel gets well, agreed?

ALL THREE: Agreed!

HARRY: And that the only way he's going to get well is to see a doctor. Agreed?

ALL THREE: Agreed.

HARRY: And it is our obligation, as his only living relatives—not counting his wife, no disrespect intended—to bear the financial responsibility of that burden. Agreed?

ALL THREE: Agreed.

HARRY: And we'll all see this thing through to the end whether it takes a week or a month or a year or even five years. Agreed? (*There is stony silence*) Okay. Our first disagreement.

PAULINE: No one's disagreeing. We're all in agreement. Except when you mention things like five years. I don't see any sense in curing Mel and ending up in the poorhouse. If, God forbid, that happened, would he be in any position to help us? He's not too able to begin with.

JESSIE: So what should we do, Harry? You know how to figure these things. What should we do?

HARRY: Well, obviously we can't afford to let Mel be sick forever. We've got to put a time limit on it. Agreed?

ALL THREE: Agreed.

HARRY: What do we give him to get better? Six months?

PAULINE: It shouldn't take six months. If that doctor's as good as Edna says, it shouldn't take six months.

(A door to the bedroom is heard closing)

PEARL: Shhh . . . She's coming.

PAULINE: We'll let Harry do the talking.

PEARL: And then we'll settle everything. Thank God, it's almost over.

(They all assume a pose of innocence and calm. EDNA *comes out of the bedroom.)*

EDNA: I'm sorry I was so long. I was just talking to Doctor Frankel. Mel's on his way home, he'll be here in a minute.

HARRY: How is Mel? What does the doctor say?

EDNA: Well, it's hard to tell. Mel is having a very rough time. He's in a very depressed state, he's not himself. He's completely withdrawn. He sits in that chair sometimes for hours without saying a word. You'll see when he comes in, he's a different person.

JESSIE: *(wipes her eyes with a hanky, sniffs)* It hurts me every time I hear it . . .

PAULINE: So what is it, a nervous breakdown? Is it a nervous breakdown? You can tell us. We're his family. It's a nervous breakdown, isn't it?

EDNA: Yes, in a way I guess you can say it's a nervous breakdown.

PEARL: I knew it, I knew it. He had the same thing in high school.

HARRY: So what's the diagnosis? What does the doctor say?

EDNA: (*shrugs*) Mel needs care and treatment. He's a very good doctor, he thinks Mel's going to be all right, but it's going to take time.

PAULINE: How much time? A month? Two months? More than two months?

EDNA: He can't tell yet.

PAULINE: He can guess, can't he? Three months? Four months? More than four months?

EDNA: There's no way of telling yet, Pauline. It could be a month, it could be two months, it could be two *years*.

PAULINE: No, two years is out of the question. I refuse to go along with two years.

EDNA: I'm not saying it will be. I'm just saying we don't know yet.

HARRY: Can I say something? Can I get a word in?

PAULINE: (*turning away from* EDNA) I wish you would say something, Harry. I wish you would do the talking.

HARRY: Thank you very much.

PAULINE: Because two years is ridiculous.

PEARL: Go on, Harry.

HARRY: We're all very concerned, Edna. Very concerned. After all, he's our brother.

JESSIE: Since he was a baby.

HARRY: Can I please do the talking?

PEARL: Will you let him do the talking, Jessie? . . . Go on, Harry.

HARRY: We're very concerned. We appreciate that you're his wife, you're going to do all you can, but we know it's not going to be enough. We want to help. We've talked it out among ourselves and . . . we're prepared to take over the financial burden of the doctor. You take care of the apartment, the food, the miscellaneous, we'll pay the doctor bills. Whatever they come to.

EDNA: I'm . . . I'm overwhelmed . . . I'll be very truthful with you, I never expected that . . . I am deeply touched and overwhelmed. I don't know what to say . . .

HARRY: You don't have to say anything.

PAULINE: Just tell us what you think the bills will come to.

EDNA: That's very generous of you all, but I couldn't let you do that. Mel wouldn't let me do it.

HARRY: Don't be ridiculous. Where you going to get the money from, a bank? You can't put up a nervous breakdown as collateral.

EDNA: I have no idea how long Mel will be in treatment. It could run into a fortune.

HARRY: Let us worry about that. The money, we'll take care of.

EDNA: But it could run as high as twenty, twenty-five thousand dollars.

(There is a long pause. The sisters all look at HARRY.*)*

PAULINE: Harry, can I say something to you in private?

HARRY: We don't need any private discussions.

PAULINE: We just found out what X is . . . Don't you think we ought to discuss X a little further?

HARRY: It's not necessary. I don't care what it's going to cost. The three of you can contribute whatever you think you can afford, *I'll* make up the deficit . . . If it's fifteen, if it's twenty, if it's twenty-five thousand, I'll see that it's taken care of, as long as Mel has the best medical treatment . . . That's all I have to say.

(He nods his head as though taking a little bow.)

EDNA: (*moved*) I'm—I'm speechless . . . What do I say?

HARRY: You don't say nothing.

PEARL: We just want to do the right thing.

EDNA: I know none of us have been very close the last few years.

PAULINE: Nine. Nine years was the last time we were invited.

EDNA: Has it been that long? I suppose it's been my fault. Maybe I haven't tried to understand you. Maybe you haven't tried to understand me. Anyway, I appreciate it more than you can imagine, but we really don't need it.

HARRY: What are you talking about? Certainly you need it.

EDNA: Over the years, we've managed to save something. I have some jewelry I can sell . . .

HARRY: You're not going to sell your jewelry.

PAULINE: Maybe she doesn't wear it anymore. Let the woman talk.

EDNA: Mel can cash in his insurance policy and I have my job. I can manage whatever the medical expenses come to, but if you really want to help ...What I'm worried about is Mel's future.

JESSIE: We all are, darling.

EDNA: It's not easy for a man of Mel's age to get a job today, to start all over again...

HARRY: If he knew lighting fixtures, I would take him in a minute.

PEARL: Certainly, my God.

EDNA: If he could just get out of New York and move to the country somewhere, he would be a hundred percent better off.

HARRY: I agree a thousand percent.

EDNA: I was thinking of a summer camp. Mel is wonderful with children and sports, I could do the cooking, the girls will help out, we can hire a small staff...There's a lovely place in Vermont that's for sale. We could have it for next summer. Don't you think Mel would be better off there?

HARRY: Again, a thousand per cent.

EDNA: They want twenty-five thousand dollars down in cash ... So instead of giving it to us for the doctor, would you lend it to us for the camp?

(There is a hush, a definite hush. HARRY *looks at* EDNA *in disbelief)*

HARRY: A summer camp? ...Twenty-five thousand dollars for a summer camp?

EDNA: The price is a hundred thousand. But they want twenty-five thousand down.

HARRY: *A hundred thousand dollars for a summer camp*?? ... Run by a man with a nervous breakdown?

EDNA: He'll be all right by next summer.

HARRY: Do you know what it is for a *normal* person to be responsible for that many boys and girls? The law suits you're open for?

EDNA: I don't understand. You were willing to give Mel the money for a doctor. Why won't you lend it to him for a camp?

HARRY: Because with a camp you can go broke. With a doctor you can go broke too, but you get better.

EDNA: All right. *You* pay for the doctor. *I'll* invest in the camp.

HARRY: You mean we should pay to get Mel healthy so you can lose your money in a camp and get him sick again? ...Then you'll come to us for more money for another doctor?

EDNA: I thought you wanted to do something. I thought you wanted to help him.

HARRY: We *do* want to help him.

EDNA: *Then help him!*

HARRY: Not when he's sick. When he's better, we'll help him.

❧

Free Trade versus Protectionism

For the past two centuries, the great majority of academic economists have supported the idea of free trade among nations for the same reasons they support free trade between individuals and regions in the same country: voluntary trade only occurs when both parties trading expect to be better off by doing so. By specializing and trading internationally as well as domestically, a nation's overall level of production is increased. Higher production translates directly into higher consumption and standards of living.

Most of the opposition to free trade comes, not surprisingly, from businesses and workers who are faced with the prospect of competing against foreign workers and producers. Can we afford to let those industries decline, and perhaps even fail? In exceptional cases, such as industries that are vital to national defense, maybe not. But in most cases, if a domestic industry can no longer compete with other firms—domestically or internationally—those resources would be better used elsewhere.

The logic behind free trade is really quite simple in some respects: We could have full employment by building a wall around the country and not importing or exporting, but we can also have full employment by allowing trade—which is just what has happened, even with the dramatic increase in the volume of international trade during the past twenty-five years. If we trade, we will specialize and produce a narrower range of goods and services, and we will export a larger part of what we produce in exchange for the goods and services we import. Free trade means getting the things we import at a lower cost, and producing more of the goods and services that are produced here at a lower cost. Not trading means paying more for the things we buy, and using more resources to produce things that can be produced at a lower cost somewhere else. As long as the fundamental economic problem is scarcity, or not being able to have all of the things we want, paying more to buy things and using more resources than necessary to produce things just doesn't make sense.

The classic fable and satire on protectionism, "Petition of the Manufacturers of Candles," was written by a French lawyer, Frédéric Bastiat, in the nineteenth century. This is one of the few literary fables that is perhaps better known to economists than to literature professors and critics.

Petition of the Manufacturers of Candles (1845)

Frédéric Bastiat

If some protectionism is a good thing, why not take it to its logical conclusion? Bastiat did just that in order to show that a nation could conceivably create jobs producing any number of products that can be imported at a lower cost, or even free. But doing so ultimately lowers the standard of living for consumers, most workers and firms, and the nation as a whole.

Gentlemen,—You are on the right road. You reject abstract theories, and have little consideration for cheapness and plenty. Your chief care is the interest of the producer. You desire to emancipate him from external competition, and reserve the *national market* for *national industry*.

We are about to offer you an admirable opportunity of applying your—what shall we call it? your theory? No; nothing is more deceptive than theory; your doctrine? your system? your principle? but you dislike doctrines, you abhor systems, and as for principles, you deny that there are any in social economy: we shall say, then, your practice, your practice without theory and without principle.

We are suffering from the intolerable competition of a foreign rival, placed, it would seem, in a condition so far superior to ours for the production of light, that he absolutely *inundates* our *national market* with it at a price fabulously reduced. The moment he shows himself, our trade leaves us—all consumers apply to him; and a branch of native industry, having countless ramifications, is all at once rendered completely stagnant. This rival, who is no other than the Sun, wages war to the knife against us, and we suspect that he has been raised up by *perfidious Albion* (good policy as times go); inasmuch as he displays towards that haughty island a circumspection with which he dispenses in our case.

What we pray for, that it may please you to pass a law ordering the shutting up of all windows, sky-lights, dormer-windows, outside and inside shutters, curtains, blinds, bull's-eyes; in a word, of all openings, holes, chinks, clefts, and fissures, by or through which the light of the sun has been in use to enter houses, to the prejudice of the meritorious manufactures with which we flatter ourselves we have accommodated our country,—a country which, in gratitude, ought not to abandon us now to a strife so unequal.

We trust, Gentlemen, that you will not regard this our request as a satire, or refuse it without at least previously hearing the reasons which we have to urge in its support.

And, first, if you shut up as much as possible all access to natural light, and create a demand for artificial light, which of our French manufactures will not be encouraged by it?

If more tallow is consumed, then there must be more oxen and sheep; and, consequently, we shall behold the multiplication of artificial meadows, meat, wool, hides, and, above all, manure, which is the basis and foundation of all agricultural wealth.

If more oil is consumed, then we shall have an extended cultivation of the poppy, of the olive, and of rape. These rich and exhausting plants will come at the right time to enable us to avail ourselves of the increased fertility which the rearing of additional cattle will impart to our lands.

Our heaths will be covered with resinous trees. Numerous swarms of bees will, on the mountains, gather perfumed treasures, now wasting their fragrance on the desert air, like the flowers from which they emanate. No branch of agriculture but will then exhibit a cheering development.

The same remark applies to navigation. Thousands of vessels will proceed to the whale fishery; and, in a short time, we shall possess a navy capable of maintaining the honour of France, and gratifying the patriotic aspirations of your petitioners, the undersigned candlemakers and others.

But what shall we say of the manufacture of *articles de Paris*? Henceforth you will behold gildings, bronzes, crystals, in candlesticks, in lamps, in lustres, in candelabra, shining forth, in spacious warerooms, compared with which those of the present day can be regarded but as mere shops.

No poor *resinier* from his heights on the seacoast, no coal-miner from the depth of his sable gallery, but will rejoice in higher wages and increased prosperity.

Only have the goodness to reflect, Gentlemen, and you will be convinced that there is, perhaps, no Frenchman, from the wealthy coalmaster to the humblest vender of lucifer matches, whose lot will not be ameliorated by the success of this our petition.

We foresee your objections, Gentlemen, but we know that you can oppose to us none but such as you have picked up from the effete works of the partisans of free trade. We defy you to utter a single word against us which will not instantly rebound against yourselves and your entire policy.

You will tell us that, if we gain by the protection which we seek, the country will lose by it, because the consumer must bear the loss.

We answer:

You have ceased to have any right to invoke the interest of the consumer; for, whenever his interest is found opposed to that of the producer, you sacrifice the former. You have done so for the purpose of *encouraging labour and increasing employment*. For the same reason you should do so again.

You have yourselves obviated this objection. When you are told that the consumer is interested in the free importation of iron, coal, corn, textile fabrics—yes, you reply, but the producer is interested in their exclusion. Well, be it so;—if consumers are interested in the free admission of natural light, the producers of artificial light are equally interested in its prohibition.

But, again, you may say that the producer and consumer are identical. If the manufacturer gain by protection, he will make the agriculturist also a gainer; and if agriculture prosper, it will open a vent to manufactures. Very well; if you confer upon us the monopoly of furnishing light during the day,—first of all, we shall purchase quantities of tallow, coals, oils, resinous substances, wax, alcohol—besides silver, iron, bronze, crystal—to carry on our manufactures; and then we, and those who furnish us with such commodities, having become rich will consume a great deal, and impart prosperity to all the other branches of our national industry.

If you urge that the light of the sun is a gratuitous gift of nature, and that to reject such gifts is to reject wealth itself under pretence of encouraging the means of acquiring it, we would caution you against giving a death-blow to your own policy. Remember that hitherto you have always repelled foreign products, *because* they approximate more nearly than home products to the character of gratuitous gifts. To comply with the exactions of other monopolists, you have only *half a motive*; and to repulse us simply because we stand on a stronger vantage-ground than others would be to adopt the equation, + x + = -; in other words, it would be to heap *absurdity* upon *absurdity*.

Nature and human labour co-operate in various proportions (depending on countries and climates) in the production of commodities. The part which nature executes is always gratuitous; it is the part executed by human labour which constitutes value, and is paid for.

If a Lisbon orange sells for half the price of a Paris orange, it is because natural, and consequently gratuitous, heat does for the one, what artificial, and therefore expensive, heat must do for the other.

When an orange comes to us from Portugal, we may conclude that it is furnished in part gratuitously, in part for an onerous consideration; in other words, it comes to us at *half-price* as compared with those of Paris.

Now, it is precisely the *gratuitous half* (pardon the word) which we contend should be excluded. You say, How can natural labour sustain competition with foreign labour, when the former has all the work to do, and the latter only does one-half, the sun supplying the remainder? But if this *half*, being *gratuitous*, determines you to exclude competition, how should the *whole*, being *gratuitous*, induce you to admit competition? If you were consistent, you would, while excluding as hurtful to native industry what is half gratuitous, exclude *a fortiori* and with double zeal, that which is altogether gratuitous.

Once more, when products such as coal, iron, corn, or textile fabrics, are sent us from abroad, and we can acquire them with less labour than if we made them ourselves, the difference is a free gift conferred upon us. The gift is more or less considerable in proportion as the difference is more or less great. It amounts to a quarter, a half, or three-quarters of the value of the product, when the foreigner only asks us for three-fourths, a half, or a quarter of the price we should otherwise pay. It is as perfect and complete as it can be, when the donor (like the sun in furnishing us with light) asks us for nothing. The question, and we ask it formally, is this, Do you desire for our country the benefit of gratuitous consumption, or the pretended advantages of onerous production? Make your choice, but be logical; for as long as you exclude as you do, coal, iron, corn, foreign fabrics, *in proportion* as their price approximates to *zero*, what inconsistency would it be to admit the light of the sun, the price of which is already at *zero* during the entire day!

U. Cost-Benefit Analysis

If there is a golden rule of economics, it is this: "When the additional benefits of doing a little more of something are greater than the additional costs, do it. When the additional costs are greater than the additional benefits, don't do it." This simple rule can be applied to the decisions made by a consumer thinking about buying another piece of pie, a producer deciding whether to increase the production of pajamas, or a government deciding whether it makes sense to try to reduce air pollution by ten percent over the next five years.

Whenever issues of life and limb are involved in these decisions, the rule of comparing additional benefits and costs becomes controversial and, for many people, uncomfortable. For example, if reducing air pollution will save lives, or even one life, can't we just say that those policies are "priceless," and worth anything? Unfortunately, no, because as soon as we say anything is infinitely valuable that means we should devote an infinite quantity of resources to producing it. We can't do that, because there are any number of things that save lives—including food, medicine, clothing, shelter, and energy for heating, as well as better environmental quality. How could we decide how many resources to use to contribute to each of these different purposes if we considered every life that could be saved to be infinitely valuable?

Consider this stark example: Would it make sense to ban all automobile travel, knowing that to do so would save thousands of lives a year? If the answer to that question is no, as most people agree that it is, then the idea that the benefits of automobile travel outweigh the costs—including the cost of having people injured and killed in automobile accidents—has been accepted. Thus, it can be determined that some policies and products may save lives at a cost low enough to make sense—for example, requiring seat belts and air bags in automobiles—while other policies and products don't—for example, building overpasses at every railroad crossing, which we could do but don't simply because it costs too much. Many people don't like to think about things in this way, but the problem can be restated in a more palatable way: How can we use some of our scarce resources to save as many lives as possible, while also producing the other kinds of goods and services people want? Of course, as discussed earlier in the section on the legal and social framework for markets, it is also important to recognize that there are some kinds of things that are, by law, removed from the realm of economic valuation.

The boundaries for what can and cannot be traded in the marketplace, or reasonably weighed in terms of costs and benefits, have attracted the attention of literary writers for centuries. Two satirical examples are provided here: Jonathan Swift's "A Modest Proposal," and Pär Lagerkvist's "A Hero's Death."

A Modest Proposal (1729)

Jonathan Swift

Swift's satire addresses and anticipates many public policy issues, some of them nearly as controversial as his actually very immodest proposal. The slave markets that operated openly and legally in some nations and for some races in Swift's time were eventually banned as a violation of basic human rights, a prohibition that garnered agreement and support from economists as much as from any other profession, and more than some. Despite that, current prohibitions against markets for organs to be used in medical transplants or research are controversial but still discussed by economists and policymakers, largely because the non-market procedures used to allocate organs and tissues are seriously and perhaps inherently flawed. And in a much wider range of settings, from wrongful death and injury lawsuits to public laws and regulations that set speed limits and safety standards for automobiles and other products, financial values are regularly established for life and limb as a necessary step in determining what outcomes are as fair and *efficient as possible.*

I am assured by our merchants, that a boy or a girl, before twelve years old, is no saleable commodity, and even when they come to this age, they will not yield above three pounds, or three pounds and half-a-crown at most on the Exchange, which cannot turn to account either to the parents or the kingdom, the charge of nutriment and rags having been at least four times that value.

I shall now therefore humbly propose my own thoughts, which I hope will not be liable to the least objection.

I have been assured by a very knowing American of my acquaintance in London, that a young healthy child, well nursed, is at a year old a most delicious, nourishing, and wholesome food; whether *stewed, roasted, baked,* or *boiled,* and I make no doubt that it will equally serve in a *fricassee*, or *ragout*.

I do therefore humbly offer it to *public consideration*, that of the hundred and twenty thousand children, already computed, twenty thousand may be reserved for breed, whereof only one fourth part to be males, which is more than we allow to *sheep, black-cattle,* or *swine*; and my reason is, that these children are seldom the fruits of marriage, *a circumstance not much regarded by our savages;* therefore *one male* will be sufficient to serve *four females*. That the remaining hundred thousand may at a year old be offered in sale to the *persons of quality* and *fortune*, through the kingdom, always advising the mother to let them suck plentifully in the last month, so as to render them plump and fat for a good table. A child will make two dishes at an entertainment for friends, and when the family dines alone the fore or hind quarter will make a reasonable dish, and seasoned with a little pepper or salt will be very good boiled on the fourth day, especially in *winter*.

I have reckoned upon a medium, that a child just born will weigh 12 pounds, and in a solar year if tolerably nursed increaseth to 28 pounds.

I grant this food will be somewhat dear, and therefore very *proper for landlords,* who, as they have already devoured most of the parents, seem to have the best title to the children.

Infants' flesh will be in season throughout the year, but more plentiful in *March*, and a little before and after, for we are told by a grave author, an eminent French physician, that *fish being a prolific diet*, there are more children born in *Roman Catholic countries* about nine months after *Lent*, than at any other season; therefore reckoning a year after *Lent*, the markets will be more glutted than usual, because the number of *Popish infants* is at least three to one in this kingdom, and therefore it will have one other collateral advantage by lessening the number of *Papists* among us.

I have already computed the charge of nursing a beggar's child (in which list I reckon all *cottagers, labourers,* and four fifths of the *farmers*) to be about two shillings *per annum*, rags included, and I believe no gentleman would repine to give ten shillings for the *carcases of a good fat child,* which, as I have said, will make four dishes of excellent nutritive meat, when he hath only some particular friend, or his own family to dine with him. Thus the Squire will learn to be a good landlord, and grow popular among his tenants, the mother will have eight shillings net profit, and be fit for work until she produces another child.

Those who are more thrifty (*as I must confess the times require*) may flay the carcass; the skin of which, artificially dressed, will make admirable *gloves for ladies,* and *summer boots for fine gentlemen*.

As to our City of Dublin; shambles may be appointed for this purpose in the most convenient parts of it, and butchers we may be assured will not be wanting, although I rather recommend buying the children alive, and dressing them hot from the knife, as we do *roasting Pigs*.

A Hero's Death
(1924)
Pär Lagerkvist

The main difference between Swift's "Modest Proposal" and this piece written two centuries later by a Nobel laureate is simply this: Lagerkvist's hero is an adult acting with full information about the consequences of his decision. Nevertheless, and whether or not his decision makes sense in purely monetary terms, legal prohibitions against this kind of market can be defended on exactly the same grounds as prohibitions against markets for slaves or, as in Swift's proposal, prohibitions against selling infants for food.

In a town where the people never seemed to get enough amusement a committee had engaged a man who was to balance on his head up on the church spire and then fall down and kill himself. He was to have 500,000 for doing it. In all levels of society, all spheres, there was keen interest in this undertaking; the tickets were snapped up in a few days and it was the sole topic of conversation. Everyone thought it was a very daring thing to do. But then, of course, the price was in keeping. It was none too pleasant to fall and kill yourself, and from such a height too. But it was also admitted that it was a handsome fee. The syndicate which had arranged everything had certainly not spared itself in any way and people were proud that it had been possible to form one like it in the town. Naturally, attention was also riveted on the man who had undertaken to perform the feat. The interviewers from the press fell on him with gusto, for there were only a few days left until the performance was to take place. He received them affably in his suite at the town's most fashionable hotel.

"Well, for me it's all a matter of business," he said. "I have been offered the sum known to you, and I have accepted the offer. That is all."

"But don't you think it's unpleasant having to lose your life? We realize the necessity, of course; otherwise it wouldn't be much of a sensation and the syndicate couldn't pay as it has done, but it can't be too nice for you."

"No, you're right there, and the thought has occurred to me, too. But one does anything for money."

On the basis of these statements long articles were written in the newspapers about the hitherto unknown man, about his past, his views, his attitude to various problems of the day, his character and private person. His picture was in every paper one opened. It showed a strong young man. There was nothing remarkable about him, but he looked spirited and healthy and had a frank, vigorous face; a typical representative of the best youth of the age, willing and sound. It was studied in all the cafés, while people made ready for the coming sensation. There was nothing wrong about it, they thought; a nice young man, the women thought he was wonderful. Those who had more sense shrugged their shoulders; smart bit of work, they said. All were unanimous on one thing, however: that the idea was strange and fantastic and that this sort of thing could only have occurred in our remarkable age with its flurry and intensity and its faculty of sacrificing all. And it was agreed that the syndicate deserved every praise for not having cavilled at expense when it came to arranging something like this and really giving the town a chance to witness such a spectacle. It would no doubt cover its expenditure by the high price of the tickets, but it took the risk at any rate.

At last the great day arrived. The space around the church was packed with people. The excitement was intense. All held their breath, in a frenzy of expectation at what was going to happen.

And the man fell; it was soon over. The people shuddered, then got up to go home. In a way they felt a certain disappointment. It had been splendid, but . . . he had only fallen and killed himself after all. It was a lot of money to pay for something that was so simple. Of course he had been frightfully mutilated, but what was the good of that? A promising young man sacrificed in that way. People went home disgruntled; the women put up their sunshades. No, awful things like that really ought to be forbidden. What pleasure did it give anyone? On second thought the whole thing was disgraceful.

Epilogue:
Mutual Gains from Exchange between Economics and Literature and Drama, or Mutual Neglect through Academic Protectionism?

George Bernard Shaw, Oscar Wilde, Dylan Thomas, Bertrand Russell, and Sir Winston Churchill have all been cited as saying that the United States and Great Britain are two nations separated by a common language.[1] The same can be said for the relationship between economics and works of literature. Economics is in some ways separated from literature and drama, and from literary criticism and history, by its development of formal definitions of terms often taken from everyday language and therefore still widely used by literary authors and critics who are also keenly interested in "the ordinary business of everyday life." Of course, economists also make use of mathematical and econometric modeling and statistical analysis, and there is no doubt that the use of these specialized methods has been productive and indeed essential in the development of economics as a separate field of academic study. But even before Adam Smith, Alexander Pope warned, in the fourth book of *The Dunciad,* about the costs of academic and scientific specialization, which can lead scholars in different fields to study microscopic pieces of the human and social scene while ignoring the "whole frame [that] is obvious to a flea."

Economists still regularly use literary and textual evidence and arguments. And for better or worse—or both—economics, literature, and literary criticism and history are constantly being pushed together because of their strong mutual interests in fundamental ideas and topics. Many of these ideas and topics deal with individual families and their roles as consumers or workers, or with businesses and the people who manage them or work for them. But like economists, literary authors, critics, and historians also frequently discuss public policy issues—or more generally the appropriate scope of, and criteria for evaluating the economic functions of government. For that reason, disagreements between economists and literary writers often deal with highly publicized and controversial issues, making the disputes more enduring and bitter.

But some of these disputes are more a matter of appearance than reality. For example, literary writers' frequent expressions of ambivalent attitudes toward wealth and material pursuits sometimes represent nothing substantially different from economists' discussions of the disutility of work, the disadvantages of specialization and the division of labor, or simply the costs that are inevitably associated with any economic choice.

It is even more important, perhaps, to recognize that literary authors and critics, like economists, are hardly a uniform, regimented lot. My own conclusion is that while some literary authors, critics, and historians are certainly more adept in describing economic material than others, there is no single literary point of view on economic topics, no uniformly pro- or anti-business attitude pervading the work of the greatest essayists, novelists, and playwrights.[2] Instead, the range of opinions on economic activity, public policy issues, and the appropriate scope of government intervention in the marketplace basically resembles the range of opinion found among economists. Given the wide range of backgrounds brought to the literary marketplace by writers, it is hardly surprising that there is expressed a wide range of social and political points of view.

Admittedly, even if the range of economic opinion is not notably different among literary writers than it is among economists, the mean and median values of literary writers' opinions on a scale of liberalism/conservatism or some such measure might be different from the economists'. To establish that would take a far more extensive review and system for evaluating writers' positions than I have presented here or in the appendices that follow; but the literary historian Neil McKendrick's conclusion that literary hostility toward businessmen owes more to a group of influential critics than to treatments in the primary works (see Appendix B) bears note.

The range of opinion to be seen in both disciplines can be viewed as a cause for optimism, despair, or cynicism. There is no reason to consider all of the implications of that statement here, but in terms of facilitating multidisciplinary initiatives across these fields, it suggests that writers from each field can probably find and quote sympathetic authors from across the disciplinary divide. In some respects, that is a pleasant idea; after all, it is not uncommon to find that the demand for economists increases when there are conflicting opinions to be heard.[3] But it also raises the question: Why should an economist bother to try to understand what novelists or essayists are saying about economics, and vice versa?

The typical rationale for initiatives that involve bringing more cultural and humane ideas into economics has occasionally been made by well-known economists from quite different backgrounds and, for that matter, different political perspectives. Admittedly, however, it is not a case that most economists embrace or even address. I will cite three of these authors below, but first let me state the basic idea, using images developed more fully in the passages from Alan Blinder that appear below:[4] The world needs the clear, hard-headed thinking offered by good economic analysis so that individuals, firms, governments, and societies can accomplish more of what they really want to do, even though the resources available to them are limited and therefore it is impossible to fulfill all of their wants. But at the same time, economics (which is to say economists) needs a more humane understanding and appreciation of people's wants and constraints, especially in presenting and explaining economics to policymakers and the public at large.

At times that humane understanding comes into play in the design of more efficient *and* equitable social policies. For example, since economists can show that free trade is good in the long run but will cause some workers to lose their jobs in the short run, they might also consider providing public assistance to help retrain or even relocate these workers. Far more often, a more humane language and framework for discussing economics would help when economists try to explain why many well-intentioned public policies should not be adopted because—despite the widespread public appeal of the good intentions that are their motive—the effects of the policies are anything but equitable or efficient. Too often, economists present only data or theoretical models to document overall effects without providing individual examples and stories to explain the shortcomings of what has been proposed, despite the fact that such illustrations are more likely to be memorable and quoted.

More importantly, a better use of literary economics might help make what many people view as the central claim of economics—that competitive markets can be both efficient and equitable, particularly when there are basic assistance programs to help poor families move into the mainstream of the market economy—more understandable and palatable to the very large number of people who apparently do not naturally embrace or perhaps even understand either Adam Smith's "invisible hand" or Keynes's "economic way of thinking." Like many specialists, economists like to preach to their own choir; but the songs they sing aren't songs that most people or policymakers are likely to continue to hum after the sermon has been preached and the service has ended. It would certainly help to teach more people, especially policymakers, the tunes and lyrics of basic economic analysis—which can't be done in one lesson or in one day, let alone in one congressional hearing or press conference. But there's also a good chance that economists will have to meet the congregation at least halfway down that road by providing memorable and well-written or well-spoken examples of fundamental concepts—some of which examples may come from literary sources like those reprinted here.

Some eminent economists have made this general case before, but not the specific case for using literature and drama. For example, Blinder's slim volume, *Hard Heads, Soft Hearts: Tough-Minded Economics for a Just Society,* was written because Blinder had concluded that "[t]hat the economist's case has not won the day in the public-policy arena can scarcely be surprising, given that we have hardly presented it. Making that case in plain English is the main reason for writing this book."[5] Blinder was later appointed to the Federal Reserve's Board of Governors during the Clinton administration, even though he had noted the problems facing economic policymaking under both Democratic and Republican administrations:

> Too often, the electorate is presented with a choice between Republican policies that are hard-headed but hard-hearted and Democratic policies that are soft-hearted but soft-headed. Faced with such meager alternatives, the electorate may justifiably yearn for a new hybrid strain of policy that combines a hard head with a soft heart. Unfortunately, neither party seems inclined to push economic policy in that direction.
>
> Traditional Republican policies, in economics and elsewhere, often evince a hard head but an equally hard heart. They are long on rational economic calculation but short on compassion. Republicans typically know their economics better than do Democrats; they more keenly appreciate the delicate workings of the free-market system and all that it can accomplish. But they manifest pitifully little pity for the unfortunate and sometimes are all too willing to tread on the downtrodden.
>
> . . . Traditional Democratic policies are not better, just different. Sympathy for the underdog is in abundant supply among Democrats and is not misplaced. But, at least before President Reagan created a permanent budget crisis, the requisite economic calculations and respect for markets was too often lacking.[6]

Blinder would very probably have disagreed with many of the specific policy prescriptions of Wilhelm Röpke, who fled Nazi Germany and later played a key role in providing policy recommendations that led to the postwar German "miracle." But like Blinder, Röpke wanted to develop and put into practice a more humane economics,[7] and he was concerned about the advantage in emotional appeal possessed by slogans popularizing bad economics, in contrast to the more abstract and complex statements usually required to explain good economics. In 1933, Röpke wrote prophetically:

> Never has the world been more thoroughly ruled by vapid catchwords resting on mass moods and sentiments and throwing up as leaders of the masses those who excel in interpreting these mass sentiments. "Liberalism" has never had any appeal for the masses: among them,

> tolerance, discussion, humanitas, reason, and fair play do not prosper, but all the more propitious is the field for violence, resentment, emotional fog, and destructive action. . . . The masses readily lap up catchwords that appeal to the emotions but are shy of the critique of reason, such as "protection of national labor," "food freedom," "Buy home-produced goods!" and other half-baked emotional arguments. By contrast, free trade, unless tangibly in the interests of the masses, has always been an aristocratic matter appealing only to the elite, since it requires serious thought and control of the emotions by reason and independent judgment.[8]

Röpke concluded this essay on the secular significance of the world crisis of the 1930s by predicting that the economic, political, and hence also the cultural future of Europe depended on whether it would be possible to achieve a degree of political integration between nations that reflected their degree of economic cooperation and trade before more trade barriers could be enacted. He saw that alternative as the only way back to "peace, prosperity, civilization, and the continuance and rise of Europe" and the only alternative to be political disintegration, followed by even more economic and cultural disintegration.[9]

While Röpke was a staunch opponent of the welfare state, he broke ranks with many of his conservative colleagues and friends in calling for government assistance to agricultural workers and craftsmen, strict antitrust policies, including the break-up of monopolies, and policies supporting a wider distribution of land (especially private homes), stocks, and other assets. He viewed this approach as constituting a truer and more defensible view of capitalism and individualism, and as distinctly contrasting with "unpalatable" attacks on capitalism and liberalism by socialists and intellectuals who, he felt

> have lost all feeling for the infinite and absolute value of individual freedom, all understanding of the truth that what the Age of Enlightenment and liberalism fought for, what men like Hume, Voltaire, Wilhelm von Humboldt, John Stuart Mill, Jefferson, or Mazzini as well as our classical poets extolled, what our grandfathers and great-grandfathers battled and suffered for, is ultimately mankind's oldest and finest intellectual heritage. All feeling for humanitas in the widest sense of the word seems to be dead to them. . . .[10]

At the time Röpke was writing these essays, economics was far less specialized than it is today, with most economists far better trained in the humanities than they are now and much less well trained in mathematics and statistics. Of course, as noted in the introduction, the animosity between some literary authors and critics and economists goes back further than the growth of specialization. So there are clearly other forces than the increasingly specialized training in economics (and for that matter in literary "theory" and criticism) at play in creating and maintaining the gulf that separates the fields, quite probably including innate differences in how different people choose to frame and study issues and problems, and in what kinds of arguments and evidence they find convincing.[11] Frankly, at times the differences between the subjects in terms of how they approach the same topics, or what they conclude about the same topics, seem to result from (or at least to reinforce) a kind of academic protectionism in which both groups seem committed not to import or export ideas to each other. Or perhaps the costs of trading are just too high, in terms of the effort needed to communicate or even to find out what is being said in the other discipline. Or maybe those high costs, including the risk of discovering or explicitly acknowledging that arguments that are widely accepted in one field are viewed as incorrect or incomplete in the other, lead both groups of specialists to play it safe by ignoring what the other group is saying.

On the other hand, it is not at all a stretch to suggest that a large part of the reason Röpke, Blinder, and many of the other economists who have proved to be unusually effective in working with policymakers and communicating with the public is that they write and speak unusually well (at least for economists), sometimes even using literary references or forms.[12] As shown in Appendix B, and in the passages in the main part of this volume, literary interest in economic ideas and issues is longstanding and quite possibly increasing. As someone who reads fairly widely in both fields, and from classic, contemporary, and popular *genres* in both literature and economics, it seems to me that the overlap of interests, content, and (to a much lesser degree) method are inevitable and permanent.

But even so, we have arrived at a point where economists know less and less about literature and drama, and literary authors know less and less about the methods and findings of modern economics. Things may well continue to get even worse in the future because, unfortunately, whether the number of economists with a literary bent will increase or even remain constant over time is doubtful, given the still-increasing stress on mathematics and statistics in economic training and analysis. That emphasis is a double-edged sword, because it makes most economics writing even less accessible to literary writers and critics. Certainly the same problems exist in math and many of the physical and biological sciences; but playwrights, essayists, and novelists typically deal less with those subjects (Tom Clancy excepted) than they do economic ideas, issues, and policies.

Finally, there is this to consider: economists may well have more at stake in using or challenging what literary writers are saying about economic ideas and issues than literary authors do in using or challenging what economists have written. Once again, this is not my original idea. In *The Commonsense of Political Economy,* Phillip Wicksteed wrote, "The prophet and the poet may regenerate the world without the economist, but the economist cannot regenerate it without them." After several pages of allusions, examples, and quotations drawn from such writers as Carroll, Wordsworth, and Goldsmith, Wicksteed acknowledged the role of poets and writers in "mak[ing] our lives worthy," and concluded, "The man who can make his fellows desire more worthily and wisely is doubtless performing a higher task than the one who enables them more amply to satisfy whatever desires they have."[13] Of course, Wicksteed believed that the economist, too, "has his place":

> He may help to guide if he cannot inspire. If he can give no strength, he may save strength from being wasted. It is his misery that he cannot glorify the purposes to which he ministers, but it is his triumph that he can be glorified by them. He works in faith, for he knows that his work is barren unless others greater than he are working too, but he believes that wherever they are he can serve them. If he can give sight to some blind reforming Samson he too has served.[14]

My hope is that this volume will increase interest among and encourage more intellectual exchange between economists and literary writers, and that it will also aid the development of humane economic understanding among general readers who feel no special allegiance to either discipline. I do worry that instead it may throw fuel on a smoldering fire; but even that might be better than having things brushed under a rug—or rather, under rugs in two different departments housed on opposite sides of campus.

Notes

1. Wilde in "The Canterbury Ghost," published in 1887; Thomas in a radio talk shortly before his death and later published in 1954; Russell in a 1944 issue of *Saturday Evening Post;* Shaw cited by *Reader's Digest* in November 1942 and in the 1951 *Treasury of Humorous Quotations*; Churchill cited—more dubiously—in recent articles of the *Times* (London) and *European*. See http://www1c.btwebworld.com/quote-unquote/p0000149.htm

2. For that matter, it would be extremely surprising had there ever been one.

3. See, for example, the first few pages in Blinder's *Hard Heads, Soft Hearts: Tough-Minded Economics for a Just Society* (Reading, Mass.: Addison Wesley, 1987), or recall the definition of a small town as someplace where one lawyer will starve but two can earn a comfortable living.

4. *Hard Heads, Soft Hearts.*

5. Ibid., 11.

6. Ibid., 13–14.

7. Röpke's last and most famous book, first published in English in 1960, is titled *A Humane Economy* (Chicago: Regnery).

8. Page 75. All of the quotations from Röpke in this volume are taken from a translated collection of some of his papers, *Against the Tide,* trans. Elizabeth Henderson (Chicago: Regnery, 1969).

9. Ibid., 76.

10. Ibid., 34.

11. If it is true that living well is the best revenge, it probably doesn't help matters that academic economists (let alone applied economists such as professors of finance and many other business disciplines) are paid significantly more, on average, than English and other humanities professors. Of course, that can just lead to another debate about what living well really means.

12. For example, see Blinder's "Christmas, Revisited," a political and economic parody of "The Night Before Christmas," in C. P. Clotfelter, ed., *On the Third Hand: Humor in the Dismal Science, an Anthology* (Ann Arbor, Mich.: University of Michigan Press, 1996), 314–15.

13. P. Wicksteed, *The Commonsense of Political Economy* (London: Macmillan, 1910), 123.

14. Ibid., 124.

Appendices

Appendix A
How Economists Have Used Literature and Drama

As noted in the introduction, and as I will describe in considerably more detail here, economists have used literary passages in a variety of applications other than teaching, including such diverse fields as economic history and the history of economic thought; empirical and public policy discussions on income distribution; monetary economics; comparative economic systems; game theory; and theoretical discussions on intergenerational bequests. Short literary quotations are sometimes used to describe human behavior and motivations more eloquently, powerfully, or humorously than economists typically do, thereby making economists' writing more interesting and effective. In other cases, literary characters or scenes are used as anecdotal evidence of individual behavior, or of economic conditions and institutions in a particular time and place. Occasionally economists evaluate whether literary authors have described characters and behaviors in ways that are in line with economists' predictions and understanding of rational behavior. And sometimes, as Veblen's suggestions about conspicuous leisure predict, economists may simply use literary allusions to make themselves look more learned than others who do not work in "intellectual" jobs, or who are not efficient enough in their regular work (intellectual or otherwise) to have time to read literature and drama.

Some economists and economic historians have claimed that there is a uniformly anti-economics, anti-market, or at least anti-business orientation in literary works. Over the past century these complaints have been extended to include movies, television programs, and print and electronic journalism. There is some evidence that these latter genres are more influential in shaping public opinion than economists,[1] and given the sales figures for leading works of fiction and periodicals as compared to even the bestselling works of economists, that is not especially surprising. It also provides more reason for economists to devote some time to learning what different groups of literary authors are saying about economic ideas.

A slightly different version of this paper was published in the *Journal of Economic Education* 33 (Fall 2002): 377–86. It is reprinted here with permission of the Helen Dwight Reid Educational Foundation.

Ultimately, the test of whether literature and drama are interesting and useful to economists is, in fact, whether economists use these materials, because as Jacob Viner once pragmatically defined the field, "Economics is what economists do."[2] It turns out that there are a surprising number of economists who have used literary sources, although as a fraction of all works by economists the level of activity can still be characterized as at best modest. With no further introduction, then, what follows is a brief review of those applications.

Economic historians and historians of economic thought have often cited passages from such authors as Swift, Defoe, DeQuincy, Coleridge, Southey, Peacock, Carlyle, Ruskin, Cobbett, Bellamy, and Shaw, who were not only prolific writers of essays as well as fiction, but also noted public speakers on social issues.[3] Particularly during the transition in the nineteenth century from an agrarian to an industrial economy in western Europe and the United States, many of these essayists became outspoken moral critics of aspects of industrialization and economics.[4] In a recent book, Levy set out to turn the moral tables against some of the literary writers, arguing that the attacks on economics by Carlyle, Ruskin, and Dickens—who tagged economics with the enduring label "the dismal science"—developed because these authors supported forms of slavery that allowed whites from Western nations to direct the lives of people of color, while the economists of the time supported the protection of minority populations under the rule of law. Levy showed how interpreting these literary writers' attacks on market economics as originating solely from a humanistic or egalitarian concern ignores their original context.[5]

Fictional works from this period have also been reviewed by economic historians,[6] as have works from earlier periods, dating back to the ancient world.[7] Some economic historians have raised the issue of bias against market activities in these sources. For example, D. C. Coleman concluded, "Look for the businessman in English fiction and either you will not find him at all or he will vary from the sinister to the absurd."[8] That claim has been disputed in much more comprehensive studies by McKendrick and other literary historians.[9] But after reviewing novels and plays by U.S. authors written between 1920 and 1960, including works by Sinclair Lewis, John Dos Passos, F. Scott Fitzgerald, John Steinbeck, Erskine Caldwell, Arthur Miller, and John P. Marquand, the economist Brandis concluded that small businessmen were often portrayed as "ambitious and hardworking, but with severely limited intellectual and cultural horizons."[10] Brandis also argued that after World War II the critical emphasis of literary authors shifted "from one which encompasses the whole system to one restricted to particular segments of that system," particularly communications (including advertising, television, publishing and the movies) and the "business aristocracy" of top executives and financiers.[11]

Of course, even if businesspeople are rarely or shallowly portrayed, a number of other economic ideas and issues are often presented in works of fiction, frequently with considerable effect. For example, Milton and Rose Friedman note the influence of Edward Bellamy's *Looking Backward* in shaping public opinion on income equality,[12] while citing more approvingly the satirical comments on this topic made by Lewis Carroll's Dodo in Chapter III of *Alice's Adventures in Wonderland*. They might also have recommended Kurt Vonnegut's story titled "Harrison Bergeron," which appears in his *Welcome to the Monkey House* and is reprinted, in part, here in section P.

The influence of literary authors on particular economists and economic ideas has also been documented in several studies. For example, Spiegel cites European studies that establish Aristophanes as an originator, or at least forerunner, of such ideas as Gresham's Law and the subjective theory of value.[13] And Schefold traces "reflections" of economic ideas in ancient Greek poetry, including the works of Homer, Hesiod, Horace, Aeschylus, Sophocles, Euripides, and Aristophanes.[14]

Jonathan Swift has been linked to supply-side economics,[15] and Swift's "Modest Proposal" is widely recognized as both an anticipation and scathing satire of cost-benefit analysis, at least when such analysis is used without any underlying legal or moral framework of human rights. Binswanger sees Goethe as a competent practical economist, a reflection of his work in the areas of taxation and finance as a member of the Privy Council at the court of Weimar.[16] In *Faust*, Goethe addressed such issues as technological unemployment, the inflationary risks associated with the creation of paper money (see the excerpt published in section Q of this volume), and environmental concerns related to industrialization, generally suggesting liberal solutions but with specific roles for government and representatives of the cultural elite. Stigler noted that George Bernard Shaw was recognized by the economist Richard Howey as one of the early "minor writers" on utility theory.[17]

Rockoff uses Littlefield's literary analysis of L. Frank Baum's *The Wonderful Wizard of Oz* to develop and then analyze a "monetary allegory" of the bimetallism debate that took place in the United States around the end of the nineteenth century.[18] He accepts Littlefield's claims—disputed by Baum's family, other literary critics, and most recently by Hansen[19]—that the Scarecrow represents Midwestern farmers, the Tin-man urban industrial workers, the Wicked Witch of the East large industrial corporations, the Wicked Witch of the West harsh and malevolent natural forces (particularly drought), the Cowardly Lion William Jennings Bryan, the Wizard any of the blustery but inept U.S. presidents of the period, and Dorothy Everyman. In Baum's novel, unlike the MGM musical, Dorothy indisputably walks down a yellow-brick (i.e., gold) road wearing silver, not ruby, slippers, and so Oz might well refer to "ounces" of precious metals.

Roback analyzes economic ideas in the writings of George Orwell, showing that Orwell's experiences in the Great Depression and two World Wars left him deeply pessimistic about both capitalism and socialism, although he held out slightly more hope for reforming socialism than capitalism. Roback concludes: "The essential missing link in Orwell's understanding of economics is that he had no notion of the price system as a coordination mechanism. . . . If there is no explicit planner, there must be no plan. And without a plan, there must be no order."[20] Hamlen uses Orwell's *Animal Farm* to predict and discuss China's experiences with communism, contrasting those who attain power (the boar "Napoleon") with those who do not (the horse "Boxer"). Using a data set on some 22,000 Chinese, Hamlen reports empirical results that "strongly support many of Orwell's predictions."[21]

Scahill adapts Mark Twain's ideas for making international comparisons of real incomes to Estonian incomes during that nation's transition from a command to a market economy. Scahill is not as pessimistic about the prospects for teaching these ideas to the general public as Twain's Connecticut Yankee eventually becomes (nor is he nearly as funny).[22]

Many links between the writings and careers of literary writers and economists have been documented, including Mandeville and Smith;[23] Twain and Veblen;[24] Bellamy and Veblen;[25] Ruskin and Jevons;[26] Goldsmith, Steinbeck, Faulkner, and Henry George;[27] Bellamy and George, Veblen, Commons, and Wesley Mitchell;[28] and Ayn Rand and Alan Greenspan.[29] Bogart uses passages from Bellamy's *Looking Backward* to help teach ideas put forth by Joseph Schumpeter.[30]

In a review of German economic thought, primarily as reflected in annual meetings of the *Dogmenhistorischer Ausschuss,* the national association of historians of economic thought, Schefold includes a summary of the first eleven volumes of the annual proceedings of the association, *Studien zur Entwicklung der ökonomischen Theorie (Studies on the Development of Economic Theory).*[31] Volume 11 in the series is primarily devoted to "The Representation of the Economy and of Economics in Belles-Lettres." In addition to Schefold's work on ancient Greek poetry and Binswanger's on Goethe, which have since been published in the English versions cited earlier, the volume includes a paper by Eisermann on economy and society in French novels by such authors as Balzac, Flaubert, Zola, and Maupassant; a paper by Kloten on literary parallels to Pareto's *Trattato di sociologia generale* in Lampedusa's novel, *Il Gattopardo*; and a paper by Harald Scherf on the role of the economy in German novels of the twentieth century, which turns out to be like the one-line treatise on snakes in Ireland: Scherf concludes that "the great modern German novel (but also novels by most of the minor authors) contains scarcely any actions, description, or consideration that would reveal either a deeper understanding or an original grasp of economic phenomena."[32] Scherf believes that this was also true of politically motivated German literature, but his conclusions were challenged by some guests at the conference from the German Democratic Republic, which was in the process of dissolution at that time.

Game theorists have frequently analyzed literary characters, plots, and situations. Brams lists twenty-two plays, operas, novels, and mysteries that have been the subject of such studies, including works by Shakespeare, Doyle, Puccini, Poe, and Conrad. After surveying those who conducted these studies, Brams concludes that in some cases the models used "indicate a sophisticated understanding of plots and character motives, but others are quite trivial or misuse game theory." He also notes that "[f]iction writers, too, vary in the intuitive understanding of game theory that they bring to their works." [33] Moldovanu and Tietzel report on Goethe's use of a second-price auction in 1797 with the publisher for his *Hermann and Dorothea*. They also report that Goethe later sold the rights to publish his *Collected Works* in an auction that included thirty-six different bidders.[34]

Hirshliefer and Becker couch a comment and reply concerning Becker's theory of altruism around a brief passage from Shakespeare's *King Lear.* Becker thanks Hirschliefer for "finding such a formidable protagonist" and asks, "Can economics now be extended to literature as well?"[35] Actually, nearly half a century earlier, a professor of economics at Yale, Henry Farnam, was admitted to the university's Elizabethan Club for his work on *Shakespeare's Economics.*[36] Kish-Goodling uses the theme of usury in Shakespeare's *Merchant of Venice* to illustrate historical lending practices and Christian and Jewish ideas on charging interest on loans.[37]

Henderson's *Economics as Literature* adopts the literary approach to economics espoused by McCloskey to study how arguments are presented in some classic and not-so-classic works published by economists between 1776 and 1936.[38] In addition to works by Smith, Ricardo, Malthus, Mill, and Keynes, Henderson studies the literary forms of arguments in such popular works as the children's stories of Maria Edgeworth, the dialogue-based textbook written by Jane Marcet, Harriet Martineau's economic stories for adults, F. Y. Edgeworth's blend of science and literature, De Quincey's introductory textbook, and Ruskin's economic essays.

Waller and Robertson use and then extend McCloskey's techniques to argue that neoclassical economists have used rhetorical methods to exclude Veblen's writings and ideas from the professional canon.[39] Hirschman, a professor of marketing, adopts the "society as text" metaphor of literary criticism to study ideas of affluence and "secular immortality," using as her basic texts for analysis Tom Wolfe's *Bonfire of the Vanities,* autobiographies by Donald Trump and Lee Iacocca, and four magazines "directed toward and consumed by the affluent."[40] Holbrook uses a literary approach to study the joys and sorrows of consumption and consumer behavior.[41]

Fletcher studies the language used by Martineau and Ayn Rand in his review of two prominent female "purpose writers" who presented economic ideas "in the guise of fiction."[42] O'Donnell also reviewed Martineau's role as an early popularizer of economics;[43] and Highfill and Weber consider her writings on arts and letters.[44]

Some economists have used literary forms other than standard technical writing, usually to present economic ideas in an interesting and different way, but sometimes purely to exercise their own literary talents and interests. A few have published poetry in their economic writings.[45] Others have written works of fiction—occasionally under pen names such as Mark Epernay, Tinker Marks, or the series of murder mysteries by Marshall Jevons[46]—but just as often under their own names, including recent works by Wolfson and Buranelli, Roberts, Wight, and McDermott and Stocks.[47] Lenin published four short articles of literary criticism on works by Tolstoy and generally opposed censorship of both old and contemporary creative works of literature and art, including attempts to produce an officially sanctioned "purely proletarian art . . . and culture."[48]

Smith, Bentham, Malthus, and Mill have been subjects of poems, Malthus by no less a figure than Wordsworth. Veblen was the subject of one of the biographical sketches in Dos Passos's *U.S.A.* ("The Bitter Drink"). John Nash was the subject of Sylvia Nasser's biography, *A Beautiful Mind,* and the award-winning film of the same title.[49] Keynes's ideas are explicitly featured in Ivan Doig's 1996 novel, *Bucking the Sun,* an excerpt from which is printed here in section S. Travis McGee's friend and neighbor in a series of more than twenty books by John D. MacDonald is an economist who lives on boats named after Keynes and Veblen.

Clotfelter's anthology on humor in economics is liberally sprinkled with excerpts from literary authors and essayists, including Mencken, Shaw, Twain, Frost, Bierce, Aesop, Pope, Dickinson, Wordsworth, Swift, and Arbuthnot.[50] It is safe to say that without these passages her anthology would have been considerably slimmer in length and more deficient in humor.

Perhaps the most prestigious indication that literary sources and practices can be useful to economists in their professional work is the *Journal of Political Economy*'s practice of reprinting literary passages on its back cover, a policy initiated in 1973 when George Stigler became the journal's coeditor.

Notes

1. W. E. Becker, W. B. Walstad, and M. Watts. "A Comparison of the Views of Economists, Economic Educators, Teachers, and Journalists on Economic Issues." In *An International Perspective on Economic Education,* W. Walstad, ed. (Boston: Kluwer Academic Publishers, 1994), 65–87.

2. Often quoted as a "famous remark" or "proposal," by Boulding (*The Skills of the Economist.* Cleveland: Howard Allen, 1958, 1), Buchanan (*What Should Economists Do?* Indianapolis: Liberty Fund, 1979, 18), and others, and giving rise to Frank Knight's circular response that "Economists are those who do economics," Viner's statement was apparently only a spoken remark, and does not appear in any of his publications.

3. In the United States, the closest parallels to these authors/essayists may be Franklin, Thoreau, and Emerson. See Rosemont, "Benjamin Franklin and the Philadelphia Typographical Strikers of 1786. *Labor History* 22 (1981): 398–429; Watanabe, "The Business Ideology of Benjamin

Franklin and Japanese Values of the 18th Century." In *Business and Economic History*, 2nd series, vol. 17, W. J. Hausman, ed. (Williamsburg, Va.: College of William and Mary, 1988), 79–90; Hodgson, "Benjamin Franklin on Population: From Policy to Theory. *Population and Development Review* 17 (1991): 639–61; Neufeldt, *The Economist: Henry Thoreau and Enterprise* (New York: Oxford University Press, 1989); and Gilmore, *American Romanticism and the Marketplace* (Chicago: University of Chicago Press, 1985).

4. W. D. Grampp, "Classical Economics and its Moral Critics." *History of Political Economy* 5 (1973): 359–74; G. J. Stigler, *The Economist as Preacher and Other Essays* (Chicago: University of Chicago Press, 1982), 27–29.

5. D. M. Levy, *How the Dismal Science Got Its Name: Classical Economics and the Ur-Text of Radical Politics* (Ann Arbor, Mich.: University of Michigan Press, 2001).

6. W. O. Aydelotte, "The England of Marx and Mill as Reflected in Fiction." *Journal of Economic History,* supplement 8, *The Tasks of Economic History* (1948): 42–58; M. Jefferson, "Industrialization and Poverty: In Fact and Fiction." In *The Long Debate on Poverty* (London: Institute of Economic Affairs, 1972).

7. J. U. Nef, *Cultural Foundations of Industrial Capitalism* (Cambridge: Cambridge University Press, 1958). F. Meijer and O. van Nijf. *Trade, Transport and Society in the Ancient World: A Sourcebook* (London: Routledge, 1992).

8. D. C. Coleman, *What Has Happened to Economic History?* (London: Cambridge University Press, 1972), 11.

9. N. McKendrick, "'Gentlemen and Players' Revisited: The Gentlemanly Ideal, the Business Ideal, and the Professional Ideal in English Literary Culture." In *Business Life and Public Policy: Essays in Honor of D.C. Coleman,* N. McKendrick and R. B. Outhwaite, eds. (Cambridge: Cambridge University Press, 1986), 98–136.

10. R. Brandis, 1961. "The American Writer Views the American Businessman. *Quarterly Review of Economics and Business* 1 (1961), 29.

11. Ibid., 34. Writing in the *Harvard Business Review,* DeMott, a humanities instructor at Amherst College, sees a similar turning point in literary treatments of business following the upheavals of the Great Depression and World War II. DeMott argues that Lionel Trilling's 1945 short story, "The Other Margaret," marked a "reinvigoration of antideterminism [that] was the intellectual change most vital to the recovery, by business, of the grip on the public imagination it had possessed before the Great Crash." B. DeMott, "Reading Fiction to the Bottom Line." *Harvard Business Review* 67 (1989), 130.

12. M. and R. Friedman, *Free to Choose* (New York: Harcourt Brace and Jovanovich, 1980). F. Cugno and M. Ferrero analyzed Bellamy's egalitarian scheme and concluded that such an economy exhibits an equilibrium "consistent with full freedom of individual choice of occupation and consumption," although "individuals have an obligation to work which deprives them of their freedom to choose between income and leisure, so that the scale of output is indeterminate and may be nonoptimal. . . ." "Individual Incentives by Adjusting Work Hours: Bellamy's Egalitarian Economy." *Journal of Comparative Economics* 8 (1984), 182.

13. H. W. Spiegel, *The Growth of Economic Thought* (Englewood Cliffs, N.J.: Prentice-Hall, 1971), 667.

14. B. Schefold, "Reflections of Ancient Economic Thought in Greek Poetry." In *Ancient Economic Thought,* vol. 1, B. B. Price, ed. (London: Routledge, 1997).

15. B. Bartlett, "Jonathan Swift: Father of Supply-Side Economics?" *History of Political Economy* 24 (1992): 745–48.

16. H. C. Binswanger, *Money and Magic: A Critique of the Modern Economy in the Light of Goethe's Faust,* trans. J. E. Harrison (Chicago: University of Chicago Press, 1994).

17. Stigler (1982), 79.

18. H. Rockoff, "*The Wizzard of Oz* as a Monetary Allegory." *Journal of Political Economy* 98 (1990): 739–60; H. M. Littlefield, "*The Wizard of Oz*: Parable on Populism." *American Quarterly* 16 (1964): 47–58.

19. B. Hansen, "The Fable of the Allegory: *The Wizard of Oz* in Economics." *Journal of Economic Education* 33 (2002): 254–64.

20. J. Roback, "The Economic Thought of George Orwell." *American Economic Review* 75 (1985), 131–32.

21. W. A. Hamlen Jr., "The Economics of *Animal Farm*." *Southern Economic Journal* 66 (2000), 942.

22. E. M. Scahill, "A Connecticut Yankee in Estonia." *Journal of Economic Education* 29 (1998): 340–46.

23. See, e.g., M. Perlman, "*The Fable of the Bees*, Considered Anew." In M. Perlman, *The Character of Economic Thought, Economic Characters, and Economic Institutions.* (Ann Arbor, Mich.: University of Michigan Press, 1996): 87–120. Originally published in German in 1990.

24. J. E. Biddle, "Veblen, Twain, and the Connecticut Yankee: A Note." *History of Political Economy* 17 (1985): 97–107.

25. R. Tilman, "The Utopian Vision of Edward Bellamy and Thorstein Veblen." *Journal of Economic Issues* 19 (1985): 879–98; C. G. Leathers, "Bellamy and Veblen's 'Christian Morals.'" *Journal of Economic Issues* 20 (1986): 1107–19.

26. H. Mass, "Pacifying the Workman: Ruskin and Jevons on Labor and Popular Culture." *History of Political Economy* 31 (1999 suppl.): 85–120.

27. T. R. DeGregori, "In Perpetuity: Some Reflections on Literary Views of Land and Other Forms of Property." *American Journal of Economics and Sociology* 38 (1979): 225–36.

28. M. Bronfenbrenner, "Early American Leaders—Institutional and Critical Traditions." *American Economic Review* 75 (1985): 13–27.

29. R. W. Bradford, "Alan Greenspan—Cultist?" *American Enterprise 8* (1997): 31–33.

30. W. T. Bogart, "Looking Backward at Feasible Socialism: Using Bellamy to Teach Schumpeter." *Journal of Economic Education* 26 (1995): 352–56.

31. B. Schefold, "The Revival of Economic Thought in Germany: The *Dogmenhistorischer Ausschuss.*" *History of Political Economy* 26 (1994): 327–35.

32. Ibid., 334–35.

33. S. J. Brams, "Game Theory and Literature." *Games and Economic Behavior* 6 (1994): 32–54.

34. B. Moldovanu and M. Tietzel, "Goethe's second-price auction." *Journal of Political Economy* 106 (1998): 854–59.

35. J. Hirshliefer, "Shakespeare vs. Becker on Altruism: The Importance of Having the Last Word." *Journal of Economic Literature* 15 (1977): 500–02; G. Becker, "Reply to Hirshliefer and Tullock." *Journal of Economic Literature* 15 (1977), 507.

36. H. W. Farnam, *Shakespeare's Economics* (New Haven, Conn.: Yale University Press, 1931).

37. D. M. Kish-Goodling, "Using *The Merchant of Venice* in Teaching Monetary Economics." *Journal of Economic Education* 29 (1998): 330–39.

38. W. Henderson, *Economics as Literature* (London: Routledge, 1995); D. McCloskey, *The Rhetoric of Economics* (Madison, Wis.: University of Wisconsin Press, 1985).

39. W. Waller and L. R. Robertson, "Why Johnny (Ph.D., Economics) Can't Read: A Rhetorical Analysis of Thorstein Veblen and a Response to Donald McCloskey's Rhetoric of Economics." *Journal of Economic Issues* 24 (1990): 1027–44.

40. E. C. Hirschman, "Secular Immorality and the American Ideology of Affluence." *Journal of Consumer Research* 17 (1990), 31–32. The magazines Hirschman reviewed are *Town & Country, Architectural Digest, Connoisseur,* and *Avenue.*

41. M. B. Holbrook, "Romanticism and Sentimentality in Consumer Behavior: A Literary Approach to the Joys and Sorrows of Consumption." In *Research in Consumer Behavior,* vol. 5., E. C. Hirschman, ed. (Greenwich, Conn.: JAI Press, 1991), 105–80.

42. M. E. Fletcher, "Harriet Martineau and Ayn Rand: Economics in the Guise of Fiction." *American Journal of Economics and Sociology 33* (1974), 367.

43. M. G. O'Donnell, "Harriet Martineau: A Popular Early Economics Educator." *Journal of Economic Education* 4 (1983): 59–64.

44. J. K. Highfill and W. V. Weber, "Harriet Martineau: An Economic View of Victorian Arts and Letters." *Journal of Cultural Economics* 15 (1991): 85–92.

45. See, e.g., K. E. Boulding, *The Skills of the Economist* (Cleveland, Ohio: Howard Allen, 1958).

46. See, e.g., J. K. Galbraith, *The McLandress Dimension* (Boston: Houghton Mifflin, 1963); I. Powell and M. Montgomery, *Theoretically Dead* (Norwich, Vt.: New Victoria Publishers, 2001); and M. Jevons (a.k.a., William Breit and Kenneth G. Elzinga), *A Deadly Indifference* (Princeton, N.J.: Princeton University Press, 1998; *The Fatal Equilibrium* (New York: Ballantine, 1986); *Murder At the Margin* (Princeton, N.J.: Princeton University Press, 1993).

47. M. Wolfson and V. Buranelli, *In the Long Run We Are All Dead* (New York: St. Martin's Press, 1984); R. Roberts, *The Choice: A Fable of Free Trade and Protectionism,* revised ed. (Upper Saddle River, N.J.: Prentice-Hall, 2000); R. Roberts, *The Invisible Heart: An Economic Romance* (Cambridge, Mass.: MIT Press, 2001); J. Wight, *Saving Adam Smith: A Tale of Wealth, Transformation, and Virtue* (Upper Saddle River, N.J.: Prentice-Hall, 2001); R. E. McDermott and K. D. Stocks, *Code Blue,* 2nd ed. (Syracuse, Utah: Traemus Books, 2001).

48. He did, however, accept the idea of control and censorship of official "party literature" dealing with political and economic policies and issues. See A. T. Rubinstein, "Lenin on Literature, Language, and Censorship." *Science and Society* 59 (1995): 368–83.

49. S. Nasser, *A Beautiful Mind: The Life of Mathematical Genius and Nobel Laureate John Nash* (New York: Touchstone, 1998).

50. C. P. Clotfelter, ed., *On the Third Hand: Humor in the Dismal Science, an Anthology* (Ann Arbor, Mich.: University of Michigan Press, 1996).

Appendix B
How Literary Critics and Historians Have Used Economics

Just as economic historians and historians of economic thought have long cited writings by literary authors, literary critics and historians have studied the influence of economic conditions, institutions, and even economic thought on literary works. Early examples include Vida Scudder's *Social Ideals in English Letters*—which offers chapters on William Langland, Sir Thomas More, Swift, Dickens and Thackeray, Carlyle, Ruskin, George Eliot, Matthew Arnold, and several U.S. poets and writers—and Leslie Stephens's *English Literature and Society in the Eighteenth Century*. Chaucer's England is discussed and illustrated by Loomis, and the Elizabethan and early Stuart periods have been studied frequently, for example in Tillyard, Knights, Hulse, Halpern, and Miller, O'Dair, and Weber. Heilman et al. explore Shakespeare's use of Elizabethan financial imagery in *Othello*. Wolfe discusses Milton's England, while the social and political/public policy background of Pope's later poetry is studied in Mack. Rigal explores artistic and literary depictions of labor and "the world of things" in the early American republic. Link uses a wide range of official and underground literature to illustrate China's "socialist literary system" of 1950–1990, drawing comparisons to a similar system that prevailed during the same period in the Soviet Union.[1]

Turning to literary history and criticism on particular topics and themes, Shell explores how both money and language are used as mediums of exchange and argues that the development of money changed both philosophical thought and language. He fits his review of symbols and inscriptions on early coins into discussions of economic thinkers such as Marx, Turgot, and Proudhon; philosophers such as Heraclitus, Plato, Aristotle, Nietzsche, and Rousseau; and literary authors such as Shakespeare, Dante, Shaw, and Sophocles. Among other issues, Shell explores why coinage, tyranny, and philosophy all developed in the same time and place.[2]

Vernon finds a duality in literary treatments of money in the nineteenth and early twentieth centuries, particularly in such authors as Balzac, Henry James, Jane Austen, Thackeray, Dickens, and Flaubert:

> This schizophrenia of money expresses moral attitudes—
> money is sordid, money gives us wings—and lends itself

> in particular to novels of social mobility. . . . Attitudes like this . . . receive a new emphasis with . . . the Industrial Revolution. . . . (C)hanges in the forms of money expressed this shift. With the growth of paper money, money of account . . . became that much more an abstract quantification, a means of weighing and measuring the value of commodities. Behind paper money, defined by virtue of its absence, metal currency became reduced to the state of leftover matter. As a representation of material existence in fiction, money always has this double aspect. . . .[3]

Predictably, the largest body of literary criticism related to economic issues deals with the works of Shakespeare, with critics from every literary and political school of thought trying to claim the Bard as their own. Also predictably, the enormous range of characters, topics, and language in Shakespeare's works gives all of them something to work with.

Tillyard's short volume titled *The Elizabethan World Picture* was an influential but controversial work for decades, describing an essentially conservative and hierarchical view of society that Tillyard claimed had not only shaped works by Shakespeare and other literary writers of the period, but also was in turn reflected and supported in those works. From the mid-1940s through the 1960s, many English and American literary critics challenged not only Tillyard's interpretation of what Shakespeare "really meant," but also the idea of searching for any single authentic and authoritative meaning of his individual or collected works. In the 1980s, Tillyard's work was attacked again, this time in works by ideological critics known as "cultural materialists."[4] In his review of these interpretations of Shakespeare and the debate over methods of literary criticism, Bradshaw writes that the cultural materialists' approach "carries on the old bad Tillyardian habit of giving particular characters and speeches a supradramatic significance, which is then identified with what the play or the dramatist 'really' thinks, and usually coincides with what the critic thinks." Differences in the conclusions of literary critics are thus not a matter of their general method but of sample selection bias: "Where Tillyard was delighted to hear His Master's Voice in any invocation of law and order, and associated the 'radical' with something nasty, the British cultural materialist knows that the 'radical,' 'subversive,' 'marginal,' or . . . 'dissident' perspective is always superior." Bradshaw reviews more problems with these approaches in critical interpretations of *Henry V, The Merchant of Venice,* and *Othello.*[5] In an earlier work he makes a case for *Shakespeare's Skepticism,* while refusing to set his critical "approach" among the competing "isms" or "ologies" that he views as "anticritical."[6]

Berry considers Shakespeare's treatment of social class, relying mainly on characters' ranks and occupations, but also on their status and income, to establish class membership. He finds that Shakespeare's treatment of the theme varied over time and in plays with different settings. Specifically, he sees the early history plays as being dominated by a single class, the nobility. The early comedies present a "straightforward, stable account of the social classes. The ranks are fixed with precision and interesting detail. The implied need is simply for the classes to get along with each other." The middle comedies are more complex and middle-class, built on the idea that society is competitive, not stable. The mature history plays display "a panorama of English society" with class tensions existing under the extreme pressures of war detailed in *Henry V*. The four major tragedies "show class as completely assimilated into character and motivation," and "Iago's hatred of Othello (and Cassio) is rooted in class resentment." The problem plays (*All's Well That Ends Well, Troilus and Cressida,* and *Measure for Measure*) show social class in relation to sex and marriage. The Roman plays offer different lines of thought, but analogies between the Roman and Elizabethan nobility appear, especially in *Coriolanus,* which Berry describes as "that bleak and unyielding analysis of the class struggle." The final romances reveal "a diminished interest in class orderings," although "(t)he core relationship of *The Tempest* is that of master and man, with the play ending in freedom for the men and freedom for the master." *Henry VIII* "closes in social accord, as all classes rejoice in the birth of a princess."[7]

A recent edited volume titled *Marxist Shakespeares* features two essays that explore Shakespearean "hauntings" and representations of revolution both in Marx (particularly using the description of Hamlet's father, "Well grubbed, old mole") and work by contemporary Marxist critics. Three essays deal with issues of gender, work, and marital property in Shakespeare's time and in some of his plays, including *Othello* and *The Merry Wives of Windsor.* An essay by Walter Cohen argues that Shakespeare's "mercantile geography" and commercial references reflect England's economic expansion. Three essays deal with the relationship between Shakespeare's works and the theatre itself—both historically and today (including the modern film industry)—considered "as commodity, institution, and shifting marker of national and transnational 'culture.'" Two final essays deal with future impacts and possible directions for Marxism, one arguing that in *Measure for Measure* Shakespeare was practicing "Marxism before Marx" by anticipating radical forms of social arrangements, and the other challenging "universal" interpretations of Shakespeare that dismiss Marxist criticism as merely ideological. This last essay is developed partly by drawing on early seventeenth-century economic writers such as Mun and Wheeler to show that Shakespeare was the "product" of a particular time and community, but one who spoke and wrote with a "singular voice in common."[8]

Turner argues that Shakespeare and other poets may have more to say than economists about what value is, because "Poets spend their lives making value out of combinations of words that have no economic worth in themselves, being common property, infinitely reproducible, and devoid of rarity value." He notes that Shakespeare "became one of the richest commoners in England—a media tycoon of his day—essentially by combining words in such a way as to persuade people to pay good money for them." In doing this, Turner feels that Shakespeare was "perhaps *the* key figure in creating that Renaissance system of meanings, values, and implicit rules that eventually gave rise to the modern world market and that still underpins it." Shakespeare's special relevance in the twenty-first century, Turner argues, is in providing the language and images to help develop a more humane version of economics and capitalism. Specifically, Turner offers as a model for that task Shakespeare's use of such words as *bond, trust, good, save, equity, value, mean, redeem, redemption, forgive, dear, obligation, interest, honor, company, credit, issue, worth, due, duty, thrift, use, will, partner, deed, fair, owe, ought, treasure, sacrifice, risk, royalty, fortune, venture,* and *grace,* because these words "preserve within them the values, patterns of action, qualities, abstract entities, and social emotions that characterize the gift and barter exchange systems upon which they are founded." The meanings of these words are "inseparable from their economic content" and "make up a large fraction of our most fundamental ethical vocabulary."[9]

McKendrick characterizes himself as one of a new group of "literary historians," including McVeaugh, Winter, and others, who have begun to trace how businessmen are portrayed in literature.[10] But even though such specialization as a literary historian is relatively new, Winter notes that "[t]he cultural context of business activity is a time-honored theme in the study of economic and social history."[11] Responding to the eminent economic historian D. C. Coleman's comment, cited in appendix A, "Look for the businessman in English fiction and either you will not find him at all or he will vary from the sinister to the absurd," and even more to claims by Wiener and others who argue that there is a pronounced, uniformly one-sided, and increasingly hostile literary opposition to capitalism,[12] McKendrick summarizes many key findings of the literary historians. He notes that there is a long history of literary writers expressing anti-business sentiments in Great Britain, dating back to at least the end of the fifteenth century, and that "far from the twentieth century representing a peak of such attacks on the businessman, there is a decline in attention to him in the literature of the last fifty years, reflecting a relative indifference to business capitalism and a preoccupation with other values." While he agrees that "few sources can tell us more about prevailing social attitudes and preferred social values," McKendrick argues that it is important to do so critically, recognizing that literary attitudes are "often partial, particular to a single class or interest group, prone to reflect specific political connections and social obsessions, and open to mimetic distortion as a result of literary convention, passing fashion, the needs of the readership, the demands of the critics, or the pressure of public opinion."[13]

Accepting the importance of what Lionel Trilling called "the rise of the adversary culture" over the past century, McKendrick nevertheless disagrees with many claims about the nature, timing, and significance of the role of literary works in bringing about that rise. He shows that there are numerous favorable treatments of businessmen and commercial activity in literature, treatments that, like the unfavorable ones, date back at least to writers in the Elizabethan and early Stuart periods, including Deloney, Heywood, and Dekker, although most writers in the period, including Jonson, Middleton, Marston, and Massinger, presented "uncompromisingly hostile" portrayals. The hostile tradition continued in Jacobean and Caroline satire; in Disraeli, Meredith, Eliot, Reade, Trollope, Hardy, Brontë, and Dickens during the Victorian period; and in the twentieth century in some works by Shaw, Wells, and D. H. Lawrence. But McKendrick finds that "the apparent unanimity of the adversary culture's response to businessmen owes more to the influential critics [most notably Ruskin, Snowden, Sidney Webb, and William Morris] than it does to the record of imaginative writing alone."[14] To support this claim, he reviews favorable portrayals of merchants and other representatives of business in such writers as Denham, Fanshawe, Weller, Dryden, Prior, Pope, Young, Gay, Steele, Addison, Mandeville, Defoe, and Austen, and the recurring theme in many of those works of noble and even heroic achievement in human endeavor.[15] He also notes cases in which particular authors (including Shakespeare, Blake, Wordsworth, Wells, Dickens, Brontë, Forster, Shaw, Wells, and Orwell) wrote both favorable and hostile portrayals of businessmen, in some cases in the same work. Sometimes these portrayals reflected specific and short-lived contemporary issues; at other times they reflected changing public tastes. He summarizes the favorable characterizations and portrayals by saying that "the English novelist has supplied such a well-stocked cast of business heroes . . . in addition [to] a rich cast of dramatic commercial heroes; one can reasonably ask why the business idea is thought to be so ill represented in English literature."[16]

But McKendrick recognizes the "pervasive acceptance" of the "adversary culture" and offers several reasons for it. Not only have pro-business English writers such as DeFoe assumed that there is a higher calling beyond business and commerce,[17] but over the last century English writers have had to acknowledge the United Kingdom's relative decline as an industrial power:

> For most modern English writers there seems little need to make the case against individual industrialists or even capital in general. . . . In a society moralized by the professional ideal, it is the mandarin class that needs detailed discussion and evaluation. The businessman offers no threat, so attitudes to him as an individual can become almost neutral—he can be charming or odious largely irrespective of his choice of career in business.[18]

> Peaks of hostility to the businessman can reflect times when his place in society, his power and his influence are seen to be at their most influential. They can, of course, also reflect widespread concern that economic decline is the result of his entrepreneurial and human failings. Troughs of apparent indifference can reflect times when his power and influence are in eclipse.[19]

McKendrick acknowledges that "[t]he accumulated verdict of the literature of the past can still be profoundly influential, especially when selected and projected by respected literary critics." He also feels that in Germany and the United States "the businessman is still the focus of serious literary debate because he is still seen as a central and important member of society."[20] He might well have added Japan to that list because there is a contemporary genre of "business novels," called *keizai-shosetsu,* that are quite popular among Japanese businessmen and their wives, as well as students and other professionals. Seven short novels from this genre are available in English translation.[21]

Turning to the United States, Gilmore sets his study of the leading American Romantic writers—Emerson, Thoreau, Hawthorne, and Melville—against the background of U.S. industrialization during the first half of the nineteenth century. He concludes that "[w]riting and publishing developed along roughly the same lines as the economy at large" because, prior to 1820, "belles-lettres had remained an upper-class or patrician pursuit" and publishers had incentives to publish foreign works on which they did not have to pay royalties (due to the absence of international copyright laws), so that "only the rare American work could sell enough copies to surmount this handicap and become a paying proposition."[22] Over the next thirty years, technological advances dramatically lowered printing costs and selling prices for large print runs, while rapid increases in the U.S. population and literacy rates increased the demand for popular fiction. As a result, the number of published fictional works by U.S. authors increased roughly tenfold between the 1820s and the 1840s.[23]

These developments were not a panacea for the most prominent writers of the period, however, as Hawthorne and Melville both became disenchanted with the necessity of wooing readers and courting public opinion.[24] Discouraged by the poor sales of their fiction, both also became distanced from their own work. While working on his last complete romance, *The Marble Faun,* Hawthorne wrote in a letter that he recognized his works did "not make their appeal to the popular mind," nor were they even to Hawthorne's own "individual taste," as he admitted that if he encountered his stories in books by different authors he would probably not have the perseverance to get through them.[25] Melville came to realize that democratic capitalism is no more congenial to the artist than the old system of aristocratic patronage. The P.I.O. man, a character in Melville's last novel, *The Confidence-Man,* his most scathing description of commercial society, says, "Confidence is the indispensable basis of all sorts of business transactions. Without it, commerce between man and man, as between country and country, would, like a watch, run down and stop." Gilmore extends this idea, writing:

> The author is in the same position as anyone else under the market regime who has goods to sell. He has to win the confidence of potential customers, in his case the reading public, to induce them to purchase his commodities. The multiple con men of Melville's novel are versions of the artist [sic] who tell stories to obtain money and use language, not to communicate truth, but to obfuscate their motives and ingratiate themselves with listeners.[26]

Gilmore finds a mixed response to economic forces by these authors: "Melville grappled with the vanishing of the human in the commodity form . . . [and] also wrote about the deepening of class divisions that accompanied the transition from a household to a rationalized economy."[27] On the other hand, Gilmore sees *The Scarlet Letter* as "the product of Hawthorne's urgent need to compose a bestseller," with the content of the novel reflecting its author's own dilemma:

> Basically Hawthorne had two roles available to him as an American man of letters in the mid-nineteenth century. He had the model of his own experience as a writer for a small coterie of admirers, a writer who enjoyed critical esteem as a truth-teller but who felt ashamed of his impoverishment. The alternative course, to follow the pen-and-ink men in appealing to the multitude, would presumably bring him fame and money but might require him to violate the integrity of his art.[28]

Ultimately, Gilmore sees these forces playing a key role in shaping the works of these Romantic writers. In the last sentences of his book, he writes, "Like the modernist novel, market society thrives on indirection and impersonality. Is it unreasonable to suppose, then, that the perdurability of the masked and difficult works of American romanticism is itself a testimony to the power of the market?"[29]

Ownby, reviewing Faulkner's treatment of the rising consumer society during the first half of the twentieth century in the American South, identifies two different responses. On the one hand, Faulkner's work portrays the escape from poverty and from restrictive traditional economic structures, as well as the greater economic equality that resulted from products formerly available only to the privileged becoming mass produced. Housing and transportation are particularly important examples of these kinds of goods because they are also important social and economic institutions and begin to take on new and different forms for different people and families. Faulkner's sympathetic view of consumerism is seen in such diverse characters as Anse and Cash Bundren, Lena Grove, Joe Christmas, and the "reivers" in Faulkner's last novel. On the other hand, there is the trilogy on the history of the Snopes family, who consume whatever they can with no sense of tradition or taste, seek wealth only as a way to acquire more wealth, and purchase (sometimes without ever using) luxury items as a matter of self-indulgence and as a means of setting themselves apart from financially less successful members of the community.[30]

Greenfield studies the theme of work in American drama from 1920 to 1970 and argues that it is not coincidental that "the American drama comes of age at precisely the same time and through the very same plays in which the theme of work comes of age in American drama." Like economists (recall Adam Smith's warnings about the costs of specialization), the playwrights recognize that there is often a considerable degree of disutility in work. Or put differently, there is a dichotomy here, too, because while work provides a sense of self-identity as well as income, it can also be a changeable and ultimately unsatisfying measure of a person, even for people in managerial and professional occupations. Plays by Clifford Odets, Robert Sherwood, Arthur Miller, Tennessee Williams, Paddy Chayesky, Edward Albee, and Neil Simon deal with characters who face that kind of disappointment, either suddenly or after a gradual accumulation of pressures and frustrations. Tellingly, Greenfield notes that the most powerful portrayals of those forces are not found when the characters are at work—the professor professing, the teacher teaching, the writer writing, or the salesman selling—but when they are at home with their families and friends, showing that "the true strength of a storm is measured not by the velocity of the winds but by the amount of damage it leaves behind."[31]

A recent anthology of writings on work by literary authors, philosophers, religious leaders, businessmen, and economists highlights many of these same themes. For example, ambivalent attitudes about work—as a curse or a source of pride, worth, and self-identity—are documented in a section on "The Yin and Yang of Work."[32]

Hapke studies American literary treatments of women and work during the Great Depression, featuring works by radical and orthodox writers including Sherwood Anderson, Fielding Burke, Erskine Caldwell, Theodore Dreiser, James T. Farrell, Mike Gold, Fannie Hurst, Zora Neale Hurston, Sinclair Lewis, Grace Lumpkin, Meredile LeSueur, Margaret Mitchell, Tillie Olsen, Agnes Smedley, John Steinbeck, and Richard Wright. Her work is a revisionist history, stressing the idea that "literature, with some notable exceptions, was enlisted in a widespread cultural campaign against changes in a woman's traditional role" because "in a time of supreme economic stress, strictures on feminine conduct narrowed." Then, ironically in Hurst's view, during World War II "the nation would be reconciled—at least for a time—to the woman at work."[33]

Addressing similar themes in his sweeping study of ideas of home, state, and history in European drama and painting since the sixteenth century, Helgerson concludes that

> the underlying social, economic, and political issues that were expressed through domestic drama and painting concerned relations between men: relations between burghers (or rich peasants) and aristocrats, between townsmen and soldiers, between men of the new regime of sentiment and fraternity and men of the old regime of hierarchy and oppression, between male subjects and their king. But the effect of representing those issues and those relations in stories about rivalry over the sexual possession of women inevitably resulted in the promotion of women to positions of great consequence. . . . The artistic power and cultural significance of this promotion of bourgeois and domestic women is undeniable. What is less clear is whether it should count as a promotion of women in any broader sense. . . . (D)oes the liberation of burghers and rich peasants mean the liberation of burgher and rich peasant women? Or does it mean their still straighter confinement in the seemingly ahistorical and apolitical realms of domesticity and sexuality?[34]

Dukore sets out to establish, or reestablish, the essential radical, anti-capitalist nature of works by Henrik Ibsen, Bernard Shaw, and Bertolt Brecht. Although most economists would never doubt that premise in the first place, Dukore shows that some Marxist social and literary critics have argued that "Shavian and Fabian notions of Socialism result in nonradicalism and nonsocialism."[35] Consequently, to such critics Brecht's Marxism makes him more truly radical than Ibsen or Shaw. Dukore sees the three authors as different—mainly because they lived at different times, under different types or stages of capitalism—and finds it pointless to argue which one is more or less (or a better or worse) radical or socialist. He also concludes that, in terms of literary and dramatic effects, the plays in which each of these three authors were most explicit about their radical diagnoses and prescriptions for society were unsuccessful, and that generally the more explicit these ideas were in the authors' plays the more unsuccessful the plays were as dramatic works.[36]

Winter deals with the treatment of businessmen in works by Shaw and Brecht, and like McKendrick challenges Wiener's view that after the 1850s English businessmen were driven away from the pursuit of profits and economic growth by a "cultural counterrevolution" reflected in the literary culture of the period, which in effect left businessmen with "a collective inferiority complex."[37] Noting that Shaw joined with the Webbs in setting up the London School of Economics to "teach the truths of the new social sciences" that "had an essential part to play in society," with the only question being "whether their contribution would be restricted to the generation of private profit or opened up to the more important realm of public service," Winter concludes that a comparison of Shaw's *Major Barbara* and Brecht's *St. Joan of the Stockyards* shows "the mildness of Shaw's attack on the capitalist system, when compared to that of Brecht."[38] Winter argues that the differences in the two writers' attacks—which in Shaw's case is mainly limited to "a nasty shower of words"—reflects differences in the character of the societies in which the two writers lived, the British socialist movement's commitment to democratic traditions, and most importantly key differences in the ideas of the groups of intellectuals with whom the two writers were associated:

> It is the very character of English intellectual life that is an essential part of the explanation as to why the cultural critique of business in [England], from Dickens to Shaw and beyond, was so relatively mild. The essential reason was that, either in the form of the literature of conversion in the novels of the 1840s or in the parody of that literature in the work of George Bernard Shaw, English writers, even the renegade Irish Protestant among them, never fully repudiated the values of their society.[39]

DeMott, a humanities instructor at Amherst College writing in the *Harvard Business Review,* sees a further turning point in literary treatments of business following the upheavals of the Great Depression and World War II. He argues that Lionel Trilling's 1945 short story, "The Other Margaret," marked a "reinvigoration of antideterminism [that] was the intellectual change most vital to the recovery, by business, of the grip on the public imagination it had possessed before the Great Crash."[40]

One of the boldest attempts to synthesize economic and literary writings is Kurt Heinzelman's *The Economics of the Imagination.*[41] Comparing the ideas and language of classical economists, including Smith, Ricardo, Malthus, Mill, Jevons, and Marx, to literary works by Spenser, Blake, Wordsworth, Thoreau, DeQuincey, Ruskin, Yeats, Frost, Pound, Williams, and (in an afterword) Shakespeare, Heinzelman attempts to develop Coleridge's idea that economics and literature are "connatural activities."[42] He makes a distinction between material labor and mental labor that most modern economists would reject, assigning the former as the subject of economic theory while regarding the latter as the endeavor that produces, and is produced by, literary work. But after exploring the shared "cognate language" of economic and poetic "systems," he concludes that economics, fully articulated, is at once a product of and a possible grammar for the imagination:

> (T)here is no simple, axiomatic reason why economics should be regarded as opposed to the production of art or why poetry should be impervious to economics. . . . Economics, in all its figural complexity, becomes an instrument which may unblock the myriad ways in which the instrumentality of the imagination is economically compromised.[43]

Notes

1. Works cited in this paragraph are, in order of their citation in the text: V. D. Scudder, *Social Ideals in English Letters* (Boston: Houghton Mifflin, 1898); L. Stephens, *English Literature and Society in the Eighteenth Century* (London: Smith, Elder and Co. and Duckworth and Co., 1907); R. S. Loomis, *A Mirror of Chaucer's World* (Princeton, N.J.: Princeton University Press, 1965); E. M. W. Tillyard, *The Elizabethan World Picture* (New York: Vintage Books, 1944); L. C. Knights, *Drama and Society in the Age of Jonson,* reprinted in 1968 (New York: Norton, 1937); C. Hulse, *The Rule of Art: Literature and Painting in the Renaissance* (Chicago: University of Chicago Press, 1990); R. Halpern, *The Poetics of Primitive Accumulation: English Renaissance Culture and the Geneology of Capital* (Ithaca, N.Y.: Cornell University Press, 1991); D. L. Miller, S. O'Dair, and H. Weber, *The Production of English Renaissance Culture* (Ithaca, N.Y.: Cornell University Press, 1994); R. B. Heilman, et al., "The Economics of Iago." *Publications of the Modern Language Association* 48 (1953): 555–71; D. M. Wolfe, *Milton and His England* (Princeton, N.J.: Princeton University Press, 1971); M. Mack, *The Garden and the City: Retirement and Politics in the Later Poetry of Pope, 1731–1743* (Toronto: University of Toronto Press, 1969); L. Rigal, *The American Manufactory: Art, Labor, and the World of Things in the Early Republic* (Princeton, N.J.: Princeton University Press, 1998); Link, *The Uses of Literature: Life in the Socialist Chinese Literary System* (Princeton, N.J.: Princeton University Press, 2000).

Link offers the following summary, sounding much like a mainstream economist:

> In China, at the peak of the Maoist fervor for the experiment, some even thought that social engineering could rework a person's innermost character, and that selfishness itself might be consigned to the dustbin of history. But by century's end it was clear that the experiment had failed. Apologists could still claim that it had not

> really had a fair trial, since the major sites of its adoption, Russia and China, had inherited strong authoritarian traditions that had skewed the experiment. But most of the people who had actually lived under the system and understood how it worked in daily life concluded that fundamental elements in its blueprint were flawed. It brought neither wealth nor freedom but often the opposite and, far from eliminating selfishness, only changed the rules under which selfishness was pursued. (3)

2. M. Shell, *The Economics of Literature* (Baltimore: Johns Hopkins University Press, 1978).

3. J. Vernon, *Money and Fiction: Literary Realism in the Nineteenth and Early Twentieth Centuries* (Ithaca, N.Y.: Cornell University Press, 1984), 66–69.

4. For example, J. Dollimore, *Radical Tragedy: Religion, Ideology, and Power in the Drama of Shakespeare and His Contemporaries* (Chicago: University of Chicago Press, 1984); J. Dollimore and A. Sinfield, eds., *Political Shakespeare: New Essays in Cultural Materialism* (Manchester: University of Manchester Press, 1985).

5. G. Bradshaw, *Misrepresentations: Shakespeare and the Materialists* (Ithaca, N.Y.: Cornell University Press, 1993), 9.

6. G. Bradshaw, *Shakespeare's Skepticism* (London: Harvester Press, 1987). Cf. Yale economist H. W. Farnam's (*Shakespeare's Economics* [New Haven, Conn.: Yale University Press, 1931], 148–49) conclusion:

> The passages quoted . . . do not prove conclusively anything with regard to Shakespeare's personal views in the matter of social economics. No one can say positively that he was or was not a snob; that he favored or did not favor inclosures; that he supported or opposed the abuse of power by the privileged classes. It does seem to be clear, however, that Shakespeare recognized the existence of the abuses of power; that he was fully aware of an ideal which would eliminate these abuses; that he knew the evils of wasteful or harmful consumption; that he was conscious of the complicated social interactions of good and evil, so that a thing in itself evil, might have some good results, and a thing in itself good, might, if abused, lead to bad results. In other words without ever having heard the words economics or sociology, he was fully aware of the reaction of economic conditions on social welfare, and of the possibility of introducing a more perfect social organism of which he formed part.

7. R. Berry, *Shakespeare and Social Class* (Atlantic Highlands, N.J.: Humanities Press International, 1988), xx–xxii.

8. J. E. Howard and S. C. Shershow, eds., *Marxist Shakespeares* (London: Routledge, 2000), 13, 15, 262–63.

9. F. Turner, *Shakespeare's Twenty-first Century Economics: The Morality of Love and Money* (New York: Oxford University Press, 1999), 11.

10. N. McKendrick, "'Gentlemen and Players' Revisited: The Gentlemanly Ideal, the Business Ideal, and the Professional Ideal in English Literary Culture." In *Business Life and Public Policy: Essays in Honor of D. C. Coleman,* N. McKendrick and R. B. Outhwaite, eds. (Cambridge: Cambridge University Press, 1986), 100. See also N. McKendrick, "Literary Luddism and the

Businessman." In *Sir Alfred Jones: Shipping Entrepreneur Par Excellence,* P. N. Davies, ed. (London: Europa Publications Limited, 1978), ix–lvi; J. McVeagh, *Tradefull Merchants: The Portrayal of the Capitalist in Literature* (London: Routledge & Kegan Paul, 1981); J. M. Winter, "Bernard Shaw, Bertold Brecht and the Businessman in Literature." In *Business Life and Public Policy: Essays in Honor of D. C. Coleman,* 185–204.

11. Winter, "Bernard Shaw, Bertold Brecht and the Businessman in Literature," 185.

12. M. J. Wiener, *English Culture and the Decline of the Industrial Spirit, 1850–1980* (Cambridge: Cambridge University Press, 1981).

13. McKendrick, "'Gentlemen and Players' Revisited," 102.

14. Ibid., 108.

15. In *Tradefull Merchants,* McVeagh has an entire chapter on "The Merchant as Hero: 1700–1750."

16. McKendrick, "'Gentlemen and Players' Revisited," 114.

17. In Defoe's *A Piece of English Commerce* (1728), he writes "Trade makes gentlemen," but then "after a generation or two the tradesman's children come to be as good statesmen, judges or bishops as those of the most antient [*sic*] families."

18. McKendrick, "'Gentlemen and Players' Revisited," 126.

19. Ibid., 102.

20. Ibid., 126.

21. T. K. Prindle, ed. and trans. *Made in Japan and Other Japanese "Business Novels"* (Armonk, N.Y.: M. E. Sharpe, 1989).

22. M. T. Gilmore, *American Romanticism and the Marketplace* (Chicago: University of Chicago Press, 1985), 3–4.

23. R. J. Zboray challenges "the illusion of a supply-driven market" selling mass-produced books to "a unified 'nation' of readers." He draws attention to many factors other than printing processes and rising literacy rates, including product distribution methods and technologies (especially railroads), management and sales practices of publishers, and especially regional and individual differences among readers/consumers. He concludes that "readers stand in the final analysis alongside writers, publishers, and booksellers in literary creation. As they employed the printed word to help cope with the social dislocations of economic development, these readers helped to forge a national identity and, not inconsequentially, to set the direction for later American cultural practices." See his *A Fictive People: Antebellum Economic Development and the American Reading Public* (Oxford: Oxford University Press, 1993), xvi, xxii.

24. L. Erickson studies the effects of the industrialization of printing on literary works in England from 1800-1850 and draws similar conclusions: "Once authors became fully aware of the market for writing, they recognized that it was organized for the publishers' benefit and not theirs." There, too, however, some authors were able to prosper in the new market structure. Erickson quotes a letter from Jane Austen to Anna Austen: "Walter Scott has no business to write novels, especially good ones.—It is not fair:—He has Fame and Profit enough as a Poet, and should not take bread out of other people's mouths." Of course, the excerpt from Washington Irving's short story shows his "Poor-Devil Author" adapting much more successfully, financially and psychologically, if not artistically. See *The Economy of Literary Form: English Literature and the Industrialization of Publishing, 1800–1850* (Baltimore: Johns Hopkins University Press, 1996), 181, 142.

25. Gilmore, *American Romanticism and the Marketplace,* 148–49.

26. Ibid., 150.

27. Ibid., 5.

28. Ibid., 72.

29. Ibid., 153.

30. T. Ownby, "The Snopes Trilogy and the Emergence of Consumer Culture." In *Faulkner and Ideology: Faulkner and Yoknapatawpha, 1992,* D. M. Kartiganer and A. J. Abadie, eds., (Jackson, Miss.: University Press of Mississippi, 1995), 95–128.

31. T. A. Greenfield, *Work and the Work Ethic in American Drama, 1920–1970* (Columbia, Mo.: University of Missouri Press, 1982), 128–129.

32. R. Sessions and J. Wortman, eds., *Working in America: A Humanities Reader* (Notre Dame, Ind.: University of Notre Dame Press, 1992).

33. L. Hapke, *Daughters of the Great Depression: Women, Work, and Fiction in the American 1930s* (Athens, Ga.: University of Georgia Press, 1995), 223.

34. R. Helgerson, *Adulterous Alliances: Home, State, and History in Early Modern European Drama and Painting* (Chicago: University of Chicago Press, 2000), 191–92.

35. B. F. Dukore, *Money and Politics in Ibsen, Shaw, and Brecht* (Columbia, Mo.: University of Missouri Press, 1980), 162–63.

36. Brecht's *The Mother*, Ibsen's *Pillars of Society*, and Shaw's *On the Rocks*. Interestingly, on the other side of the spectrum, similar claims have been made concerning the literary merits of Ayn Rand's works. See M. E. Fletcher, "Harriet Martineau and Ayn Rand: Economics in the Guise of Fiction." *American Journal of Economics and Sociology* 33 (1974), 378

37. Winter, "Bernard Shaw, Bertold Brecht and the Businessman in Literature," 185–86.

38. Ibid., 203.

39. Ibid., 204.

40. B. DeMott, "Reading Fiction to the Bottom Line." *Harvard Business Review* 67 (1989), 130. An economist considering anti-business sentiment in American literature pointed to the same kind of turning point, occurring at exactly the same time. Brandis concluded that after World II the critical emphasis of literary authors shifts "from one which encompasses the whole system to one restricted to particular segments of that system"—especially communications (including advertising, television, publishing, and the movies) and the "business aristocracy" of top executives and financiers. See "The American Writer Views the American Businessman." *Quarterly Review of Economics and Business 1* (1961), 34.

41. K. Heinzelman, *The Economics of the Imagination* (Amherst, Mass.: University of Massachusetts Press, 1980).

42. From Coleridge's *The Friend*. Coleridge used the word trade, not economics.

43. Heinzelman, *The Economics of the Imagination,* 275.

Sources

A. Scarcity, Wants, and Resources

Milton, John. *Comus.* In *L'Allegro, Il-Penseroso, Comus And Lycidas,* edited by Tuley Francis Huntington, 38–39. Boston: A. M. Ginn & Company Publishers, The Athenaeum Press, 1902.

B. Choice and Opportunity Cost

Frost, Robert. "The Road Not Taken." In *The Road Not Taken,* edited by Louis Untermeyer, 270–71. New York: Henry Holt and Company, 1951.

C. Self-Interest and Economic Systems

Mandeville, Bernard. "The Grumbling Hive: Or, Knaves turn'd Honest." In *The Fable of the Bees: or, Private Vices, Publick Benefits,* vol. 1, with commentary by F. B. Kaye, 17–37. London: Oxford University Press, Amen House, 1924.

Brontë, Emily. *Wuthering Heights,* 135–36. Edinburgh: John Grant, 1907.

Rand, Ayn. *Atlas Shrugged,* 660–63. New York: Random House, 1957.

White, T. H. *The Book of Merlyn,* 135–42. New York: Ace Books, 1999.

Bellamy, Edward. "The Parable of the Water Tank." In *The Parable Of The Water Tank,* 195–203. New York: Equality Greenwood Press Publishers, 1969.

Mann, Thomas. *Doctor Faustus: The Life of the German Composer Adrian Leverkühn As Told by a Friend,* 128–32. Translated by John E. Woods. New York: Vintage Books, 1999.

D. Property Rights and Incentives

Frost, Robert. "Mending Wall." In *The Road Not Taken,* 112–13.

Junger, Sebastian. *The Perfect Storm,* 66–69. From *The Perfect Storm* by Sebastian Junger. Copyright © 1997 by Sebastian Junger. Used by permission of W.W. Norton & Company, Inc.

Doig, Ivan. *Ride with Me, Mariah Montana,* 39, 109–10, 132–35, 312–14. New York: Penguin Books, 1991. Reprinted with the permission of Scribner, a division of Simon & Schuster, from *Ride with Me, Mariah Montana* by Ivan Doig. Copyright © 1990 Ivan Doig.

Caldwell, Erskine. *God's Little Acre,* 18–20, 38–39. New York: Viking Press, 1933. Used by permission of the University of Georgia Press.

Steinbeck, John. *The Grapes of Wrath,* 49–53. New York: Sun Dial Press, 1941. From *The Grapes of Wrath* by John Steinbeck, copyright © 1939, renewed copyright © 1967 by John Steinbeck. Used by permission of Viking Penguin, a division of Penguin Group (USA) Inc.

E. Specialization, the Division of Labor, and Economies and Diseconomies of Scale

Anderson, Sherwood. *Winesburg, Ohio: A Group of Tales of Ohio Small-Town Life,* 8–12. New York: Modern Library, 1919.

Steinbeck, John. *East of Eden,* 540–41. New York: Viking Press, 1952. From *East of Eden* by John Steinbeck, copyright © 1952, renewed copyright © 1980 by Elaine Steinbeck, John Steinbeck IV, and Thom Steinbeck. Used by permission of Viking Penguin, a division of Penguin Group (USA) Inc.

Masters, Edgar Lee. *Spoon River Anthology,* 21, 45, 116–17, 136, 178, 203. New York: MacMillan, 1915.

Dreiser, Theodore. *Sister Carrie,* 266–72. New York: Harper & Row, 1965.

Steinbeck, John. *Travels with Charley: In Search of America,* 81–85, 96–97, 126–28, 162–63. New York: Viking Press, 1962. From *Travels with Charley: In Search of America* by John Steinbeck, copyright © 1961, 1962 by the The Curtis Publishing Co, © 1962 by John Steinbeck, renewed copyright © 1990 by Elaine Steinbeck, John Steinbeck IV, and Thom Steinbeck. Used by permission of Viking Penguin, a division of Penguin Group (USA) Inc.

F. Entrepreneurship and Profits

Shakespeare, William. *The Merchant of Venice,* 3–5. Cambridge: Cambridge University Press, 1953.

Pope, Alexander. "Moral Essays." In *The Complete Poetical Works of Pope,* 169–70, 173. Boston: Houghton Mifflin Co., 1903.

Dos Passos, John. "Tin Lizzie." In *U.S.A., The 42nd Parallel,* 264–65. New York: Modern Library, 1937. Used by permission of Lucy Dos Passos Coggin.

Dos Passos, John. "Prince of Peace." In *U.S.A., The Big Money,* 47–57. New York: Modern Library, 1937. Used by permission of Lucy Dos Passos Coggin.

Heller, Joseph. *Catch-22,* 63–66, 226–29. New York: Simon and Schuster, 1961.

Francis, Dick. *Banker,* 80–82. New York: G. P. Putnam's Sons, 1983. From *Banker* by Dick Francis, copyright © 1982 Dick Francis. Used by permission of G.P. Putnam's Sons, a division of Penguin Group (USA) Inc.

Miller, Arthur. *All My Sons,* 66–69, 79–83. New York: Reynal & Hitchcock, 1947. *All My Sons*, copyright © 1947, renewed copyright © 1975 by Arthur Miller, from *Arthur Miller's Collected Plays* by Arthur Miller. Used by permission of Viking Penguin, a division of Penguin Group (USA) Inc.

G. Markets, Prices, Supply, and Demand

Gilbert, William S. *Songs of a Savoyard.* In *Plays and Poems of W. S. Gilbert,* 565. New York: Random House, 1932.

Norris, Frank. *The Octopus: A Story of California,* 576. New York: Doubleday, Page and Company, 1901.

Stoppard, Tom. *Arcadia,* 60–62. London and Boston: Faber and Faber, 1993.

Emerson, Ralph Waldo. *Journals,* 377–78, 528–29. Edited by Edward Waldo Emerson and Waldo Emerson Forbes. Boston and New York: Houghton Mifflin Company, 1912.

Steinbeck, John. *East of Eden,* 542–44. From *East of Eden* by John Steinbeck, copyright © 1952, renewed copyright © 1980 by Elaine Steinbeck, John Steinbeck IV, and Thom Steinbeck. Used by permission of Viking Penguin, a division of Penguin Group (USA) Inc.

Irving, Washington. "The Poor-Devil Author." In *The Complete Tales Of Washington Irving,* edited by Charles Neider, 277–81, 290–91. New York: Doubleday & Company, 1975.

Doig, Ivan. *Dancing at the Rascal Fair,* 128–31. New York: Atheneum Publishers, 1987. Reprinted with permission of Scribner, a division of Simon & Schuster from *Dancing at the Rascal Fair* by Ivan Doig. Copyright © 1987 by Ivan Doig.

Junger, Sebastian. *The Perfect Storm,* 33–35, 41–46, 75–76, 121–22. From *The Perfect Storm* by Sebastian Junger. Copyright © 1997 by Sebastian Junger. Used by permission of W.W. Norton & Company, Inc.

Tan, Amy. *The Joy Luck Club,* 28–30. New York: G.P. Putnam's Sons, 1989. From *The Joy Luck Club* by Amy Tan, copyright © 1989 by Amy Tan. Used by permission of G.P Putnam's Sons, a division of Penguin Group (USA) Inc.

Steinbeck, John. *The Pearl,* 21–22, 28–30, 32–37, 40–41, 57–59, 64–72. New York: Viking Press, 1947. From *The Pearl* by John Steinbeck, copyright © 1945, renewed copyright © 1980 by Elaine Steinbeck, John Steinbeck IV, and Thom Steinbeck. Used by permission of Viking Penguin, a division of Penguin Group (USA) Inc.

Atwood, Margaret. *The Robber Bride,* 58–63. New York: Anchor Books, Doubleday, 1993. From *The Robber Bride* by Margaret Atwood, copyright © 1993 O.W.Todd Ltd. Used by permission of Doubleday, a division of Random House Inc.

H. Substitution and Income Effects, Elasticity

Krakauer, Jon. *Into Thin Air,* 22-23. New York: Random House, 1997. From *Into Thin Air* by Jon Krakauer, copyright © 1997 by Jon Krakauer. Used by permission of Villard Books, a division of Random House Inc.

Pope, Alexander. *Imitations of Horace,* 167. Edited by John Butt. New York: Oxford University Press, 1946.

I. Public Goods, Externalities, and the Coase Theorem

Steinbeck, John. *Travels with Charley,* 168–69. From *Travels with Charley: In Search of America* by John Steinbeck, copyright © 1961, 1962 by the The Curtis Publishing Co, © 1962 by John Steinbeck, renewed copyright © 1990 by Elaine Steinbeck, John Steinbeck IV, and Thom Steinbeck. Used by permission of Viking Penguin, a division of Penguin Group (USA) Inc.

Rabelais, Francois. *Gargantua and Pantagruel,* 193–95. Translated by Sir Thomas Urquhart and Peter Le Motteux. New York: AMS Press, 1967.

Dickens, Charles. *Hard Times,* 26–27. London: Thomas Nelson and Sons, n.d.

Krakauer, Jon. *Into Thin Air,* 60, 76–77. From *Into Thin Air* by Jon Krakauer, copyright © 1997 by Jon Krakauer. Used by permission of Villard Books, a division of Random House Inc.

Roy, Arundhati. *The God of Small Things,* 118–19. New York: Harper Perennial, 1997. From *The God of Small Things* by Arundhati Roy, copyright © 1997 by Arundhati Roy. Used by permission of Random House Inc.

J. Government Regulation and the Legal and Social Framework for Markets

Shakespeare, William. *The Merchant of Venice,* 63–77.

Sinclair, Upton. *The Jungle,* 160–62. New York: Grosset & Dunlap, 1906.

Solzhenitsyn, Aleksandr. *The Cancer Ward,* 490–92. Translated by Rebecca Frank. New York: Dial Press, 1968. From *The Cancer Ward* by Aleksandr L. Solzhenitsyn, translated by Rebecca Frank, copyright © 1968 by Doubleday, a division of Random House Inc. Used by permission of Doubleday, a division of Random House Inc.

K. Principal-Agent Problems

Hugo, Victor. *Les Miserables,* 149–53. Translated by Charles E. Wilbour. New York: Modern Library, 1931.

L. Government Failure and the Economics of Public Choice

Adams, Henry. *Democracy: An American Novel,* 1–12, 366–67. New York: Henry Holt and Company, 1908.

Heller, Joseph. *Good As Gold,* 116–22. New York: Simon and Schuster, 1979. Used by permission of the estate of Joseph Heller.

M. Labor Markets, Unions, and Human Capital

Franklin, Benjamin. *Autobiography,* 8–11, 12–17. New York: Harper & Brothers, 1956.

Fitzgerald, F. Scott. *The Great Gatsby,* 208–09. New York: Modern Library, 1934.

Sedaris, David. "Something For Everyone," from *Naked,* 202–08. Boston: Little, Brown, & Co., 1997.

Krakauer, Jon. *Into Thin Air,* 45–46. From *Into Thin Air* by Jon Krakauer, copyright © 1997 by Jon Krakauer. Used by permission of Villard Books, a division of Random House Inc.

Junger, Sebastian. *The Perfect Storm,* 13–15, 33, 46–49. From *The Perfect Storm* by Sebastian Junger. Copyright © 1997 by Sebastian Junger. Used by permission of W.W. Norton & Company, Inc.

Orwell, George. *The Road to Wigan Pier,* 22–34. London: Victor Gollancz Ltd., 1937. From *The Road to Wigan Pier* by George Orwell. Copyright © 1937 by George Orwell. Used by permission of Bill Hamilton as the literary executor for the estate of the late Sonia Brownell Orwell and Martin Secker & Warburg Ltd.

Shelley, Percy Bysshe. "Song to the Men of England." In *The Complete Poetical Works of Percy Bysshe Shelley,* vol. 3, edited by George Edward Woodberry, 226–28. Cambridge: Houghton, Mifflin and Company, The Riverside Press, 1892.

Steinbeck, John. *In Dubious Battle,* 31–33. New York: Modern Library, 1936. From *In Dubious Battle* by John Steinbeck, copyright © 1936, renewed copyright © 1964 by John Steinbeck. Used by permission of Viking Penguin, a division of Penguin Group (USA) Inc.

Caldwell, Erskine. *God's Little Acre,* 74–76, 103–07, 256–59. Used by permission of the University of Georgia Press.

N. Discrimination

Roy, Arundhati. *The God of Small Things,* 70–74. From *The God of Small Things* by Arundhati Roy, copyright © 1997 by Arundhati Roy. Used by permission of Random House Inc.

Steinbeck, John. *Travels with Charley,* 217–19, 220, 223–29. From *Travels with Charley: In Search of America* by John Steinbeck, copyright © 1961, 1962 by the The Curtis Publishing Co, © 1962 by John Steinbeck, renewed copyright © 1990 by Elaine Steinbeck, John Steinbeck IV, and Thom Steinbeck. Used by permission of Viking Penguin, a division of Penguin Group (USA) Inc.

Twain, Mark. *Adventures of Huckleberry Finn,* 281–84. New York: Harper & Brothers, 1903.

O. Immigration

Ivan Doig, *Dancing at the Rascal Fair,* 2–11. New York: Atheneum Publishers, 1987. Reprinted with permission of Scribner, a division of Simon & Schuster from *Dancing at the Rascal Fair* by Ivan Doig. Copyright © 1987 by Ivan Doig.

P. Income Inequality, Poverty, and Income Redistribution Policies

Shakespeare, William. *Troilus and Cressida.* In *The Works Of William Shakespeare,* vol. 6, edited by William Aldis Wright, 26–28. London and New York: MacMillan, 1892.

Emerson, Ralph Waldo. *Journals,* 166–67.

Orwell, George. *The Road to Wigan Pier,* 78–83. From *The Road to Wigan Pier* by George Orwell. Copyright © 1937 by George Orwell. Used by permission of Bill Hamilton as the literary executor for the estate of the late Sonia Brownell Orwell and Martin Secker & Warburg Ltd.

Norris, Frank. *The Octopus,* 601–07.

Hemingway, Ernest. *A Moveable Feast,* 50–51. New York: Touchstone, 1996.

Caldwell, Erskine. *Tobacco Road,* 146–51. New York: Grosset & Dunlap, 1932. Used by permission of the University of Georgia Press.

Vonnegut, Kurt. "Harrison Bergeron." In *Welcome to the Monkey House: A Collection of Short Works,* 7–13. New York: Delacorte Press, 1968. "Harrison Bergeron" by Kurt Vonnegut, from *Welcome to the Monkey House* by Kurt Vonnegut Jr., copyright © 1961 by Kurt Vonnegut Jr. Used by permission of Dell Publishing, a division of Random House Inc.

Q. Barter, Money, and Inflation

Frazier, Charles. *Cold Mountain,* 71–74, 191–92. Boston: Atlantic Monthly Press, 1997. From *Cold Mountain* by Charles Frazier, copyright © 1997 by Charles Frazier. Used by permission of Grove/Atlantic Inc.

Remarque, Erich Maria. *The Black Obelisk,* 4, 6–10. Translated by Denver Lindley. New York: Harcourt, Brace and Company, 1957.

Goethe, Johann. *Faust Parts I & II,* 66–73. Edited by Ernest Rhys. Translated by Albert G. Latham. New York: Everyman's Library, n.d.

Stein, Gertrude. "Money." *Saturday Evening Post,* June 13, 1936, 88.

R. Real versus Nominal Values

Twain, Mark. *A Connecticut Yankee in King Arthur's Court,* 420–25. New York: Charles L. Webster & Co., 1889.

S. Unemployment and Fiscal Policy

Doig, Ivan. *Bucking the Sun,* 33, 37–38, 132–33, 174. New York: Simon & Schuster, 1997. Reprinted with permission of Simon & Schuster from *Bucking the Sun* by Ivan Doig. Copyright © 1987 by Ivan Doig.

Simon, Neil. *The Prisoner of Second Avenue,* 48–54, 61–71. New York: Random House, 1972. Excerpt from *The Prisoner of Second Avenue,* copyright © 1972 by Neil Simon. Professionals and amateurs are hereby warned that *The Prisoner of Second Avenue* is fully protected under the Berne Convention and the Universal Copyright Convention and is subject to royalty. All rights, including without limitation professional, amateur, motion picture, television, radio, recitation, lecturing, public reading and foreign translation rights, computer media rights and the right of reproduction, and electronic storage or retrieval, in whole or in part and in any form, are strictly reserved and none of these rights can be exercised or used without written permission from the copyright owner. Inquiries for stock and amateur performances should be addressed to Samuel French, Inc., 45 West 25th Street, New York, NY 10010. All other inquiries should be addressed to Gary N. DaSilva, 111 N. Sepulveda Blvd., Suite 250, Manhattan Beach, CA 90266-6850.

T. Free Trade versus Protectionism

Bastiat, Frédéric. "Petition of the Manufacturers of Candles." In *Economic Sophisms,* translated from the fifth edition by Patrick James Stirling, 49–53. Edinburgh: Oliver and Boyd, 1873.

U. Cost-Benefit Analysis

Swift, Jonathan. *A Modest Proposal,* 8–11. London: S. Harding, 1729.

Lagerkvist, Pär. "A Hero's Death." In *The Marriage Feast,* 37–38. London: Chatto & Windus, 1955.